ACCA

Applied Skills

Performance Management (PM)

Practice & Revision Kit

For exams in September 2022, December 2022, March 2023 and June 2023

First edition 2008
Fifteenth edition February 2022

ISBN: 9781509747566
(previous ISBN 9781 5097 3802 1)
e-ISBN: 9781509744626

Cataloguing-in-Publication Data
A catalogue record for this book is available
from the British Library

Published by

BPP Learning Media Ltd
BPP House, Aldine Place
London W12 8AA

www.bpp.com/learningmedia

Printed in the United Kingdom

Your learning materials, published by BPP
Learning Media Ltd, are printed on paper
obtained from traceable, sustainable sources.

The contents of this book are intended as a
guide and not professional advice. Although
every effort has been made to ensure that the
contents of this book are correct at the time of
going to press, BPP Learning Media makes no
warranty that the information in this book is
accurate or complete and accept no liability for
any loss or damage suffered by any person
acting or refraining from acting as a result of
the material in this book.

We are grateful to the Association of Chartered
Certified Accountants for permission to
reproduce past examination questions. The
suggested solutions in the Practice & Revision Kit
have been prepared by BPP Learning Media Ltd,
except where otherwise stated.

Contents

Finding questions

Revising Performance Management viii

Helping you with your revision xiii

Essential skill areas in Performance Management xiv

---

Questions and answers

Exam practice

Exam formulae 455

BPP
LEARNING
MEDIA

Question index

The headings in this checklist/index indicate the main topics of questions, but questions often cover several different topics.

Past exam questions are designated with the date of the exam in which they featured, although some have been amended to reflect subsequent changes to the syllabus or in the format of the exam. Prior to September 2018, Performance Management (PM) was known as F5 Performance Management.

Since September 2015 there have been four exam sittings per year, but ACCA only publish two exams' worth of questions per year. These releases are compiled from questions selected from the preceding sessions. These compilation exams are denoted as 'Mar/Jun' and 'Sept/Dec' in the index below.

BPP
LEARNING
MEDIA

BPP
LEARNING
MEDIA

Mock exam 1 (September 2016 exam)

Mock exam 2 (Specimen exam)

Mock exam 3 (December 2016 exam)

Mock exam 4

Revising Performance Management (PM)

Topics to revise

All questions are compulsory so you must revise the **whole** syllabus. Since the exam includes 15 objective test questions in Section A, you should expect questions to cover a large part of the syllabus. Selective revision **will limit** the number of questions you can answer and hence reduce your chances of passing. It is better to go into the exam knowing a reasonable amount about most of the syllabus rather than concentrating on a few topics to the exclusion of the rest.

Question practice

Question practice is a core part of learning new topic areas. When you practise questions, you should focus on improving the Exam success skills – personal to your needs – by obtaining feedback or through a process of self-assessment.

Sitting this exam as a computer-based exam and practising as many exam-style questions as possible in the ACCA CBE practice platform will be the key to passing this exam. You should attempt questions under timed conditions and ensure you produce full answers to the discussion parts as well as doing the calculations. Also ensure that you attempt all mock exams under exam conditions.

ACCA have launched a free on-demand resource designed to mirror the live exam experience helping you to become more familiar with the exam format. You can access the platform via the Study Support Resources section of the ACCA website navigating to the CBE question practice section and logging in with your myACCA credentials.

Passing your PM exam

Displaying the right qualities

- You are expected to have a core of management accounting knowledge from your previous studies of MA.

- You will be required to identify the requirements of multiple choice questions quickly, so that you can make your answers confidently within the available time.

- You will be required to carry out calculations, with clear workings and a logical structure.

- You will be required to interpret data.

- You will be required to explain management accounting techniques and discuss whether they are appropriate for a particular organisation.

- You must be able to apply your skills in a practical context.

- You must understand what numbers tell you about the performance of an organisation.

Avoiding weaknesses

- There is no choice in this exam all questions have to be answered. You must therefore study the entire syllabus, there are no short-cuts.

- Ability to answer multiple choice questions and cases improves with practice. Try to get as much practice with these questions as you can.

- The longer questions will be based on simple scenarios and answers must be focused and specific to the organisation.

Section A Objective test questions (OTQs)

Some OTQs are easier than others. Answer those that you feel fairly confident about as quickly as you can. Come back later to those you find more difficult. This could be a way of making use of the time in the examination most efficiently and effectively. Some questions are more time-consuming than others.

The first more time-consuming OTQ will involve doing a computation. You will probably need to jot down a quick proforma to answer a computational question. If the OTQ is a multiple choice question, remember that the wrong answers will usually involve common errors so don't assume that because you have the same answer as one of the options that your answer is necessarily correct! Double check to make sure you haven't made any silly mistakes. If you haven't got the same answer as any of the options, rework your computation, thinking carefully about what errors you could have made. If you still haven't got one of the options, choose the one which is nearest to your answer.

The second more time-consuming OTQ is one where you are asked to consider a number of statements and identify which one (or more) of them is correct. Make sure that you read each statement at least twice before making your selection. Be careful to follow the requirements of the OTQ exactly, for example if you are asked to identify two correct statements. Make sure that you understand the wording of 'written' OTQs before selecting your answer.

Note that the exam software contains a 'flag' functionality, meaning that you can flag any questions that you want to return to and review, if you have spare time at the end.

Section B Objective test questions (OTQs)

The general advice for Section A OTQs stands for Section B. Additional advice is to make sure that you read the whole case scenario. Make a note of any specific instructions or assumptions, then skim through the requirements of the five questions. The questions are independent of each other and can be answered in any order.

Calculations in Section C questions

There will be some relatively straightforward calculations at the start of the question and they will then probably get progressively more difficult. If you get stuck, make an assumption, state it and move on. Do not miss out on easy marks by not learning your proformas properly.

Discussions in Section C questions

A Section C question may separate discussion requirements from calculations, so that you do not need to do the calculations first in order to answer the discussion part. This means that you should be able to gain marks from making sensible, practical comments without having to complete the calculations.

Discussions that are focused on the specific organisation in the question will gain more marks than regurgitation of knowledge. Read the question carefully and more than once, to ensure you are actually answering the specific requirements.

Pick out key words such as 'describe', 'evaluate' and 'discuss'. These all mean something specific.

- 'Describe' means to communicate the key features of
- 'Evaluate' means to assess the value of
- 'Discuss' means to examine in detail by argument

Clearly label the points you make in discussions so that the marker can identify them all rather than getting lost in the detail.

Provide answers in the form requested. Use a report format if asked for and give recommendations if required.

Exam information

Computer-based exams

Applied Skills exams are all computer-based exams.

Format of the exam

The exam format will comprise three exam sections:

Section	Style of question type	Description	Proportion of exam, %
A	Objective test (OT)	15 questions × 2 marks	30
B	Objective test (OT) case	3 questions × 10 marks Each question will contain 5 subparts each worth 2 marks	30
C	Constructed Response (Long questions)	2 questions × 20 marks	40
Total			100

Section A and B questions will be selected from the entire syllabus. The responses to each question or subpart in the case of OT cases are marked automatically as either correct or incorrect by computer.

Section A and B questions will be selected from the entire syllabus. The responses to each question or subpart in the case of OT cases are marked automatically as either correct or incorrect by computer.

Section C questions will mainly focus on the following syllabus areas:

- Decision-making techniques (syllabus area C)
- Budgeting and control (syllabus area D)
- Performance measurement and control (syllabus area E)

However, these questions may also include requirements related to the information systems area of the syllabus. The responses to Section C questions are human marked.

Additional information

The Study Guide provides more detailed guidance on the syllabus and can be found by visiting the exam resource finder on the ACCA website.

Useful websites

The websites below provide additional sources of information of relevance to your studies for Performance Management.

- www.accaglobal.com

  ACCA's website. The students' section of the website is invaluable for detailed information about the qualification, past issues of Student Accountant (including technical articles) and a free downloadable Student Planner App.
- www.bpp.com

  Our website provides information about BPP products and services, with a link to the ACCA website.

Helping you with your revision

BPP Learning Media – ACCA Approved Content Provider

As an ACCA Approved Content Partner, BPP Learning Media gives you the opportunity to use revision materials reviewed by the ACCA examining team. By incorporating the examining team comments and suggestions regarding the depth and breadth of syllabus coverage, the BPP Learning Media Practice & Revision Kit provides excellent, ACCA-approved support for your revision.

These materials are reviewed by the ACCA examining team. The objective of the review is to ensure that the material properly covers the syllabus and study guide outcomes, used by the examining team in setting the exams, in the appropriate breadth and depth. The review does not ensure that every eventuality, combination or application of examinable topics is addressed by the ACCA Approved Content. Nor does the review comprise a detailed technical check of the content as the Approved Content Provider has its own quality assurance processes in place in this respect.

BPP Learning Media do everything possible to ensure the material is accurate and up to date when sending to print. In the event that any errors are found after the print date, they are uploaded to the following website: www.bpp.com/learningmedia/Errata.

The structure of this Practice and Revision Kit

Using feedback obtained from ACCA examining team review:

- We look at the dos and don'ts of revising for, and taking, ACCA exams

- We focus on Performance Management; we discuss revising the syllabus, what to do (and what not to do) in the exam, how to approach different types of question and ways of obtaining easy marks

- There are also four mock exams which provide you the opportunity to refine your knowledge and skills as part of your final exam preparations.

Selecting questions

We provide a full question index to help you plan your revision.

Making the most of question practice

At BPP Learning Media we realise that you need more than just questions and model answers to get the most from your question practice.

- Our top tips included for certain questions provide essential advice on tackling questions, presenting answers and the key points that answers need to include.

- We show you how you can pick up easy marks on some questions, as we know that picking up all readily available marks often can make the difference between passing and failing.

- We include marking guides to show you what the examining team rewards.

- We include comments from the examining team to show you where students struggled or performed well in the actual exam.

- We refer to the 2022 BPP Workbook (for exams in September 2022, December 2022, March 2023 and June 2023) for detailed coverage of the topics covered in questions.

Attempting mock exams

There are four mock exams that provide practice at coping with the pressures of the exam day. We strongly recommend that you attempt them under exam conditions. Mock exam 1 is the Specimen exam paper. Mock exam 2 is the September 2016 exam. Mock exam 3 is the December 2016 exam. Mock exam 4 is a mixture of exam standard questions, some of which have come from past papers.

BPP LEARNING MEDIA

Essential skill areas to be successful in Performance Management

There are three areas you should develop in order to achieve exam success in the Performance Management (PM):

(1) Knowledge application
(2) Specific PM skills
(3) Exam success skills.

At the revision and final exam preparation phases these **should be developed together as part of a comprehensive study plan of focused question practice**.

Take some time to revisit the Specific **PM skills** and **Exam success skills**. These are shown in the diagram below and followed by tutorial guidance of how to apply them.

Specific PM skills

These are the skills specific to PM that we think you need to develop in order to pass the exam. In the BPP Workbook for PM there are five **Skills Checkpoints** which define each skill and show how it is applied in answering a question. A brief summary of each skill is given below.

Skill 1: Approach to objective test (OT) questions

Skills Checkpoint 1 in the BPP Workbook for PM covers the various types of OT question through application to an exam-standard Section B question. Consider revisiting Skills Checkpoint 1 to improve your OT skills.

Skill 2: Using the scenario

Skills Checkpoint 2 in the BPP Workbook for PM covers this technique in detail through application to an exam-standard question. Consider revisiting Skills Checkpoint 2 to specifically improve this skill.

Skill 3: How to approach your PM exam

Skills Checkpoint 3 in the BPP Workbook for PM covers the approach to your PM exam. Consider revisiting Skills Checkpoint 3 to specifically improve your exam technique.

Skill 4: Effective use of spreadsheets

Skills Checkpoint 4 in the BPP Workbook for PM covers spreadsheets in detail through application to an exam-standard question. Consider revisiting Skills Checkpoint 4 to specifically improve this skill. Note that there is detailed commentary on the use of spreadsheets for the Mar/Jun 19 sample question 'Belton Park', found on the ACCA website. You should read this to build on the skills discussed in this Checkpoint.

Skill 5: Performance management questions

Skills Checkpoint 5 in the BPP Workbook for PM covers performance management questions in detail through application to an exam-standard question. Consider revisiting Skills Checkpoint 5 to specifically improve this skill. Note that there are exam technique technical articles on the ACCA website relating to the PM exam.

Essential skill areas

Exam success skill 1

Managing information

Questions in the exam will present you with a lot of information. The skill is how you handle this information to make the best use of your time. The key is determining how you will approach the exam and then actively reading the questions.

Advice on developing Managing information

Approach

The exam is three hours long. There is no designated 'reading' time at the start of the exam.

However, one approach that can work well is to start the exam by spending 10–15 minutes carefully reading through all of the questions to familiarise yourself with the exam.

Once you feel familiar with the exam consider the order in which you will attempt the questions; always attempt them in your order of preference. For example, you may want to leave to last the question you consider to be the most difficult.

If you do take this approach, remember to adjust the time available for each question appropriately – see Exam success skill 6: Good time management.

If you find that this approach doesn't work for you, don't worry – you can develop your own technique.

Active reading

You must take an active approach to reading each question. In Section C questions in particular, focus on the requirement first, making a note of key verbs such as 'explain' and 'discuss', to ensure you answer the question properly. Then read the rest of the question, making notes on important and relevant information you think you will need.

Exam success skill 2

Correct interpretation of the requirements

The active verb used often dictates the approach that written answers should take (eg 'explain', 'discuss'). It is important you identify and use the verb to define your approach. The **correct interpretation of the requirements** skill means correctly producing only what is being asked for by a requirement. Anything not required will not earn marks.

Advice on developing correct interpretation of the requirements

This skill can be developed by analysing question requirements and applying this process:

Step 1 Read the requirement

Firstly, read the requirement a couple of times slowly and carefully and note the active verbs. Use the active verbs to define what you plan to do. Make sure you identify any sub-requirements.

Step 2 Read the rest of the question

By reading the requirement first, you will have an idea of what you are looking out for as you read through the scenario. This is a great time saver and means you don't end up having to read the whole question in full twice. You should do this in an active way – see Exam success skill 1: Managing Information.

Step 3 Read the requirement again

Read the requirement again to remind yourself of the exact wording before starting your answer. This will capture any misinterpretation of the requirements or any missed requirements entirely. This should become a habit in your approach and, with repeated practice, you will find the focus, relevance and depth of your answer plan will improve.

Exam success skill 3

Answer planning: Priorities, structure and logic

This skill requires the planning of the key aspects of an answer which accurately and completely responds to the requirement.

Advice on developing Answer planning: Priorities, structure and logic

Everyone will have a preferred style for an answer plan. For example, it may be a mind map, bullet pointed lists or simply making some notes. Choose the approach that you feel most comfortable with, or, if you are not sure, try out different approaches for different questions until you have found your preferred style.

Exam success skill 4

Efficient numerical analysis

This skill aims to maximise the marks awarded by making clear to the marker the process of arriving at your answer. This is achieved by laying out an answer such that, even if you make a few errors, you can still score subsequent marks for follow-on calculations. It is vital that you do not lose marks purely because the marker cannot follow what you have done.

Advice on developing Efficient numerical analysis

This skill can be developed by applying the following process:

Step 1 Use a standard proforma working where relevant

If answers can be laid out in a standard proforma then always plan to do so. This will help the marker to understand your working and allocate the marks easily. It will also help you to work through the figures in a methodical and time-efficient way.

Step 2 Show your workings

Keep your workings as clear and simple as possible and ensure they are cross referenced to the main part of your answer. Where it helps, provide brief narrative explanations to help the marker understand the steps in the calculation. This means that if a mistake is made you do not lose any subsequent marks for follow-on calculations.

Step 3 Keep moving!

It is important to remember that, in an exam situation, it can sometimes be difficult to get every number 100% correct. The key is therefore ensuring you do not spend too long on any single calculation. If you are struggling with a solution then make a sensible assumption, state it and move on.

Exam success skill 5

Effective writing and presentation

Written answers should be presented so that the marker can clearly see the points you are making. The skill is to provide efficient written answers with sufficient breadth of points that answer the question, in the right depth, in the time available.

Advice on developing Effective writing and presentation

Step 1 Use headings

Using the headings and sub-headings from your answer plan will give your answer structure, order and logic. This will ensure your answer links back to the requirement and is clearly signposted, making it easier for the marker to understand the different points you are making. Making your headings bold will also help the marker.

Step 2 Type your answer in short, but full, sentences

Use short, punchy sentences with the aim that every sentence should say something different and generate marks. Type in full sentences, ensuring your style is professional.

Step 3 Do your calculations first and explanation second

Questions sometimes ask for a discussion or explanation with suitable calculations. The best approach is to prepare the calculation first then add the explanation.

Performing the calculation first should enable you to explain what you have done.

Exam success skill 6

Good time management

This skill means planning your time across all the requirements so that all tasks have been attempted at the end of the 3 hours available and actively checking on time during your exam. This is so that you can flex your approach and prioritise requirements which, in your judgement, will generate the maximum marks in the available time remaining.

Advice on developing Good time management

The exam is 3 hours long, which translates to 1.8 minutes per mark. Therefore a 10-mark requirement should be allocated a maximum of 18 minutes to complete your answer before you move on to the next task. At the beginning of a question, work out the amount of time you should be spending on each requirement. If you take the approach of spending 10–15 minutes reading and planning at the start of the exam, adjust the time allocated to each question accordingly.

Keep an eye on the clock

Aim to attempt all requirements, but be ready to be ruthless and move on if your answer is not going as planned. The challenge for many is sticking to planned timings. Be aware this is difficult to achieve in the early stages of your studies and be ready to let this skill develop over time.

If you find yourself running short on time and know that a full answer is not possible in the time you have, consider recreating your plan in overview form and then add key terms and details as time allows. Remember, some marks may be available, for example, simply stating a conclusion which you don't have time to justify in full.

Questions

Section A questions

OTQ bank – Information, technologies and systems for organisation performance
54 mins

1 The cost of running a company's IT department is $2.4m per annum. 90% of the processing time in the department is spent on recording accounting transactions and 10% on responding to online information requests from managers.

There are two types of information request: full reports and specific queries. A full report takes twice the processing time as a specific query and each month there are 4,000 specific queries and 500 requests for full reports. Costs are apportioned on the basis of processing time.

What is the estimated cost per specific query (to the nearest $)?

O $4

O $20

O $48

O $40   (2 marks)

2 The following statements have been made about data and information.

(1)   Automated systems for data capture are generally more reliable than data capture requiring input by individuals.

(2)   As a general rule, secondary information is more expensive to collect than primary data.

Which of the above statements is/are true?

O   1 only

O   2 only

O   Neither 1 nor 2

O   Both 1 and 2   (2 marks)

3 Indicate, by selecting the relevant boxes, whether each of the following controls help to ensure the security of highly confidential information.

Logical access controls	YES	NO
Database controls	YES	NO
Hierarchical passwords	YES	NO
Range checks	YES	NO

(2 marks)

BPP LEARNING MEDIA

4   The following statements have been made about management information and management information systems.

(1)   Management information is often produced from transaction processing systems.

(2)   The data used in management information systems comes mainly from sources within the organisation and its operations.

Which of the above statements is/are true?

O   1 only

O   2 only

O   Neither 1 nor 2

O   Both 1 and 2   (2 marks)

5   Are the following statements about management information systems true or false?

They are designed to report on existing operations.	TRUE	FALSE
They have an external focus.	TRUE	FALSE

(2 marks)

6   The following statements have been made about operational control.

(1)   Budgeting is commonly associated with decision-making at the operational planning level within a management hierarchy.

(2)   Operational control decisions in general are more narrowly focused and have a shorter time horizon than management control decisions.

Which of the above statements is/are true?

O   1 only

O   2 only

O   Neither 1 nor 2

O   Both 1 and 2   (2 marks)

7   Which of the following terms is used to describe an information system that provides senior executives with online access to important information obtained from both internal and external sources?

O   Executive information system

O   Enterprise resource planning system

O   Management information system

O   Transaction processing system   (2 marks)

8   A company's board of directors were recently embarrassed when a very unhappy junior human resources employee emailed details of their salaries to the entire company. An investigation revealed that the human resources director had lent his username and password to the junior employee so that routine maintenance of the human resources database could be conducted whilst the director was on vacation. During the director's vacation, the junior employee had used the director's username and password to access the board's salary records.

Which of the following controls could have helped to prevent this breach of confidential information?

○   Monitoring the database system logs on a daily basis to see what information is being accessed

○   Building levels of access into the database so that only senior staff have access to board records

○   Keeping all the human resource records for salaries on a separate server

○   Having a policy of regularly updating the passwords required to access the system

(2 marks)

9   Big data analytics usually involves the analysis of unstructured data.

Which of the following is an example of unstructured data?

○   Data tables showing monthly purchases figures

○   Spreadsheet analysis of annual sales

○   Email communications between a customer and the customer services department

○   A table of supplier names and addresses

(2 marks)

10   The following statements have been made about information systems.

(1)   Feedback is information produced from a system that is used by management to take action to control further inputs to the system.

(2)   Information for benchmarking purposes may be obtained from both internal and external sources.

Which of the above statements is/are true?

○   1 only

○   2 only

○   Neither 1 nor 2

○   Both 1 and 2

(2 marks)

11   Coff Co operates a chain of coffee shops. It has an interactive website where customers can leave feedback, and has recently introduced a customer loyalty card that is swiped at the till whenever a purchase is made. Coff Co is keen to make use of this new data.

Which **TWO** of the following are ways that Coff Co could use the information collected from the website and customer loyalty cards?

☐   Understand individual customer preferences

☐   Update its inventory records

☐   Analyse the take-up of targeted promotions

☐   Compile branch sales forecasts   **(2 marks)**

---

12   The following costs relate to management accounting information for Kite Co for April 20X8:

Cost	$
Employee time spent filling in purchase requisitions	600
Use of barcodes and scanners to record inventory	200
Storage of sales information no longer needed	400
Time taken by staff to input data into production system	900

What were the total direct data capture costs for Kite Co for April 20X8?

O $200

O $800

O $1,700

O $2,100   **(2 marks)**

---

13   An education department has a statutory obligation to report on the number of students on site throughout the day. In order to produce this information, a swipe card system has been introduced.

The following table details the costs of the swipe card system in its first year:

	$	Notes
Purchase price of the swipe system (vendor list price)	100,000	Invoiced and paid
Installation costs of the system (negotiated with vendor)	20,000	Invoiced and paid
Pre-launch testing costs (in-house)	17,000	Salaries time spent on testing
Cost per 100 swipe cards	5,000	1,000 cards purchased in the first year
Apportionment of the technology insurance cost	9,000	Fixed cost
Salary of clerk employed to collate and distribute swipe card system information	36,000	Fixed cost

What is the indirect cost of producing the information required in the first year of the swipe card system?

| $ | | **(2 marks)**

14　Which of the following is an example of local networking?

○　　Internet

○　　File server

○　　Intranet

○　　Ethernet　　　　　　　　　　　　　　　　　　　　　　**(2 marks)**

15　Which **TWO** of the following are benefits of wireless technology?

☐　　Better decision-making

☐　　Increased productivity

☐　　Increased security

☐　　Reduced costs as businesses expand　　　　　　　　**(2 marks)**

OTQ bank – Information, technologies and systems for organisation performance　　　54 mins

16　Which of the following statements is NOT a benefit of using data mining by an online book retailer?

○　　Better understanding of customer behaviour

○　　Targeted marketing based on previous browsing history

○　　Fewer staff required in the finance function to analyse data

○　　Better control of inventories from real time inventory reports　　**(2 marks)**

17　Which **TWO** of the following are true of customer relationship management (CRM) systems?

☐　　They analyse a customer's interactions with an organisation throughout the customer life cycle

☐　　The software subscription and purchase fees are inexpensive

☐　　They allow marketing communication to be tailored to the customer's interests

☐　　CRM systems require no staff training　　　　　　　　**(2 marks)**

18　Match the following levels in the data pyramid to the appropriate explanation.

Levels
Data
Information
Knowledge
Wisdom

Level	Explanation
	Adding value
	Revealing relationships
	Providing insights
	Making measurements

(2 marks)

19   Which of the following is an external source of information?

    O   Value of sales, analysed for each customer

    O   Value of purchases, analysed for each supplier

    O   Prices of similar products, analysed for each competitor company

    O   Hours worked, analysed for each employee   (2 marks)

20   Are the following statements about data and information systems true or false?

In-depth analysis of data on a database in order to identify undiscovered trends or patterns in the data is known as data mining.	TRUE	FALSE
Large public databases are a major source of feedback for many commercial organisations.	TRUE	FALSE

           (2 marks)

21   Which of the following statements concerning big data analytics is correct?

    O   It relies on digital information

    O   It relies on written information

    O   It relies on verbal information

    O   It relies on confidential information   (2 marks)

22   Are the following statements about management information systems true or false?

Budgetary control information comes mainly from sources outside the organisation.	TRUE	FALSE
An EIS provides an integrated database system for the management of operations.	TRUE	FALSE

           (2 marks)

23   Match the information system with the appropriate level on the data pyramid.

Information system
Expert system
Transaction processing system
Decision support system
Management information system

Information system	Level
	Data
	Information
	Knowledge
	Wisdom

           (2 marks)

24   Which of the following statements is/are true?

    (1)   Enterprise Resource Planning (ERP) systems use complex computer systems, usually comprehensive databases, to provide plans for every aspect of the business.

    (2)   Enterprise Resource Planning (ERP) systems are accounting oriented information systems which aid in identifying and planning the enterprise wide resources needed to resource, make, account for and deliver customer orders.

    ○   1 only

    ○   2 only

    ○   Both 1 and 2

    ○   Neither 1 nor 2   **(2 marks)**

25   Which **TWO** of the following are risks of using big data?

    ☐   Veracity of data used

    ☐   Volume of data used

    ☐   Security of data collected

    ☐   The use of real time data   **(2 marks)**

26   Which of the following controls is used to ensure accuracy of data?

    ○   Dial-back

    ○   Firewall

    ○   Encryption

    ○   Validation   **(2 marks)**

27   Which **TWO** of the following are ways that big data can be used to improve performance?

    ☐   Reducing the number of data analysts (reducing labour costs)

    ☐   Stocking products that customers want (increasing sales)

    ☐   Being able to apply target advertising (increasing sales)

    ☐   Costs saved by collecting less data (reducing costs)   **(2 marks)**

28   Are the following statements about big data and data analytics true or false?

Big data can be used to provide insights into costs.	TRUE	FALSE
Social media is a source of big data.	TRUE	FALSE
Predictive analytics is a branch of data analytics.	TRUE	FALSE

        (2 marks)

29 Which of the following systems helps managers to see trends and make strategic decisions?

Picklist:

Transaction processing system (TPS)
Management information system (MIS)
Executive information system (EIS)
Enterprise resource planning systems (ERPS)   (2 marks)

---

30 Are the following statements about big data analytics true or false?

It enables large quantities of data to be examined quickly.	TRUE	FALSE
It improves organisational decision-making.	TRUE	FALSE
It enables cost reduction.	TRUE	FALSE
It requires adherence to data privacy laws	TRUE	FALSE

(2 marks)

Section C question

31 Story   36 mins

Story is a well-established, global publishing conglomerate. The corporation is structured to allow each country of operation to function as an autonomous business unit, that reports back to head office. The data from each business unit is entered onto the mainframe computer at head office. Each business unit can make use of any service offered by other business units and can also offer services to the other units. The services include translation into different languages, typesetting, printing, storage and so forth. In each country of operation there is at least one, and usually several, retail outlets.

The core business was traditionally based upon the provision of fictional stories for the mass market. For the past decade Story has diversified into publishing textbooks and technical literature. The organisation currently enjoys a good reputation in both areas of the business and global sales are increasing annually at a rate of 5% for fictional books and 2% for textbooks. Last year 700 million fictional works and 25 million textbooks were sold.

The corporate management team wish to increase the growth in sales of textbooks but realise that they cannot afford to allocate significant resources to this task as the market, and profit margin, for textbooks is very much smaller than for fiction. They also wish to improve the sales performance of the fictional books.

Story is currently having trouble in maintaining a corporate image in some countries of operation. For example, several business units may be unaware of additions to the product range. Another example is that a price change in a book is not simultaneously altered by all the business units, leading to pricing discrepancies.

Some members of the corporate management team see possible advantages to upgrading the existing computer system to one that is fully networked. Other members are more sceptical and are reluctant to consider enhancing the system. Some members have also wondered whether big data could provide useful information to aid decision-making for Story but others think there may be problems with actually using big data.

Required

(a)   Discuss the issues involved in upgrading the existing information system and the proposed changes, with reference to both the wider business environment and the decision-making process.   **(8 marks)**

(b)   Explain the problems Story may have trying to capture and use big data.   **(6 marks)**

(c)   Management information systems (MIS) allow managers to make timely and effective decisions using data in an appropriate form. List three types of MIS and how they would be used in an organisation.   **(6 marks)**

(Note that syllabus learning outcome A on Information, technologies and systems for organisational performance, can form **parts** of a Section C question. However, you will never see a full 20 mark Section C question from this area. This question is just to help you practise the subject.)

(Total = 20 marks)

Section A questions

OTQ bank – Specialist cost and management accounting techniques

54 mins

32   The following costs have arisen in relation to the production of a product:

(1)   Planning and concept design costs

(2)   Testing costs

(3)   Production costs

(4)   Distribution and customer service costs

In calculating the life cycle costs of a product, which of the above items would be included?

O   3 only

O   1, 2 and 3

O   1, 2 and 4

O   All of the above   (2 marks)

33   Which **TWO** of the following activities are environmental INTERNAL failure costs?

☐   Quality control inspections to monitor pollution levels in water leaving a production process.

☐   Water purification treatment to clean waste water before it leaves the factory.

☐   Fitting of carbon filters to machine processes to reduce carbon emissions.

☐   Power usage measuring system to monitor energy consumption within the factory.

☐   Payment of fines for breaching environmental regulations in the industry

☐   Insulation of heating pipes in the factory to reduce heat loss

☐   Public relations costs to remedy reputational damage caused by accidental river pollution.

☐   Capturing and recycling of waste exhaust gases to generate energy.   **(2 marks)**

34   One of the products manufactured by a company is Product X, which sells for $40 per unit and has a material cost of $10 per unit and a direct labour cost of $7 per unit. The total direct labour budget for the year is 50,000 hours of labour time at a cost of $12 per hour. Factory overheads are $2,920,000 per year.

The company is considering the introduction of a system of throughput accounting. It has identified that machine time is the bottleneck in production. Product X needs 0.01 hours of machine time per unit produced. The maximum capacity for machine time is 4,000 hours per year.

What is the throughput accounting ratio for Product X (to two decimal places)?

    [   ]

                                                                                          (2 marks)

35 Are the following statements about material flow cost accounting (MFCA) true or false?

In material flow cost accounting, waste is treated as a negative product and given a cost.	TRUE	FALSE
Material flow cost accounting should encourage management to focus on ways of achieving the same amount of finished output with less material input.	TRUE	FALSE

(2 marks)

36 Which of the following statements about activity based costing is true?

○ The cost driver for quality inspection is likely to be batch size.

○ The cost driver for materials handling and despatch costs is likely to be the number of orders handled.

○ In the short run, all the overhead costs for an activity vary with the amount of the cost driver for the activity.

○ A cost driver is an activity based cost. (2 marks)

37 The following data refers to a soft drinks manufacturing company that passes its product through four processes and is currently operating at optimal capacity.

Process	Washing	Filling	Capping	Labelling
Time per dozen units	6 mins	3 mins	1.5 mins	2 mins
Machine hours available	1,200	700	250	450

Product data	$ per unit
Selling price	0.60
Direct material	0.18
Direct labour	0.02
Factory fixed cost	$4,120

Which process is the bottleneck?

Picklist:

Washing
Filling
Capping
Labelling

(2 marks)

38 A manufacturing company uses machine C, which is operational for five hours a day to manufacture four products: W, X, Y and Z. Factory costs are $150,000 per day. The company uses throughput accounting and its objective is to maximise profits.

Information relating to these products is as follows:

Product	Production rate per machine hours (units)	Selling price per unit ($)	Material cost per unit ($)	Conversion cost per unit ($)
W	200	350	120	40
X	500	190	95	25
Y	400	270	160	20
Z	350	215	75	35

If the company is not able to increase the availability of machine C's operational hours, what is the production ranking of product Y?

○ First

○ Second

○ Third

○ Forth   .   (2 marks)

---

39 Which **THREE** of the following statements about activity-based costing (ABC) and traditional costing systems (absorption costing and marginal costing) are correct?

☐ No over-absorption or under-absorption of overheads can occur under ABC.

☐ ABC is useful for businesses which have high overheads in their cost structure.

☐ ABC is not suitable for use in businesses that provide services.

☐ Marginal costing understates the true cost of a product when compared to ABC.

☐ ABC is better than absorption costing in understanding what causes costs to be incurred.

☐ Both ABC and marginal costing treat all fixed costs as product costs.   (2 marks)

---

40 When activity based costing is used for environmental accounting, which statement is correct for environment-related costs and environment-driven costs?

○ Environment-related costs can be attributed to joint cost centres and environment-driven costs cannot be

○ Environment-driven costs can be attributed to joint cost centres and environment-related costs cannot be

○ Both environment-related costs and environment-driven costs can be attributed to joint cost centres

○ Neither environment-related costs nor environment-driven costs can be attributed to joint cost centres   (2 marks)

41   The following statements have been made about traditional absorption costing and activity based costing (ABC).

(1)   Traditional absorption costing may be used to set prices for products, but activity based costing cannot.

(2)   Traditional absorption costing tends to allocate too many overhead costs to low-volume products and not enough overheads to high-volume products.

(3)   Implementing ABC is expensive and time consuming

Which of the above statements is/are true?

○   1 only

○   3 only

○   1, 2 and 3

○   1 and 2 only   (2 marks)

42   Are the following statements about environmental cost accounting true or false?

The majority of environmental costs are already captured within a typical organisation's accounting system. The difficulty lies in identifying them.	TRUE	FALSE
Input/output analysis divides material flows within an organisation into three categories: material flows; system flows; and delivery and disposal flows.	TRUE	FALSE

(2 marks)

43   Which of the following statements about target costing is **NOT** true?

○   Target costing is better suited to assembly orientated industries than service industries that have a large fixed cost base.

○   Costs may be reduced in target costing by removing product features that do not add value.

○   A target cost gap is the difference between the target cost for a product and its projected cost.

○   Products should be discontinued if there is a target cost gap.   (2 marks)

44   Budget information relating to a company that manufactures four products is as follows.

Product	Maximum sales demand	Machine hours per unit	Maximum machine hours required	Sales price per unit	Material cost per unit
	Units			$	$
A	1,000	0.1	100	15	6
B	500	0.2	100	21	10
C	2,000	0.3	600	18	9
D	1,000	0.2	200	25	16
			1,000		

Only 750 machine hours are available during the period. Applying the principles of throughput accounting, how many units of Product B should be made if the company produces output to maximise throughput and profit?

[   ] units   (2 marks)

45   ABC is felt to give a more useful product cost than classic absorption costing (with overheads absorbed on labour hours) if which of the following **TWO** apply?

        ☐   Labour costs are a relatively minor proportion of total costs

        ☐   Overheads vary with many different measures of activity

        ☐   Overheads are difficult to predict

        ☐   Cost drivers are difficult to identify   **(2 marks)**

---

46   A company has a target mark up of 25% and sells into a competitive market where the market price is $120 per unit. The company's current costs per unit are $46 for variable costs and $60 for fixed costs, and it has a budgeted output of 10,000 units.

       What is the minimum production required to close the target cost gap?

       ○   11,778 units

       ○   13,636 units

       ○   11,042 units

       ○   12,000 units   **(2 marks)**

                                          (Total = 30 marks)

OTQ bank – Specialist cost and management accounting techniques   54 mins

47   In which of the following ways might financial returns be improved over the life cycle of a product?

      (1)   Maximising the breakeven time

      (2)   Minimising the time to market

      (3)   Minimising the length of the life cycle

      ○   1 and 2

      ○   1 and 3

      ○   2 only

      ○   2 and 3   **(2 marks)**

---

48   Which **TWO** of the following statements about throughput accounting and the theory of constraints are true?

        ☐   A principle of throughput accounting is that a buffer inventory should be built up for output from the bottleneck resource.

        ☐   Unless output capacity is greater than sales demand, there will always be a binding constraint.

        ☐   The production capacity of a bottleneck resource should determine the production schedule for the organisation as a whole.

        ☐   Idle time should be avoided in areas of production that are not a bottleneck resource.   **(2 marks)**

---

49   The following information relates to the expected cost of a new product over its expected three-year life.

	Year 0	Year 1	Year 2	Year 3
Units made and sold		25,000	100,000	75,000
R&D costs	$850,000	$90,000		
Production costs				
Variable per unit		$30	$25	$20
Fixed costs		$500,000	$500,000	$500,000
Selling and distribution costs				
Variable per unit		$6	$5	$4
Fixed costs		$700,000	$500,000	$300,000
Customer service costs				
Variable per unit		$4	$3	$2

What is the expected average life cycle cost per unit?

O $35.95

O $46.25

O $48.00

O $50.95   (2 marks)

50   Are the following statements about target costing true or false?

A risk with target costing is that cost reductions may affect the perceived value of the product.	TRUE	FALSE
An effective way of reducing the projected cost of a new product is to simplify the design.	TRUE	FALSE
The value of target costing depends on having reliable estimates of sales demand.	TRUE	FALSE
Target costing may be applied to services that are provided free of charge to customers, such as costs of call centre handling.	TRUE	FALSE

(2 marks)

51   In flow cost accounting, which of the following is **NOT** a category used?

O   Output flows

O   Material flows

O   Delivery and disposal flows

O   System flows   (2 marks)

52   Which **TWO** of the following statements about life cycle costing are true?

☐   A product is usually most profitable during the growth phase of its life cycle.

☐   Life cycle costing is useful for deciding the selling price for a product.

☐   An important use of life cycle costing is to decide whether to go ahead with the development of a new product.

☐   Life cycle costing encourages management to find a suitable balance between investment costs and operating expenses.   (2 marks)

53   The following statements have been made about throughput accounting.

(1)   Direct labour should always be treated as a factory cost when measuring throughput.

(2)   If machine time is the bottleneck resource, there is no value in taking measures to improve direct labour efficiency.

Which of the above statements is/are true?

O   1 only

O   2 only

O   Neither 1 nor 2

O   Both 1 and 2   (2 marks)

54   The selling price of Product X is set at $550 for each unit and sales for the coming year are expected to be 800 units.

A return of 30% on the investment of $500,000 in Product X will be required in the coming year.

What is the target cost for each unit of Product X (to two decimal places)?

$ [   ]   (2 marks)

55   Which of the following should be categorised as environmental failure costs by an airline company?

(1)   Compensation payments to residents living close to airports for noise pollution caused by their aircraft

(2)   Air pollution due to the airline's carbon emissions from their aircraft engines

(3)   Penalties paid by the airline to the government for breaching environmental regulations

O   2 only

O   1, 2 and 3

O   1 and 3 only

O   2 and 3 only   (2 marks)

56   The following estimates have been produced for a new product with an expected life of four years.

	Year 1	Year 2	Year 3	Year 4
Units made and sold	5,000	10,000	25,000	10,000
	$	$	$	$
R&D costs	0.9 million	0.3 million	–	–
Marketing costs	0.3 million	0.3 million	0.1 million	0.1 million
Production cost per unit	80	40	30	30
Customer service cost per unit	20	15	10	5
Disposal costs	–	–	–	0.2 million

What is the expected life cycle cost per unit (to two decimal places)?

$ [   ]   (2 marks)

57 Product YZ2 is made in a production process where machine time is a bottleneck resource. Production of one unit of Product YZ2 takes 0.25 machine hours. The costs and selling price of Product YZ2 are as follows:

	$
Materials	10
Labour (0.5 hours)	7
Other factory costs	7
	24
Sales price	30
Profit	6

In a system of throughput accounting, what is the return per factory hour (to two decimal places)?

$ [   ]

(2 marks)

---

58 A company manufactures Product Q, which sells for $50 per unit and has a material cost of $14 per unit and a direct labour cost of $10 per unit. The total direct labour budget for the year is 18,000 hours of labour time at a cost of $10 per hour. Factory overheads are $1,620,000 per year. The company has identified machine time as the bottleneck in production. Product Q needs 0.05 hours of machine time per unit produced. The maximum capacity for machine time is 6,000 hours per year.

What is the throughput accounting ratio for Product Q (to one decimal place)?

[   ]

(2 marks)

---

59 Which **TWO** of the following statements about activity based costing (ABC) are true?

☐ ABC recognises the complexity of modern manufacturing by the use of multiple cost drivers.

☐ ABC establishes separate cost pools for support activities.

☐ ABC reapportions support activity costs.

☐ ABC is an appropriate costing system when overheads vary with time spent on production.

(2 marks)

---

60 In the theory of constraints and throughput accounting, which of the following methods may be used to elevate the performance of a binding constraint?

Method 1: Acquire more of the resource that is the binding constraint

Method 2: Improve the efficiency of usage of the resource that is the binding constraint

O   Method 1 only

O   Method 2 only

O   Method 1 and Method 2

O   Neither method would be effective

(2 marks)

61   Which **TWO** of the following costs are likely to rise when just-in-time (JIT) manufacturing is
        introduced?

        ☐   Set-up costs

        ☐   Raw material handling costs

        ☐   Raw material storage costs

        ☐   Customer order costs   (2 marks)

_____

(Total = 30 marks)

Section B OT case questions

Brick by Brick   **18 mins**

The following scenario relates to the next five questions.

Brick by Brick (BBB) is a building business that provides a range of building services to the public.
Recently it has been asked to quote for garage conversions (GC) and extensions to properties
(EX) and has found that it is winning fewer GC contracts than expected. In addition, BBB also
produces and sells different types of brick to the construction industry. The three types of brick
produced are clay, concrete and reclaimed bricks.

BBB has a policy to price all jobs at budgeted total cost plus 50%. Overheads are currently
absorbed on a labour hour basis. BBB thinks that a switch to activity based costing (ABC) to
absorb overheads would reduce the costs associated with GC and hence make them more
competitive.

You are provided with the following data:

Overhead category	Annual overheads $	Activity driver	Total number of activities per year
Supervisors	90,000	Site visits	500
Planners	70,000	Planning documents	250
Property related	240,000	Labour hours	40,000
Total	400,000		

A typical GC takes 300 labour hours to complete. A GC requires only one site visit by a supervisor
and needs only one planning document to be raised. An EX requires six site visits and five
planning documents.

62   What are the total overheads assigned to a GC using labour hours to absorb the
        overheads?

        GC $ [   ]   (2 marks)

_____

63   What are the total overheads assigned to a GC using ABC principles in respect of
        supervisor costs?

        GC $ [   ]   (2 marks)

_____

64 What are the total overheads assigned to an EX using ABC principles in respect of planning costs?

EX $ [   ]   (2 marks)

---

65 The absorption cost and ABC cost per service have now been correctly calculated as follows:

	GC	EX
Absorption cost	$11,000	$20,500
ABC cost	$10,260	$20,980

Are the following statements true or false?

Changing to a system of ABC costing should lead to a more competitive price being charged for the GC.	TRUE	FALSE
Using ABC would cause total overhead costs to increase.	TRUE	FALSE

(2 marks)

---

66 Which of the following statements about Brick by Brick and the use of ABC is true?

○ The traditional absorption approach gives a better indication of where cost savings can be made.

○ ABC is a cheaper system for BBB than absorption costing.

○ ABC eliminates the need for cost apportionment.

○ ABC improves pricing decisions.   (2 marks)

(Total = 10 marks)

Midhurst Co (Sep/Dec 2020)   18 mins

The following scenario relates to the next five questions.

Midhurst Co manufactures air conditioning units and is considering an investment in a new unit that will be used in modern office buildings. Advances in technology mean that this unit is more sensitive to changes and variations in temperature and therefore it can regulate airflow and heating more efficiently. Midhurst Co's competitors currently do not have an equivalent product that can offer these features.

Midhurst Co expects to sell 10,000 units over the predicted five-year life cycle of the unit. The finance director has just prepared the initial costings for the unit as follows:

	$'000
Research and development costs	6,200
Design costs	33,450
Marketing costs	177,685
Variable production cost per unit	42
Fixed production cost	98,470
Variable distribution cost	9
Fixed distribution cost	10,300
Variable selling cost per unit	4
Fixed selling cost	7,790
Administration cost	23,450

The finance director plans to use life-cycle costing to measure the profitability of the new product. The chief executive has asked for more information about life-cycle costing, as she is not sure whether it is the right method to use.

The production director has reviewed the costings in detail and suggested a couple of changes. He is enthusiastic about the product and believes that modifications could be made to prolong the product's life but wonders when the best time would be to make changes to the product.

67 According to the life-cycle costing method, which TWO of the following statements regarding the stages of the life-cycle are true?

☐ At the introduction stage, further capital expenditure will be needed as production capacity will need to increase to meet demand

☐ The maturity stage occurs when the market has reached 'saturation point' and bought enough of the product

☐ The majority of a product's life-cycle costs are determined by decisions which are made at the design and development stage

☐ The growth stage, when sales will have reached their peak and become stable, will be the most profitable stage (2 marks)

---

68 What is the cost per unit for the new air conditioning unit using life-cycle costing (to the nearest $)?

O $35,740

O $51,847

O $88,390

O $90,735 (2 marks)

---

69 The production director has suggested the following change for the costing of the new unit:

Currently material costs are 20% of the variable production costs per unit. One of the materials used is stainless steel which is budgeted at $2,000 per unit but an alternative corrosion-resistant metal costing 25% less can be used. The production director believes a 15% discount can be negotiated for the remainder of the materials.

What would be the revised material cost per unit (to the nearest whole $)?

$ [   ] (2 marks)

---

70 The production director has also asked about the implications for production planning if the company wishes to extend the product's life-cycle.

At what stage of the life-cycle is the new unit most likely to undergo product development?

O Introduction.

O Growth.

O Maturity.

O Decline. (2 marks)

---

71   The chief executive wants to be briefed on the advantages of using life-cycle costing.

Which of the following statements relating to the advantages of life-cycle costing are correct?

(1)   It draws management's attention to all costs related to a product which other costing methods usually treat as period costs

(2)   It focuses on measuring a product's costs from concept to withdrawal rather than reviewing costs on a period by period basis

(3)   It focuses on what consumers are prepared to pay for a product and establishes cost budgets based on an expected selling price

(4)   It aids understanding of the relationship between decisions at the design stage and the cost of other functions, such as marketing

O   2, 3 and 4 only

O   1, 2 and 4 only

O   1 and 3 only

O   1, 2, 3 and 4   (2 marks)

(Total = 10 marks)

Jola Publishing Co   18 mins

The following scenario relates to the next five questions.

Jola Publishing Co publishes two forms of book.

The company publishes a children's book (CB), which is sold in large quantities to government-controlled schools. The book is produced in four large production runs. The second book is a comprehensive technical journal (TJ). It is produced in monthly production runs, 12 times a year.

The directors are concerned about the performance of the two books and are wondering what the impact would be of a switch to an activity based costing (ABC) approach to accounting for overheads. They currently use absorption costing, based on number of books produced for all overhead calculations. Overheads amount to $2,880,000.

The CB will be inspected on 180 occasions next year, whereas the TJ will be inspected just 20 times.

Machine time per unit is six minutes for the CB and ten minutes for the TJ.

Jola Publishing will produce its annual output of 1,000,000 CBs in four production runs and approximately 10,000 TJs per month in each of 12 production runs.

Required

72   What is the overhead cost per unit of the CB using the current system of absorption costing?

$ [   ] per unit   (2 marks)

BPP
LEARNING
MEDIA

73   Jola Publishing Co has decided to adopt ABC. Management has put together a list of steps. Match each of the steps in ABC to the correct order in which they should be carried out.

Steps	Correct order	
Calculate the overhead cost per unit of CB and TJ.	Step 1	
Calculate the absorption rate for each 'cost driver'.	Step 2	
Determine what causes the cost of each activity – the 'cost driver'.	Step 3	
Identify major activities within each department which creates cost.	Step 4	
Create a cost centre/cost pool for each activity – 'the activity cost pool'.	Step 5	

(2 marks)

74   The overheads involved have been analysed as follows:

Overhead	$	Activity driver
Production costs	2,160,000	Machine hours
Quality control	668,000	Number of inspections
Production set up costs	52,000	Number of set ups
	2,880,000	

What is the total activity based apportionment of production costs for production of the CB?

$ [   ]   (2 marks)

75   What is the total activity based apportionment of quality control overheads for production of the TJ?

$ [   ]   (2 marks)

76   If Jola Publishing Co decides to introduce an ABC costing system, which of the following is an advantage of ABC that they can expect to benefit from?

○   A reduction in overhead costs

○   Cost savings compared to absorption costing

○   Simplification of the costing process

○   More accurate costs per unit   (2 marks)

(Total = 10 marks)

Corrie

The following scenario relates to the next five questions.

Corrie produces three products, X, Y and Z and uses throughput accounting. The capacity of Corrie's plant is restricted by process alpha. Process alpha is expected to be operational for eight hours per day and can produce 1,200 units of X per hour, 1,500 units of Y per hour and 600 units of Z per hour.

Selling prices and material costs for each product are as follows.

Product	Selling price $ per unit	Material cost $ per unit	Throughput contribution $ per unit
X	150	70	80
Y	120	40	80
Z	300	100	200

Conversion costs are $720,000 per day.

Required

77   What is the profit per day if daily output achieved is 6,000 units of X, 4,500 units of Y and 1,200 units of Z?

$ [   ]

(2 marks)

78   What is the efficiency of the bottleneck process given the output achieved is 6,000 units of X, 4,500 units of Y and 1,200 units of Z?

[   ] %

(2 marks)

79   What are the conversion costs per factory hour?

$ [   ]

(2 marks)

80   A change in factory cost arose, giving a new figure for conversion costs per factory hour of $80,000. What is the revised throughput accounting (TPAR) ratio for each product?

X [   ]

Y [   ]

Z [   ]

(2 marks)

81   Which **TWO** of the following statements about using throughput accounting (TA) are true?

☐   Corrie Co's priority, using TA, should be given to products with the highest throughput contribution per unit.

☐   TA assumes that labour costs are largely fixed.

☐   The TA ratio for each product should be less than 1.

☐   TA assumes that material costs can be controlled in the short term.

(2 marks)

(Total = 10 marks)

A Co

The following scenario relates to the next five questions.

A Co makes two products, B1 and B2. Its machines can only work on one product at a time. The two products are worked on in two departments by differing grades of labour. The labour requirements for the two products are as follows:

	B1	B2
	Minutes per unit of product	
Department 1	12	16
Department 2	20	15

There is currently a shortage of labour and the maximum times available each day in Departments 1 and 2 are 480 minutes and 840 minutes, respectively. The bottleneck or limiting factor is labour in Department 1. The current selling prices and costs for the two products are shown below:

	B1	B2
	$ per unit	$ per unit
Selling price	50.00	65.00
Direct materials	10.00	15.00
Direct labour	10.40	6.20
Variable overheads	6.40	9.20
Fixed overheads	12.80	18.40
Profit per unit	10.40	16.20

As part of the budget-setting process, A Co needs to know the optimum output levels. All output is sold.

Required

82   What is the maximum number of each product that could be produced each day?

B1 Department 1 [   ] units

B1 Department 2 [   ] units

B2 Department 1 [   ] units

B2 Department 2 [   ] units   (2 marks)

83   Using limiting factor analysis, what is the contribution per unit of limiting factor of B1 (to two decimal places)?

$ [   ]   (2 marks)

84   What is the throughput per minute of bottleneck resource of B2 (to two decimal places)?

$ [   ]   (2 marks)

85 A Co needs to decide whether to base its decisions about optimum levels of production using a throughput accounting approach, or a limiting factor approach.

Which of the following is an example of an advantage of choosing a throughput accounting approach?

O   The throughput accounting approach eliminates employee idle time.

O   The throughput accounting approach eliminates bottlenecks in manufacturing.

O   The throughput accounting approach eliminates the cost of holding inventory.

O   The throughput accounting approach is more suitable for short-term decision-making than limiting factor analysis.   (2 marks)

86 If A Co decides to apply the theory of constraints, match each of the steps to the correct order in which they should be carried out.

Steps	Correct order	
Subordinate everything else to the decisions made about exploiting the bottlenecks.	Step 1	
Elevate the system's bottlenecks.	Step 2	
Identify A Co's bottlenecks.	Step 3	
Decide how to exploit the system's bottlenecks.	Step 4	

(2 marks)

(Total = 10 marks)

Cam Co   18 mins

The following scenario relates to the next five questions.

Cam Co manufactures webcams, devices which can provide live video and audio streams via personal computers. It has recently been suffering from liquidity problems and hopes that these will be eased by the launch of its new webcam, which has revolutionary audio and video quality.

The webcam is expected to have a product life cycle of two years. Market research has already been carried out to establish a target selling price and projected lifetime sales volumes for the product. Cost estimates have also been prepared, based on the current proposed product specification. Cam Co uses life cycle costing to work out the target costs for its products. You are provided with the following relevant information for the webcam:

Projected lifetime sales volume   50,000 units
Target selling price per unit $200
Target profit margin   35%
Note. Estimated lifetime cost per unit:

	$	$
Manufacturing costs		
Direct material (bought in parts)	40	
Direct labour	26	
Machine costs	24	
Quality control costs	10	
		100
Non-manufacturing costs		60
Estimated lifetime cost per unit		160

The following information has been identified as relevant:

(1) Direct material cost: all of the parts currently proposed for the webcam are bespoke parts. However, most of these can actually be replaced with standard parts costing 55% less. However, three of the bespoke parts, which currently account for 20% of the estimated direct material cost, cannot be replaced, although an alternative supplier charging 10% less has been sourced for these parts.

(2) Direct labour cost: the webcam uses 45 minutes of direct labour, which costs $34.67 per hour. The use of more standard parts, however, will mean that while the first unit would still be expected to take 45 minutes, there will now be an expected rate of learning of 90% (where 'b' = − 0.152). This will end after the first 100 units have been completed.

Required

87 What is the target cost of the new webcam?

$ [   ]   (2 marks)

___

88 What is the direct material cost per unit in light of the new information in point (1)?

$ [   ]   (2 marks)

___

89 What is the average direct labour cost per unit in light of the new information in point (2)?

$ [   ]   (2 marks)

___

90 Are the following statements about Cam Co's target costing system true or false?

	TRUE	FALSE
Target costing ensures that new product development costs are recovered in the target price for the webcam.	TRUE	FALSE
A cost gap is the difference between the target price and the target cost of the webcam.	TRUE	FALSE

(2 marks)

___

91 Which of the following in the drop down list represents a possible method for closing the target cost gap for the webcam?

[▼]

Picklist:

Increase its selling price
Employ more specialist staff in its production
Use cheaper labour
Increase the number of bespoke components   (2 marks)

___

(Total = 10 marks)

Yam Co

The following scenario relates to the next five questions.

Yam Co uses throughput accounting. The company is involved in the processing of sheet metal into products A, B and C using three processes: pressing, stretching and rolling. The factory has many production lines, each of which contains the three processes. Raw material for the sheet metal is first pressed, then stretched and finally rolled. The processing capacity varies for each process and the factory manager has provided the following data:

| | Processing time per metre in hours | | |
	Product A	Product B	Product C
Pressing	0.50	0.50	0.40

The total annual processing hours for the factory is 225,000. On average, one hour of labour is needed for each of the 225,000 hours of factory time. Labour is paid $10 per hour.

The raw materials cost per metre is $2.50 for product B. Other factory costs (excluding labour and raw materials) are $18,000,000 per year. Selling prices per metre are $60 for product B. The return per factory hour of product A is $134.

Yam carries very little inventory. Pressing has been identified as the bottleneck.

Required

92   What is the maximum output capacity per year for the bottleneck 'pressing' for each product?

Product A

[   ] metres $225000/.50$

Product B

[   ] metres

Product C

[   ] metres

(2 marks)

---

93   What is the conversion cost per factory hour?

$ [2025 0000] / 225000

90

$7250000 + 18000000$

20 (2 marks)

---

94   What is the return per factory hour of product B?

$ [115]

TP $60 - 2.5 = 57.50$

$57.50/.5$ (2 marks)

---

95   Yam Co is considering increasing the labour rate per hour. This would result in a conversion cost per factory hour of $95.

What is the throughput accounting ratio (TPAR) for product A assuming that this change occurs and the bottleneck process is fully utilised? (to two decimal points)

(2 marks)

96   Are the following statements about throughput accounting in Yam Co true or false?

When the bottleneck 'pressing' is overcome ('elevated'), a new bottleneck will appear.	TRUE	FALSE
It should be expected that the throughput accounting ratio for any product in Yam Co will exceed 1.	TRUE	FALSE

(2 marks)

(Total = 10 marks)

Ivey Co   18 mins

The following scenario relates to the next five questions.

Ivey Co is an electronics business operating within an advanced manufacturing technology environment, producing fitness watches, weighing scales and other electronic items. It uses life cycle costing (LCC).

Ivey Co is about to launch a new electronic gadget called the Diam, for measuring health statistics in patients who are unwell. It intends to sell the gadget to hospitals.

	20X1	20X2
Number of Diams	5,000	7,500
Components cost per unit	$12.00	$10.00
Labour cost per unit	$14.00	$12.00
Total fixed production costs	$5,000	$4,500
Total fixed selling and distribution costs	$1,000	$1,200

Ivey Co is also thinking of developing 'smart' weighing scales that scan food labels and give nutrients based on the weight.

Required

97   What is the life cycle cost per unit for the Diam (to two decimal places)?

$ [   ] per unit   (2 marks)

98   Which of the following costs would be included in the life cycle cost of the smart weighing scales?

Scales concept design costs	INCLUDED	NOT INCLUDED
Scales testing costs	INCLUDED	NOT INCLUDED
Scales production costs	INCLUDED	NOT INCLUDED
Scales distribution costs	INCLUDED	NOT INCLUDED

(2 marks)

99 Which **TWO** of the following statements about using LCC for the Diam are true?

☐ LCC aims to ensure that a profit is generated over the entire life of the Diam

☐ LCC focuses on the short-term by identifying costs at the beginning of the Diam's life cycle

☐ LCC writes off costs to each stage of the Diam's life cycle

☐ LCC ensures that the price set for the Diam is based on better knowledge of costs

(2 marks)

---

100 Are the following statements true or false?

(1) Ivey Co uses an expensive costing system

(2) Ivey Co's costing system is quicker to use than traditional absorption costing

○ Both statements are true

○ Both statements are false

○ Statement 1 is true and Statement 2 is false

○ Statement 1 is false and Statement 2 is true

(2 marks)

---

101 When would the bulk of Ivey Co's products' life cycle costs normally be determined?

○ At the design and development stage

○ On disposal of the products

○ When the product is introduced to the market

○ When the product is in its growth stage

(2 marks)

(Total = 10 marks)

Section A questions

OTQ bank – Decision-making techniques   **54 mins**

102   A decision tree is a way of representing decision choices in the form of a diagram. It is usual for decision trees to include probabilities of different outcomes.

The following statements have been made about decision trees.

(1)   Each possible outcome from a decision is given an expected value.

(2)   Each possible outcome is shown as a branch on a decision tree.

Which of the above statements is/are true?

○   1 only

○   2 only

○   Neither 1 nor 2

○   Both 1 and 2   **(2 marks)**

---

103   A business produces three products, Z1, Z2 and Z3. Each of these products requires different amounts of material (material X), which is a scarce resource. The following budgeted data relates to the three products:

Per unit:	Z1	Z2	Z3
	$	$	$
Selling price	200	150	100
Materials ($5 per kg)	(35)	(20)	(10)
Labour ($20 per hour)	(50)	(25)	(10)
Variable overheads	(45)	(45)	(30)
Fixed overheads	(30)	(25)	(20)
Profit per unit	40	35	30

Match the products to the order in which they should be manufactured to ensure profit is maximised.

Product
Z1
Z2
Z3

Ranking	
1st	
2nd	
3rd	

(2 marks)

---

104 The following statements have been made about cost plus pricing.

(1) A price in excess of full cost per unit will ensure that a company will cover all its costs and make a profit.

(2) Cost plus pricing is an appropriate pricing strategy when jobs are carried out to customer specifications.

Which of the above statements is/are true?

○ 1 only

○ 2 only

○ Neither 1 nor 2

○ Both 1 and 2 (2 marks)

---

105 H Co uses a marginal cost plus pricing system to determine the selling price for one of its products, Product X.

Product X has the following costs:

	$
Direct materials	12
Direct labour	5
Variable overheads	3
Fixed overheads	40

Fixed overheads are $20,000 for the year. Budgeted output and sales for the year are 500 units and this should be sufficient for Product X to break even.

What profit mark-up would H Co need to add to the marginal cost to allow H Co to break even?

[   ] % (2 marks)

---

106 The standard costs and revenues of Log Co's only product are as follows:

	$ per unit
Sales price	60
Direct materials	12
Direct labour	15
Variable production overhead	3
Fixed production overhead	15
Profit	15

Fixed overheads are absorbed on budgeted production and sales of 10,000 units per year. Sales staff receive a sales commission of 5% of sales revenue.

What is Log Co's margin of safety (to the nearest whole %)?

○ 80%

○ 50%

○ 44%

○ 55% (2 marks)

BPP
LEARNING
MEDIA

107   A company is making product P with the following cost card:

	$	$
Selling price		100
Marginal	25	
Labour	30	
Variable overheads	20	
Fixed overheads	10	
		(85)
Profit		15

Each unit of P takes one hour to make and the available labour and machinery are fully used in its current production of P. The company is considering making a new product, Q, but would have to divert labour and machine use from product P.

What is the relevant total cost per hour for labour and variable overheads which should be included in the cost of product Q?

$ [   ]   (2 marks)

---

108   A company has fixed costs of $1.3 million. Variable costs are 55% of sales up to a sales level of $1.5 million, but at higher volumes of production and sales, the variable cost for incremental production units falls to 52% of sales.

What is the breakeven point in sales revenue, to the nearest $1,000?

○ $1,977,000

○ $2,027,000

○ $2,708,000

○ $2,802,000   (2 marks)

---

109   A benefit sacrificed by taking one course of action instead of the most profitable alternative course of action is known as which of the following?

[▼]

Picklist:

Opportunity cost
Incremental cost
Relevant cost
Sunk cost   (2 marks)

BPP
LEARNING
MEDIA

110 A manufacturing company makes two joint products, CP1 and CP2, in a common process. These products can be sold at the split-off point in an external market, or processed further in separate processes to produce products FP1 and FP2. Details of these processes are shown in the diagram.

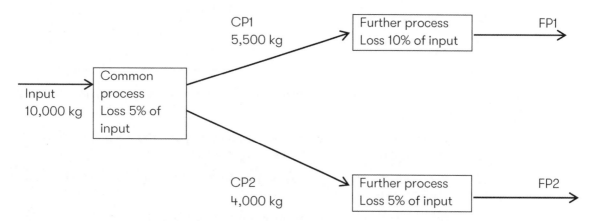

CP1 has a market price of $6 per kg and CP2 has a market price of $5 per kg. Relevant further processing costs are $2 per input kg in the process to make FP1 and $3 per input kg in the process to make FP2. Both FP1 and FP2 sell for $9 per kg.

For each 10,000 kg input to the common process, how much additional profit is obtained by further processing each of the joint products instead of selling them at the split-off point?

O $2,750

O $4,450

O $8,750

O $9,500 (2 marks)

111 The following decision tree shows four decision options: 1, 2, 3 and 4

		Probability	Benefit $
1		1.0	9,500
2		0.3	14,000
		0.3	10,000
		0.4	5,000
3		0.4	10,000
		0.6	9,000
4		0.7	8,000
		0.3	14,000

Using the expected value rule, which choice should be made so as to optimise the expected benefit?

Choice	

(2 marks)

112 Analysing the range of different possible outcomes from a particular situation, with a computer model that uses random numbers, is known as which of the following?

○ Probability analysis

○ Sensitivity analysis

○ Simulation modelling

○ Stress testing (2 marks)

---

113 Which of the following statements about graphical linear programming with the objective of maximising profit is true?

(1) If a resource constraint line does not pass through the optimum point on the graph, then the shadow price of that resource is zero

(2) The shadow price is the maximum amount a company should pay for one more unit of a scarce resource

(3) The slope or gradient of the objective function depends on the amount of resources available to the organisation

○ 1 only

○ 1 and 2 only

○ 1, 2 and 3

○ 2 and 3 only (2 marks)

---

114 A company uses linear programming to decide on the production and sales budget that will maximise total contribution and profit for a financial period. The optimal solution involves using all available direct labour hours, for which the shadow price is $4.50 per hour, and machine hours, for which the shadow price is $3 per machine hour. Direct labour is paid $8 per hour.

If the objective of the company is to maximise total contribution and profit in each period, how much should the company be willing to pay per hour to obtain additional direct labour hours of production capacity?

○ Up to but not including $4.50

○ Up to but not including $9.50

○ Up to but not including $12.50

○ Up to but not including $15.50 (2 marks)

---

115 Which **TWO** pieces of information are required when deciding, purely on financial grounds, whether or not to process a joint product further?

☐ The final sales value of the joint product

☐ The further processing cost of the joint product

☐ The value of the common process costs

☐ The method of apportioning the common costs between the joint products

(2 marks)

116 A company makes two products, X and Y, using the same type of direct labour. Production capacity per period is restricted to 60,000 direct labour hours. The contribution per unit is $8 for Product X and $6 for Product Y. The following constraints apply to production and sales:

x $\leq 10,000$ (Sales demand for Product X)

y $\leq 12,000$ (Sales demand for Product Y)

$5x + 4y$ $\leq 60,000$ (Direct labour hours)

The contribution-maximising output is to produce and sell 10,000 units of Product X and 2,500 units of Product Y.

What is the shadow price per direct labour hour and for how many additional hours of labour does this shadow price per hour apply?

O $1.50 per hour for the next 38,000 direct labour hours

O $1.50 per hour for the next 47,500 direct labour hours

O $1.60 per hour for the next 38,000 direct labour hours

O $1.60 per hour for the next 47,500 direct labour hours   **(2 marks)**

(Total = 30 marks)

OTQ bank – Decision-making techniques   **72 mins**

117 The price elasticity of demand for a product at its current price level is inelastic.

What will happen to the total revenue and the profit if the price of the product is reduced?

	Increase	Fall
Total revenue	☐	☐
Profit	☐	☐

(2 marks)

118 The following statements have been made about price elasticity of demand.

(1)   When sales demand is inelastic, a company can increase profits by raising the selling price of its product.

(2)   Price elasticity of demand is measured as the amount of change in sales price (measured as a percentage of the current sales price) divided by the amount of change in quantity demanded (measured as a percentage of the current sales volume).

Which of the above statements is/are true?

O   1 only

O   2 only

O   Neither 1 nor 2

O   Both 1 and 2   **(2 marks)**

119 A company makes and sells four products. Direct labour hours are a scarce resource, but the company is able to sub-contract production of any products to external suppliers. The following information is relevant.

Product	W $ per unit	X $ per unit	Y $ per unit	Z $ per unit
Sales price	10	8	12	14
Variable cost	8	5	8	12
Cost of external purchase	9	7.1	10	13
Direct labour hours per unit	0.1	0.3	0.25	0.2

Match the products to the order of priority in which the company should make them in-house, rather than purchase them externally.

Product
W
X
Y
Z

Ranking	
1st	
2nd	
3rd	
4th	

(2 marks)

---

120 Which method of pricing is most easily applied when two or more markets for the product or service can be kept entirely separate from each other?

  O   Price discrimination

  O   Product line pricing

  O   Skimming

  O   Volume discounting

(2 marks)

---

121 Indicate, by clicking on the relevant boxes in the table below, whether each of the statements made about short-term decisions are true or false.

	TRUE	FALSE
Joint costs are relevant in decisions about whether to sell a joint product at the split-off (separation) point or after further processing.	TRUE	FALSE
The relevant costs and revenues in decisions relating to the operating of internal service departments or the use of external services, are the differential costs between the two options.	TRUE	FALSE

(2 marks)

122 A company wishes to go ahead with one of three mutually exclusive projects, but the profit outcome from each project will depend on the strength of sales demand, as follows.

	Strong demand Profit $	Moderate demand Profit $	Weak demand Profit/(Loss) $
Project 1	70,000	10,000	(7,000)
Project 2	25,000	12,000	5,000
Project 3	50,000	20,000	(6,000)
Probability of demand	0.1	0.4	0.5

What is the value to the company of obtaining this perfect market research information, ignoring the cost of obtaining the information?

  O $3,000

  O $5,500

  O $6,000

  O $7,500   (2 marks)

---

123 A special job for a customer will require eight tonnes of a Material M. The company no longer uses this material regularly although it holds 3 tonnes in inventory. These originally cost $44 per tonne, and could be resold to a supplier for $35 per tonne. Alternatively these materials could be used to complete another job instead of using other materials that would cost $126 to purchase. The current market price of Material M is $50 per tonne.

The company must decide whether to agree to the customer's request for the work, and to set a price. What would be the relevant cost of Material M for this job?

$ [   ]   (2 marks)

---

124 A company makes and sells a single product. When sales per month are $6.8 million, total costs are $6.56 million. When sales per month are $5.2 million, total costs are $5.44 million. There is a step cost increase of $400,000 in fixed costs when sales are $6.0 million, but variable unit costs are constant at all levels of output and sales.

What is the breakeven point for sales revenue per month?

  O $6.0 million

  O   There are two breakeven points: $5.64 million and $6.36 million

  O $5.64 million only

  O $6.36 million only   (2 marks)

125 A company wishes to decide on a selling price for a new product. Weekly sales of each product will depend on the price charged and also on customers' response to the new product. The following pay-off table has been prepared.

	Probability	Price P1 $	Price P2 $	Price P3 $	Price P4 $
Price		5.00	5.50	6.00	6.50
Unit contribution		3.00	3.50	4.00	4.50
Weekly demand		Units	Units	Units	Units
Best possible	0.3	10,000	9,000	8,000	7,000
Most likely	0.5	8,000	7,500	7,000	6,000
Worst possible	0.2	6,000	5,000	4,000	3,000

If the choice of selling price is based on a maximin decision rule, which price would be selected?

| P | |

(2 marks)

126 A company produces and sells a single product. Budgeted sales are $2.4 million, budgeted fixed costs are $360,000 and the margin of safety is $400,000. What are budgeted variable costs?

○ $1.640 million

○ $1.728 million

○ $1.968 million

○ $2.040 million

(2 marks)

127 A company wants to decide whether to make its materials in-house or to sub-contract production to an external supplier. In the past it has made four materials in-house, but demand in the next year will exceed in-house production capacity of 8,000 units. All four materials are made on the same machines and require the same machine time per unit: machine time is the limiting production factor.

The following information is available.

Material	W	X	Y	Z
Units required	4,000	2,000	3,000	4,000
Variable cost of in-house manufacture	$8 per unit	$12 per unit	$9 per unit	$10 per unit
Directly attributable fixed cost expenditure	$5,000	$8,000	$6,000	$7,000
Cost of external purchase	$9 per unit	$18 per unit	$12 per unit	$12 per unit

Directly attributable fixed costs are fixed cash expenditures that would be saved if production of the material in-house is stopped entirely.

If a decision is made solely on the basis of short-term cost considerations, what materials should the company purchase externally?

Picklist:

4,000 units of W and 1,000 units of Z
4,000 units of W and 4,000 units of Z
3,000 units of Y and 2,000 units of Z
1,000 units of Y and 4,000 units of Z

(2 marks)

BPP LEARNING MEDIA

128   A company makes two products with the following characteristics.

	Product X	Product Y
Contribution to sales ratio	0.3	0.5
Selling price per unit	$3.00	$4.80
Maximum demand	8,000 units	3,000 units

Fixed costs are $9,000.

What is the minimum revenue required for production to break even?

○ $20,400

○ $25,800

○ $29,400

○ $24,000   (2 marks)

---

129   The demand for a product at its current price has a price elasticity greater than 1.0 (ignoring the minus sign). Which of the following statements must be correct?

(1)   A reduction in the sales price will increase total revenue.

(2)   A reduction in the sales price by x% will result in a percentage increase in sales demand which is greater than x%.

(3)   An increase in the selling price will increase total profit.

○   Statements 1 and 2 only

○   Statements 1 and 3 only

○   Statements 2 and 3 only

○   Statements 1, 2 and 3   (2 marks)

---

130   A company wishes to go ahead with one of two mutually exclusive projects, but the profit outcome from each project will depend on the strength of sales demand, as follows.

	Strong demand Profit $	Moderate demand Profit $	Weak demand Profit/(Loss) $
Project 1	80,000	50,000	(5,000)
Project 2	60,000	25,000	10,000
Probability of demand	0.2	0.4	0.4

The company could purchase market research information, at a cost of $4,500. This would predict demand conditions with perfect accuracy.

What is the value to the company of obtaining this perfect market research information?

$ _____   (2 marks)

---

131   A company budgets to sells its three products A, B and C in the ratio 2:3:5 respectively, measured in units of sales. Unit sales prices and variable costs are as follows.

Product	A $ per unit	B $ per unit	C $ per unit
Sales price	20	18	24
Variable cost	11	12	18

Budgeted fixed costs are $1.2 million. What sales will be needed to achieve a target profit of $400,000 for the period? Give your answer in millions, to 3 decimal points.

$ _____ m   (2 marks)

---

132   What is the main purpose of sensitivity analysis?

    ○   To calculate the expected value of an outcome that is uncertain

    ○   To predict the future outcome from an uncertain situation

    ○   To gain insight into which assumptions or variables in a situation are critical

    ○   To determine the outcome from a situation in the event of the worst possible outcome

    (2 marks)

---

133   Market research into demand for a product indicates that when the selling price per unit is $145, demand in each period will be 5,000 units; if the price is $120, demand will be 11,250 units. It is assumed that the demand function for this product is linear. The variable cost per unit is $27.

What selling price should be charged in order to maximise the monthly profit?

$ [   ]   **(2 marks)**

---

134   Lauda Co has two divisions with the following results in the table below:

	Division A	Division B
	$ million	$ million
Sales revenue	1,000	1,240
Variable costs	400	500
Contribution	600	740
Divisional fixed costs	650	600
Allocated head office costs	50	150
Divisional net loss	(100)	(10)

If a division is shut down, then Lauda Co will avoid all the division's specific costs and half of the head office costs allocated to the division.

What will be the revised total divisional net loss if Lauda Co chooses to shut down Division A?

$ [   ] million   **(2 marks)**

---

135   In a linear programming problem to determine the contribution-maximising production and sales volumes for two products, X and Y, the following information is available.

	Product X per unit	Product Y per unit	Total available per period
Direct labour hours	2 hours	4 hours	10,000 hours
Material X	4 kg	2 kg	14,000 kg
Contribution per unit	$12	$18	

The profit-maximising level of output and sales is 3,000 units of Product X and 1,000 units of Product Y.

What is the shadow price of a direct labour hour?

    ○ $1.00

    ○ $2.40

    ○ $4.00

    ○ $4.50   **(2 marks)**

136 Which **TWO** statements are true when using linear programming to solve production problems?

☐ If the aim is to minimise costs, the solution is where the total cost line touching the feasible area at a tangent is as far away from the origin as possible.

☐ If the aim is to minimise costs, the solution is where the total cost line touching the feasible area at a tangent is as close to the origin as possible.

☐ If the aim is to maximise profit, the solution is where the total cost line touching the feasible area at a tangent is as far away from the origin as possible.

☐ If the aim is to maximise profit, the solution is where the total contribution line touching the feasible area at a tangent is as close to the origin as possible.

☐ If the aim is to maximise profit, the solution is where the total contribution line touching the feasible area at a tangent is as far away from the origin as possible.

(2 marks)

(Total = 40 marks)

Section B questions

OT case questions

Home Electrics Co (Mar/Jun 2021)   18 mins

The following scenario relates to the next five questions.

Home Electrics Co manufactures electrical appliances for domestic use. It is made up of two divisions:

Small Appliances division

Two of the products manufactured by the Small Appliances division are the Blender (Product B) and the Toaster (Product T). The standard cost cards per unit for each of the products is as follows:

	B	T
	$	$
Selling price	80	120
Direct materials ($5 per kg)	10	15
Direct labour ($7 per hour)	21	35
Variable overheads	12	18
Fixed overheads	8	10
Profit	29	42

In the first quarter of the year the supply of materials was restricted to 2,000 kg per month. This was due to a global shortage.

It is now April and it has been identified that material will continue to be limited to 2,000 kg per month but also labour hours will be restricted to 3,200 hours per month. The management accountant has supplied formulas for the production constraints as follows:

Materials: 2B + 3T = 2,000
Labour: 3B + 5T = 3,200

Large Appliances divsion

This division also manufactures two products; a Freezer (Product F) which earns a contribution of $150 per unit and a Dishwasher (Product D) which earns a contribution of $200 per unit. Both products use the same resources, several of which are in short supply.

In April only 4,000 labour hours, 2,500 kg of material and 3,200 machine hours will be available. The management accountant has applied linear programming and defined the following constraints:

Materials: 4F + 6D = 2,500
Labour: 10F + 8D = 4,000
Machine time: 5F + 10D = 3,200
Demand for D: 250

Labour and machine time have been identified as the binding constraints and an optimum production plan of 240 units of F and 200 units of D has been calculated.

Required

137   What is the contribution per unit of limiting factor for Product T in the first quarter of the year (to the nearest whole $)?

$ [   ]   (2 marks)

138   Using simultaneous equations, what is the total contribution to be earned from Products B and T in April?

O $28,400

O $35,600

O $62,000

O $77,200   (2 marks)

139   Which of the following statements about the use of linear programming to resolve limiting factor problems are true?

(1)   The linear programming method helps to identify the optimum selling price for a product

(2)   Slack occurs when more than the maximum available of the limited resource is required

O   1 only

O   2 only

O   Both 1 and 2

O   Neither 1 nor 2   (2 marks)

140   What would be the shadow price of material in the Large Appliances division (to the nearest whole $)?

$ [   ]   (2 marks)

---

141   Which of the following statements about the linear programming method in the Large Appliances division are true?

(1)   Product D has a slack value

(2)   Contribution of $76,000 will be earned from the optimum production plan

(3)   Labour and machine time intersect at the optimum point if shown on a graph

O   1, 2 and 3

O   2 and 3 only

O   1 and 3 only

O   2 only   (2 marks)

(Total = 10 marks)

Cuckoo Co   18 mins

The following scenario relates to the next five questions.

Period 1

In Period 1, manufacturing company Cuckoo Co produced a single product called the Gamma. The budget details for 1,200 units for Period 1 were as follows:

	$ per unit
Sales price	27
Variable cost	15
Fixed overhead cost	8
Profit	4

Period 2

In period 2, fixed costs were calculated as $10,000

Periods 3 and 4

At the end of period 3, a competitor launched a cheaper, yet superior product to Gamma. Cuckoo Co decided to cease production of Gamma, implement a large expansion project, and focus on new products, C, S, and D. The budget for period 4 is as follows:

Product	C	S	D
	$ per unit	$ per unit	$ per unit
Sales price	30	20	37
Variable cost	12	3	19
	18	17	18
Fixed cost	10	9	10
Profit	8	8	8
Number of units	15,000	20,000	10,000

Period 5

In Period 5, new suppliers were found and the sales prices and the costs for products C, S and D were changed. The following profit volume (PV) chart was drawn:

Period 5 Multi-product PV chart

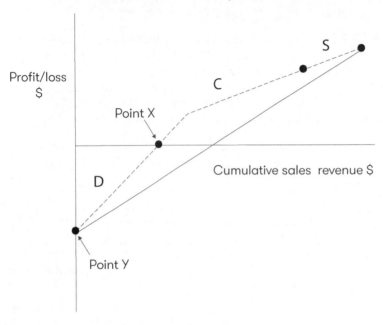

Required

142   What is the budgeted breakeven point in units for Period 1?

| | units |

(2 marks)

143   How many units need to be produced and sold to achieve a profit of $6,600 for Period 2 (rounded up to the nearest whole unit)?

| | units |

(2 marks)

144   What is the breakeven sales revenue for Period 4 to the nearest $'000?

○ $790,000

○ $278,000

○ $430,000

○ $664,000   (2 marks)

145   Based on the Period 5 PV chart, are the following statements true or false?

	TRUE	FALSE
Point X is the breakeven point.	TRUE	FALSE
Product D is the most profitable product in terms of C/S ratio.	TRUE	FALSE
Point Y is the fixed cost amount	TRUE	FALSE

(2 marks)

146   What does the solid line of the Period 5 PV chart indicate?

      O   The cumulative sales as each product's sales are in turn added to the sales mix

      O   The cumulative profit/loss as each product's contribution are in turn added to the sales mix

      O   The average variable costs which will be in incurred in the production and sale of the three products in this mix

      O   The average profit which will be earned from the sales of three products in this mix

(2 marks)

(Total = 10 marks)

BDU Co   **18 mins**

The following scenario relates to the next five questions.

BDU Co is a manufacturer of baby equipment and is planning to launch a revolutionary new style of sporty pushchair. The company has commissioned market research to establish possible demand for the pushchair and the following information has been obtained.

If the price is set at $425, demand is expected to be 1,000 pushchairs; at $500 it will be 730 pushchairs and at $600 it will be 420 pushchairs. Variable costs are estimated at $170, $210 or $260.

A decision needs to be made on what price to charge.

The following contribution table has been produced showing the possible outcomes.

Price		$425	$500	$600
Variable cost	$170	255,000	240,900	180,600
	$210	215,000	211,700	163,800
	$260	165,000	175,200	142,800

147   What price would be set if BDU were to use a maximin decision criterion?

      $ [   ]   **(2 marks)**

---

148   What price would be set if BDU were to use a minimax regret decision criterion?

      $ [   ]   **(2 marks)**

---

149   If the probabilities of the variable costs are $170: 0.4; $210: 0.25; and $260: 0.35, which price would the risk-neutral decision maker choose?

      $ [   ]   **(2 marks)**

150 Which **TWO** of the following, used by BDU Co, reduce uncertainty in decision-making?

☐ Expected value analysis

☐ Market research

☐ Focus groups

☐ Relevant costing (2 marks)

151 Indicate, by selecting the relevant boxes in the table below, whether each of the following statements regarding BDU Co's use of expected values is correct or incorrect.

Expected values are more valuable for decision making when they refer to outcomes that occur many times over.	CORRECT	INCORRECT
The average profit calculated will correspond to one of the possible outcomes.	CORRECT	INCORRECT

(2 marks)

(Total = 10 marks)

Metallica Co   18 mins

The following scenario relates to the next five questions.

Metallica Co is an engineering company that manufactures a number of products, using a team of highly skilled workers and a variety of different metals. A supplier has informed Metallica Co that the amount of M1, one of the materials used in production, will be limited for the next three-month period.

The only items manufactured using M1 and their production costs and selling prices (where applicable) are shown below.

	Product P4 $/unit	Product P6 $/unit
Selling price	125	175
Direct materials:		
M1*	15	10
M2	10	20
Direct labour	20	30
Variable overhead	10	15
Fixed overhead	20	30
Total cost	75	105

* Material M1 is expected to be limited in supply during the next three months. These costs are based on M1 continuing to be available at a price of $20 per square metre. The price of M2 is $10 per square metre.

Required

152 What is the contribution per unit for each product?

$	P4	
$	P6	

(2 marks)

153 Metallica Co carried out some market research which suggested that a change should be made to the selling price of both Product P4 and P6. As a result, the new contribution per unit for P4 is $85 and for P6 it is $95. Which of the following answers is correct?

- O The contribution per limiting factor of P4 and P6 is $85 and $47.50 respectively, therefore P4 should be produced first.

- O The contribution per limiting factor of P4 and P6 is $113.33 and $190 respectively, therefore P6 should be produced first.

- O The contribution per limiting factor of P4 and P6 is $85 and $47.50 respectively, therefore P6 should be produced first.

- O The contribution per limiting factor of P4 and P6 is $113.33 and $190 respectively, therefore P4 should be produced first. **(2 marks)**

154 Indicate, by selecting the relevant boxes in the table below, whether each of the following items would be included in the calculation of throughput contribution if Metallica Co operated in a throughput accounting environment.

	YES	NO
Selling price	YES	NO
Direct materials	YES	NO
Direct labour	YES	NO

(2 marks)

155 Indicate, by selecting the relevant boxes in the table below, which of the following constraints would necessitate the performance of limiting factor analysis by Metallica Co.

	YES	NO
Limited demand for P4 or P6	YES	NO
Limited M1 or M2	YES	NO
Limited labour	YES	NO

(2 marks)

156 Once a scarce resource is identified, Metallica Co carries out a limiting factor analysis using four steps. Match each of the steps to the correct order in which they should be carried out.

Steps	Correct order	
Rank the products in order of the contribution per unit of the scarce resource.	Step 1	
Allocate resources using the ranking.	Step 2	
Calculate the contribution per unit of the scarce resource for each product.	Step 3	
Calculate the contribution per unit for each product.	Step 4	

(2 marks)

(Total = 10 marks)

T Co

The following scenario relates to the next five questions.

The Telephone Co (T Co) is a company specialising in the provision of telephone systems for commercial clients.

T Co has been approached by a potential customer, Push Co, which wants to install a telephone system in new offices it is opening. While the job is not a particularly large one, T Co is hopeful of future business in the form of replacement systems and support contracts for Push Co. T Co is therefore keen to quote a competitive price for the job. The following information should be considered:

(1) One of the company's salesmen has already been to visit Push Co, to give them a demonstration of the new system, together with a complimentary lunch, the costs of which totalled $400.

(2) The installation is expected to take one week to complete and would require three engineers, each of whom is paid a monthly salary of $4,000. The engineers have just had their annually renewable contract renewed with T Co. One of the three engineers has spare capacity to complete the work, but the other two would have to be moved from Contract X in order to complete this one. Contract X generates a contribution of $200 per engineer per week. There are no other engineers available to continue with Contract X if these two engineers are taken off the job. It would mean that T Co would miss its contractual completion deadline on Contract X by one week. As a result, T Co would have to pay a one-off penalty of $500. Since there is no other work scheduled for their engineers in one week's time, it will not be a problem for them to complete Contract X at this point.

(3) 120 telephone handsets would need to be supplied to Push Co. The current cost of these is $18.20 each, although T Co already has 80 handsets in inventory. These were bought at a price of $16.80 each. The handsets are the most popular model on the market and are frequently requested by T Co's customers.

(4) Push Co would also need a computerised control system called 'Swipe 2'. The current market price of Swipe 2 is $10,800, although T Co has an older version of the system, 'Swipe 1', in inventory, which could be modified at a cost of $4,600. T Co paid $5,400 for Swipe 1 when it ordered it in error two months ago and has no other use for it. The current market price of Swipe 1 is $5,450, although if T Co tried to sell the one it has, it would be deemed to be 'used' and therefore only worth $3,000.

Required

157 What figure should be included in the relevant cost statement for engineers' costs?

$ _____ (2 marks)

158 What figure should be included in the relevant cost statement for telephone handsets?

$ _____ (2 marks)

159 What figure should be included in the relevant cost statement for the computerised control system?

- $7,600
- $10,800
- $10,050
- $10,000 (2 marks)

160   Indicate, by selecting the relevant boxes in the table below, whether each of the following statements about T Co's decision to quote for the contract are true or false?

	TRUE	FALSE
The opportunity cost is defined as the relevant cost of taking a business opportunity to install the telephone system for Push Co.	TRUE	FALSE
The decision to install the telephone system should be taken purely on the basis of whether it improves profit or reduces costs for T Co.	TRUE	FALSE

(2 marks)

161   Use the drop down list to select the type of cost that is detailed in point (1).

[▼]

Picklist:

Sunk cost
Opportunity cost
Relevant cost
Committed cost

(2 marks)

(Total = 10 marks)

Rotanola Co   18 mins

The following scenario relates to the next five questions.

Rotanola Co manufactures mobile phones. It has been extremely successful in the past but the market has become extremely competitive. The company is considering a number of different strategies to improve its profitability.

The most successful product is the RTN99 which is sold for $110. Weekly demand is currently 20,000 phones. Market research has revealed that if Rotanola Co reduced the price of the RTN99 by $10, demand would increase by 2,000 phones.

Each time the phone is produced, Rotanola Co incurs extra costs of $30 for materials, $18 for labour, $14 for variable overheads and $23 for fixed costs, based on expected weekly output of 20,000 phones.

Another phone produced by Rotanola Co is the CTF99. At a price of $250, demand is 12,000 units and demand will rise or fall by 5 units for every $1 fall or rise in the selling price. The marginal cost of the CTF99 is $80.

Required

162   What is the straight line demand equation for the RTN99?

P = [   ] – [   ] Q   (2 marks)

163   What is the total cost function for the RTN99?

TC = [   ] + [   ] Q   (2 marks)

164 If marginal revenue = a - 2bQ when the selling price is P = a - bQ, what is the profit-maximising demand for CTF99?

	units	(2 marks)

165 Rotanola Co produces another phone with a price elasticity of demand equal to one.

Indicate, by selecting the relevant boxes in the table below, whether each of the following statements are true or false.

Demand will remain constant despite price changes.	TRUE	FALSE
If price increases by 5%, demand will fall by 10%.	TRUE	FALSE
Total expenditure will remain constant despite price changes.	TRUE	FALSE

(2 marks)

166 When is a market penetration pricing policy appropriate for Rotanola Co?

- ○ If the mobile phone is new and different
- ○ If demand for the phone is highly elastic
- ○ If high development costs need to be recovered quickly
- ○ If there is no possibility of economies of scale

(2 marks)

(Total = 10 marks)

Section C questions

167 Health Nuts (Sep/Dec 2020)   36 mins

Health Nuts is a fitness centre, offering 'pay as you go' gym facilities. It has a fully fitted gym with the capacity to accommodate 200 users at one time. It also has 100 car parking spaces and an onsite café, both of which are only for customers using the gym. The fitness centre has shower facilities for customers and Health Nuts provides all customers with a clean towel to use on entry. It is open 360 days a year, from 7.00am until 9.00pm.

Customers pay $8.40 for access to the gym for one hour plus unlimited time in the café. If customers want to use the car park, they have to pay an additional $1 per visit and 80% of visiting customers use the car park. Health Nuts has been monitoring the number of customers attending throughout each day for the month of June, which was considered to be an average month, and for which Health Nuts was open for 30 days. It has determined that the average number of customers per day is 330 with 40 of these customers attending during the time of 9.00am to 5.00pm.

The total costs of the fitness centre for June, **excluding the café**, have also been recorded and analysed as follows:

Fixed costs per month	$48,000
Variable cost per customer	$1.20

On average, half of the customers also used the café in June, with an average spend per customer of $2.20. Of this spend, 60% related to drinks, which have a profit margin of 60%, and the remainder related to food items, which have a profit margin of 40%. The specific fixed costs associated with running the café are $3,600 for the month.

Crèche proposal

After reviewing all of the above information, the manager of Health Nuts has put together a proposal to close the café at the fitness centre and convert it into a crèche for children. This would mean that parents could leave their children in the crèche whilst they use the fitness centre between the hours of 9.00am and 5.00pm **only**. The charge for the crèche would be $4 per child, per hour.

Initial research suggests that customers have an average of two children each. The crèche is expected to attract new customers and increase the average number of customers between 9.00am and 5.00pm by 300%. Only these new customers will use the crèche facilities. Car park usage is expected to continue to be 80%. The fixed costs associated with running the crèche are estimated to be $8,000 per month, with a variable cost of $0.50 per child, per hour.

(a) Calculate both the number of customers Health Nuts needs to break even and the margin of safety as a percentage for the month of June for:

    (i)   The gym; and   **(3 marks)**
    (ii)   The café.   **(2 marks)**

(b) Explain what each of your calculations in (a) tells Health Nuts about the performance of the gym and the café.   **(3 marks)**

(c) Calculate the budgeted total weighted average contribution/sales (C/S) ratio and the budgeted profit per month for Health Nuts if it closes the café and opens a crèche instead.   **(6 marks)**

(d) Advise Health Nuts, considering both financial and non-financial factors, whether it should replace the café with a crèche and whether the calculations in part (c) provide enough information to make such a decision.   **(6 marks)**

(Total = 20 marks)

168 Belton Park Resort (Mar/Jun 2019)   36 mins

Belton Park Resort is a new theme park resort located in the country of Beeland. The resort is made up of a theme park, a hotel and an indoor water park. The resort opened two months ago and is already very popular.

As all theme parks in Beeland are required, by law, to shut down in the colder month of January because of the risk of accidents, Belton Park Resort must decide whether to shut down the whole resort or just the theme park. It could choose to keep open the hotel and/or the water park.

Since Belton Park Resort has not been open for long, there is limited historical data available about costs and revenues. However, based on the last two months, the following average monthly data is available:

Hotel

Number of rooms	120
Average room rate per night	$100
Average occupancy rate per month	90%
Average nightly spend on 'extras' per room	$20
Contribution margin for 'extras'*	60%

Water park

Number of visitors per month	12,000
Admission price per visitor	$21
Average spend on 'extras' per visitor	$12
Contribution margin for 'extras'*	60%

*'Extras' includes anything purchased by the customer not included in the room rate or admission price.

Management estimates that, for January, the average room rate per night would need to decrease by 30% and the admission price for the water park by 20%. With such reductions, it is estimated that an occupancy rate of 50% would be achieved for the hotel and that the number of visitors to the water park would be 52% lower than current levels. The average nightly spend on 'extras' per room of $20 at the hotel and $12 per customer at the water park is expected to remain unchanged.

The running costs for the hotel and water park for each of the last two months are as follows:

	Notes	Hotel	Water park $
Staff costs	1	120,000	75,600
Maintenance costs	2	14,600	6,000
Power costs	3	20,000	18,000
Security costs	4	13,600	8,000
Water costs	5	12,900	12,100

Notes

(1) Staff costs

Permanent staff Included in the staff costs for the hotel is the salary of $30,000 per annum for the hotel manager and $24,000 per annum for the head chef. These are both permanent members of staff who are paid for the full year regardless of their working hours.

The water park employs one permanent member of staff, the manager, on a salary of $24,000 who is also paid for the full year regardless of his working hours.

Temporary staff

The remaining staff costs relate to temporary staff who are only paid for the hours they work. If the hotel stays open in January, half of these staff members will continue to work their current hours because their jobs are largely unaffected by guest occupancy rates. However, the other half of the staff will work proportionately less hours to reflect the 50% occupancy rate in January as opposed to the 90% occupancy rate of the last two months.

At the water park, the temporary staff's working hours will fall according to the number of visitors, hence a fall of 52% would be expected for January.

(2) Maintenance costs

Maintenance is undertaken by a local company, 'Techworks', which bills Belton Park Resort for all work carried out each month. If the hotel and water park are closed, Techworks will instead be paid a flat fee for the month of $4,000 for the hotel and $2,000 for the water park.

(3) Power costs

Electricity Belton

Park Resort pays a fixed monthly charge for electricity of $8,000 for the hotel and $7,000 for the water park, all year round.

Gas

The gas charges relate to heating and include a fixed charge of $2,200 per month for the hotel and $1,500 per month for the water park. The remainder of the gas charges is based solely on usage and would be expected to increase by 50% in January because of the colder weather.

(4) Security costs

If the hotel and water park close, no changes will be made to the current arrangements for security whilst the premises are empty.

(5)   Water costs

It is estimated that water costs for the hotel would fall to $6,450 for the month if it remains open in January. However, the water costs for the water park would be expected to remain at their current level. If the hotel and water park were closed, all water would be turned off and no charges would arise.

Required

(a)   Calculate the incremental cash flows, for the month of January (31 days), if Belton Park Resort decides to keep open:

(i)   The hotel;
(ii)   The water park.

In each case, state whether it should remain open or should close.   **(15 marks)**

(b)   Discuss any other factors which Belton Park Resort should consider when making the decision in part (a).   **(5 marks)**

(Total = 20 marks)

169 Robber (June 2012)   36 mins

Robber Co manufactures control panels for burglar alarms, a very profitable product. Every product comes with a one-year warranty offering free repairs if any faults arise in this period.

It currently produces and sells 80,000 units per annum, with production of them being restricted by the short supply of labour. Each control panel includes two main components – one key pad and one display screen. At present, Robber Co manufactures both of these components in-house. However, the company is currently considering outsourcing the production of keypads and/or display screens. A newly established company based in Burgistan is keen to secure a place in the market, and has offered to supply the keypads for the equivalent of $4.10 per unit and the display screens for the equivalent of $4.30 per unit. This price has been guaranteed for two years.

The current total annual costs of producing the keypads and the display screens are:

	Keypads	Display screens
Production	80,000 units	80,000 units
	$'000	$'000
Direct materials	160	116
Direct labour	40	60
Heat and power costs	64	88
Machine costs	26	30
Depreciation and insurance costs	84	96
Total annual production costs	374	390

Notes

(1)   Materials costs for keypads are expected to increase by 5% in six months' time; materials costs for display screens are only expected to increase by 2%, but with immediate effect.

(2)   Direct labour costs are purely variable and not expected to change over the next year.

(3)   Heat and power costs include an apportionment of the general factory overhead for heat and power as well as the costs of heat and power directly used for the production of keypads and display screens. The general apportionment included is calculated using 50% of the direct labour cost for each component and would be incurred irrespective of whether the components are manufactured in-house or not.

(4)   Machine costs are semi-variable; the variable element relates to set-up costs, which are based upon the number of batches made. The keypads' machine has fixed costs of $4,000 per annum and the display screens' machine has fixed costs of $6,000 per annum. Whilst both components are currently made in batches of 500, this would need to change, with immediate effect, to batches of 400.

(5)   60% of depreciation and insurance costs relate to an apportionment of the general factory depreciation and insurance costs; the remaining 40% is specific to the manufacture of keypads and display screens.

Required

(a)   Advise Robber Co whether it should continue to manufacture the keypads and display screens in-house or whether it should outsource their manufacture to the supplier in Burgistan, assuming it continues to adopt a policy to limit manufacture and sales to 80,000 control panels in the coming year.   **(8 marks)**

(b)   Robber Co takes 0.5 labour hours to produce a keypad and 0.75 labour hours to produce a display screen. Labour hours are restricted to 100,000 hours and labour is paid at $1 per hour. Robber Co wishes to increase its supply to 100,000 control panels (ie 100,000 each of keypads and display screens).

Advise Robber Co as to how many units of keypads and display panels they should either manufacture and/or outsource in order to minimise their costs.   **(7 marks)**

(c)   Discuss the non-financial factors that Robber Co should consider when making a decision about outsourcing the manufacture of keypads and display screens.   **(5 marks)**

(Total = 20 marks)

170 Gam Co (June 2014)   36 mins

Gam Co sells electronic equipment and is about to launch a new product onto the market. It needs to prepare its budget for the coming year and is trying to decide whether to launch the product at a price of $30 or $35 per unit. The following information has been obtained from market research:

Price per unit $30		Price per unit $35	
Probability	Sales volume	Probability	Sales volume
0.4	120,000	0.3	108,000
0.5	110,000	0.3	100,000
0.1	140,000	0.4	94,000

Notes

(1)   Variable production costs would be $12 per unit for production volumes up to and including 100,000 units each year. However, if production exceeds 100,000 units each year, the variable production cost per unit would fall to $11 for all units produced.

(2)   Advertising costs would be $900,000 per annum at a selling price of $30 and $970,000 per annum at a price of $35.

(3)   Fixed production costs would be $450,000 per annum.

Required

(a)   Calculate each of the six possible profit outcomes which could arise for Gam Co in the coming year.   **(8 marks)**

(b)   Calculate the expected value of profit for each of the two price options and recommend, on this basis, which option Gam Co would choose.   **(3 marks)**

(c)   Briefly explain the maximin decision rule and identify which price should be chosen by management if they use this rule to decide which price should be charged.   **(3 marks)**

(d)   Discuss the factors which may give rise to uncertainty when setting budgets.   **(6 marks)**

(Total = 20 marks)

171 Cardio Co (Sep/Dec 2015 amended)   36 mins

Cardio Co manufactures three types of fitness equipment: treadmills (T), cross trainers (C) and rowing machines (R). The budgeted sales prices and volumes for the next year are as follows:

	T	C	R
Selling price	$1,600	$1,800	$1,400
Units	420	400	380

The standard cost card for each product is shown below.

	T	C	R
	$	$	$
Material	430	500	360
Labour	220	240	190
Variable overheads	110	120	95

Labour costs are 60% fixed and 40% variable. General fixed overheads excluding any fixed labour costs are expected to be $55,000 for the next year.

Required

(a)   Calculate the weighted average contribution to sales ratio for Cardio Co.   **(4 marks)**

(b)   Calculate the margin of safety in $ revenue for Cardio Co.   **(3 marks)**

Chart

(c) A chart has been drawn assuming that the products are sold in a constant mix. State the type of chart shown, the axis labels and point A, length B, length C, line D, line E and line F.

(6 marks)

(d) Explain what would happen to the breakeven point if the products were sold in order of the most profitable products first.

(2 marks)

(e) Explain the limitations of cost volume profit (CVP) analysis.

(5 marks)

(Total = 20 marks)

172 TR Co (Sep/Dec 2017)   36 mins

TR Co is a pharmaceutical company which researches, develops and manufactures a wide range of drugs. One of these drugs, 'Parapain', is a pain relief drug used for the treatment of headaches and until last month TR Co had a patent on Parapain which prevented other companies from manufacturing it. The patent has now expired and several competitors have already entered the market with similar versions of Parapain, which are made using the same active ingredients.

TR Co is reviewing its pricing policy in light of the changing market. It has carried out some market research in an attempt to establish an optimum price for Parapain. The research has established that for every $2 decrease in price, demand would be expected to increase by 5,000 batches, with maximum demand for Parapain being one million batches.

Each batch of Parapain is currently made using the following materials:

Material Z: 500 grams at $0·10 per gram

Material Y: 300 grams at $0·50 per gram

Each batch of Parapain requires 20 minutes of machine time to make and the variable running costs for machine time are $6 per hour. The fixed production overhead cost is expected to be $2 per batch for the period, based on a budgeted production level of 250,000 batches.

The skilled workers who have been working on Parapain until now are being moved onto the production of TR Co's new and unique anti-malaria drug which cost millions of dollars to develop. TR Co has obtained a patent for this revolutionary drug and it is expected to save millions of lives. No other similar drug exists and, whilst demand levels are unknown, the launch of the drug is eagerly anticipated all over the world.

Agency staff, who are completely new to the production of Parapain and cost $18 per hour, will be brought in to produce Parapain for the foreseeable future. Experience has shown there will be a significant learning curve involved in making Parapain as it is extremely difficult to handle. The first batch of Parapain made using one of the agency workers took five hours to make. However, it is believed that an 80% learning curve exists, in relation to production of the drug, and this will continue until the first 1,000 batches have been completed. TR Co's management has said that any pricing decisions about Parapain should be based on the time it takes to make the 1,000th batch of the drug.

Note. The learning co-efficient, b = −0·321928

Required

(a) Calculate the optimum (profit-maximising) selling price for Parapain and the resulting annual profit which TR Co will make from charging this price.

   Note. If P = a − bQ, then MR = a − 2bQ   (12 marks)

(b) Discuss and recommend whether market penetration or market skimming would be the most suitable pricing strategy for TR Co when launching the new anti-malaria drug.

(8 marks)

(Total = 20 marks)

173 The Alka Hotel (Mar/Jun 2018)

The Alka Hotel is situated in a major city close to many theatres and restaurants.

The Alka Hotel has 25 double bedrooms and it charges guests $180 per room per night, regardless of single or double occupancy. The hotel's variable cost is $60 per occupied room per night.

The Alka Hotel is open for 365 days a year and has a 70% budgeted occupancy rate. Fixed costs are budgeted at $600,000 a year and accrue evenly throughout the year.

During the first quarter (Q1) of the year the room occupancy rates are significantly below the levels expected at other times of the year with the Alka Hotel expecting to sell 900 occupied room nights during Q1. Options to improve profitability are being considered, including closing the hotel for the duration of Q1 or adopting one of two possible projects as follows:

Project 1 – Theatre package

For Q1 only the Alka Hotel management would offer guests a 'theatre package'. Couples who pay for two consecutive nights at a special rate of $67·50 per room night will also receive a pair of theatre tickets for a payment of $100. The theatre tickets are very good value and are the result of long negotiation between the Alka Hotel management and the local theatre. The theatre tickets cost the Alka Hotel $95 a pair. The Alka Hotel's fixed costs specific to this project (marketing and administration) are budgeted at $20,000.

The hotel's management believes that the 'theatre package' will have no effect on their usual Q1 customers, who are all business travellers and who have no interest in theatre tickets, but will still require their usual rooms.

Project 2 – Restaurant

There is scope to extend the Alka Hotel and create enough space to operate a restaurant for the benefit of its guests. The annual costs, revenues and volumes for the combined restaurant and hotel are illustrated in the following graph:

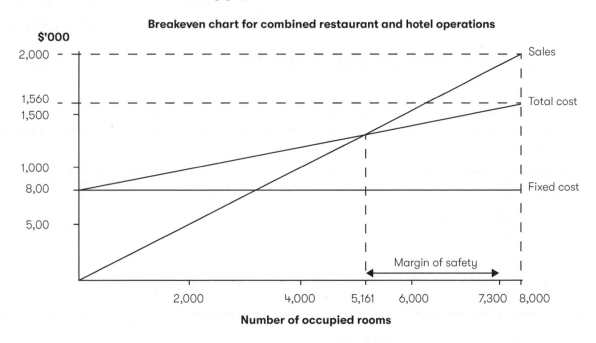

Breakeven chart for combined restaurant and hotel operations

Note. The graph does not include the effect of the 'Theatre package' offer.

Required

(a)   Using the current annual budgeted figures, and ignoring the two proposed projects, calculate the breakeven number of occupied room nights and the margin of safety as a percentage.   **(4 marks)**

(b) Ignoring the two proposed projects, calculate the budgeted profit or loss for Q1 and explain whether the hotel should close for the duration of Q1. **(4 marks)**

(c) Calculate the breakeven point in sales value of Project 1 and explain whether the hotel should adopt the project. **(4 marks)**

(d) Using the graph, quantify and comment upon the financial effect of Project 2 on the Alka Hotel. **(8 marks)**

Note. There are up to four marks available for calculations.

(Total = 20 marks)

174 HMF Co   36 mins

HMF Co manufactures children's scooters and is soon to launch its new MX model with GPS tracking and electronic display, showing the number of miles travelled. HMF Co is yet to decide on a price for the new MX. To reduce the risk of uncertainty, it has commissioned some research on the expected level of demand, based on varying selling price levels. The research suggests that if the price is $400, demand is expected to be 2,000, at $450, demand is expected to be 1,750 and at $500, demand is expected to be 1,500. Variable costs are estimated to be either $120, $160 or $210.

Required

(a) Produce a table showing the expected contribution for each of the nine possible outcomes.

(4 marks)

(b) Explain what is meant by maximax, maximin and minimax regret decision rules, using the information in the scenario to illustrate your explanations. **(10 marks)**

(c) Explain the use of expected values and sensitivity analysis and suggest how HMF Co could make use of such techniques. **(6 marks)**

(Total = 20 marks)

175 Cut and Stitch (June 2010)   36 mins

Cut and Stitch (CS) make two types of suits using skilled tailors (labour) and a delicate and unique fabric (material). Both the tailors and the fabric are in short supply and so the accountant at CS has correctly produced a linear programming model to help decide the optimal production mix.

The model is as follows:

Variables:

Let W = the number of work suits produced
Let L = the number of lounge suits produced

Constraints:

Tailors' time: $7W + 5L \leq 3,500$ (hours) – this is line T on the diagram
Fabric: $2W + 2L \leq 1,200$ (metres) – this is line F on the diagram
Production of work suits: $W \leq 400$ – this is line P on the diagram

Objective is to maximise contribution subject to:

$C = 48W + 40L$

On the diagram provided the accountant has correctly identified OABCD as the feasible region and point B as the optimal point.

CS – Production Plan

Feasible region   OABCD
Optimal point   B

Required

(a)   Find by appropriate calculation the optimal production mix and related maximum contribution that could be earned by CS. **(6 marks)**

(b)   Calculate the shadow prices of the fabric per metre and the tailor time per hour. **(6 marks)**

The tailors have offered to work an extra 500 hours provided that they are paid three times their normal rate of $1.50 per hour at $4.50 per hour.

Required

(c)   Briefly discuss whether CS should accept the offer of overtime at three times the normal rate. **(6 marks)**

(d)   Calculate the new optimum production plan if maximum demand for W falls to 200 units. **(2 marks)**

(Total = 20 marks)

Section A questions

OTQ bank – Budgeting and control   54 mins

176   Based on the last 15 periods, the underlying trend of sales is $y = 345.12 - 1.35x$, where y is the number of items sold and x represents the period number.

If the 16th period has a seasonal factor of -23.62, assuming an additive forecasting model, what is the sales forecast for that period, to the nearest whole unit?

   ○   247 units

   ○   300 units

   ○   324 units

   ○   347 units   (2 marks)

---

177   Which **TWO** of the following statements correctly describe an attainable standard?

   ☐   This standard is the least useful and most rarely used type of standard.

   ☐   This standard makes allowances for expected wastage and inefficiencies.

   ☐   This standard is based on perfect operating conditions.

   ☐   This standard should give employees a realistic, but challenging target of efficiency

(2 marks)

---

178   The correlation coefficient between advertising expenditure and sales revenue is calculated to be 0.85.

Which of the following statements is true?

   ○   There is a weak relationship between advertising expenditure and sales revenue

   ○   85% of the variation in sales revenue can be explained by the corresponding variation in advertising expenditure

   ○   72% of the variation in sales revenue can be explained by the corresponding variation in advertising expenditure

   ○   Sales revenue will increase by 85% more than advertising expenditure will increase

(2 marks)

---

179   The following information is given about standard and actual material costs during one
      month for a production process.

Material	Standard cost	Actual cost	Standard mix	Actual mix
	per kg	per kg		kg
P	3.00	3.50	10%	820
Q	2.50	2.75	20%	1,740
R	4.00	3.50	30%	2,300
S	5.25	5.00	40%	2,640
				7,500

What was the favourable materials mix variance?

$ [   ]   (2 marks)

---

180   The following statements have been made about flexed budgets.

      (1)   Flexed budgets enable proper comparisons to be made between actual and
            expected revenues and costs.

      (2)   In every variance reporting system with flexed budgets that compares budgeted and
            actual profit, there must be a sales volume variance.

      Which of the above statements is/are true?

      O   1 only

      O   2 only

      O   Neither 1 nor 2

      O   Both 1 and 2   (2 marks)

---

181   Which **TWO** of the following are arguments that variance analysis from a standard costing
      system is redundant in a total quality management environment?

      ☐   For standard costing to be useful for control purposes, it requires a reasonably
            stable environment.

      ☐   The ethos behind a system of standard costing is that performance is satisfactory if
            it meets predetermined standards.

      ☐   The control aspect of standard costing systems is achieved by making individual
            managers responsible for the variances relating to their part of the organisation's
            activities.

      ☐   Standard costs are set based on ideal standards rather than attainable ones.
                                                                         (2 marks)

182 The standard material input for making 100 kg of a product is as follows.

80 kg of material Z at $5 per kg	$400
45 kg of material Y at $9 per kg	$405
Total	$805

During the last period, 5,000 kg of Z costing $4.80 per kg and 2,500 kg of Y costing $9 per kg were used to produce 6,200 kg of product.

What was the total yield variance?

O $2,410 favourable

O $800 favourable

O $1,610 favourable

O $2,570 favourable   (2 marks)

---

183 The following budgeted data for a particular period was available for a company selling two products:

	Sales price per unit	Variable cost per unit	Sales volume in units
Product A	$20	$8	15,840
Product B	$24	$11	10,560

The actual results for the period were as follows:

	Sales price per unit	Variable cost per unit	Sales volume in units
Product A	$22	$8	14,200
Product B	$26	$11	12,500

What is the sales quantity contribution variance?

O $3,720 F

O $3,720 A

O $4,320 F

O $4,320 A   (2 marks)

184   The following statements have been made about the application of standard costing
       systems.

       (1)   Standard costing systems are compatible with a Total Quality Management
              approach to operations.

       (2)   Standard costing systems are less commonly used in an industry that operates in a
              rapidly changing environment.

       Which of the above statements is/are true?

       O   1 only

       O   2 only

       O   Neither 1 nor 2

       O   Both 1 and 2   (2 marks)

185   By linear regression, the relationship between the monthly quantity produced (x) and total
       production cost (y) was found to be y = 15,000 + 286x

       What is the variable production cost if output is 400 units?

       O $114,400

       O $100,000

       O $129,400

       O $14,400   (2 marks)

186   Under which of the following circumstances would a multiplicative model be preferred to an
       additive model in a time series?

       O   When a model easily understood by non-accountants is required

       O   When the trend is increasing or decreasing

       O   When the trend is steady

       O   When very accurate forecasts are required   (2 marks)

187   Which **TWO** of the following statements are true in the context of a just in time (JIT)
       inventory system?

       ☐   It can result in much reduced inventory holding costs

       ☐   It inevitably increases the need for safety inventories

       ☐   It requires suppliers to operate sound quality control procedures

       ☐   It works best if supplies are obtained from a number of different suppliers
                                                                                      (2 marks)

188   Vibrant Paints Co manufactures and sells paints. Business Unit A of the company makes a paint called Micra. Micra is made using three key materials: R, S and T.

At the end of period 1, a total material cost variance of $4,900 adverse was correctly recorded for Micra.

The following information relates to Micra for period 1:

Material	Standard cost per litre ($)	Actual cost per litre ($)	Actual usage (litres)
R	63	62	1,900
S	50	51	2,800
T	45	48	1,300

The standard ratio of mixing material R, material S and material T is 30:50:20.

The material price variance for Micra has been correctly calculated as $4,800 adverse.

What is the total material yield variance for Micra for period 1?

O $700 favourable

O $800 adverse

O $800 favourable

O $900 adverse   (2 marks)

---

189   A company operates in export and import markets, and its operational cash flows are affected by movements in exchange rates, which are highly volatile. As a result, the company has great difficulty in establishing a budgeting system that is reliable for more than three months ahead.

Which of the following approaches to budgeting would be most appropriate for this company's situation?

Picklist:

Flexible budget
Incremental budget
Rolling budget
Zero-based budget   (2 marks)

---

190   The regression equation y = 3 + 2x has been calculated from 6 pairs of values, with x ranging from 1 to 10. The correlation coefficient is 0.8. It is estimated that y = 43 when x = 20.

Which of the following are true?

(1)   x is outside the range of the data and this makes the estimate unreliable.

(2)   The correlation is low and this makes the estimate unreliable.

(3)   The sample is small and this makes the estimate unreliable.

O   1 and 2

O   2 and 3

O   1 and 3

O   1, 2 and 3   (2 marks)

(Total = 30 marks)

OTQ bank – Budgeting and control

54 mins

191 The following cost information relates to product XY, which is produced in a continuous process from several different materials.

	$
Actual quantity of materials at standard price	19,960
Actual quantity of materials at actual price	23,120
Actual yield at standard materials cost	20,800
Standard yield from actual input of materials at standard cost	19,552

What is the favourable materials yield variance for the period?

$ [   ] (2 marks)

192 $\sum x = 100$, $\sum y = 400$, $\sum x^2 = 2,040$, $\sum y^2 = 32,278$, $\sum xy = 8,104$ and n = 5.

Which of the following values for a and b are correct in the formula y = a + bx?

○ a = 28, b = -2.6

○ a = 28, b = 2.6

○ a = -28, b = -2.6

○ a = -28, b = 2.6 (2 marks)

193 The first item of a new product took 2,000 hours to manufacture (at a labour cost of $15 per hour). A 90% learning curve was expected to apply, and it was decided to establish a standard time as the time required to manufacture the 50th item of the product, rounded to the nearest hour. The 50th item actually took 980 hours.

Select two boxes to indicate the labour efficiency variance for the 50th unit produced and whether it is favourable or adverse.

Value ($)	Sign
645	Favourable
43	Adverse
1,860	
1,905	

(2 marks)

194 $\sum x = 440$, $\sum y = 330$, $\sum x^2 = 17,986$, $\sum y^2 = 10,366$, $\sum xy = 13,467$ and n = 11

What is the value of the correlation coefficient, r?

$ [   ] (2 marks)

195 A company makes and sells three products. Budgeted and actual results for the period just ended were as follows.

Product	Budgeted sales	Budgeted profit per unit	Actual sales	Actual profit per unit
	Units	$	Units	$
X	800	10	700	8
Y	1,000	6	1,200	6
Z	600	12	350	16
	2,400		2,250	

What was the adverse sales mix variance?

$ [   ]   (2 marks)

196 Using data from twelve countries, the correlation between the level of car ownership and the number of road accidents has been calculated as 0.73.

Which **TWO** of the following statements are correct?

☐ High levels of car ownership cause high levels of road accidents

☐ There is a strong relationship between the level of car ownership and the number of road accidents

☐ 53% of the variation in the level of road accidents from one country to the next can be explained by the corresponding variation in car ownership

☐ 73% of the variation in the level of road accidents from one country to the next can be explained by the corresponding variation in the level of car ownership

                                                                       (2 marks)

197 A standard product uses 3 kg of direct material costing $4 per kg. During the most recent month, 120 units of the product were manufactured. These required 410 kg of material costing $4.50 per kg. It is decided in retrospect that the standard usage quantity of the material should have been 3.5 kg, not 3 kg.

What is the favourable materials operational usage variance, if it is chosen to use planning and operational variances for reporting performance?

$ [   ]   (2 marks)

198 The following statements have been made about learning curves.

(1) Learning curves are easier to apply in companies with a high labour turnover than those with a lower rate of staff turnover.

(2) Learning rates are not affected by time gaps between the production of additional units of a product.

Which of the above statements is/are true?

O 1 only

O 2 only

O Neither 1 nor 2

O Both 1 and 2   (2 marks)

199   In which **TWO** of the following ways might a budgetary control be a disincentive to management to achieve targeted performance?

☐   Control reports are provided too late

☐   Targets are too easy

☐   Targets are not communicated

☐   Budgets are prepared on a bottom-up basis   **(2 marks)**

200   For which of the following reasons is zero-based budgeting (ZBB) often considered more suitable for public sector service organisations than for private sector companies?

O   ZBB is more suited to costs where there is little discretionary spending, as in the public sector services.

O   The public sector is better able to afford the high cost of ZBB.

O   ZBB is used in a top-down approach to budgeting, which is more common in the public sector than the private sector.

O   It is easier to put public sector activities into decision packages because they are more easily definable than in the private sector.   **(2 marks)**

201   In a time series analysis, the multiplicative model is used to forecast sales and the following seasonal variations apply:

Quarter	1	2	3	4
Seasonal variation	1.3	1.4	0.5	0.8

The actual sales for the first two quarters of the year 20X0 were:

Quarter 1: $520,000

Quarter 2: $630,000

What are the trend values for quarter 1 and quarter 2?

Quarter 1 [   ]

Quarter 2 [   ]

                          (2 marks)

202   Which of the following correctly describes a standard hour?

O   An hour during which only standard units are made

O   An hour during which no machine breakdowns occur

O   The quantity of work achievable at standard performance in an hour

O   An hour for which standard labour rates are paid   **(2 marks)**

203   Broad Co produces quarterly rolling budgets and had forecast the costs of material purchases for the next four quarters (quarters 1, 2, 3 and 4). Purchases for quarter 1 were budgeted to be $220,000 and it was anticipated that the cost of materials would rise at a rate of 2% per quarter.

At the end of quarter 1:

Actual material purchases were recorded as $210,000. This was due to a change of material supplier during the quarter.

- A revised estimate for the increase in material purchase costs was made. The rise was now predicted to be only 1% per quarter.

- The budget was updated.

What estimate for total annual material purchases should be recorded in the updated budget (to the nearest whole $)?

$	

(2 marks)

---

204   What is an attainable standard?

    O   A standard which is based on currently attainable working conditions.

    O   A standard which is established for use over a long period, which is used to show trends.

    O   A standard which can be attained under perfect operating conditions, and which includes no allowance for wastage, spoilage, machine breakdowns and other inefficiencies.

    O   A standard which can be attained if production is carried out efficiently, machines are operated properly and/or materials are used properly. Some allowance is made for waste and inefficiencies.

(2 marks)

---

205   For some quarterly sales data, the trend has been calculated as increasing by 6 each quarter and the average seasonal variation for the 3rd quarter as -22.5. The most recent data available is for the second quarter of Year 3 when sales were 370 units, and a centred moving average for the fourth quarter of Year 2 was 330.625 units.

Using the additive model, what are predicted sales for the third quarter of Year 3?

    O   376 units

    O   349 units

    O   308 units

    O   326 units

(2 marks)

(Total = 30 marks)

OTQ bank – Budgeting and control

206 A regression equation y = a + bx is used to forecast the value of y for a given value of x.

Which of the following increase the reliability of the forecast?

○ A large sample used to calculate the regression equation

○ Forecasting for values of x outside the range of those in the sample used to calculate the equation

○ Working to a higher number of decimal places of accuracy

○ A correlation coefficient numerically close to 0 **(2 marks)**

207 Which of the following is the **LEAST** likely reason why standard costs might not easily be applied to road haulage and distribution services?

○ It is difficult to measure labour times reliably

○ Variable costs are negligible

○ It is difficult to identify a standard item for costing

○ Standard costing applies to manufacturing industries only **(2 marks)**

208 For which of the following variances should a production manager usually be held responsible?

○ Material price planning variance

○ Material price operational variance

○ Material usage planning variance

○ Material usage operational variance **(2 marks)**

209 Tech World is a company which manufactures mobile phone handsets. From its past experiences, Tech World has realised that whenever a new design engineer is employed, there is a learning curve with a 75% learning rate which exists for the first 15 jobs.

A new design engineer has just completed their first job in five hours.

Note. At the learning rate of 75%, the learning factor (b) is equal to −0.415.

How long would it take the design engineer to complete the sixth job?

○ 2.377 hours

○ 1.442 hours

○ 2.564 hours

○ 5 hours **(2 marks)**

210   The following statements have been made about standard mix and yield variances.

(1)   Mix variances should be calculated whenever a standard product contains two or more direct materials.

(2)   When a favourable mix variance is achieved, there may be a counterbalancing adverse yield variance.

Which of the above statements is/are true?

○   1 only

○   2 only

○   Neither 1 nor 2

○   Both 1 and 2   (2 marks)

211   Which of the following provides the most suitable definition of the controllability principle in business?

○   A fundamental principle of management is the responsibility to control the organisation

○   Managers should be held accountable only for costs and revenues over which they have some influence or control

○   Organisations should be divided into budget centres for the purpose of operational control

○   Performance measures should be reported to managers to enable them to control operations   (2 marks)

212   An ice cream supplier has recorded some sales data which they believe shows a relationship between temperature (x) and sales (y). The results shown below are for ten sample days in the summer.

$\sum x=210$, $\sum y = 187$, $\sum x^2 = 4,634$, $\sum y^2 = 3,865$, $\sum xy = 4,208$.

What is the correlation coefficient of temperature and sales (to two decimal places)?

[   ]

(2 marks)

213   Capacity levels used in setting standard absorption rates for production overheads are often related to performance standards.

To which performance standard is budgeted capacity often associated?

○   Basic standard

○   Attainable standard

○   Ideal standard

○   Current standard   (2 marks)

214   In a time series analysis, the multiplicative model is used to forecast sales and the following seasonal variations apply:

Quarter	1	2	3	4
Seasonal variation	1.3	1.4	0.5	?

What is the seasonal variation for the fourth quarter (to one decimal place)?

| |

(2 marks)

215   Which **TWO** of the following points state why it is generally regarded to be more difficult to set standards for service function costs than for manufacturing costs?

☐   There is often no measurable output from service functions

☐   The activities of many service functions are of a non-standard nature

☐   The costs of many service functions are predominantly variable

☐   Tasks in many service industries are usually quick and simple   (2 marks)

216   Are the following statements about zero-based budgeting true or false?

Employees will focus on eliminating wasteful expenditure.	TRUE	FALSE
Short-term benefits could be emphasised over long-term benefits.	TRUE	FALSE

(2 marks)

217   Which of the following defines a trend?

O   A medium-term change in results caused by circumstances which repeat in cycles

O   An underlying long-term movement over time in the values of the data recorded

O   A short-term fluctuation due to different circumstances which affect results at different points in time

O   A non-recurring fluctuation caused by unforeseen circumstances   (2 marks)

218   Are the following statements about regression true or false?

Extrapolation is inherently risky.	TRUE	FALSE
The pattern of trend is expected to continue into the future.	TRUE	FALSE
The nearer in the future the forecast is for, the more unreliable it is.	TRUE	FALSE

(2 marks)

219 Total production costs for 900 units of output are $58,200 and total production costs for 1,200 units are $66,600.

The variable cost per unit is constant up to a production level of 2,000 units per month, but a step up of $6,000 in the monthly total fixed cost occurs when production reaches 1,100 units per month.

What is the total cost for a month when 1,000 units are produced?

$ [   ]

(2 marks)

220 A company sells two products X and Y. Product X sells for $30 per unit and achieves a standard contribution of $12 per unit, which is 40% of the selling price. Product Y, a new product, sells for $80 per unit and achieves a standard contribution of just $10 per unit, which is 12.5% of the selling price. Budgeted sales are 5,000 units of X and 3,000 units of Y.

However, the sudden cancellation of an advertising campaign for Product Y has meant that sales for the product will be well below budget, and there has been some price discounting in an attempt to obtain sales for the product. Sales of X were in line with the budget.

Which of the following sales variances, if calculated, would you expect to show a favourable variance for the period?

O   Sales mix variance

O   Sales price variance

O   Sales quantity variance

O   Sales volume variance

(2 marks)

(Total = 30 marks)

Section B questions

OT case questions

Crush Co

18 mins

The following scenario relates to the next five questions.

Crush Co has developed a new product. The first batch of 100 units will take 1,500 labour hours to produce. Crush Co has estimated that there will be an 85% learning curve that will continue until 6,400 units have been produced. Batches after this level will each take the same amount of time as the 64th batch. The batch size will always be 100 units.

Note. The learning index for an 85% learning curve is −0.2345

Ignore the time value of money.

221 What is the cumulative average time per batch for the first 64 batches?

- ○ 567.7 hours
- ○ 565.6 hours
- ○ 433.3 hours
- ○ 570 hours (2 marks)

---

222 The total time for the first 16 batches of 100 units was 9,000 hours.

What was the actual learning rate closest to (to the nearest %)?

| | %

(2 marks)

---

223 The following statements have been made about Crush Co and the learning curve:

(1) Decisions about allocating resources and costing the new product should be based on the time taken to produce the 64th batch.

(2) The learning process does not start until the second batch comes off the production line.

Which of the above statements is/are true?

- ○ 1 only
- ○ 2 only
- ○ Neither 1 nor 2
- ○ Both 1 and 2 (2 marks)

---

224 Are the following statements about the learning curve true or false?

The learning curve must assume a certain degree of motivation among employees of Crush Co.	TRUE	FALSE
The learning curve phenomenon is not always present.	TRUE	FALSE

(2 marks)

---

225 Which of the following conditions, if present in Crush Co, would allow the learning curve to flourish?

○ The process is a repetitive one

○ There is a continuity of workers

○ There are no prolonged breaks during the production process

○ All of the above (2 marks)

(Total = 10 marks)

BBB Co 18 mins

The following scenario relates to the next five questions.

BBB Co has developed a new product. The first batch of 50 units will take 750 labour hours to produce. There will be an 90% learning curve that will continue until 3,550 units have been produced. Batches after this level will each take the same amount of time as the 71st batch. The batch size will always be 50 units.

Note. The learning index for a 90% learning curve is –0.152

Ignore the time value of money.

226 What is the time taken for the 71st batch?

○ 392.35 hours

○ 330.75 hours

○ 393.23 hours

○ 345.65 hours (2 marks)

227 The total time for the first 16 batches of units was 8,500 hours.

What was the actual learning rate closest to (to the nearest %)?

┌────────────────┐
│   │ % (2 marks)
└────────────────┘

228 The following statements have been made about BBB Co and the learning curve:

(1) The learning effect comes to an end in BBB Co after the 71st unit; however, some learning effects can continue indefinitely.

(2) The learning curve is restricted to the manufacturing industry.

Which of the above statements is/are true?

○ 1 only

○ 2 only

○ Neither 1 nor 2

○ Both 1 and 2 (2 marks)

229   The costs of producing more units in BBB Co has been reduced due to the following factors. Which factor from those below is due to the learning curve effect?

    O   Bulk quantity discounts received from the supplier

    O   Lower labour costs

    O   A reduction in materials price

    O   Economies of scale achieved in energy costs   (2 marks)

230   The learning curve effect in BBB Co could be extended by which of the following?

    O   Increasing staff turnover

    O   Increasing the level of staff training

    O   Allowing extended breaks in production

    O   Introducing a new mechanised process   (2 marks)

(Total = 10 marks)

Mistletoe Co   18 mins

The following scenario relates to the next five questions.

Mistletoe Co currently prepares an annual fixed budget using incremental budgeting but is considering changing to a quarterly rolling budget. The accounts department consists of one part-qualified accountant who is always very busy. However, management want to improve the budget forecasts and improve performance over the year. There is some degree of uncertainty in Mistletoe Co's industry but the level of uncertainty is quantifiable.

The sales and cost of sales budgets for the year to 30 June 20X9 were as follows:

	Q1	Q2	Q3	Q4
	$	$	$	$
Sales	80,000	81,600	83,232	84,897
Cost of sales	56,000	57,120	58,262	59,428

However, at the end of Quarter 1, actual sales were $110,000 because a competitor went out of business. Senior management suggested that the revised assumption for sales growth should be 3% per quarter.

231   Using a rolling budget, what should the budget for Quarter 3 sales be?

$ [   ]   (2 marks)

232   Based on the actual sales for Quarter 1, what should the budget for Quarter 1 cost of sales be?

$ [   ]   (2 marks)

233 Which **THREE** of the following are advantages for Mistletoe Co of implementing rolling budgets?

☐ They are quicker to prepare than fixed budgets

☐ They reduce the element of uncertainty in budgeting

☐ There is always a budget which extends for several months ahead

☐ They are more realistic

☐ They are cheaper to prepare than fixed budgets

(2 marks)

234 Are the following statements about incremental budgeting for Mistletoe Co true or false?

It compounds budgetary slack.	TRUE	FALSE
It discourages efforts to improve performance.	TRUE	FALSE
It involves more time and effort than other methods.	TRUE	FALSE

(2 marks)

235 Which **TWO** of the following methods could Mistletoe Co use to reduce the element of uncertainty in its budgets?

☐ Zero-based budgeting

☐ Probabilistic budgeting

☐ Sensitivity analysis

☐ Activity-based budgeting

(2 marks)

(Total = 10 marks)

Birch Co   18 mins

The following scenario relates to the next five questions.

Birch Co budgeted to make and sell 20,000 units of Product X in a four-week period, as follows:

	$
Budgeted sales ($4 per unit per week)	80,000
Variable costs ($2.50 per unit)	50,000
Contribution	30,000
Fixed costs	3,000
Profit	27,000

The actual results for the period were as follows.

	$
Budgeted sales ($4 per unit)	64,000
Variable costs ($2.50 per unit)	40,000
Contribution	24,000
Fixed costs	3,000
Profit	21,000

In retrospect, it is decided that the optimum budget would have been to sell only 17,500 units in the period.

236 Select two boxes to indicate the sales volume planning variance and whether it is favourable or adverse.

Value ($)	Sign
2,250	Favourable
3,750	Adverse

(2 marks)

237 Select two boxes to indicate the sales volume operational variance and whether it is favourable or adverse.

Value ($)	Sign
2,250	Favourable
3,750	Adverse

(2 marks)

238 In a subsequent 4-week period, Birch Co decided to adopt absorption costing and actual fixed costs were $3,500. There were 18,000 units produced. The budgeted fixed costs were $3,000 based on budgeted production of 17,500 units.

Select two boxes to indicate the fixed production overhead total variance and whether it is favourable or adverse.

Value ($)	Sign
440	Favourable
500	Adverse
525	

(2 marks)

239 Which of the following factors would contribute to a planning variance in Birch Co?

○ A better negotiation of the material price with the supplier

○ An increase in wage costs due to unplanned overtime worked

○ An improvement in technology that led to an international reduction in sales price of Product X

○ A break in production due to a machine breakdown, which was caused by human error

(2 marks)

240 A manager in Birch Co asked for the market share variance. Which of the following variances was she looking for?

Picklist:

The sales volume planning variance
The sales volume operational variance
The sales price planning variance
The sales price operational variance

(2 marks)

(Total = 10 marks)

Organic Bread Co (Sep/Dec 2015 amended)   18 mins

The following scenario relates to the next five questions.

The Organic Bread Company (OBC) makes a range of breads for sale direct to the public. The production process begins with workers weighing out ingredients on electronic scales and then placing them in a machine for mixing. A worker then manually removes the mix from the machine and shapes it into loaves by hand, after which the bread is placed into the oven for baking.

All baked loaves are then inspected by OBC's quality inspector before they are packaged up and made ready for sale. Any loaves which fail the inspection are donated to a local food bank.

The standard cost card for OBC's 'Mixed Bloomer', one of its most popular loaves, is as follows:

			$
White flour	450 grams	at $1.80 per kg	0.81
Wholegrain flour	150 grams	at $2.20 per kg	0.33
Yeast	10 grams	at $20 per kg	0.20
Total	610 grams		1.34

Budgeted production of Mixed Bloomers was 1,000 units for the quarter, although actual production was only 950 units. The total actual quantities used and their actual costs were:

	Kg	$ per kg
White flour	408.50	1.90
Wholegrain flour	152.0	2.10
Yeast	10.0	20.00
Total	570.5	

241 What is the favourable materials usage variance (to two decimal places)?

$ [   ]

(2 marks)

242 Select two boxes to indicate the material mix variance and whether it is favourable or adverse.

Value ($)	Sign
14.17	Favourable
16.51	Adverse

(2 marks)

243 Select two boxes to indicate the material yield variance and whether it is favourable or adverse.

Value ($)	Sign
3.30	Favourable
19.77	Adverse

(2 marks)

244 Indicate, by selecting the relevant boxes in the table below, whether each of the following statements would result in an adverse material yield variance in Organic Bread Company?

Not fully removing the mix out of the machine, leaving some behind.	YES	NO
Errors in the mix causing sub-standard loaves and rejections by the quality inspector.	YES	NO
An unexpected increase in the cost of flour introduced by the supplier.	YES	NO

(2 marks)

245 Indicate, by selecting the relevant boxes in the table below, whether each of the following statements would result in a material mix variance in Organic Bread Company?

The production manager in Organic Bread Co deviates from the standard mix.	YES	NO
The selling price of the Mixed Bloomer changes.	YES	NO
An inferior quality of flour or yeast is used unknowingly.	YES	NO

(2 marks)

(Total = 10 marks)

Elm Co

18 mins

The following scenario relates to the next five questions.

Elm Co is a company which operates in Sealand. Elm Co budgeted to sell 25,000 units of a new product during the year. The budgeted sales price was $8 per unit, and the variable cost $4 per unit.

Actual sales during the year were 22,000 units and variable costs of sales were $88,000. Sales revenue was only $9 per unit. With the benefit of hindsight, it is realised that the budgeted sales price of $8 was too low, and a price of $10 per unit would have been much more realistic.

Required

246 What is the favourable sales price planning variance?

$ [   ]

(2 marks)

247 What is the adverse sales price operational variance?

$ [   ]   (2 marks)

---

248 In a subsequent year, the cost of labour was $73,000. 4,000 hours were worked. The budgeted cost of labour was $15 per labour hour.

What is the adverse labour rate variance for this subsequent year?

$ [   ]   (2 marks)

---

249 Are the following statements about Elm Co true or false?

	TRUE	FALSE
The sales manager of Elm Co should be held responsible if an unfavourable planning sales price variance is found.	TRUE	FALSE
It is possible for the revised price to be manipulated and revised to a level whereby a favourable operational sales price could be found.	TRUE	FALSE

(2 marks)

---

250 Are the following statements about Elm Co true or false?

	TRUE	FALSE
The operational manager of Elm Co should examine each variance in isolation only.	TRUE	FALSE
A change in economic conditions in Sealand will result in operational variances.	TRUE	FALSE

(2 marks)

(Total = 10 marks)

Maple Co   18 mins

The following scenario relates to the next five questions.

A company made a product called Bark. Bark had a standard direct material cost in the budget of:

2.5 kg of Material X at $4 per kg = $10 per unit.

The average market price for Material X during the period was $5 per kg, and it was decided to revise the material standard cost to allow for this.

During the period, 8,000 units of Bark were manufactured. They required 22,000 kg of Material X, which cost $123,000.

Required

251 What is the adverse material price planning variance?

$ [   ]   (2 marks)

---

252 What is the adverse material price operational variance?

$ [   ]   (2 marks)

253 What is the adverse material usage operational variance?

$ [   ]   (2 marks)

254 Are the following possible reasons for a material price planning variance valid or invalid?

Maple Co failed to order a sufficient amount of Material X for production from the main supplier. They sourced the rest of the material from another supplier at a higher price to make up for this.	VALID	INVALID
There was a disruption to the supply of Material X to the market.	VALID	INVALID

(2 marks)

255 Are the following statements about variances in Maple Co true or false?

Any operational variances arising should be a realistic measure of what the causes of the variances have cost Maple Co.	TRUE	FALSE
The causes of the planning variances should be investigated immediately by the operational manager in Maple Co.	TRUE	FALSE

(2 marks)

(Total = 10 marks)

Pine Co   **18 mins**

The following scenario relates to the next five questions.

Pine Co makes a single product. At the beginning of the budget year, the standard labour cost was established as $45 per unit, and each unit should take three hours to make.

However, during the year, the standard labour cost was revised. The labour rate was reduced to $14 per hour, and the revised labour time was 4.5 hours per unit.

In the first month after revision of the standard cost, budgeted production was 10,000 units but only 8,000 units were actually produced. These took 24,300 hours of labour time, which cost $352,350.

Required

256 What is the favourable labour rate planning variance?

$ [   ]   (2 marks)

257 What is the adverse labour efficiency planning variance?

$ [ ]   (2 marks)

258 What is the adverse labour rate operational variance?

$ [ ]   (2 marks)

259 What is the favourable labour efficiency operational variance?

$ [ ]   (2 marks)

260 Are the following statements about labour variances in Pine Co true or false?

	TRUE	FALSE
Production management's motivation is likely to increase if they know they will not be held responsible for poor planning and faulty standard setting.	TRUE	FALSE
Planning variances will provide a more realistic and fair reflection of actual performance.	TRUE	FALSE

(2 marks)

(Total = 10 marks)

Kiss Co   **18 mins**

The following scenario relates to the next five questions.

Kiss Co has developed a new product. The first batch of 200 units will take 3,500 labour hours to produce. There will be a 75% learning curve that will continue until 4,800 units have been produced. Batches after this level will each take the same amount of time as the 24th batch. The batch size will always be 200 units.

Note. The learning index for a 75% learning curve is –0.415

Ignore the time value of money.

261 What is the time taken for the 24th batch (to the nearest hour)?

[ ] hours   (2 marks)

262 The total time for the first 16 batches of units was 22,000 hours.

What was the actual learning rate, to the nearest %?

[ ] %   (2 marks)

263   Kiss Co makes another product, the Lyco. The learning effect stopped after the 16th batch of product, and a 'steady state' was reached. Workers in Kiss Co received $15 per hour. The first batch of Lyco took 0.75 hours to produce. The 16th batch of Lyco took 0.5 hours, and the standard cost was revised to this figure once the 'steady state' was reached. Kiss Co produced 10,000 batches of Lyco during the year.

What is the favourable labour efficiency planning variance?

$	

(2 marks)

264   Are the following statements about Kiss Co true or false?

Because of the learning effect, the labour efficiency planning variance of Lyco will always be favourable.	TRUE	FALSE
A standard labour cost should only be established when a 'steady state' is reached.	TRUE	FALSE

(2 marks)

265   In which of the following ways might an operational manager in Kiss Co try to improve labour efficiency and achieve favourable labour efficiency variances?

O   Increase output volumes

O   Increase inspection and testing of products

O   Provide workers with training

O   Arrange for overtime working

(2 marks)

(Total = 10 marks)

Hollie Hotels Co   18 mins

The following scenario relates to the next five questions.

Hollie Hotels Co operates a chain of upmarket hotels across the country of Westland. Each hotel manager is responsible for producing an annual budget, based on targets set by head office. Online budget training is available for all managers. Hollie Hotels Co has recently updated its information system and it is capable of providing extensive cost information for managers. Managers find the new system easy to use.

20X0 and 20X1

In 20X1, Hollie Hotels Co used incremental budgeting based on the previous year's actual results. Estimated cost inflation was 5% and occupancy was estimated to be two percentage points higher than 20X0. Hollie Hotel – Northwest is a typical hotel in the chain and opens for 360 days a year. The budgeted and actual results for Hollie Hotel – Northwest in 20X0 were as follows:

		Budget (Y/e Nov 20X0)	Actual (Y/e Nov 20X0)
Number of rooms available	20		
Occupancy		80%	75%
Revenue per room per night (average)		$120	$110
Variable cost per room per night (average)		$30	$40
Fixed costs		$125,000	$130,000

BPP
LEARNING
MEDIA

20X2

According to targets set by head office for 20X2, the company hoped to raise total revenue by 7% and total profit by 14%. By the end of the year, total profits had only increased by 9% because of a lack of cost control.

20X3

Hollie Hotels Co is considering whether zero-based budgeting (ZBB) would be beneficial, given the 20X2 results.

266 What is the total budgeted profit for Hollie Hotel – Northwest for 20X1 (to the nearest whole dollar)?

$ [   ]   (2 marks)

---

267 If Hollie Hotels Co changed to zero-based budgeting, match the steps in the correct order in which they should be carried out.

List of steps	Correct order	
Allocation of resources	Step 1	
Identification of decision packages – base level	Step 2	
Evaluation and ranking of each activity	Step 3	
Identification of decision packages – incremental packages	Step 4	

(2 marks)

---

268 Are the following statements about zero-based budgeting for Hollie Hotels Co true or false?

ZBB is particularly useful for cost reduction exercises.	TRUE	FALSE
ZBB is particularly useful for cost structures such as Hollie Hotels Co's.	TRUE	FALSE

(2 marks)

---

269 Which **TWO** of the following problems relating to ZBB would apply to Hollie Hotels Co?

☐ Managers may not have the necessary skills

☐ Short term benefits may be to the detriment of long term benefits

☐ ZBB is more time consuming than incremental budgeting

☐ Hollie Hotels Co may not be able to provide relevant information to managers

(2 marks)

---

270   Three months into 20X3, Hollie Hotels Co looks at the results and forecasts of its hotels.

Which of the following situations describes feedforward control?

O   Hotel Southwest: Fixed costs have deviated from plan and must be brought back on course

O   Hotel Southeast: Revenues and costs are going according to plan and no corrective action is necessary

O   Hotel Northeast: Forecast profits are poor and control action is taken in advance

O   Hotel Midwest: Variable costs are more than budget and must be reduced as they are deviating from plan   (2 marks)

(Total = 10 marks)

Section C questions

271 Mic Co (December 2013)   36 mins

Mic Co produces microphones for mobile phones and operates a standard costing system. Before production commenced, the standard labour time per batch for its latest microphone was estimated to be 200 hours. The standard labour cost per hour is $12 and resource allocation and cost data were therefore initially prepared on this basis.

Production of the microphone started in July and the number of batches assembled and sold each month was as follows:

Month	No of batches assembled and sold
July	1
August	1
September	2
October	4
November	8

The first batch took 200 hours to make, as anticipated, but, during the first four months of production, a learning effect of 88% was observed, although this finished at the end of October. The learning formula is shown on the formula sheet and at the 88% learning rate the value of b is -0.1844245.

Mic Co uses 'cost plus' pricing to establish selling prices for all its products. Sales of its new microphone in the first five months have been disappointing. The sales manager has blamed the production department for getting the labour cost so wrong, as this, in turn, caused the price to be too high. The production manager has disclaimed all responsibility, saying that, 'as usual, the managing director prepared the budgets alone and didn't consult me and, had he bothered to do so, I would have told him that a learning curve was expected.'

Required

(a)   Calculate the actual total monthly labour costs for producing the microphones for each of the five months from July to November.   (9 marks)

(b)   Discuss the implications of the learning effect coming to an end for Mic Co, with regard to costing, budgeting and production.   (4 marks)

(c)   Discuss the potential advantages and disadvantages of involving senior staff at Mic Co in the budget-setting process, rather than the managing director simply imposing budgets on them.   (7 marks)

(Total = 20 marks)

272 Yumi Co (Sep/Dec 2019)   36 mins

Yumi Co owns a number of restaurants. It is a well-established company, and its restaurants have gained a favourable reputation for the quality of their meals.

Yumi Co's restaurants are all set in rural locations, where there is limited competition and this enabled them to develop a loyal customer base. Restaurants design their own menus and décor to fit with the requirements of their local market.

Yumi Co has been consistently profitable, however as is the case across the restaurant industry, profit margins are quite low and there is still a constant need for Yumi Co to monitor costs.

One of Yumi Co's restaurants is located in the small town of Cowly. Cowly has recently been the location for the filming of a popular television series and visitor numbers to the town have increased significantly as a result. Yumi Co's restaurant in Cowly has noticed a similar increase in customer numbers.

At the start of the current month a new restaurant opened in Cowly. The manager of Yumi Co's restaurant in Cowly has expressed concerns about the impact this new competitor will have on their ability to achieve profit targets for the rest of the year.

Budgets for all of Yumi Co's restaurants are prepared by the head office. At the start of each year, restaurant managers are given an annual budget, which is split into months. At the end of each month, the manager receives a statement comparing actual monthly performance against budget.

The statement for the Cowly restaurant for the most recent completed month is as follows:

	Actual	Budget	Variance
Number of customers	1,800	1,500	
	$	$	$
Revenue	87,300	75,000	12,300 F
Costs:			
Food and drink	26,100	22,500	3,600 A
Staff wages	38,250	31,500	6,750 A
Heat, light and power	8,100	7,500	600 A
Rent, rates and other overheads	12,600	12,000	600 A
Profit	2,250	1,500	750 F

Notes:

(1) Rent, rates and other overheads are apportioned to its restaurants by Yumi Co's head office, based on a fixed annual charge.

(2) All other budgeted costs are treated as variable costs, based on the expected number of customers.

Yumi Co currently adopts an incremental approach to budgeting, with the annual budget figures for each year being based on the previous year's figures. However, a new finance director has recently joined the company, and he has questioned whether this is suitable for all Yumi Co's restaurants.

The new finance director has also suggested that the company should adopt a more participative approach to budgeting.

Required

(a)   (i)   Prepare a flexed budget for the Cowly restaurant.   (3 marks)

      (ii)   With reference to your answer from part (i), explain the main weaknesses in the current monthly budget statements issued to the restaurants as a basis for managing performance.   (4 marks)

(b)　Discuss whether an incremental approach to budgeting is appropriate for Yumi Co.

(6 marks)

(c)　Define a participative approach to budgeting and explain the potential advantages and disadvantages of introducing this approach at Yumi Co. **(7 marks)**

(Total = 20 marks)

273 Crumbly Cakes (June 2009 amended)　　36 mins

Crumbly Cakes makes cakes, which are sold directly to the public. The new production manager (a celebrity chef) has argued that the business should use only organic ingredients in its cake production. Organic ingredients are more expensive but should produce a product with an improved flavour and give health benefits for the customers. It was hoped that this would stimulate demand and enable an immediate price increase for the cakes.

Crumbly Cakes operates a responsibility-based standard costing system which allocates variances to specific individuals. The individual managers are paid a bonus only when net favourable variances are allocated to them.

The new organic cake production approach was adopted at the start of March 20X9, following a decision by the new production manager. No change was made at that time to the standard costs card. The variance reports for February and March are shown below (Fav = Favourable and Adv = Adverse).

Manager responsible	Allocated variances	February variance $	March variance $
Production manager	Material price (total for all ingredients)	25 Fav	2,100 Adv
	Material mix	0	600 Adv
	Material yield	20 Fav	400 Fav
Sales manager	Sales price	40 Adv	7,000 Fav
	Sales contribution volume	35 Adv	3,000 Fav

The production manager is upset that they seem to have lost all hope of a bonus under the new system. The sales manager thinks the new organic cakes are excellent and is very pleased with the progress made.

Crumbly Cakes operates a JIT inventory system and holds virtually no inventory.

Required

(a)　Assess the performance of the production manager and the sales manager and indicate whether the current bonus scheme is fair to those concerned. **(7 marks)**

In April 20X9 the following data applied:

Standard cost card for one cake (not adjusted for the organic ingredient change)

Ingredients	Kg	$
Flour	0.10	0.12 per kg
Eggs	0.10	0.70 per kg
Butter	0.10	1.70 per kg
Sugar	0.10	0.50 per kg
Total input	0.40	
Normal loss (10%)	(0.04)	
Standard weight of a cake	0.36	

The budget for production and sales in April was 50,000 cakes. Actual production and sales was 60,000 cakes in the month, during which the following occurred:

Ingredients used	Kg	$
Flour	5,700	$741
Eggs	6,600	$5,610
Butter	6,600	$11,880
Sugar	4,578	$2,747
Total input	23,478	$20,978
Actual loss	(1,878)	
Actual output of cake mixture	21,600	

All cakes produced must weigh 0.36 kg, as this is what is advertised.

Required

(b)   Calculate the material price, mix and yield variances for April. You are not required to make any comment on the performance of the managers.   **(9 marks)**

With the benefit of hindsight the management of Crumbly Cakes realises that a more realistic standard cost for current conditions would be $0.40 per cake. The planned standard cost is unrealistically low.

Required

(c)   Calculate the total cost planning and operational variances for April. Briefly comment on each variance.   **(4 marks)**

(Total = 20 marks)

274 Medical Temp Co (Mar/Jun 2021)   36 mins

Medical Temp Co (MTC) is one of several agencies in Sictopia supplying medical staff, both nurses and doctors, under temporary weekly contracts to local hospitals.

Information regarding the size of the market in Sictopia for the supply of medical staff is as follows:

	Quarter 1 $m	Quarter 2 $m
Size of national market for supply of temporary nurses	14	18.9
Size of national market for supply of temporary doctors	8	8.2

The increase in the national market for the supply of temporary nurses is due to a shortage of full-time nurses in Sictopia.

All agencies in Sictopia, including MTC, charge a single market rate for the supply of each type of staff: $1,000 per week for supplying a nurse and $2,000 per week for supplying a doctor. In quarter 1, MTC held 30% of the market for the supply of temporary nurses and 40% for the supply of temporary doctors.

MTC uses quarterly rolling budgets. At the end of quarter 1, it prepared its budgeted revenue figures for quarter 2. It based these budgeted figures on the assumption that the company would continue to maintain the market share it had in quarter 1. It also assumed that it would maintain its standard contribution margin of 80% for both nurses and doctors.

MTC's actual figures for quarter 2 are as follows:

	Actual
Total revenue from supply of nurses	$5.3m
Total revenue from supply of doctors	$3.6m
Actual contribution margin from both nurses and doctors	75%

This part of the scenario relates to requirement (c).

Cheat Co

The market size and market share variances have also been calculated for quarter 2 for one of MTC's competitors, Cheat Co. These variances are as follows:

	Nurses $'000	Doctors $'000	Total $'000
Market size	185 A	724 A	909 A
Market share	1,065 F	1,043 F	2,108 F

Cheat Co holds the same percentage of each market as MTC. It also uses rolling budgets and prepares its budgeted revenue figures using exactly the same assumptions as MTC. However, when Cheat Co's sales director had to provide the market size figures for quarter 2 to the accounts department, he deliberately reported these figures 30% lower by excluding the market segment relating to maternity units. The accounts department were unaware of this.

Required

(a) Explain why businesses calculate market size and market share variances. **(4 marks)**

(b) Calculate the total market size (planning) variance and the total market share (operational) variance for MTC for quarter 2. **(10 marks)**

(c) Discuss the actions of the sales director at Cheat Co and how this may have impacted on the variances which have been calculated. **(6 marks)**

(Total = 20 marks)

275 Clear Co (Mar/Jun 2020)   36 mins

Clear Co is an eye treatment specialist, founded in 20X4, which runs five clinics nationwide. It is based in Zeeland, a country in which 20% of the population is over 65 years old, compared to only 15% ten years ago.

Clear Co offers two eye treatment procedures: laser treatment and lens treatment. Laser treatment is the less complex of the two procedures. Technology changes rapidly in this industry and as a result 90% of patients now qualify for laser treatment, compared to only 80% five years ago.

The remaining 10% of patients are only able to have lens treatment, of which there are two types: 'refractive lens exchange' (RLE) and 'implantable contact lenses' (ICL). Clear Co started providing RLE, a treatment most effective for patients aged 40 or older, in 20X4 when it was founded. Two years ago, it also began providing ICL, a treatment recommended for patients under the age of 40.

The market for eye treatment procedures in Zeeland is dominated by a few main suppliers, of which Clear Co is one. Until two years ago, Clear Co was the largest supplier but, following the merger of two other companies, it is now the second largest. The merged company, Eos Co, has recently released its financial statements for the year, showing profits which were 10% higher than forecast. Eos Co's press release stated that it has achieved this despite offering reduced prices for the ICL treatment. It has been able to offer reduced prices because of the economies of scale achieved by the merger.

The following information relates to the two types of lens treatments offered by Clear Co for the year just ended:

Lens treatment	RLE		ICL	
	Budget	Actual	Budget	Actual
Number of treatments	3,750	4,130	1,320	960
Selling price per treatment ($)	3,000	2,900	3,650	3,400
Variable cost treatment ($)	600	590	1,150	1,200

BPP
LEARNING
MEDIA

Required

(a) Calculate the following TOTAL variances for Clear Co's lens treatments:

    (i)   The sales mix contribution variance   **(4 marks)**

    (ii)   The sales quantity contribution variance.   **(4 marks)**

(b) Explain what each of the sales mix contribution variance and sales quantity contribution variance measures.   **(2 marks)**

(c) Using your answer from part (a) and any other relevant calculations, discuss Clear Co's SALES performance for the year just ended.   **(10 marks)**

Note: There are up to four marks available for additional calculations relevant to SALES performance and six marks available for discussion.

(Total = 20 marks)

276 Truffle Co (December 2012)   **36 mins**

Truffle Co makes high quality, hand-made chocolate truffles which it sells to a local retailer. All chocolates are made in batches of 16, to fit the standard boxes supplied by the retailer. The standard cost of labour for each batch is $6.00 and the standard labour time for each batch is half an hour. In November, Truffle Co had budgeted production of 24,000 batches; actual production was only 20,500 batches. 12,000 labour hours were used to complete the work and there was no idle time. All workers were paid for their actual hours worked. The actual total labour cost for November was $136,800. The production manager at Truffle Co has no input into the budgeting process.

At the end of October, the managing director decided to hold a meeting and offer staff the choice of either accepting a 5% pay cut or facing a certain number of redundancies. All staff subsequently agreed to accept the 5% pay cut with immediate effect.

At the same time, the retailer requested that the truffles be made slightly softer. This change was implemented immediately and made the chocolates more difficult to shape. When recipe changes such as these are made, it takes time before the workers become used to working with the new ingredient mix, making the process 20% slower for at least the first month of the new operation.

The standard costing system is only updated once a year, in June, and no changes are ever made to the system outside of this.

Required

(a) Calculate the total labour rate and total labour efficiency variances for November, based on the standard cost provided above.   **(4 marks)**

(b) Analyse the total labour rate and total labour efficiency variances into component parts for planning and operational variances in as much detail as the information allows.   **(8 marks)**

(c) Assess the performance of the production manager for the month of November. **(8 marks)**

(Total = 20 marks)

277 Block Co (June 2013)

Block Co operates an absorption costing system and sells three types of product – Commodity 1, Commodity 2 and Commodity 3. Like other competitors operating in the same market, Block Co is struggling to maintain revenues and profits in face of the economic recession which has engulfed the country over the last two years. Sales prices fluctuate in the market in which Block Co operates. Consequently, at the beginning of each quarter, a market specialist, who works on a consultancy basis for Block Co, sets a budgeted sales price for each product for the quarter, based on their expectations of the market. This then becomes the 'standard selling price' for the quarter. The sales department itself is run by the company's sales manager, who negotiates the actual sales prices with customers. The following budgeted figures are available for the quarter ended 31 May 20X3.

Product	Budgeted production and sales units	Standard selling price per unit	Standard variable production costs per unit
Commodity 1	30,000	$30	$18
Commodity 2	28,000	$35	$28.40
Commodity 3	26,000	$41.60	$26.40

Block Co uses absorption costing. Fixed production overheads are absorbed on the basis of direct machine hours and the budgeted cost of these for the quarter ended 31 May 20X3 was $174,400. Commodities 1, 2 and 3 use 0.2 hours, 0.6 hours and 0.8 hours of machine time respectively.

The following data shows the actual sales prices and volumes achieved for each product by Block Co for the quarter ended 31 May 20X3 and the average market prices per unit.

Product	Actual production and sales units	Actual selling price per unit	Average market price per unit
Commodity 1	29,800	$31	$32.20
Commodity 2	30,400	$34	$33.15
Commodity 3	25,600	$40.40	$39.10

The following variances have already been correctly calculated for Commodities 1 and 2:

Sales price operational variances

Commodity 1: $35,760 Adverse

Commodity 2: $25,840 Favourable

Sales price planning variances

Commodity 1: $65,560 Favourable

Commodity 2: $56,240 Adverse

Required

(a) Calculate, for Commodity 3 only, the sales price operational variance and the sales price planning variance. **(4 marks)**

(b) Using the data provided for Commodities 1, 2 and 3, calculate the total sales mix variance and the total sales quantity variance. **(11 marks)**

(c) Briefly discuss the performance of the business and, in particular, that of the sales manager for the quarter ended 31 May 20X3. **(5 marks)**

(Total = 20 marks)

278 Newtown School (June 2013)

Newtown School's head teacher has prepared the budget for the year ending 31 May 20X4. The government pays the school $1,050 for each child registered at the beginning of the school year, which is June 1, and $900 for any child joining the school part-way through the year. The school does not have to refund the money to the government if a child leaves the school part-way through the year. The number of pupils registered at the school on 1 June 20X3 is 690, which is 10% lower than the previous year. Based on past experience, the probabilities for the number of pupils starting the school part-way through the year are as follows:

Probability	No of pupils joining late
0.2	50
0.3	20
0.5	26

The head teacher admits to being 'poor with numbers' and does not understand probabilities so, when calculating budgeted revenue, he just calculates a simple average for the number of pupils expected to join late. His budgeted revenue for the year ending 31 May 20X4 is therefore as follows:

	Pupils	Rate per pupil	Total income
Pupils registered at beginning of school year	690	$1,050	$724,500
Average expected number of new joiners	32	$900	$28,800
			$753,300

The head teacher uses incremental budgeting to budget for his expenditure, taking actual expenditure for the previous year as a starting point and simply adjusting it for inflation, as shown below.

	Note	Actual cost for y/e 31 May 20X3 $	Inflationary adjustment	Budgeted cost for y/e 31 May 20X4 $
Repairs and maintenance	1	44,000	+ 3%	45,320
Salaries	2	620,000	+ 2%	632,400
Capital expenditure	3	65,000	+ 6%	68,900
Total budgeted expenditure				746,620
Budget surplus				6,680

Notes

(1) $30,000 of the costs for the year ended 31 May 20X3 related to standard maintenance checks and repairs that have to be carried out by the school every year in order to comply with government health and safety standards. These are expected to increase by 3% in the coming year. In the year ended 31 May 20X3, $14,000 was also spent on redecorating some of the classrooms. No redecorating is planned for the coming year.

(2)   One teacher earning a salary of $26,000 left the school on 31 May 20X3 and there are no plans to replace her. However, a 2% pay rise will be given to all staff with effect from 1 December 20X3.

(3)   The full $65,000 actual costs for the year ended 31 May 20X3 related to improvements made to the school gym. This year, the canteen is going to be substantially improved, although the extent of the improvements and level of service to be offered to pupils is still under discussion. There is a 0.7 probability that the cost will be $145,000 and a 0.3 probability that it will be $80,000. These costs must be paid in full before the end of the year ending 31 May 20X4.

The school's board of governors, who review the budget, are concerned that the budget surplus has been calculated incorrectly. They believe that it should have been calculated using expected income, based on the probabilities provided, and using expected expenditure, based on the information provided in Notes 1 to 3. They believe that incremental budgeting is not proving a reliable tool for budget setting in the school since, for the last three years, there have been shortfalls of cash despite a budget surplus being predicted. Since the school has no other source of funding available to it, these shortfalls have had serious consequences, such as the closure of the school kitchen for a considerable period in the last school year, meaning that no hot meals were available to pupils. This is thought to have been the cause of the 10% fall in the number of pupils registered at the school on 1 June 20X3.

Required

(a) Considering the views of the board of governors, recalculate the budget surplus/deficit for the year ending 31 May 20X4. **(6 marks)**

(b) Discuss the advantages and disadvantages of using incremental budgeting. **(4 marks)**

(c) Briefly outline the three main steps involved in preparing a zero-based budget. **(6 marks)**

(d) Discuss the extent to which zero-based budgeting could be used by Newtown School to improve the budgeting process. **(4 marks)**

(Total = 20 marks)

279 Bedco (December 2013) 36 mins

Bedco manufactures bed sheets and pillowcases, which it supplies to a major hotel chain. It uses a just-in-time system and holds no inventories.

The standard cost for the cotton which is used to make the bed sheets and pillowcases is $5 per m^2.

Each bed sheet uses 2 m^2 of cotton and each pillowcase uses 0.5 m^2. Production levels for bed sheets and pillowcases for November were as follows:

	Budgeted production levels	Actual production levels
	Units	Units
Bed sheets	120,000	120,000
Pillow cases	190,000	180,000

The actual cost of the cotton in November was $5.80 per m^2. 248,000 m^2 of cotton was used to make the bed sheets and 95,000 m^2 was used to make the pillowcases.

The world commodity prices for cotton increased by 20% in the month of November. At the beginning of the month, the hotel chain made an unexpected request for an immediate design change to the pillowcases. The new design required 10% more cotton than previously. It also resulted in production delays and therefore a shortfall in production of 10,000 pillowcases in total that month.

The production manager at Bedco is responsible for all buying and any production issues which occur, although they are not responsible for the setting of standard costs.

Required

(a) Calculate the following variances for the month of November, for both bed sheets and pillow cases, and in total:

(i)	Total material price planning variance	**(3 marks)**
(ii)	Total material price operational variance	**(3 marks)**
(iii)	Total material usage planning variance	**(3 marks)**
(iv)	Total material usage operational variance	**(3 marks)**

(b) Assess the performance of the production manager for the month of November. **(8 marks)**

(Total = 20 marks)

280 Valet Co (June 2014)

36 mins

Valet Co is a car valeting (cleaning) company. It operates in the country of Strappia, which has been badly affected by the global financial crisis. Petrol and food prices have increased substantially in the last year and the average disposable household income has decreased by 30%. Recent studies have shown that the average car owner keeps their car for five years before replacing it, rather than three years as was previously the case. Figures over recent years also show that car sales in Strappia are declining, while business for car repairs is on the increase.

Valet Co offers two types of valet – a full valet and a mini valet. A full valet is an extensive clean of the vehicle, inside and out; a mini valet is a more basic clean of the vehicle. Until recently, four similar businesses operated in Valet Co's local area, but one of these closed down three months ago after a serious fire on its premises. Valet Co charges customers $50 for each full valet and $30 for each mini valet and this price never changes. Their budget and actual figures for the last year were as follows:

	Budget		Actual	
Number of valets:				
Full valets	3,600		4,000	
Mini valets	2,000		3,980	
	$	$	$	$
Revenue		240,000		319,400
Variable costs:				
Staff wages	(114,000)		(122,000)	
Cleaning materials	(6,200)		(12,400)	
Energy costs	(6,520)		(9,200)	
		(126,720)		(143,600)
Contribution		113,280		175,800
Fixed costs:				
Rent, rates and depreciation		(36,800)		(36,800)
Operating profit		76,480		139,000

The budgeted contribution to sales ratios for the two types of valet are 44.6% for full valets and 55% for mini valets.

Required

(a) Using the data provided for full valets and mini valets, calculate:

    (i)   The total sales mix contribution variance   **(4 marks)**

    (ii)   The total sales quantity contribution variance   **(4 marks)**

(b) Briefly describe the sales mix contribution variance and the sales quantity contribution variance.   **(2 marks)**

(c) Discuss the **SALES** performance of the business for the period, taking into account your calculations from part (a) **AND** the information provided in the scenario.   **(10 marks)**

(Total = 20 marks)

281 Glove Co (Mar/Jun 2016 amended)

Glove Co makes high quality, hand-made gloves which it sells for an average of $180 per pair. The standard cost of labour for each pair is $42 and the standard labour time for each pair is three hours. In the last quarter, Glove Co had budgeted production of 12,000 pairs, although actual production was 12,600 pairs in order to meet demand. 37,000 hours were used to complete the work and there was no idle time. The total labour cost for the quarter was $531,930.

At the beginning of the last quarter, the design of the gloves was changed slightly. The new design required workers to sew the company's logo onto the back of every glove made and the estimated time to do this was 15 minutes for each pair. However, no-one told the accountant responsible for updating standard costs that the standard time per pair of gloves needed to be changed. Similarly, although all workers were given a 2% pay rise at the beginning of the last quarter, the accountant was not told about this either. Consequently, the standard was not updated to reflect these changes.

When overtime is required, workers are paid 25% more than their usual hourly rate.

Required

(a)   Calculate the total labour rate and total labour efficiency variances for the last quarter.

(2 marks)

(b)   Analyse the above total variances into component parts for planning and operational variances in as much detail as the information allows.   **(6 marks)**

(c)   Explain what is meant by the controllability principle and assess the performance of the production manager for the last quarter.   **(12 marks)**

(Total = 20 marks)

282 SU Co (Mar/Jun 2017)

36 mins

The School Uniform Company (SU Co) manufactures school uniforms. One of its largest contracts is with the Girls' Private School Trust (GPST), which has 35 schools across the country, all with the same school uniform.

After a recent review of the uniform at the GPST schools, the school's spring/summer dress has been re-designed to incorporate a dropped waistband. Each new dress now requires 2.2 metres of material, which is 10% more material than the previous style of dress required. However, a new material has also been chosen by the GPST which costs only $2.85 per metre which is 5% cheaper than the material used on the previous dresses. In February, the total amount of material used and purchased at this price was 54,560 metres.

The design of the new dresses has meant that a complicated new sewing technique needed to be used. Consequently, all staff required training before they could begin production. The manager of the sewing department expected each of the new dresses to take ten minutes to make as compared to eight minutes per dress for the old style. SU Co has 24 staff, each of whom works 160 hours per month and is paid a wage of $12 per hour. All staff worked all of their contracted hours in February on production of the GPST dresses and there was no idle time. No labour rate variance arose in February.

Activity levels for February were as follows:

Budgeted production and sales (units) 30,000
Actual production and sales (units) 24,000

The production manager at SU Co is responsible for all purchasing and production issues which occur. SU Co uses standard costing and usually, every time a design change takes place, the standard cost card is updated prior to production commencing. However, the company accountant responsible for updating the standards has been off sick for the last two months. Consequently, the standard cost card for the new dress has not yet been updated.

Required

(a) Calculate the material variances in as much detail as the information allows for the month of February. **(7 marks)**

(b) Calculate the labour efficiency variances in as much detail as the information allows for the month of February. **(5 marks)**

(c) Assess the performance of the production manager for the month of February. **(8 marks)**

(Total = 20 marks)

283 Kappa Co (Sep/Dec 2018)   36 mins

Kappa Co produces Omega, an animal feed made by mixing and heating three ingredients: Alpha, Beta and Gamma.

The company uses a standard costing system to monitor its costs.

The standard material cost for 100 kg of Omega is as follows:

Input	Kg	Cost per kg	Cost per 100 kg of Omega
		$	$
Alpha	40	2.00	80.00
Beta	60	5.00	300.00
Gamma	20	1.00	20.00
Total	120		400.00

Notes

(1) The mixing and heating process is subject to a standard evaporation loss.

(2) Alpha, Beta and Gamma are agricultural products and their quality and price varies significantly from year to year. Standard prices are set at the average market price over the last five years. Kappa Co has a purchasing manager who is responsible for pricing and supplier contracts.

(3) The standard mix is set by the finance department. The last time this was done was at the product launch which was five years ago. It has not changed since.

Last month 4,600 kg of Omega was produced, using the following inputs:

Input	Kg	Cost per kg	Total cost
		$	$
Alpha	2,200	1.80	3,960
Beta	2,500	6.00	15,000
Gamma	920	1.00	920
	5,620		19,880

At the end of each month, the production manager receives a standard cost operating statement from Kappa Co's performance manager. The statement contains material price and usage variances, labour rate and efficiency variances, and overhead expenditure and efficiency variances for the previous month. No commentary on the variances is given and the production manager receives no other feedback on the efficiency of the Omega process.

Required

(a) Calculate the following variances for the last month:

    (i) the material usage variance for each ingredient and in total   **(4 marks)**
    (ii) the total material mix variance   **(4 marks)**
    (iii) the total material yield variance   **(3 marks)**

(b) Discuss the problems with the current system of calculating and reporting variances for assessing the performance of the production manager. **(9 marks)**

(Total = 20 marks)

Section A questions

OTQ bank – Performance measurement and control
54 mins

284 The following statements have been made about a transfer pricing system where Division A transfers output to Division B.

(1) Internal transfers should be preferred when there is an external market for the transferred item, because there will be more control over quality and delivery.

(2) The transfer price will determine how profits will be shared between the two divisions.

Which of the above statements is/are true?

○ 1 only

○ 2 only

○ Neither 1 nor 2

○ Both 1 and 2   **(2 marks)**

285 In a company with a divisionalised structure, Division A transfers its output to Division B. Division A produces just one item, Component X. Division B makes and sells an end product that requires one unit of Component X.

	$ per unit of X
Marginal cost of production in Division A	8
Fixed overhead cost of production	3
Cost of selling in the external market	1
Market price in the external market	16
Division B contribution from further processing Component X, before deducting the transfer cost	25

Division A is working at full capacity.

What should be the minimum transfer price per unit of Component X in this situation?

$ [   ]   **(2 marks)**

286 The following statements have been made about performance measurements in not-for-profit organisations.

(1) Not-for-profit organisations do not have financial objectives.

(2) The outputs produced by not-for-profit organisations are easier to measure than output of commercial companies.

Which of the above statements is/are true?

○ 1 only

○ 2 only

○ Neither 1 nor 2

○ Both 1 and 2   **(2 marks)**

BPP
LEARNING
MEDIA

287 Which of the following figures would be the most suitable for divisional profit for the purpose of performance measurement?

○ Gross profit

○ Profit before interest and tax

○ Profit before tax

○ Profit after tax   (2 marks)

288 Organisations may need to develop performance measures to ensure that the needs of stakeholders are met.

Which **TWO** of the following measures are geared towards customer needs?

☐ Profit margin

☐ Percentage of repeat customers

☐ Number of warranty claims

☐ Dividend yield   (2 marks)

289 A hospital wishes to establish a performance measurement for its 'quality of care', and in particular its adherence to appointment times for patients receiving medical checks.

Which of the following performance measurements would be the most suitable for this purpose?

○ Average length of appointments

○ Average number of appointments per day

○ Average number of days from making an appointment to the appointment date

○ Average waiting time at the hospital   (2 marks)

290 A company that uses a balanced scorecard approach to performance measurement has recorded the following data for the previous financial year.

	Products made and sold for at least two years	Products introduced to market within the previous two years = 'new products'	Total
Number of products	16	4	
Annual sales	$3.0 million	$0.50 million	$3.50 million
Cost of sales	$2.4 million	$0.42 million	$2.82 million
Hours worked	27,500	4,500	
Research and development costs			$150,000

Which of the following would be the most suitable measure of performance from the innovation and learning perspective in a balanced scorecard?

○ Development cost per new product

○ Sales revenue per new product

○ Sales revenue from new products as a percentage of total revenue

○ Sales revenue per hour worked on new products   (2 marks)

291 Which of the following measures of performance for public sector services is a measure of efficiency?

O   Number of patients treated per $1 spent on the state hospital service

O   Percentage reduction in the spending budget of a government department compared with the previous year

O   Proportion of reported crimes that are solved by the police service

O   Proportion of students in a state-owned college achieving good pass grades in their examinations   **(2 marks)**

292 Which **TWO** of the following bases for setting a transfer price are most likely to result in goal congruent behaviour by BOTH the selling and receiving divisions?

☐   Opportunity cost

☐   Market price

☐   Actual cost

☐   Standard full cost plus   **(2 marks)**

293 A company had budgeted sales of $30.9 million within a market worth $61.8 million. When the budget was drafted, it was assumed that inflation would be 3%. After the end of the budget period, it was discovered that inflation had been 2% and that the market had been worth $65 million.

What is the sales revenue figure which should be used when assessing company performance (to one decimal place)?

$ [   ] million   **(2 marks)**

294 In a balanced scorecard system of performance measurement, which of the following is most likely to be used as a measure of performance from the customer perspective?

O   Increase in size of product range

O   Percentage of customers making repeat orders

O   Number of orders won per sales representative

O   Speed of processing an order   **(2 marks)**

295   The following statements have been made about performance measurements in not-for-profit organisations.

(1)   Providing value for money (VFM) means providing a service that is cheap, efficient and effective.

(2)   For the refuse collection department of a local government authority, the efficiency of operations can be measured by the proportion of collected refuse that is recycled.

Which of the above statements is/are true?

O   1 only

O   2 only

O   Neither 1 nor 2

O   Both 1 and 2   (2 marks)

296   The following statements have been made about divisionalisation and performance measurement systems.

(1)   Residual income as a measure of performance enables fair comparisons to be made between the performances of different divisions in the company.

(2)   When a transfer price is based on cost because there is no external market for the transferred item, at least one of the divisional managers is likely to consider the transfer price as 'unfair'.

Which of the above statements is/are true?

O   1 only

O   2 only

O   Neither 1 nor 2

O   Both 1 and 2   (2 marks)

297   Binny Co has annual sales of $960,000 and a current ratio of 3.2:1. All of its sales are for cash and are priced at a mark-up on cost of 50%. The average cash balance is $40,000 and the inventory turnover period is 90 days.

Assuming 360 days in a year, what is Binny Co's quick ratio (acid test ratio)?

O   0.64

O   0.53

O   0.80

O   1.56   (2 marks)

298   In the Fitzgerald and Moon model of performance measurement in service businesses, which of the following dimensions of performance reflects past results or achievements, rather than provides a guide or determinant for future performance?

O   Competitiveness

O   Flexibility

O   Quality

O   Resource utilisation   (2 marks)

(Total = 30 marks)

OTQ bank – Performance measurement and control

299   In a company with a divisionalised structure, Division A transfers its output to Division B. Division A produces just one item, Component X. Division B makes and sells an end product that requires one unit of Component X.

	$ per unit of X
Marginal cost of production in Division A	8
Fixed overhead cost of production	3
Market price in the external market	16
Division B contribution from further processing Component X, before deducting the transfer cost	25

Division A is not working at full capacity, and can meet in full the external market demand and the demand from Division B for internal transfers.

What should be the minimum transfer price per unit and the maximum transfer price per unit for Component X in this situation?

minimum transfer price $ [   ]

maximum transfer price $ [   ]   (2 marks)

---

300   Which of the following is a dimension of performance in a service business, as identified by Fitzgerald and Moon?

   O   Controllability

   O   Innovation

   O   Rewards

   O   Standards   (2 marks)

---

301   On which **TWO** of the following matters would the manager of an investment centre make decisions?

   ☐   Granting credit to customers.

   ☐   Administration of centralised departments

   ☐   Settling inter-departmental disputes

   ☐   Inventory carrying decisions   (2 marks)

BPP LEARNING MEDIA

302 At the beginning of 20X2, a division has capital employed, consisting of non-current assets of $2 million (at carrying value) and working capital of $0.2 million. These are expected to earn a profit in 20X2 of $0.5 million, after depreciation of $0.4 million. A new machine will be installed at the beginning of 20X2. It will cost $0.8 million and will require an additional $0.1 million in working capital. It will add $0.35 million to divisional profits before deducting depreciation. This machine will have a four-year life and no residual value: depreciation is by the straight-line method. When calculating ROI, capital employed is taken at its mid-year value.

What is the expected ROI of the division in 20X2?

   O   21.7%

   O   23.2%

   O   24.1%

   O   26.0%   (2 marks)

---

303 A company has two Divisions, A and B. Division A manufactures a component which is transferred to Division B. Division B uses two units of the component from Division A in every item of finished product that it makes and sells. The transfer price is $43 per unit of the component.

	$ per unit
Selling price of finished product made in Division B	154
Variable production costs in Division B, excluding the cost of transfers from Division A	32
Variable selling costs, chargeable to the division	1
	33
Fixed costs	$160,000
External sales in units	7,000
Investment in the division	$500,000

The company uses 16% as its cost of capital.

What is the residual income of Division B for the period?

$ [   ]   (2 marks)

---

304 A company has a divisionalised structure in which Division A transfers its output to Division B. There is no external market for the transferred item and cost will be used as the basis for setting a transfer price.

Which of the following will be the most appropriate basis for negotiating and agreeing a transfer price?

   O   Actual cost

   O   Actual cost plus a profit margin equal to a percentage of cost

   O   Standard cost

   O   Standard cost plus a profit margin equal to a percentage of cost   (2 marks)

305 An investment centre has prepared the following forecasts for the next financial year.

	$
Operating profit before depreciation	85,000
Depreciation	20,000
Net current assets at beginning of year	30,000
Carrying value of non-current assets at beginning of year	180,000

The centre manager is now considering whether to sell a machine that is included in these forecasts. The machine would add $2,500 to divisional profit next year after depreciation of $500. It has a carrying value of $6,000 and could be sold for this amount. They would use the proceeds from the sale plus additional cash from Head Office to purchase a new machine for $15,000. This new machine would add $5,200 to divisional profit next year after depreciation of $2,000.

What will be the expected return on investment (ROI) for the division next year, assuming that the manager acquires the new machine and that non-current assets are valued at the start of year carrying amount for the purpose of the ROI calculation?

[   ] %

(2 marks)

306 Which of the following is **NOT** usually a consequence of divisionalisation?

○ Duplication of some activities and costs

○ Goal congruence in decision-making

○ Faster decision-making at operational level

○ Reduction in head office control over operations

(2 marks)

307 Classify the following into qualitative and quantitative aspects of non-financial performance.

Volume of customer complaints	☐ Quantitative ☐ Qualitative
Employee revenue	☐ Quantitative ☐ Qualitative
Defective products per batch	☐ Quantitative ☐ Qualitative
Customer needs	☐ Quantitative ☐ Qualitative
Employee morale	☐ Quantitative ☐ Qualitative
Brand recognition	☐ Quantitative ☐ Qualitative
Customer satisfaction	☐ Quantitative ☐ Qualitative
Repeat business	☐ Quantitative ☐ Qualitative

(2 marks)

308 A typical balanced scorecard measures performance from four different perspectives. Which perspective is concerned with measuring 'What must we excel at?'

○ Customer perspective

○ Financial perspective

○ Innovation and learning perspective

○ Internal business perspective

(2 marks)

309 The 3Es are often used to assess performance in non-profit making organisations, especially in relation to value for money.

Which **THREE** of the following Es are used?

☐ Efficiency

☐ Effectiveness

☐ Economy

☐ Enterprise

☐ Efficacy

☐ Expediency

☐ Endurance   (2 marks)

---

310 A division is considering investing in capital equipment costing $2.7 million. The useful economic life of the equipment is expected to be 50 years, with no resale value at the end of the period. The forecast return on the initial investment is 15% per annum before depreciation. The division's cost of capital is 7%?

What is the expected annual residual income of the initial investment?

O $0

O ($270,000)

O $162,000

O $216,000   (2 marks)

---

311 The following statements have been made about transfer pricing.

(1) Transfer pricing is almost inevitably required when a business is structured as more than one division and some divisions provide goods or services to other divisions.

(2) Where a perfect external market price exists and unit variable costs and unit selling prices are constant, the opportunity cost of transfer will be external market price or external market price less savings in selling costs.

Which of the above statements is/are true?

O 1 only

O 2 only

O Neither 1 nor 2

O Both 1 and 2   (2 marks)

---

312 If the performance of a local fire service is judged in terms of its inputs rather than its outputs, which one of the following would be a suitable measure of performance?

O Average response times to call-outs

O Cost of the local fire service per member of the local population

O Number of emergency calls answered per month

O Average length of time between call-outs   (2 marks)

313 Which of the following could lead to an increase in management bonus, without benefiting the organisation?

(1) A manager holds on to heavily depreciated assets in order to avoid heavy investment in the period

(2) A manager in a manufacturing division uses absorption costing and builds up high levels of inventory

(3) A sales manager changes their fixed target to a relative target based on market share

○ 1 and 2 only

○ 1, 2 and 3

○ 1 only

○ 2 and 3 only (2 marks)

(Total = 30 marks)

Section B questions

OT case questions

Cherry Co   18 mins

The following scenario relates to the next five questions.

Cherry Co has two independent divisions, A and B. Division A produces product X. B is a new division which produces product Y. It requires units of product X to produce product Y. Last year, A sold X exclusively to the external market. Management at Cherry Co did not wish to disrupt the operations of A as B was an experimental division. However, due to the success of product Y, B is now a permanent division of Cherry Co. Management wants A to provide at least some units of product X to B.

The table below shows the contribution margin for each division when B purchases X from an outside supplier.

	B	A
	$	$
Selling price per unit	150	37
Variable cost per unit		
(Div B does not include the cost of X)	65	30
Cost of X purchased from outside suppliers	35	—
Contribution margin per unit	50	7

314   What would the minimum transfer price per unit of product X be if A sold 12,000 units of X, assuming that A has capacity for 15,000 units?

$ [   ]   (2 marks)

---

315   What would the minimum transfer price per unit of product X be if A sold 12,000 units of X, assuming that A has no spare capacity?

○ $36

○ $30

○ $37

○ $35   (2 marks)

---

316   If there was no external market for product X, which of the following approaches could be used to negotiate a transfer price?

○   Full cost

○   Management estimate of market cost

○   Scrap value of product X

○   All of the above   (2 marks)

---

317   Are the following two statements about Cherry Co true or false?

Cherry Co's transfer pricing system should seek to establish a transfer price for X that will provide an incentive for the managers of A and B to make and sell quantities of products that will maximise sales of Product Y.	TRUE	FALSE
The manager of division B is likely to be more motivated if she is given freedom in which to operate and is able to purchase from outside suppliers if prices are cheaper.	TRUE	FALSE

(2 marks)

318   Are the following statements about Cherry Co true or false?

The performance of the managers of A and B will be easier to assess in an environment in which managers are able to control greater elements of the business.	TRUE	FALSE
In a competitive market, it is likely that suppliers will offer product X to Division B significantly cheaper than Division A can, for a sustained period of time.	TRUE	FALSE

(2 marks)

(Total = 10 marks)

Jamair (December 2014 amended)   18 mins

The following scenario relates to the next five questions.

Jamair is one of a growing number of low-cost airlines in the country of Shania.

Jamair's strategy is to operate as a low-cost, high-efficiency airline.

The airline was given an 'on time arrival' ranking of seventh best by the country's aviation authority, which ranks all 50 of the country's airlines based on the number of flights which arrive on time at their destinations.

The average 'ground turnaround time' for airlines in Shania is 50 minutes, meaning that, on average, planes are on the ground for cleaning, refuelling, etc for 50 minutes before departing again.

The number of passengers carried by the airline has grown from 300,000 passengers on a total of 3,428 flights in 2007 to 920,000 passengers on 7,650 flights in 2013.

The overall growth of the airline has been helped by the limited route licensing policy of the Shanian government, which has given Jamair almost monopoly status on some of its routes. However, the government is now set to change this policy with almost immediate effect, and it has become more important than ever to monitor performance effectively.

319   The [▼] perspective considers whether the management in Jamair meets the expectations of its shareholders and how it creates value for them.

Which of the following words is missing from the above statement?

Picklist:

Customer
Internal business
Innovation and learning
Financial

(2 marks)

320 The following performance measure has been suggested for Jamair:

Improve on the 'on time arrival' ranking of seventh best in the country's aviation authority ratings.

To which perspective of the balanced scorecard does this measure belong?

○   Customer perspective

○   Internal business perspective

○   Innovation and learning perspective

○   Financial perspective   (2 marks)

321 The following performance objective has been suggested for Jamair:

Improve the turnaround time on the ground

To which perspective of the balanced scorecard does this objective belong?

○   Customer perspective

○   Internal business perspective

○   Innovation and learning perspective

○   Financial perspective   (2 marks)

322 The following performance objective has been suggested for Jamair:

Increase seat revenue per plane

To which perspective of the balanced scorecard does this objective belong?

○   Customer perspective

○   Internal business perspective

○   Innovation and learning perspective

○   Financial perspective   (2 marks)

323 Are the following statements about Jamair's performance measurement system true or false?

When performance is not quantified, it is difficult to target and monitor.	TRUE	FALSE
Jamair is more likely to have a reliable and comprehensive system for collecting data about qualitative aspects of performance than a well-established system for measuring quantitative data.	TRUE	FALSE

(2 marks)

(Total = 10 marks)

Stickleback Co

The following scenario relates to the next five questions.

Kingfisher is an investment centre within Stickleback Co. Kingfisher has an operating profit of $30,000, and operating assets of $150,000. The cost of capital is 15%. There is a proposed investment of $15,000 which will increase the operating income by $1,900.

324   What is the return on investment (ROI) for Kingfisher with and without the proposed investment?

  ○ Before investment: 20%, After investment 17%

  ○ Before investment: 17%, After investment 19.3%

  ○ Before investment: 19.3%, After investment 20%

  ○ Before investment: 20%, After investment 19.3% **(2 marks)**

325   What is the residual income (RI) for Kingfisher with and without the proposed investment?

  ○ Before investment: $3,350, After investment $7,150

  ○ Before investment: $7,500, After investment $3,350

  ○ Before investment: $7,500, After investment $7,150

  ○ Before investment: $7,150, After investment $7,500 **(2 marks)**

326   The following statements have been made about the use of ROI as a performance measure in Stickleback Co.

  (1) If a manager's performance is being evaluated, a portion of head office assets should be included in the calculation of ROI in Stickleback Co's investment centres.

  (2) It may lead to short termism.

  Which of the above statements is/are correct?

  ○ 1 only

  ○ 2 only

  ○ Both 1 and 2

  ○ Neither 1 nor 2 **(2 marks)**

327   The divisional manager for Kingfisher wants to increase the ROI for the next period.

  Which **TWO** of the following options would increase the ROI?

  ☐ Increase payables

  ☐ Reduce interest payments

  ☐ Accept all projects with a positive NPV

  ☐ Keep Kingfisher's old machinery **(2 marks)**

328 The following statements have been made about Stickleback Co's divisionalised structure.

(1) There is a danger that managers in the divisions may use their decision-making freedom to make decisions that are not in the best interests of the overall company.

(2) Stickleback Co's top management must have involvement in the day-to-day operations of the divisions.

Which of the above statements is/are correct?

○ 1 only

○ 2 only

○ Both 1 and 2

○ Neither 1 nor 2 (2 marks)

(Total = 10 marks)

Squarize (June 2013 amended) 18 mins

The following scenario relates to the next five questions.

Squarize is a large company which started as a pay-TV broadcaster and then started offering broadband and telephone services to its pay-TV customers. Customers could take advantage of discounts for 'bundle' packages of all three services.

All contracts to customers of Squarize are for a minimum three-month period. The pay-TV box is sold to the customer at the beginning of the contract; however, the broadband and telephone equipment is only rented to them.

In the first few years after product bundling was introduced, the company saw a steady increase in profits. Then, Squarize saw its revenues and operating profits fall. Several reasons were identified for the deterioration of results:

(1) In a bid to save cash, many pay-TV customers were cancelling their contracts after the minimum three-month period as they were then able to keep the pay-TV box. The box comes with a number of free channels, which the customer can continue to receive free of charge, even after the cancellation of their contract.

(2) Some bundle customers found that the broadband service that they had subscribed to did not work. As a result, they were immediately cancelling their contracts for all services within the 14-day cancellation period permitted under the contracts.

In a response to the above problems and in an attempt to increase revenues and profits, Squarize made the following changes to the business:

(1) It made a strategic decision to withdraw the bundle package from the market and, instead, offer each service as a standalone product.

(2) It investigated and resolved the problem with customers' broadband service.

It is now one year since the changes were made and the finance director wants to use a balanced scorecard to assess the extent to which the changes have been successful in improving the performance of the business.

329 The following performance objective has been suggested for Squarize:

Reduce the number of contracts cancelled due to the broadband service not working

To which perspective of the balanced scorecard does this objective belong?

[▼]

Picklist:

Customer
Internal business
Innovation and learning
Financial

(2 marks)

330 The following performance measure has been suggested for Squarize:

Volume of sales to new customers for each product/service

To which perspective of the balanced scorecard does this measure belong?

[▼]

Picklist:

Customer
Internal business
Innovation and learning
Financial

(2 marks)

331 Which of the following would be the most suitable measure of performance from the innovation and learning perspective in Squarize's balanced scorecard?

○ Development cost per new standalone service

○ Sales revenue per new standalone service

○ Sales revenue from new standalone service as a percentage of total revenue

○ Sales revenue per hour worked on new standalone service (2 marks)

332 Which of the following is most likely to be used as a measure of performance from the customer perspective in Squarize's balanced scorecard?

○ Increase in size of the product range

○ Percentage of customers renewing their subscription or making repeat orders

○ Number of orders won per sales representative

○ Speed of processing an order (2 marks)

333 Squarize has been advised that it could also use the Fitzgerald and Moon building block model to attempt to overcome the problems associated with performance measurement of service businesses.

Which of the following is not a building block included in this performance management system?

- O   Rewards
- O   Innovation
- O   Standards
- O   Dimensions of performance   (2 marks)

(Total = 10 marks)

Alder Co   18 mins

The following scenario relates to the next five questions.

An investment centre with capital employed of $750,000 is budgeted to earn a profit of $200,000 next year. A proposed non-current asset investment of $125,000, not included in the budget at present, will earn a profit next year of $20,000. The company's cost of capital is 15%.

334 What is the budgeted ROI for next year, both before and after the investment is made (to the nearest %)?

Before investment: [   ] %

After investment: [   ] %   (2 marks)

---

335 What is the residual income for next year, both before and after the investment is made?

Before investment: $ [   ]

After investment: $ [   ]   (2 marks)

---

336 Are the following statements about the divisionalised structure in Alder Co true or false?

	TRUE	FALSE
The authority to act to improve performance motivates the divisional managers in Alder Co, more so than if the company was centralised.	TRUE	FALSE
Alder Co's top management must have involvement in the day-to-day operations of Alder Co.	TRUE	FALSE

(2 marks)

---

337 Are the following statements about the use of ROI in Alder Co true or false?

If a manager's performance is being evaluated, a portion of head office assets should be included in the calculation of ROI in Alder Co's investment centres.	TRUE	FALSE
If the performance of the investment centre is being appraised, head office assets or investment centre assets controlled by head office should not be included in the calculation of ROI.	TRUE	FALSE

(2 marks)

338 Are the following statements about the use of ROI in Alder Co true or false?

The profit figure for ROI should always be the amount before any interest is charged.	TRUE	FALSE
The asset base of the ratio can be altered by increasing/decreasing payables and receivables (by speeding up or delaying payments and receipts).	TRUE	FALSE

(2 marks)

(Total = 10 marks)

Apple Co   18 mins

The following scenario relates to the next five questions.

An investment centre in Apple Co generates a profit of $24,000. You have been given the following additional information about the investment centre.

Working capital		20,000
Non-current assets at cost	230,000	
Accumulated depreciation	170,000	
Carrying value		60,000

339 What is the ROI for the investment centre? (to the nearest %)

[   ] %   (2 marks)

340 An investment in a non-current asset could be made which would result in a capital employed figure of $100,000. The investment would result in a new profit figure of $35,000 for the division. If the investment is made, what would the residual income be for the investment centre if the cost of capital is 12%?

$ [   ]   (2 marks)

341 Are the following statements about the use of different performance measures in Apple Co true or false?

Residual income is more flexible, since a different cost of capital can be applied to investments with different risk characteristics.	TRUE	FALSE
Residual income does not facilitate comparisons between investment centres.	TRUE	FALSE

(2 marks)

342 Apple Co operates a transfer pricing system between two divisions based on market price. Are the following statements about this true or false?

The market price acts as an incentive to use up any spare capacity in the selling division of Apple Co.	TRUE	FALSE
Using the market price as the transfer price encourages selling and buying decisions which appear to be in the best interests of the division's performance. This leads to the company as a whole achieving optimal results as each division optimises its performance.	TRUE	FALSE

(2 marks)

343 Apple Co has two divisions which are set to begin buying and selling a product between themselves. It has been suggested that a cost-based approach to transfer pricing be used.

Are the following statements about this suggestion true or false?

A cost-based approach is suitable for Apple Co in this scenario if there is no external market for the product that is being transferred.	TRUE	FALSE
A cost-based approach is suitable for Apple Co in this scenario if an imperfect market exists.	TRUE	FALSE

(2 marks)

(Total = 10 marks)

Box Co   18 mins

The following scenario relates to the next five questions.

Box Co has an operating profit of $20,000, and operating assets of $95,000. The cost of capital is 12%. There is a proposed investment of $10,000 which will increase the operating profit by $1,400.

344 What is the ROI with and without the proposed investment? (to one decimal point)

Without investment: [   ] %

With investment: [   ] %

(2 marks)

345 What is the RI with and without the proposed investment?

Without investment: $ [   ]

With investment: $ [   ]   (2 marks)

346 One of the managers in Box Co is critical of the performance measures used. She has said that they are too focused on financial performance and do not take into account any non-financial performance measures.

Are the following statements she has made true or false?

	TRUE	FALSE
Financial performance measures do not necessarily provide sufficient information about ongoing problems with product quality. As a result, there is little attention paid to the generation of information on quality in Box Co.	TRUE	FALSE
Non-financial performance indicators can give a better indication of future prospects.	TRUE	FALSE

(2 marks)

347 Which of the following methods would encourage the managers of Box Co to take a short-term view?

○ Link managers' rewards to share price

○ Set quality-based targets as well as financial targets

○ Keep managers informed about the short-term budget targets

○ Make long-term targets realistic   (2 marks)

348 Are the following statements about Box Co's divisionalised structure true or false?

	TRUE	FALSE
There is a danger that managers in Box Co may use their decision-making freedom to make decisions that are not in the best interests of the overall company.	TRUE	FALSE
A good performance measure for the divisional managers in Box Co should include a portion of head office costs in the calculations.	TRUE	FALSE

(2 marks)

(Total = 10 marks)

Willow Co

The following scenario relates to the next five questions.

An investment centre with capital employed of $600,000 is budgeted to earn a profit of $100,000 next year. A proposed fixed asset investment of $150,000, not included in the budget at present, will earn a profit next year of $23,000 after depreciation. The company's cost of capital is 13%.

Required

349   What is the budgeted return on investment (ROI) for next year, both before and after the investment is made (to the nearest %)?

	% before investment

| | % after investment | (2 marks)
|---|---|

350   What is the residual income (RI) for next year, both before and after the investment is made?

$ [   ] before investment

$ [   ] after investment   (2 marks)

351   Due to its size, Willow Co operates a divisionalised structure. One of the manager's area of responsibility is 'decisions over costs, revenues, and assets'. The typical financial performance measures used by this manager is return on investment and residual income.

Which of the following centres best describes the manager's responsibility area?

○   Profit centre

○   Responsibility centre

○   Cost centre

○   Investment centre   (2 marks)

352   Two of the divisional managers in Willow Co disagree on the performance measure which should be used to determine their bonus for the year. Manager 1 is the manager of a large division, while manager 2 is manager of a small division. Manager 1 prefers to use residual income and has given the following examples of limitations of ROI to support this decision.

Which of the following is a valid reason for Willow Co choosing to use RI and not ROI?

○   ROI requires an estimate of the cost of capital, a figure which can be difficult to calculate.

○   ROI can over-emphasise short-term performance at the expense of long-term performance.

○   If assets are valued at carrying value, ROI figures generally improve as assets get older. This can encourage managers to retain outdated plant and machinery.

○   ROI is a relative measure, therefore small investments with a high rate of return may appear preferable to a larger investment with lower ROI. However, the larger investment may be worth more in absolute terms.   (2 marks)

353 Manager 2 wishes to use ROI as a performance measure.

Which of the following reasons is a valid reason for Willow Co choosing to use ROI and not RI?

- O Identifying controllable (traceable) profits and investment can be difficult.

- O RI attempts to measure divisional performance in a single figure.

- O ROI ties in with NPV, theoretically the best way to make investment decisions.

- O Manager 1 will show a higher RI because of the size of the division rather than superior managerial performance. **(2 marks)**

(Total = 10 marks)

Section C questions

354 Biscuits and Cakes (June 2012) 36 mins

The Biscuits division (Division B) and the Cakes division (Division C) are two divisions of a large, manufacturing company. While both divisions operate in almost identical markets, each division operates separately as an investment centre. Each month, operating statements must be prepared by each division and these are used as a basis for performance measurement for the divisions.

Last month, senior management decided to recharge head office costs to the divisions. Consequently, each division is now going to be required to deduct a share of head office costs in its operating statement before arriving at 'net profit', which is then used to calculate return on investment (ROI). Prior to this, ROI has been calculated using controllable profit only. The company's target ROI, however, remains unchanged at 20% per annum. For each of the last three months, Divisions B and C have maintained ROIs of 22% per annum and 23% per annum respectively, resulting in healthy bonuses being awarded to staff. The company has a cost of capital of 10%.

The budgeted operating statement for the month of July is shown below:

	B	C
	$'000	$'000
Sales revenue	1,300	1,500
Less variable costs	(700)	(800)
Contribution	600	700
Less controllable fixed costs	(134)	(228)
Controllable profit	466	472
Less apportionment of head office costs	(155)	(180)
Net profit	311	292
Divisional net assets	$23.2m	$22.6m

Required

(a) Calculate the expected annualised return on investment (ROI) using the new method as preferred by senior management, based on the above budgeted operating statements, for each of the divisions. **(2 marks)**

The divisional managing directors are unhappy about the results produced by your calculations in (a) and have heard that a performance measure called 'residual income' may provide more information.

(b) Calculate the annualised residual income (RI) for each of the divisions, based on the net profit figures for the month of July. **(3 marks)**

(c)   Discuss the expected performance of each of the two divisions, using both ROI and RI, and making any additional calculations deemed necessary. Conclude as to whether, in your opinion, the two divisions have performed well. **(6 marks)**

Division B has now been offered an immediate opportunity to invest in new machinery at a cost of $2.12 million. The machinery is expected to have a useful economic life of four years, after which it could be sold for $200,000. Division B's policy is to depreciate all of its machinery on a straight-line basis over the life of the asset. The machinery would be expected to expand Division B's production capacity, resulting in an 8.5% increase in contribution per month.

Required

(d)   Recalculate Division B's expected annualised ROI and annualised RI, based on July's budgeted operating statement after adjusting for the investment. State whether the managing director will be making a decision that is in the best interests of the company as a whole if ROI is used as the basis of the decision. **(5 marks)**

(e)   Explain any behavioural problems that will result if the company's senior management insist on using solely ROI, based on net profit rather than controllable profit, to assess divisional performance and reward staff. **(4 marks)**

(Total = 20 marks)

355 Hammer (June 2010)   36 mins

Hammer is a large garden equipment supplier with retail stores throughout Toolland. Many of the products it sells are bought in from outside suppliers but some are currently manufactured by Hammer's own manufacturing division 'Nail'.

The prices (a transfer price) that Nail charges to the retail stores are set by head office and have been the subject of some discussion. The current policy is for Nail to calculate the total variable cost of production and delivery and add 30% for profit. Nail argues that all costs should be taken into consideration, offering to reduce the mark-up on costs to 10% in this case. The retail stores are unhappy with the current pricing policy arguing that it results in prices that are often higher than comparable products available on the market.

Nail has provided the following information to enable a price comparison to be made of the two possible pricing policies for one of its products.

Garden shears

Steel: the shears have 0.4 kg of high quality steel in the final product. The manufacturing process loses 5% of all steel put in. Steel costs $4,000 per tonne (1 tonne = 1,000 kg)

Other materials: Other materials are bought in and have a list price of $3 per kg although Hammer secures a 10% volume discount on all purchases. The shears require 0.1 kg of these materials.

The labour time to produce shears is 0.25 hours per unit and labour costs $10 per hour.

Variable overheads are absorbed at the rate of 150% of labour rates and fixed overheads are 80% of the variable overheads.

Delivery is made by an outsourced distributor that charges Nail $0.5 per garden shear for delivery.

Required

(a)   Calculate the price that Nail would charge for the garden shears under the existing policy of variable cost plus 30%. **(6 marks)**

(b)   Calculate the increase or decrease in price if the pricing policy switched to total cost plus 10%. **(4 marks)**

(c)   Discuss whether or not including fixed costs in a transfer price is a sensible policy. **(4 marks)**

(d)   Discuss whether the retail stores should be allowed to buy in from outside suppliers if the prices are cheaper than those charged by Nail. **(6 marks)**

(Total = 20 marks)

356 Tonford School (Sep/Dec 2020)

All schools in the country of Ducland are funded by the state and are accountable to the Department of Education (DoE) which oversees educational standards and monitors performance of the schools.

The DoE's objectives, which are also the objectives for all the schools in Ducland, are to:

(1) Strive for continuous improvement in performance standards

(2) Provide a supportive learning environment, which encourages a high standard of pupil achievement

(3) Ensure pupils are prepared for adult life and have the skills and character necessary to contribute to society and the economy

(4) Provide all children with access to high quality education, regardless of their location or background

Summary performance data for each school is accessible via the DoE's website. Parents in Ducland have the right to choose which school their child should attend and many parents use the performance data to help with their selection.

Inspectors from the DoE visit each school in Ducland at the end of every five years. The DoE believes that to gain a better insight into the quality of the teaching and learning environment, inspectors should attend a selection of lessons and speak to some of the pupils.

Tonford School has recently had its inspection visit, and the school's data entry on the DoE's website has been updated following that visit. The revised entry is shown below:

Performance factor	Notes	Tonford School Actual (2017)	National target (2017)	Tonford School Actual (2012)
Exam results	1	62%	65%	64%
Pupil progress	2	0.4	0.25	0.3
Inspection grade	3, 4	Very good	Good	Good
Pupil numbers	-	662	n/a	627
Number of teaching staff	5	35	n/a	33

Notes:

(1) The 'exam results' indicator shows the percentage of pupils leaving school with at least five final exams including compulsory subjects of mathematics, science and languages at Grade A-C (the top three grades).

(2) 'Pupil progress' is an indicator of how well pupils have performed in compulsory subjects in their final exams at age 16 compared to their performance in intermediate exams at age 11.

     Academic grades are given numerical values, and the 'pupil progress' score is the movement in the average of pupils' grades. Scores typically range between -0.5 and +0.5.

(3) There are six inspection grades: excellent; very good; good; average; poor and very poor.

(4) The inspector's summary report for Tonford School concluded: "There is a very strong sense of community values and citizenship. Pupils appear to have a genuine respect for their teachers, and for one another, despite their diverse backgrounds."

(5) The DoE recommends that the pupil/teacher ratio should be less than 22:1.

Required

(a) Explain the problems which not-for-profit organisations face as a result of having multiple objectives. **(4 marks)**

(b) Assess Tonford School's performance against the objectives set by the DoE, using the performance data published on the DoE's website.

Note: Use the four objectives in the template provided to structure your answer.

(12 marks)

Objective 1 – Strive for continuous improvement in performance standards.
Objective 2 – Provide a supportive learning environment, which encourages a high standard of pupil achievement.
Objective 3 – Ensure pupils are prepared for adult life and have the skills and character necessary to contribute to society and the economy.
Objective 4 – Provide all children with access to high quality education, regardless of their location or background.

(c) Explain the difficulties in assessing performance of schools in Ducland due to the qualitative nature of their objectives. **(4 marks)**

(Total = 20 marks)

357 Ties Only Co (December 2007)　　　36 mins

Ties Only Co is a new business, selling high quality imported men's ties through the internet. The managers, who also own the company, are young and inexperienced but they are prepared to take risks. They are confident that importing quality ties and selling through a website will be successful and that the business will grow quickly. This is despite the well-recognised fact that selling clothing is a very competitive business.

They were prepared for a loss-making start and decided to pay themselves modest salaries (included in administration expenses in Table 1 below) and pay no dividends for the foreseeable future.

The owners are so convinced that growth will quickly follow that they have invested enough money in website server development to ensure that the server can handle the very high levels of predicted growth. All website development costs were written off as incurred in the internal management accounts that are shown below in Table 1.

Significant expenditure on marketing was incurred in the first two quarters, to launch both the website and new products. It is not expected that marketing expenditure will continue to be as high in the future.

Customers can buy a variety of styles, patterns and colours of ties at different prices.

The business's trading results for the first two quarters of trade are shown below in Table 1.

Table 1

	Quarter 1		Quarter 2	
	$	$	$	$
Sales		420,000		680,000
Less cost of sales		(201,600)		(340,680)
Gross profit		218,400		339,320

	Quarter 1		Quarter 2	
	$	$	$	$
Less expenses				
Website development	120,000		90,000	
Administration	100,500		150,640	
Distribution	20,763		33,320	
Launch marketing	60,000		40,800	
Other variable expenses	50,000		80,000	
Total expenses		(351,263)		(394,760)
Loss for quarter		(132,863)		(55,440)

Required

(a)   Assess the financial performance of the business during its first two quarters, using only the data in Table 1 above. **(10 marks)**

(b)   Briefly consider whether the losses made by the business in the first two quarters are a true reflection of the current and likely future performance of the business. **(3 marks)**

The owners are well aware of the importance of non-financial indicators of success and therefore have identified a small number of measures to focus on. These are measured monthly and then combined to produce a quarterly management report.

The data for the first two quarters' management reports is shown below:

Table 2

	Quarter 1	Quarter 2
Number of ties sold	27,631	38,857
On-time delivery	95%	89%
Sales returns	12%	18%
System downtime	2%	4%

The industry average for sales returns was 13%.

Required

(c)   Comment on each of the non-financial data in Table 2 above, taking into account, where appropriate, the industry averages provided, providing your assessment of the performance of the business. **(7 marks)**

(Total = 20 marks)

358 Best Night Co (Mar/Jun 2019)   36 mins

Best Night Co operates a chain of 30 hotels across the country of Essland. It prides itself on the comfort of the rooms in its hotels and the quality of service it offers to guests.

The majority of Best Night Co's hotels are located in major cities and have previously been successful in attracting business customers. In recent years, however, the number of business customers has started to decline as a result of tough economic conditions in Essland.

Best Night Co's policy is to set standard prices for the rooms in each of its hotels, with that price reflecting the hotel's location and taking account of competitors' prices. However, hotel managers have the authority to offer discounts to regular customers, and to reduce prices when occupancy rates in their hotel are expected to be low. The average standard price per night, across all the hotels, was $140 in 20X7, compared to $135 in 20X6.

In addition to room bookings, the hotels also generate revenue from the additional services available to customers, such as restaurants and bars.

BPP
LEARNING
MEDIA

Summary from Best Night Co's management accounts:

	Year ended 30 June 20X7 $'000	Year ended 30 June 20X6 $'000
Revenue – rooms at standard price per night	111,890	104,976
Room discounts or rate reductions given	(16,783)	(11,540)
Other revenue: food, drink	24,270	23,185
Total revenue	119,377	116,621
Operating costs	(95,462)	(92,379)
Operating profit	23,915	24,242

Other performance information:

	Year ended 30 June 20X7	Year ended 30 June 20X6
Capital employed (Note 1)	$39.5m	$39.1m
Average occupancy rates (Note 2)	74%	72%
Average customer satisfaction score (Note 3)	4·2	4·5

Notes

(1) Capital employed is calculated using the depreciated cost of non-current assets at all Best Night Co's hotels.

(2) Occupancy rates for the year ended 30 June 20X7 were budgeted to be 72%.

(3) Customer satisfaction scores are graded on a scale of 1–5 where '5' represents 'Excellent'. On average, in any given town in Essland, the top 10% of hotels earn a score of 4·5 or above and the top 25% of hotels earn a score of 4·2 or above.

Two themes are becoming increasingly frequent in the comments Best Night Co's customers make alongside the scores:

(1) Repeat customers have said that the standard of service in recent visits has not been as good as in previous visits.

(2) The rooms need redecorating, and the fixtures and fittings need replacing. For example, the beds need new mattresses to improve the level of comfort they provide.

Best Night Co had planned a two-year refurbishment programme beginning in 20X7 of all the rooms in each hotel. However, this programme has been put on hold, due to the current economic conditions, and in order to reduce expenditure.

Required

Using the information provided, discuss Best Night Co's financial and non-financial performance for the year ended 30 June 20X7.

Note: There are five marks available for calculations and 15 marks available for discussion.

(Total = 20 marks)

359 Jump (June 2010)   36 mins

Jump has a network of sports clubs which are managed by local managers reporting to the main board. The local managers have a lot of autonomy and are able to vary employment contracts with staff and offer discounts for membership fees and personal training sessions. They also control their own maintenance budget, but do not have control over large amounts of capital expenditure.

A local manager's performance and bonus is assessed relative to three targets. For every one of these three targets that is reached in an individual quarter, $400 is added to the manager's bonus, which is paid at the end of the year. The maximum bonus per year is therefore based on 12 targets (three targets in each of the four quarters of the year). Accordingly, the maximum bonus that could be earned is 12 × $400 = $4,800, which represents 40% of the basic salary of a local manager. Jump has a 31 March year end.

The performance data for one of the sports clubs for the last four quarters is as follows.

	Qtr to 30 June 20X1	Qtr to 30 September 20X1	Qtr to 31 December 20X1	Qtr to 31 March 20X2
Number of members	3,000	3,200	3,300	3,400
Member visits	20,000	24,000	26,000	24,000
Personal training sessions booked	310	325	310	339
Staff days	450	480	470	480
Staff lateness days	20	28	28	20
Days in quarter	90	90	90	90

Agreed targets are:

(1) Staff must be on time over 95% of the time (no penalty is made when staff are absent from work).

(2) On average 60% of members must use the clubs' facilities regularly, by visiting at least 12 times per quarter.

(3) On average 10% of members must book a personal training session each quarter.

Required

(a) Calculate the amount of bonus that the manager should expect to be paid for the latest financial year. **(6 marks)**

(b) Discuss to what extent the targets set are controllable by the local manager (you are required to make a case for both sides of the argument). **(9 marks)**

(c) Describe two methods as to how a manager with access to the accounting and other records could unethically manipulate the situation so as to gain a greater bonus. **(5 marks)**

(Total = 20 marks)

360 Bridgewater Co (June 2008 amended)   36 mins

Bridgewater Co provides training courses for many of the mainstream software packages on the market.

The business has many divisions within Waterland, the one country in which it operates. The senior managers of Bridgewater Co have very clear objectives for the divisions and these are communicated to divisional managers on appointment and subsequently in quarterly and annual reviews. These are:

- Each quarter, sales should grow and annual sales should exceed budget
- Trainer (lecture staff) costs should not exceed $180 per teaching day
- Room hire costs should not exceed $90 per teaching day
- Each division should meet its budget for profit per quarter and annually

It is known that managers will be promoted based on their ability to meet these targets. A member of the senior management is to retire after Quarter 2 of the current financial year, which has just begun. The divisional managers anticipate that one of them may be promoted at the beginning of Quarter 3 if their performance is good enough.

The manager of the Northwest division is concerned that their chances of promotion could be damaged by the expected performance of their division. They are a firm believer in quality and they think that if a business gets this right, growth and success will eventually follow.

The current quarterly forecasts, along with the original budgeted profit for the Northwest division, are as follows:

	Q1 $'000	Q2 $'000	Q3 $'000	Q4 $'000	Total $'000
Sales	40.0	36.0	50.0	60.0	186.0
Less:					
Trainers	8.0	7.2	10.0	12.0	37.2
Room hire	4.0	3.6	5.0	6.0	18.6
Staff training	1.0	1.0	1.0	1.0	4.0
Other costs	3.0	1.7	6.0	7.0	17.7
Forecast net profit	24.0	22.5	28.0	34.0	108.5
Original budgeted profit	25.0	26.0	27.0	28.0	106.0
Annual sales budget	——	——	——	——	180.0
Teaching days	40	36	50	60	

Required

(a) Assess the financial performance of the Northwest division against its targets and reach a conclusion as to the promotion prospects of the divisional manager. **(8 marks)**

The manager of the Northwest division has been considering a few steps to improve the performance of their division.

Voucher scheme

As a sales promotion, vouchers will be sold for $125 each, a substantial discount on normal prices. These vouchers will entitle the holder to attend four training sessions on software of their choice. They can attend when they want to but are advised that one training session per quarter is sensible. The manager is confident that, if the promotion took place immediately, they could sell 80 vouchers and that customers would follow the advice given to attend one session per quarter. All voucher holders would attend planned existing courses and all will be new customers.

Software upgrade

A new important software programme has recently been launched for which there could be a market for training courses. Demonstration programs can be bought for $1,800 in Quarter 1. Staff training would be needed, costing $500 in each of Quarters 1 and 2 but in Quarters 3 and 4 extra courses could be offered selling this training. Assuming similar class sizes and the usual sales prices, extra sales revenue amounting to 20% of normal sales are expected (measured before the voucher promotion above). The manager is keen to run these courses at the same tutorial and room standards as they normally provide. Software expenditure is written off in the income statement as incurred.

Delaying payments to trainers

The manager is considering delaying payment to the trainers. They think that, since their commitment to quality could cause them to miss out on a well-deserved promotion, the trainers owe them a favour. They intend to delay payment on 50% of all invoices received from the trainers in the first two quarters, paying them one month later than is usual.

Required

(b) Revise the forecasts to take account of all three of the proposed changes. **(6 marks)**

(c) Comment on each of the proposed steps and reach a conclusion as to whether, if all the proposals were taken together, the manager will improve their chances of promotion. **(6 marks)**

(Total = 20 marks)

361 One Stop Car Co (Sep/Dec 2018)

The One Stop Car Co (OSC Co) offers a range of services for car owners at its 55 service centres across the country. The car maintenance business is extremely competitive in all regions across the country. Each service centre operates autonomously and managers are able to choose how to package up the services they offer. OSC Co's aim is to 'make the task of car maintenance a pleasure and not a chore'.

Its national website states the following:

- Range of service packs available, including express service and full valet
- 'We work whilst you wait' service, with average wait times of only two hours
- Watch our friendly, experienced mechanics producing high quality work
- Freshly made tea and coffee and free internet in our comfortable lounges
- Monthly free prize draw for all customers completing an online feedback form

Customers initially access the national website, but depending on their location, they are automatically redirected to the website of their nearest service centre so that they can view the offers available at that centre. All bookings are made through the OSC website.

Results for one of the service centres, the Midlands Service Centre (MSC), for the year which has just ended are given below. The column headed 'OSC' shows the average figures for all of OSC Co's 55 service centres:

	Notes	MSC	OSC Average
Sales revenue ($)		760,500	890,365
Gross profit ($)		304,200	328,146
Number of mechanics: senior	1	7	7.8
Number of mechanics: junior	2	5	5.2
Number of new service packs developed	3	3	2
Number of website hits		14,000	18,260
Total number of jobs booked and completed		9,506	11,870
Number of jobs from repeat customers only		1,500	1,660
Total time spent completing jobs (hours)		23,100	24,800
Percentage of customer feedback forms showing score of 9 or 10	4	80%	70%

Notes

(1) Mechanics are classified as 'senior' if they have been qualified for more than five years.

(2) 'Junior' mechanics includes both trainee mechanics who are unqualified and mechanics who have been qualified for less than five years.

(3) The MSC introduced three new service packs during the year:

- free valets for orders over $100

- a safety check costing only $20, instead of the usual $40, for all customers booking a full service

- a $10 air conditioning efficiency check, which usually costs $20, for all customers booking an oil change.

These three new service packs produced revenues of $66,000, $58,000 and $54,000 respectively. Two comparable new service packs developed by other centres produced revenues of $44,000 and $42,000.

(4) The online feedback form asks customers to rate the centre from one to ten, with ten being the best.

The CEO of OSC Co has recently attended a business seminar and heard about Fitzgerald and Moon's building block model of performance management. The CEO is interested in how the dimensions block could be applied at OSC Co. The dimensions of performance identified in the model are: competitiveness, financial performance, quality of service, flexibility, resource utilisation and innovation.

Required

(a) For each of the dimensions of the building block model, calculate one performance indicator for MSC and one for the OSC average using the data available. Briefly justify your choice of performance indicator and discuss MSC's performance relative to the other OSC service centres. **(16 marks)**

(b) Explain how the standards and rewards blocks support the dimensions block in Fitzgerald and Moon's building block model. **(4 marks)**

(Total = 20 marks)

362 Web Co (December 2012) $\qquad$ 36 mins

Web Co is an online retailer of fashion goods and uses a range of performance indicators to measure the performance of the business. The company's management have been increasingly concerned about the lack of sales growth over the last year and, in an attempt to resolve this, made the following changes right at the start of Quarter 2.

Advertising: Web Co placed an advert on the webpage of a well-known online fashion magazine at a cost of $200,000. This had a direct link from the magazine's website to Web Co's online store.

Search engine: Web Co also engaged the services of a website consultant to ensure that, when certain key words are input by potential customers onto key search engines, such as Google and Yahoo, Web Co's website is listed on the first page of results. This makes it more likely that a customer will visit a company's website. The consultant's fee was $20,000.

Website availability: During Quarter 1, there were a few problems with Web Co's website, meaning that it was not available to customers some of the time. Web Co was concerned that this was losing them sales and the IT department therefore made some changes to the website in an attempt to correct the problem.

The following incentives were also offered to customers:

Incentive 1: A free 'Fast Track' delivery service, guaranteeing delivery within two working days, for all continuing customers who subscribe to Web Co's online subscription newsletter. Subscribers are thought by Web Co to become customers who place further orders.

Incentive 2: A $10 discount to all customers spending $100 or more at any one time.

The results for the last two quarters are shown below, Quarter 2 being the most recent. The results for Quarter 1 reflect the period before the changes and incentives detailed above took place and are similar to the results of other quarters in the preceding year.

	Quarter 1	Quarter 2
Total sales revenue	$2,200,000	$2,750,000
Net profit margin	25%	16.7%
Total number of orders from customers	40,636	49,600
Total number of visits to website	101,589	141,714
Conversion rate – visitor to purchaser	40%	35%
The percentage of total visitors accessing website through magazine link	0	19.9%
Website availability	95%	95%
Number of customers spending more than $100 per visit	4,650	6,390
Number of subscribers to online newsletter	4,600	11,900

Required

Assess the performance of the business in Quarter 2 in relation to the changes and incentives that the company introduced at the beginning of this quarter. State clearly where any further information might be necessary, concluding as to whether the changes and incentives have been effective.

(Total = 20 marks)

363 PAF Co (December 2013)

36 mins

Protect Against Fire Co (PAF Co) manufactures and sells fire safety equipment and also provides fire risk assessments and fire safety courses to businesses. It has been trading for many years in the country of Calana, where it is the market leader.

Five years ago, the directors of PAF Co established a similar operation in its neighbouring country, Sista, renting business premises at various locations across the country. The fire safety market in Sista has always been dominated by two other companies, and when PAF Co opened the Sista division, its plan was to become market leader there within five years. Both the Calana division (Division C) and the Sista division (Division S) usually restrict themselves to a marketing budget of $0.5 million per annum but in 20X3, Division S launched a $2 million advertising campaign in a final push to increase market share. It also left its prices for products and services unchanged in 20X3 rather than increasing them in line with its competitors.

Although the populations of both countries are similar, geographically, the country of Sista is twice as large as Calana and its customers are evenly spread across the country. The products and services offered by the two divisions to their customers require skilled staff, demand for which is particularly high in Sista. Following the appointment of a new government in Sista at the end of 20X2, stricter fire safety regulations were immediately introduced for all companies. At the same time, the government introduced a substantial tax on business property rents which landlords passed on to their tenants.

International shortages of fuel have led to a 20% increase in fuel prices in both countries in the last year.

Summary statements of profit or loss for the two divisions for the two years ended 30 November 20X2 and 30 November 20X3 are shown below.

	Division S 20X3 $'000	Division S 20X2 $'000	Division C 20X3 $'000	Division C 20X2 $'000
Revenue	38,845	26,937	44,065	40,395
Material costs	(3,509)	(2,580)	(4,221)	(3,385)
Payroll costs	(10,260)	(6,030)	(8,820)	(7,700)
Property costs	(3,200)	(1,800)	(2,450)	(2,320)
Gross profit	21,876	16,527	28,574	26,954
Distribution and marketing (D&M) costs	(10,522)	(7,602)	(7,098)	(5,998)
Administrative overheads	(7,024)	(6,598)	(12,012)	(11,974)
Operating profit	4,330	2,327	9,464	8,982
Employee numbers	380	241	420	385
Market share	30%	25%	55%	52%

Required

Using all the information above, assess the financial performance of Division S in the year ended 30 November 20X3. State clearly where further information might be required in order to make more reasoned conclusions about the division's performance.

Note. Up to seven marks are available for calculations.

(20 marks)

364 CIM Co (Sep/Dec 2015 amended)   36 mins

Cardale Industrial Metal Co (CIM Co) is a large supplier of industrial metals. The company is split into two divisions: Division F and Division N. Each division operates separately as an investment centre, with each one having full control over its non-current assets. In addition, both divisions are responsible for their own current assets, controlling their own levels of inventory and cash and having full responsibility for the credit terms granted to customers and the collection of receivables balances. Similarly, each division has full responsibility for its current liabilities and deals directly with its own suppliers.

Each divisional manager is paid a salary of $120,000 per annum plus an annual performance-related bonus, based on the return on investment (ROI) achieved by their division for the year. Each divisional manager is expected to achieve a minimum ROI for their division of 10% per annum. If a manager only meets the 10% target, they are not awarded a bonus. However, for each whole percentage point above 10% which the division achieves for the year, a bonus equivalent to 2% of annual salary is paid, subject to a maximum bonus equivalent to 30% of annual salary.

The following figures relate to the year ended 31 August 20X5:

	Division F $'000	Division N $'000
Sales	14,500	8,700
Controllable profit	2,645	1,970
Less apportionment of Head Office costs	(1,265)	(684)
Net profit	1,380	1,286
Non-current assets	9,760	14,980
Inventory, cash and trade receivables	2,480	3,260
Trade payables	2,960	1,400

During the year ending 31 August 20X5, Division N invested $6.8 million in new equipment, including a technologically advanced cutting machine, which is expected to increase productivity by 8% per annum. Division F has made no investment during the year, although its computer system is badly in need of updating. Division F's manager has said that they have already had to delay payments to suppliers (ie accounts payables) because of limited cash and the computer system 'will just have to wait', although the cash balance at Division F is still better than that of Division N.

Required

(a) For each division, for the year ended 31 August 20X5, calculate the appropriate closing return on investment (ROI) on which the payment of management bonuses will be based. Briefly justify the figures used in your calculations.

   Note. There are three marks available for calculations and two marks available for discussion. **(5 marks)**

(b) Based on your calculations in part (a), calculate each manager's bonus for the year ended 31 August 20X5. **(3 marks)**

(c) Discuss whether ROI is providing a fair basis for calculating the managers' bonuses and the problems arising from its use at CIM Co for the year ended 31 August 20X5. **(7 marks)**

(d) Briefly explain steps that could be taken by CIM Co to encourage managers to take a long-term view in decision-making. **(5 marks)**

(Total = 20 marks)

365 Man Co (Mar/Jun 2016 amended)   36 mins

A manufacturing company, Man Co, has two divisions: Division L and Division M. Both divisions make a single standardised product. Division L makes component L, which is supplied to both Division M and external customers. Division M makes product M using one unit of component L and other materials. It then sells the completed product M to external customers. To date, Division M has always bought component L from Division L.

The following information is available:

	Component L $	Product M $
Selling price	40	96
Direct materials:		
Component L		(40)
Other	(12)	(17)
Direct labour	(6)	(9)
Variable overheads	(2)	(3)
Selling and distribution costs	(4)	(1)
Contribution per unit before fixed costs	16	26
Annual fixed costs	$500,000	$200,000
Annual external demand (units)	160,000	120,000
Capacity of plant	300,000	130,000

Division L charges the same price for component L to both Division M and external customers. However, it does not incur the selling and distribution costs when transferring internally.

Division M has just been approached by a new supplier who has offered to supply it with component L for $37 per unit. Prior to this offer, the cheapest price at which Division M could have bought component L from outside the group was $42 per unit.

It is head office policy to let the divisions operate autonomously without interference at all.

Required

(a) Calculate the incremental profit/(loss) per component for the group if Division M accepts the new supplier's offer and recommend how many components Division L should sell to Division M if group profits are to be maximised. **(3 marks)**

(b) Using the quantities calculated in (a) and the current transfer price, calculate the total annual profits of each division and the group as a whole. **(6 marks)**

(c) Discuss the problems which will arise if the transfer price remains unchanged and advise the divisions on a suitable alternative transfer price for component L. **(6 marks)**

(d) Discuss the advantages of allowing divisions to operate autonomously. **(5 marks)**

                                                            (Total = 20 marks)

366 Rotech group (June 2014)   36 mins

The Rotech group comprises two companies, W Co and C Co.

W Co is a trading company with two divisions: The Design division, which designs wind turbines and supplies the designs to customers under licences, and the Gearbox division, which manufactures gearboxes for the car industry.

C Co manufactures components for gearboxes. It sells the components globally and also supplies W Co with components for its Gearbox manufacturing division.

The financial results for the two companies for the year ended 31 May 20X4 are as follows:

	Design division $'000	W Co Gearbox division $'000	C Co $'000
External sales	14,300	25,535	8,010
Sales to Gearbox division			7,550
			15,560
Cost of sales	(4,900)	(16,200)*	(5,280)
Administration costs	(3,400)	(4,200)	(2,600)
Distribution costs	–	(1,260)	(670)
Operating profit	6,000	3,875	7,010
Capital employed	23,540	32,320	82,975

* Includes cost of components purchased from C Co.

Required

(a) Discuss the performance of C Co and each division of W Co, calculating and using the following three performance measures:

    (i)   Return on capital employed (ROCE)

    (ii)   Asset turnover

    (iii)   Operating profit margin

    Note. There are 4.5 marks available for calculations and 5.5 marks available for discussion.

(10 marks)

C Co is currently working to full capacity. The Rotech group's policy is that group companies and divisions must always make internal sales first, before selling outside the group. Similarly, purchases must be made from within the group wherever possible. However, the group divisions and companies are allowed to negotiate their own transfer prices without interference from Head Office.

C Co has always charged the same price to the Gearbox division as it does to its external customers. However, after being offered a 5% lower price for similar components from an external supplier, the manager of the Gearbox division feels strongly that the transfer price is too high and should be reduced. C Co currently satisfies 60% of the external demand for its components. Its variable costs represent 40% of revenue.

Required

(b) Advise, using suitable calculations, the total transfer price or prices at which the components should be supplied to the Gearbox division from C Co.
(10 marks)

(Total = 20 marks)

367 Bus Co (Sep/Dec 2015 amended)   36 mins

Bus Co is a large bus operator, operating long-distance bus services across the country. There are two other national operators in the country. Bus Co's mission is to 'be the market leader in long-distance transport providing a greener, cleaner service for passengers nationwide'. Last month, an independent survey of 40,000 passengers was carried out, the results of which are shown in the table below:

Table: Bus passenger satisfaction % by national operator

Operator	Overall satisfaction	Value for money	Punctuality	Journey time
Bus	*	67	80	82
Prime	*	58	76	83
Express	*	67	76	89

* denotes that the percentage has not yet been calculated.

The 'overall satisfaction' percentages, which have not yet been inserted into the table, are calculated using a weighted average which reflects the importance customers place on each of the other three criteria above. The weightings used are as follows:

Value for money   40%

Punctuality   32%

Journey time   28%

The managing director (MD) of Bus Co has said: 'Independent research has shown that our customers are the most satisfied of any national bus operator. We are now leading the way on what matters most to customers – value for money and punctuality.'

Required

(a)   Calculate the 'overall satisfaction' percentage for each operator.   **(2 marks)**

(b)   Taking into account all the data in the table and your calculations from part (a), discuss whether the managing director's statement is true.   **(4 marks)**

When measuring performance using a 'value for money' approach, the criteria of economy, efficiency and effectiveness can be used.

Required

(c)   Briefly define 'efficiency' and 'effectiveness' and suggest one performance measure for **EACH**, which would help Bus Co assess the efficiency and effectiveness of the service it provides.   **(4 marks)**

(d)   Describe the balanced scorecard approach to performance measurement and suggest a performance measure for Bus Co for each perspective of the balanced scorecard.
          (10 marks)

          (Total = 20 marks)

368 People's Bank (Mar/Jun 2017)   36 mins

The People's Bank is a bank based in the country of Nawkrei. It has a total of 65 branches across the country and also offers online banking (access to services via computer) and telephone banking (access to customer service agents over the telephone) to its customers. Recently, The People's Bank also began offering its customers a range of mobile banking services, which can be accessed from customers' smartphones and tablet computers. Its customer-base is made up of both private individuals and business customers. The range of services it offers includes:

Current accounts
Savings accounts
Credit cards
Business and personal loans
Mortgages (loans for property purchases)

The People's Bank's vision is to be 'the bank that gives back to its customers' and their purpose is 'to help the people and businesses of Nawkrei to live better lives and achieve their ambitions'. In order to achieve this, the bank's values are stated as:

(1)   Putting customers' needs first, which involves anticipating and understanding customers' needs and making products and services accessible to as many customers as possible. The People' Bank has recently invested heavily in IT security to prevent fraud and also invested to make more services accessible to disabled and visually impaired customers

(2)   Making business simple, which involves identifying opportunities to simplify activities and communicating clearly and openly

(3)   Making a difference to the communities they serve, which involves primarily helping the disadvantaged and new homeowners but also supporting small and medium-sized businesses (SMEs) and acting fairly and responsibly at all times

Extracts from The People's Bank's balanced scorecard are shown below:

Performance measure	20X6 Actual	20X6 Target
Financial perspective		
Return on capital employed (ROCE)	11%	12%
Interest income	$7.5m	$7m
Net interest margin (margin achieved on interest income)	2.4%	2.5%
Amount of new lending to SMEs	$135m	$150m
Customer perspective		
Number of first-time homebuyers given a mortgage by The People's Bank	86,000	80,000
Number of complaints (per 1,000 customers)	1.5	2
Number of talking cashpoints installed for the visually impaired	120	100
Number of wheelchair ramps installed in branches	55	50
Internal processes		
Number of business processes within The People's Bank re-engineered and simplified	110	100
Number of new services made available through 'mobile banking'	2	5
Incidences of fraud on customers' accounts or credit cards (per 1,000 customers)	3	10
Total carbon dioxide emissions (tonnes)	430,000	400,000
Learning and growth		
Number of colleagues trained to provide advice to SMEs	1,300	1,500
Number of hours (paid for by The People's Bank) used to support community projects	1,020,000	1,000,000
Number of trainee positions taken up by candidates from Nawkrei's most disadvantaged areas	1,990	2,000
Number of community organisations supported (either through funding or by volunteers from The People's Bank)	7,250	7,000

Required

(a) Explain why the balanced scorecard approach to performance measurement is more useful to measure performance for The People's Bank than a traditional approach using solely financial performance measures. **(4 marks)**

(b) Using all of the information provided, including The People's Bank's vision and values, discuss the performance of The People's Bank in 20X6.

Note. Use each of the four headings of the balanced scorecard to structure your discussion. **(16 marks)**

(Total = 20 marks)

369 Sports Co (Sep/Dec 2017)

36 mins

Sports Co is a large manufacturing company specialising in the manufacture of a wide range of sports clothing and equipment. The company has two divisions: Clothing (Division C) and Equipment (Division E). Each division operates with little intervention from Head Office and divisional managers have autonomy to make decisions about long-term investments.

Sports Co measures the performance of its divisions using return on investment (ROI), calculated using controllable profit and average divisional net assets. The target ROI for each of the divisions is 18%. If the divisions meet or exceed this target the divisional managers receive a bonus.

Last year, an investment which was expected to meet the target ROI was rejected by one of the divisional managers because it would have reduced the division's overall ROI. Consequently, Sports Co is considering the introduction of a new performance measure, residual income (RI), in order to discourage this dysfunctional behaviour in the future. Like ROI, this would be calculated using controllable profit and average divisional net assets.

The draft operating statement for the year, prepared by the company's trainee accountant, is shown below:

	Division C $'000	Division E $'000
Sales revenue	3,800	8,400
Less variable costs	(1,400)	(3,030)
Contribution	2,400	5,370
Less fixed costs	(945)	(1,420)
Net profit	1,455	3,950
Opening divisional controllable net assets	13,000	24,000
Closing divisional controllable net assets	9,000	30,000

Notes

(1) Included in the fixed costs are depreciation costs of $165,000 and $460,000 for Divisions C and E respectively. 30% of the depreciation costs in each division relates to assets controlled but not owned by Head Office. Division E invested $2m in plant and machinery at the beginning of the year, which is included in the net assets figures above, and uses the reducing balance method to depreciate assets. Division C, which uses the straight-line method, made no significant additions to non-current assets. It is the policy of both divisions to charge a full year's depreciation in the year of acquisition.

(2) Head Office recharges all of its costs to the two divisions. These have been included in the fixed costs and amount to $620,000 for Division C and $700,000 for Division E.

(3) Sports Co has a cost of capital of 12%.

Required

(a) (i) Calculate the return on investment (ROI) for each of the two divisions of Sports Co.

(6 marks)

(ii) Discuss the performance of the two divisions for the year, including the main reasons why their ROI results differ from each other. Explain the impact the difference in ROI could have on the behaviour of the manager of the worst performing division.

(6 marks)

(b) (i) Calculate the residual income (RI) for each of the two divisions of Sports Co and briefly comment on the results of this performance measure. **(4 marks)**

(ii) Explain the advantages and disadvantages of using residual income (RI) to measure divisional performance. **(4 marks)**

(Total = 20 marks)

370 Portable Garage Co (Mar/Jun 2018)

36 mins

The Portable Garage Co (PGC) is a company specialising in the manufacture and sale of a range of products for motorists. It is split into two divisions: the battery division (Division B) and the adaptor division (Division A). Division B sells one product – portable battery chargers for motorists which can be attached to a car's own battery and used to start up the engine when the car's own battery fails. Division A sells adaptors which are used by customers to charge mobile devices and laptops by attaching them to the car's internal power source.

Recently, Division B has upgraded its portable battery so it can also be used to rapidly charge mobile devices and laptops. The mobile device or laptop must be attached to the battery using a special adaptor which is supplied to the customer with the battery. Division B currently buys the adaptors from Division A, which also sells them externally to other companies.

The following data is available for both divisions:

Division B

Selling price for each portable battery, including adapter	$180
Costs per battery:	
Adaptor from Division A	$13
Other materials from external suppliers	$45
Labour costs	$35
Annual fixed overheads	$5,460,000
Annual production and sales of portable batteries (units)	150,000
Maximum annual market demand for portable batteries (units)	180,000

Division A

Selling price per adaptor to Division B	$13
Selling price per adaptor to external customers	$15
Costs per adaptor:	
Materials	$3
Labour costs	$4
Annual fixed overheads	$2,200,000
Current annual production capacity and sales of adaptors - both internal and external sales (units)	350,000
Maximum annual external demand for adaptors (units)	200,000

In addition to the materials and labour costs above, Division A incurs a variable cost of $1 per adaptor for all adaptors it sells externally. Currently, Head Office's purchasing policy only allows Division B to purchase the adaptors from Division A but Division A has refused to sell Division B any more than the current level of adaptors it supplies to it. The manager of Division B is unhappy. He has a special industry contact who he could buy the adaptors from at exactly the same price charged by Division A if he were given the autonomy to purchase from outside the group. After discussions with both of the divisional managers and to ensure that the managers are not demotivated, Head Office has now agreed to change the purchasing policy to allow Division B to buy externally, provided that it optimises the profits of the group as a whole.

Required

(a) Under the current transfer pricing system, prepare a profit statement showing the profit for each of the divisions and for The Portable Garage Co (PGC) as a whole. Your sales and costs figures should be split into external sales and inter-divisional transfers, where appropriate.
(9 marks)

(b) Assuming that the new group purchasing policy will ensure the optimisation of group profits, calculate and discuss the number of adaptors which Division B should buy from Division A and the number of adaptors which Division A should sell to external customers.

Note. There are three marks available for calculations and three marks for discussion.
(6 marks)

Assume now that no external supplier exists for the adaptors which Division B uses.

(c) Calculate and discuss what the minimum transfer price per unit would be for any additional adaptors supplied above the current level by Division A to Division B so that Division B can meet its maximum annual demand for the new portable batteries.

Note. There are two marks available for calculations and three marks available for discussion.

(5 marks)

(Total = 20 marks)

371 Robinholt University (Sep/Dec 2019)   36 mins

The following scenario relates to one requirement.

Robinholt University is one of the largest and most popular universities in the country of Richpori. It had 27,000 registered students in 20X6, whereas in 20X5, the number of registered students was only 24,000. Robinholt University managed to increase its student numbers in 20X6 by making the entry requirements for students slightly lower than in previous years. All courses at the university last for three years.

Robinholt University has five strategic aims:

(1) To provide education which promotes intellectual initiative and produces confident and ambitious graduates who have reached the highest academic standards to prepare them for success in life and the workplace

(2) To provide an organised, efficient learning environment with access to cutting edge technology and facilities

(3) To be a leader in sustainable business practices which protect the environment and support local people

(4) To provide attractive, innovative conference and event facilities, attracting clients both nationally and internationally

(5) To be recognised both nationally and internationally for the scope and relevance of their research

Extracts from the university's income statement for the last two years are as follows:

	20X6	20X5
	$ million	$ million
Income		
Tuition fees	148.0	135.6
Research grants	3.5	4.5
Conferences and other events	18.0	16.0
Total income	169.5	156.1
Expenditure		
Academic staff costs	80.8	76.2
Administration staff costs	50.4	48
Premises, facilities and technology costs	7.6	8.4
Events and conference costs	8.3	8.0
Research grants	3.1	4.0
Sustainability and community assistance	1.2	2.4
Total expenditure	151.4	147.0
Surplus	18.1	9.1

Every year, final year students complete an external survey run by the National Organisation for Students. In this, they have to agree or disagree with statements made. Extracts from this for the last two years are shown below (the percentage rates show the number of students who agreed with the statements made):

	20X6	20X5
Teaching		
(1) The course is intellectually stimulating and quality of teaching high	83%	86%
Academic support		
(2) I have received good advice and support with my studies from academic staff	82%	86%
Organisation and management		
(3) The course is well organised and its administration is good	81%	90%
Learning resources		
(4) The standard of rooms, facilities and equipment is good	83%	92%
Personal development		
(5) The course has helped me develop as a person	82%	80%
Overall satisfaction		
(6) Overall, I am satisfied with the quality of the course	81%	83%

The 'overall satisfaction' percentage is used by the Education Authority to set the maximum level of tuition fees that a university can charge each year and is seen as the main measure of success both internally and externally.

Other key information	20X6	20X5
Students graduating with a First Class Honours degree (highest class attainable)	20%	28%
Employers happy with the graduates from Robinholt University	72%	75%
Ratio of students to staff members	40:1	35:1
Staff retention rate	75%	90%

The staff retention rate in 20X5 was consistent with previous years. Data gathered from students who graduated in 20X5 showed that 65% of students found a graduate job within one year of leaving compared to 68% of 20X4's graduates.

In 20X5, Robinholt University won the 'Green Environmental' award for their campuses, which all have extensive recycling facilities. Students were also involved in a local 'Grow to Give' food sharing project that year, which provided thousands of pounds worth of fresh produce to food banks offering food to poorer residents. Due to staff shortages, the university was not involved in this project in 20X6. The recycling bins have also been abandoned because of the cost of using them.

Every year, the University Research Council issues a range of prestigious awards for contributions to research. One of Robinholt University's main competitors in the area won an award in 20X5 for their contribution to some pioneering research on genetics. Robinholt University has yet to win an award for research. However, in 20X5 it did win an 'Innovation' award for its new, innovative conference facilities which have attracted a number of new clients in the last year.

Required

Using Robinholt University's five strategic aims, assess its performance for 20X6.   **(20 marks)**

Note: There are four marks available for calculations and 16 marks for discussion.

372 Hammocks Co (Mar/Jun 2020)

36 mins

The following scenario relates to three requirements.

Hammocks Co own and operate a small chain of four luxury vacation resorts. All four resorts are located on islands that enjoy a hot, sunny climate for nine months of the year. Each resort has gourmet restaurants, water sports and spa facilities, as well as sun terraces and pools.

Hammocks Co's management currently focus on two distinct stakeholder groups: shareholders and customers, and has two objectives:

(1)   To make a profit long term; and

(2)   To create customer loyalty.

All operational (non-management) staff at the resorts receive comprehensive training and are employed in secure, long-term contracts, which is unusual in this industry.

Guests who visit the resorts pay one upfront fee and then enjoy unlimited food, drink and use of the resort facilities. When a guest arrives at a resort they are personally greeted by a concierge, offered a drink and cold towel while their luggage is transferred to their luxury room. All rooms are scrupulously clean and contain complimentary drinks, snacks, toiletries, bathrobes and slippers. The rooms are all equipped with appliances, which Hammock Co's management believe that guests need during their stay, including satellite television, coffee-maker, refrigerator and hairdryer. If a guest requests something that is not available in the room, a call to the reception ensures that it arrives within ten minutes.

An extract from Hammocks Co's management accounting data is as follows:

	Budget 20X7	Actual 20X7*	Actual 20X6	Actual 20X6 Competitor 'Loungers'
Average number of guests per week	2,000	1,960	1,940	1,700
Average revenue per week ($)	4,000,000	3,920,000	3,880,000	3,060,000
Average staff costs per week:				
- Maintenance ($)	480,000	480,000	470,588	455,000
- Service ($)	960,000	960,000	941,176	800,000
Average weekly spend on repairs ($)	200,000	160,000	196,078	180,000
Ratio of operational staff to guests	1.50	1.53	1.50	1.30
Average rooms available per week**	1,200	1,200	1,200	1,100
Market share %	29	28	29	23

*The actual 20X7 figures are based on the year to date figures (ten weeks).

** Rooms are designed for double occupancy.

Note: General inflation is 2% higher in 20X7 compared to 20X6.

Extracts from TripEvent, an influential online customer forum:

'I love Hammocks Co; the service and attention to detail is exemplary and the resorts are always pristine. However, their competitor "Loungers" has full body dryers, ionised water taps and a range of professional haircare equipment in all their rooms.'

BPP
LEARNING
MEDIA

'Our third time back to Hammocks Co this year and we continue to be amazed by the wonderful level of service. One thing though is the menus don't seem to have changed much from one visit to the next.'

'We booked Hammocks Co on the spur of the moment but then found that we couldn't get a flight. We called Hammocks Co's administrative centre to change our booking to another resort where we could get a flight to and were told that it would not be a problem. However, it took two more calls and three emails to get confirmation and then our credit card was charged twice in error. Of course it was eventually all resolved, the incorrect charge refunded, a complimentary limousine provided to and from the airport and we received the most amazing customer service at the resort, but it was frustrating at the time.'

'When I made my booking I was assured that my bed would be made with the special anti-allergenic bedding which I need for a good night's sleep and that my favourite blend of tea would be available. When I arrived, neither of these requirements were met. To be fair to Hammocks Co though, everything was in order two hours later when I went to bed.'

Required

(a) Based on the limited information available, discuss the performance of Hammocks Co in light of its two existing objectives. **(8 marks)**

(b) (i) Explain TWO advantages of Hammocks Co using the balanced scorecard approach to performance management. **(3 marks)**

(ii) Suggest and justify ONE goal and TWO performance measures for each of the TWO perspectives of the balanced scorecard which are not currently addressed by Hammocks Co's objectives. **(9 marks)**

(Total = 20 marks)

373 Medcomp (Mar/Jun 2021)   36 mins

The following scenario relates to two requirements.

Medcomp is a charity based in Ceeland. It provides medical treatment to prevent and cure blindness caused by cataracts, to thousands of people in less developed countries. This disease is relatively easy to cure when treatment is available, but the majority of people who need treatment cannot afford to pay for it. For over 10 years Medcomp has provided free treatment from 12 treatment centres based in fixed locations worldwide.

Medcomp employs a small number of paid permanent staff who consist of medical practitioners, medical administrators and fundraisers, but the majority of its workforce is voluntary. The charity has built relationships with several teaching hospitals in Ceeland, from where it recruits newly qualified doctors and nurses. These doctors and nurses volunteer to work unpaid for a year in Medcomp's treatment centres before returning home to work in one of Ceeland's many hospitals. Mecomp believes that using newly qualified medical staff will promote the use of the most effective and up-to-date techniques and procedures.

Financial donations are sourced from large businesses in Ceeland and most of the equipment and other medical supplies needed are donated by hospitals and manufacturers. Thus, it is rare for the treatment centres to run short of supplies.

Medcomp keeps accounts with a year end of 31 August as well as detailed operating data. Data extracts from its management accounts for the current year (20X8) and from 20X7 and 20X6 are as follows:

	20X8	20X7	20X6
Average size of donation ($)	600	535	500
Number of donations	2,850	3,000	2,950
Total operating costs ($'000)	1,730	1,550	1,430
New procedures as a percentage of total procedures (**Note**)	20%	5%	5%

	20X8	20X7	20X6
Number of treatments performed	5,600	5,000	4,600
Number of successful treatments	4,312	4,300	4,002
Average number of days taken to deliver drugs and equipment to treatment centres	7	7	7

Note: New procedures are procedures which are introduced within the year.

Medcomp is about to introduce a balanced scorecard to help implement its strategy and measure performance. The critical success factors (CSFs), which relate to the four perspectives of the balanced scorecard have been identified as: **positive cash flow, innovation, medical effectiveness and function efficiency.**

Required

(a) For each perspective of the balanced scorecard, select the appropriate critical success factor (CSF) which relates to the perspective, suggest ONE key performance indicator (KPI) which will help to measure the CSF and use the KPI to analyse Medcomp's performance from 20X6 to 20X8. **(16 marks)**

Note: Use the balanced scorecard template provided below to structure your answer.

(b) Explain the benefits of an organisation using the balanced scorecard to measure performance instead of using solely financial measures. **(4 marks)**

(Total = 20 marks)

Template

Financial	CSF:
	KPI:
	Performance analysis:
Customer	CSF:
	KPI:
	Performance analysis:
Internal business process	CSF:
	KPI:
	Performance analysis:
Innovation and learning	CSF:
	KPI:
	Performance analysis:

Section A questions

OTQ bank – mixed bank   54 mins

374   A company has entered two different new markets.

In market A, it is initially charging low prices so as to gain rapid market share while demand is relatively elastic.

In market B, it is initially charging high prices so as to earn maximum profits while demand is relatively inelastic.

Which price strategy is the company using in each market?

O   Penetration pricing in market A and price skimming in market B

O   Price discrimination in market A and penetration pricing in market B

O   Price skimming in market A and penetration pricing in market B

O   Price skimming in market A and price discrimination in market B   **(2 marks)**

375   A company makes a single product which it sells for $2 per unit.

Fixed costs are $13,000 per month.

The contribution/sales ratio is 40%.

Sales revenue is $62,500.

What is the margin of safety (in units)?

[   ] units   **(2 marks)**

376   Which of the following statements is NOT consistent with the theory of constraints?

O   There is no inventory of work in progress or finished goods held

O   Raw materials are converted into sales as quickly as possible

O   Operations prior to the bottleneck operate at the same level as the bottleneck

O   Conversion costs and investment costs are kept to a minimum   **(2 marks)**

377   The following statements have been made about changing budgetary systems. Are they true or false?

The costs of implementation may outweigh the benefits.	TRUE	FALSE
Employees will always welcome any new system which improves planning and control within the organisation.	TRUE	FALSE

(2 marks)

378 At the start of the year, a company has non-current assets amounting to $6 million and by the end of the year this figure has risen to $8 million after depreciation of $600,000 has been charged at the end of the year. Working capital at the start of the year has been reported at $0.5 million and by the year end had increased by $0.2 million. Profit for the same period is $1.6 million before any depreciation charges had been deducted.

What was the ROI of the company for the year, based on average capital employed?

- ○ 11.49%
- ○ 13.16%
- ○ 14.29%
- ○ 21.05% **(2 marks)**

---

379 Mabel Co manufactures and sells tables and chairs in a standard mix of one table to four chairs. The following information is available:

Product	Table	Chair
Variable cost per unit ($)	120	16
Contribution to sales ratio	0.4	0.6

Annual fixed costs are $100,000.

What is the breakeven point in sales revenue (to the nearest hundred dollars)?

$ [   ] **(2 marks)**

---

380 The following are types of management accounting techniques.

(1) Flow cost accounting
(2) Input/output analysis
(3) Life cycle costing
(4) Activity-based costing

Which of the above techniques could be used by a company to account for its environmental costs?

- ○ 1 only
- ○ 1 and 2
- ○ 2 and 3
- ○ All of the above **(2 marks)**

---

381 Which of the following statements describes target costing?

- ○ It allocated the expected cost of a product and then adds a margin to it to arrive at the target selling price
- ○ It allocates overhead costs to products by collecting the costs into pools and sharing them out according to each product's usage of the cost-driving activity
- ○ It identifies the market price of a product and then subtracts a desired profit margin to arrive at the target cost
- ○ It identifies different markets for a product and then sells that same product at different prices in each market **(2 marks)**

---

382 C Co uses material B, which has a current market price of $0.80 per kg. In a linear program, where the objective is to maximise profit, the shadow price of material B is $2 per kg. Are the following statements true or false?

Contribution will be increased by $2 for each additional kg of material B purchased at the current market price.	TRUE	FALSE
The maximum price which should be paid for an additional kg of material B is $2.	TRUE	FALSE
Contribution will be increased by $1.20 for each additional kg of material B purchased at the current market price	TRUE	FALSE
The maximum price which should be paid for an additional kg of material B is $2.80	TRUE	FALSE

(2 marks)

383 S Company is a manufacturer of multiple products and uses target costing. It has been noted that Product P currently has a target cost gap and the company wishes to close this gap.

Which of the following may be used to close the target cost gap for Product P?

○ Use overtime to complete work ahead of schedule

○ Substitute current raw materials with cheaper versions

○ Raise the selling price of P

○ Negotiate cheaper rent for S Company's premises

(2 marks)

384 An investment centre in a manufacturing group produced the following results in the previous financial year:

	$'000
Operating profit	360
Capital employed: non-current assets	1,500
current assets	100

For the purpose of performance measurement, non-current assets are valued at cost. The investment centre is considering a new investment that will increase annual operating profit by $25,000, and will require an investment of $100,000 in a non-current asset and an additional $30,000 in working capital.

Will the performance measurement criteria of (1) return on investment (ROI) and (2) residual income (RI) motivate the centre manager to undertake the investment? Assume a notional capital charge of 18% on divisional capital.

	Yes	No
ROI	☐	☐
RI	☐	☐

(2 marks)

385 Which of the following may be used to study possible future outcomes when there are many different variables in the situation and the relationships between variables are not predictable?

(1) Sensitivity analysis
(2) Pay-off table
(3) Simulation model

○ (1) and (3) only
○ (3) only
○ (1) and (2) only
○ (1), (2) and (3)   (2 marks)

386 B Co operates a production process which generates a contribution of $4 per hour. Wages are paid at $7 per hour and labour is fully utilised. During busy periods workers are offered the chance to work overtime, which is paid $10 per hour. However, workers are currently refusing to work overtime because of an industrial dispute.

B Co has just received an additional order which must be fulfilled immediately and which will require ten hours of labour to fulfil.

What is the total relevant cost of labour for the additional order?

$ [   ]   (2 marks)

387 A company has two divisions. The divisions are identical in terms of the number and type of machines they have and the operations they carry out. However, one division was set up four years ago and the other was set up one year ago. Head office appraises the division using both the return on investment (ROI) and residual income (RI).

Which of the following statements is correct in relation to the outcome of the appraisal for each division?

○ Both ROI and RI will favour the older division
○ ROI will favour the older division, but RI will treat each fairly
○ RI will favour the newer division and ROI will favour the older division
○ Both RI and ROI will favour the newer division   (2 marks)

388 A bank has developed a new type of account called the Gold Account. Development and advertising costs were $50,000. At the start of each of the next four years, 1,000 customers are expected to open a Gold Account and to pay the bank $300 each year that they use it. Of the 1,000 customers who open a Gold Account, 500 are expected to close the account after one year and 500 after two years. The bank estimates it will cost $400 per customer to administer the Gold Account in the customer's first year reducing to $50 per customer in the second year.

Ignoring the time value of money, what is the lifecycle profit per customer of Gold Account?

○ $8.33
○ $25.00
○ $12.50
○ $16.67   (2 marks)

(Total = 30 marks)

Answers

Section A answers

OTQ bank – Information, technologies and systems for organisation performance

1   This question appeared in the Mar/Jun 2021 exam.

   The correct answer is: $4

   Examination team comments

   The total cost of responding to information requests = $2.4m × 10% = $240,000. This cost relates to both full reports and specific queries. As the full report takes double the time of the specific query, the total number of equivalent requests can be calculated as 4,000 + (500 × 2) = 5,000. This is the number of requests per month, therefore 5,000 × 12 = 60,000 equivalent requests per year.

   The cost per specific query = $240,000/60,000 = $4.

2   The correct answer is: 1 only

   For example, systems for recording attendance times at work are more reliable when recorded automatically by a card reader system than if individuals sign in and sign out in a manual attendance record. However, time-recording systems (such as time sheets for recording time spent on different jobs) must sometimes rely on human records. Secondary information is usually much cheaper to collect than primary data.

3   The correct answers are:

Logical access controls	YES	
Database controls	YES	
Hierarchical passwords	YES	
Range checks		NO

   A range check is a control within specific IT applications to check that an input item of data has a value within an acceptable range, and any input items with a value outside the range are reported as errors.

4   The correct answer is: Both 1 and 2

   Management information, often of an operational nature, is often produced as summary data output from a transaction processing system. Management information systems are based mainly on internal data sources rather than sources that are external to the organisation.

5   The correct answer is:

   They are designed to report on existing operations.   **TRUE**

   They have an external focus.   FALSE

   Management information systems provide information to management about existing operations, and have an internal focus.

6   The correct answer is: 2 only

   Budgeting is commonly associated with decision-making at the tactical planning level (management control level) within a management hierarchy.

7   The correct answer is: Executive information system

   EIS systems often present key information in a 'visually friendly' format.

8   **This question appeared in the March 2019 exam.**

   The correct answer is: Monitoring the database system logs on a daily basis to see what information is being accessed

   Monitoring the usage and access logs on a regular basis would have revealed that the human resource director's account was being accessed whilst he was on vacation and that confidential information was being looked at and copied. This would have enabled the company to investigate immediately and the individual could have been identified sooner, which could have prevented the sensitive information from being divulged to everyone in the company.

9   The correct answer is: Email communications between a customer and the customer services department

Structured data refers to any data that is contained within a field in a data record or file. This includes data contained in databases and spreadsheets. Unstructured data is data that is not easily contained within structured data fields: pictures, videos, webpages, PDF files, emails, blogs etc.

10   The correct answer is: Both 1 and 2

Feedback is information produced by a system as control information for management. Benchmarking means comparing performance of an organisation, or part of an organisation, with a 'benchmark'. The benchmark may be an external organisation, such as a competitor company, or another department or division within the same organisation.

11   The correct answers are:

- Understand individual customer preferences
- Analyse the take-up of targeted promotions

Coff Co can use information from the interactive website and loyalty cards to track individual purchases and see which customers are taking advantage of the offers that are targeted at them. The updating of inventory records would take place as part of the standard point of sale and inventory accounting systems, and branch sales forecasts are likely to be built up from historical sales figures, rather than from the sales to those customers who use loyalty cards.

12   **This question appeared in the December 2018 exam.**

The correct answer is: $200

Only the cost of the use of bar coding and scanners is a direct data capture cost. The correct answer is therefore $200.

13   **This question appeared in the March 2017 exam.**

The correct answer is: $9,000

There are two types of costs of producing information in this case – direct and indirect. A direct cost can be completely attributed to obtaining the information. An indirect cost is required in order to produce the information, but can't be completely attributed to it.

In this example, only the apportionment of the technology insurance cost is indirect – all of the others are solely related to producing the information.

14   The correct answer is: Intranet

The internet is an example of a global network (not a local network). A file server is a computer within a network. Ethernet cables are cables connecting networks.

15   The correct answers are:

- Increased productivity
- Reduced costs

Increased productivity occurs because employees can work together wherever they need to. Costs are reduced as the business expands because it is easier to add new users to a wireless network than to install new cabling.

If using wireless technology in public places, it may not always be possible to find secure networks therefore security can be an issue. Wireless technology will not necessarily lead to better decision-making.

OTQ bank – Information, technologies and systems for organisation performance

16 The correct answer is: Fewer staff required in the finance function to analyse data.

More staff may be required to process the information and make decisions with the information gleaned from the data obtained. All the other options are benefits from using data mining.

17 The correct answers are: They analyse a customer's interactions with an organisation throughout the customer life cycle and They allow marketing communication to be tailored to the customer's interests

One of the disadvantages of a CRM system is its total costs. Costs can include software, upgrades, customisation and IT resources as well as the costs of training staff.

18 The correct answer is:

Level	Explanation
Wisdom	Adding value
Information	Revealing relationships
Knowledge	Providing insights
Data	Making measurements

This is just text book knowledge that you should learn.

19 **This question appeared in the June 2015 exam.**

The correct answer is: Prices of similar products, analysed for each competitor company

All of the others are internal sources of information.

20 The correct answers are:

In-depth analysis of data on a database in order to identify undiscovered trends or patterns in the data is known as data mining.	TRUE	
Large public databases are a major source of feedback for many commercial organisations.		FALSE

Feedback is information captured within an organisation by measuring output from the system. Information from an external source cannot be feedback.

21 The correct answer is: It relies on digital information

Information may be written, verbal or confidential, but if it is not digitised it cannot be analysed by big data analytics.

22 The correct answers are:

Budgetary control information comes mainly from sources outside the organisation.		FALSE
An EIS provides an integrated database system for the management of operations.		FALSE

Budgetary control information comes mainly from sources **inside** the organisation.

An **Enterprise Resource Planning (ERP)** system provides an integrated database system for the management of operations.

23 The correct answer is:

Information system	Level
Transaction processing system	Data
Management information system	Information
Decision support system	Knowledge
Expert system	Wisdom

24 The correct answer is: Both 1 and 2

They are both true.

25 The correct answers are: Veracity of data used and security of data collected

The veracity of data (its validity) is likely to be compromised unless there are effective cleansing procedures to remove incomplete, obsolete or duplicated data records.

Data protection and privacy issues must be considered with regard to data collected to ensure it complies with current legislation in these areas.

The volume of data is one of the characteristics of big data. The use of real time data is a benefit of using big data.

26 The correct answer is: Validation

Validation is used to ensure that data is accurate, for example, that a credit card has the correct number of digits. The other options are all security measures.

27 The correct answers are: Stocking products that customers want and Being able to apply target advertising

Big data requires skilled data analysts and therefore reducing the number would not improve performance. Big data means collecting more data, not less data.

28 The correct answers are:

Big data can be used to provide insights into costs.	TRUE
Social media is a source of big data.	TRUE
Predictive analytics is a branch of data analytics.	TRUE

Big data can be used to find patterns and make predictions of future costs.

Social media can be a useful source of big data for businesses. For example, it can be used to see what customers are saying about certain products.

Predictive analytics is a branch of data analytics that uses a variety of statistical techniques (eg data mining, machine learning, regression, decision trees) to make predictions.

29 The correct answer is: Executive information system (EIS)

The EIS provides a generalised computing and communication environment for senior managers to support strategic decisions.

30   The correct answers are:

It enables large quantities of data to be examined quickly.	TRUE
It improves organisational decision-making.	TRUE
It enables cost reduction.	TRUE
It requires adherence to data privacy laws	TRUE

All of the statements are true. The first three are benefits of big data analytics and the last one is a risk of using big data analytics.

Section C question

31 Story

(a) **Issues in upgrading the existing information system**

The issues involved in an upgrade of the existing information system include achieving the potential advantages at minimum cost and anticipating and managing necessary changes.

(i) **Advantages of upgrade**

A networked system would allow the **transmission** of information both to and from the business units and head office at Story. As such it is likely that performance indicators, financial statistics and similar **information** could be **rapidly gathered, processed and disseminated. Improved communication** between units and head office should improve, leading to **rapid reaction** to changes both within the organisation and outside it. This should result in a responsive, evolving organisation capable of meeting the challenges of the market place. It would also get rid of the problems currently experienced where some countries do not have the most up-to-date information on products and prices.

(ii) **Costs**

The **costs** of providing a fully networked computer system, changeover costs and the costs of future maintenance and training must be evaluated and budgeted for. The development and implementation of **security measures** to prevent the misuse of corporate data, and to prevent fraud by unauthorised users (who may be employees or external to the organisation) have to be considered and costed. In addition, there may be a possible need to **recruit** specialised staff to implement the changes to the existing information system. All of these costs are foreseeable and can be planned.

(iii) **Changes**

Upgrading corporate information systems usually results in many unforeseen changes to the **culture** of the organisation and to the **working practices** of staff at all levels. For example, would greater efficiency be achieved by allowing staff to have more flexible hours of attendance? Can costs be reduced by allowing some staff to telecommute on a regular basis, thus allowing hot-desking to take place? Is it likely that morale will be adversely affected by staff who may be concerned about using new technology or staff who fear that they may lose their jobs through the changes?

The proposed changes are unlikely to change the **role and remit of management** in relation to the directing of staff, although it is likely that there will be some impact upon organising staff tasks as new needs arise. **Strategic and tactical planning** are likely to change in response to the improved, and more rapid, flow of information that the information system will provide.

Operational decisions can be taken at lower levels of the corporate hierarchy as information becomes available more rapidly and in an appropriate format. As well as providing a swift response to changes in the business environment, it is possible that the organisation will, in time, evolve into one with a **flatter hierarchy**. This would particularly suit the autonomous business unit structure in Story which already operates with devolved decision-making. However, there is always the danger of **'information overload'** which can reduce efficiency and morale within the organisation.

(b) Although big data could potentially provide useful information for Story in relation to the growth of textbook sales, there are several considerations to be assessed.

Volume/variety - Capacity

Two of the features of big data are volume and variety. These characteristics may mean that a larger information system capacity is required in order to capture and store data correctly. If data is not captured and stored correctly it can lead to misleading information and therefore incorrect decision-making. The information derived from big data needs to be reliable.

Volume - Analytical tools

As well as having the capacity to store big data, Story will need the right analytical tools and technologies to be able to analyse it, because it is too large and unstructured to be analysed through traditional means.

Velocity

If the volume and variety of the data means that Story's current information systems are not able to process it, the 'velocity' aspect of big data will be undermined. If IT teams or business analysts become burdened with increasing requests for ad hoc analysis and one-off reports (because the systems cannot process the data automatically), the information and analysis from big data will not be available for decision makers as quickly as they might want.

(c) **Three types of MIS and how they would be used in an organisation**

Type of MIS	Detail
Transaction processing systems (TPS)	Collect, store, modify and retrieve the transactions of an organisation. A **transaction** is an event that generates or modifies data that is eventually stored on an information system. There are two types of TPS:
	Batch transaction processing (BTP) collects transaction data as a group and processes it later, after a time delay, as batches of identical data.
	Real time transaction processing (RTTP) is the immediate processing of data. It involves using a terminal or workstation to enter data and display results and provides instant confirmation.

Type of MIS	Detail
Executive information systems (EIS)	Give executives a straightforward means of access to **key internal and external data**. They provide summary-level data, captured from the organisation's main systems (which might involve integrating the executive's desktop PC with the organisation's mainframe), data manipulation facilities (such as comparison with budget or prior year data and trend analysis) and user-friendly presentation of data.
Enterprise resource planning systems (ERP)	Integrate the **key processes** in an organisation so that a single system can serve the information needs of all functional areas. They primarily support business operations including Finance, HR, Marketing and Accounting and work in real time, meaning that the exact status of everything is always available to all users. ERP systems can be deployed at sites around the world; they can work in multiple languages and currencies. When they are used this way, you can immediately see, for example, exactly how much of a particular part is to hand at the warehouse in Japan and what its value is in yen or dollars.

Part B answers

OTQ bank – Specialist cost and management accounting techniques

32   The correct answer is: All of the above.

A product's life cycle costs are incurred from its design stage through development to market launch, production and sales, and finally to its eventual decline and withdrawal from the market.

33   **This question appeared in the Sep/Dec 2020 exam.**

The correct answers are: Water purification treatment to clean waste water before it leaves the factory and Capturing and recycling of waste exhaust gases to generate energy.

Examination team comments.

Environmental costs can be categorised as prevention costs, detection cost, internal failure costs and external failure costs.

This question asks for the identification of the two environmental internal failure costs. These are costs relating to an environmental failure, for example pollution or wastage but where the failure has been identified and dealt with within the organisation before it manages to affect the external environment. Water purification treatment to clean waste water before it leaves the factory and capturing and recycling of waste exhaust gases to generate energy would be examples of environmental internal failure costs.

The key here is that waste water has been produced which is a failure cost, but it has been cleaned before leaving the factory, making it an internal failure cost. Likewise, waste exhaust gases have been produced, but these have been captured and recycled within the factory.

Environmental prevention costs relate to activities or measure which aim to avoid the pollution or wastage occurring. Insulation of heating pipes in the factory to reduce heat loss and fitting of carbon filters to machine processes to reduce carbon emissions would come under this heading.

Environmental detection costs relate to the costs incurred to test the levels of emissions and wastage to ensure that the organisation is being compliant with internal standards and external regulations. Quality control inspections to monitor pollution levels in water leaving a production process and power usage measuring system to monitor energy consumption within the factory would come under this heading.

External failure costs relate to pollution which has affected the outside environment. Payment of fines for breaching environmental regulations in the industry and public relations costs to remedy reputational damage caused by accidental river pollution would be examples of environmental external failure costs.

A number of candidates did not answer the question which was asked and instead gave the answer for the two environmental prevention costs, or the two environmental detection costs or the two environmental external failure costs.

Environmental management accounting is an important area and candidates should ensure that they are familiar with the different categories of environmental costs. They should also read the requirements of the question carefully.

34   The correct answer is: 3.41

Throughput per unit of Product X = $(40 − 10) = $30
Throughput per bottleneck hour = $30/0.01 hours = $3,000
Factory costs per year = $2,920,000 + (50,000 × $12) = $3,520,000
Factory cost per bottleneck hour = $3,520,000/4,000 hours = $880
Throughput accounting ratio = $3,000/$880 = 3.41

35 The correct answer is: Both are true

In MFCA, a distinction is made between good finished output (positive output) and waste and emissions (negative output). Both types of output are given a cost. Performance can be improved by finding ways to reduce the amount of negative output – and so achieve the same amount of output with less input materials.

36 The correct answer is: The cost driver for materials handling and despatch costs is likely to be the number of orders handled.

'The cost driver for quality inspection is likely to be batch size' is incorrect. The cost driver for quality inspection costs is likely to be either the number of units produced or the number of batches produced, depending on whether quality inspection is linked to batches produced or total production output. The batch size is not a factor that drives total inspection costs.

'In the short run, all the overhead costs for an activity vary with the amount of the cost driver for the activity' is incorrect. Some costs of activities may vary with the volume of the activity, but other costs of the activity will be fixed costs. ' A cost driver is an activity based cost' is incorrect. A cost driver is not the cost itself; it is a measure of the volume or quantity of an activity.

37 The correct answer is: Capping.

Operation		Wash Units	Fill Units	Cap Units	Label Units
(a)	Capacity in mins	(1,200 × 60) 72,000	(700 × 60) 42,000	(250 × 60) 15,000	(450 × 60) 27,000
(b)	Time in minutes per 12 units	6	3	1.5	2
Capacity in groups of 12 units ((a)/(b))		12,000	14,000	10,000	13,500

Therefore capping is the bottleneck as it is the process which determines the maximum number of units which can be produced.

38 **This question appeared in the Mar/Jun 2021 exam.**

The correct answer is: Forth

Examination team comments

As the products are all produced in the same factory the cost per machine hour will be the same across all the products so they can be ranked on their throughput return per machine hour (otherwise they should be ranked ion their throughput accounting ratio).

Product	Production rate per machine hours (units)	Throughput per unit (selling price - material cost per unit) $	Throughput per machine hour ($)	Ranking of products
W	200	230	(200 × $230) = 46,000	3rd
X	500	95	(500 × $95) = 47,500	2nd
Y	400	110	(400 × $110) = 44,000	4th
Z	350	140	(350 × $140) = 49,000	1st

The products would be ranked in order: Z, X, W and Y. Product Y would be ranked forth (last).

39 **This question appeared in the Sep/Dec 2020 exam.**

The correct answers are:

- ABC is useful for businesses which have high overheads in their cost structure

- Marginal costing understates the true cost of a product when compared to ABC

- ABC is better than absorption costing in understanding what causes costs to be incurred

If budgeted level of activity differs from actual level of activity, over-absorption or under-absorption of overheads may occur under ABC just as under absorption costing. This will have to be accounted for when reconciling the budgeted and actual profit under ABC. Hence, this answer option is incorrect.

ABC leads to a rational absorption of overheads and therefore it is particularly useful when overheads are high in the overall cost structure of a business. Hence, this answer option is correct.

ABC can be applied to both manufacturing and service industry. In fact, ABC is relevant in service industries where overheads account for a significant share of the total cost. Hence, this answer option is incorrect.

Marginal costing takes into account only variable costs whereas ABC accounts for all costs when computing the cost of a product. This means that ABC gives a better reflection of the true cost of a product unlike marginal costing which computes a lower cost. Hence, this answer option is correct.

ABC absorbs costs on the basis of cost driver units consumed in the making of a product or provision of a service. Cost drivers are specific actions that cause the costs to be incurred. As a result, ABC helps to understand what really drives costs. In contrast, absorption costing absorbs costs using rather generic or blanket factors for absorbing overheads. This does not help to ascertain what is driving costs. Hence, this answer option is correct.

ABC considers all costs, including fixed costs, when computing the cost of a product or service. This means ABC treats fixed costs as product costs. On the other hand, marginal costing does not absorb any fixed costs when computing the cost of a product; in fact, it treats all fixed costs as period costs i.e. relating to a specific time period. Hence, this answer option is incorrect.

40 The correct answer is: Environment-related costs can be attributed to joint cost centres and environment-driven costs cannot be

This is the correct option as environment-driven costs are allocated to general overheads, not joint cost centres.

41 The correct answer is: 3 only

ABC can be used for cost-plus pricing. Traditional absorption costing tends to allocate insufficient overhead costs to low-volume products that use up a disproportionate amount of time for order handling, production runs and set-ups. ABC is expensive and time-consuming to implement. It is therefore important to assess whether the benefits will outweigh the costs before implementing ABC.

42 The correct answers are: 'The majority of environmental costs are already captured within a typical organisation's accounting system. The difficulty lies in identifying them' is **true**. 'Input/output analysis divides material flows within an organisation into three categories: material flows; system flows; and delivery and disposal flows' is **false**.

Statement 2 refers to flow cost accounting rather than input/output analysis. Under the flow cost accounting technique, material flows within an organisation are divided into three categories: material flows; system flows; and delivery and disposal flows.

43   The correct answer is: Products should be discontinued if there is a target cost gap.

If there is a target cost gap that cannot be eliminated, management may consider whether or not to continue with the product, since it will not be achieving the required profit margin. However, a decision to discontinue a product, or whether to continue making it, should not be based on target costs or profit margins alone. Therefore the statement 'Products should be discontinued if there is a target cost gap' is NOT true and this is the correct answer.

For services that have a large fixed cost base, other methods of cost control may be more appropriate, such as activity-based management, and a key to reducing costs is often increasing sales volumes rather than reducing expenditure. To achieve a target cost, one approach is to remove design features from a product specification that do not add value for customers (so do not affect the price that customers are willing to pay).

44   The correct answer is: 500 units.

	A	B	C	D
Maximum sales demand	1,000	500	2,000	1,000
Selling price per unit	$15	$21	$18	$25
Material cost per unit	$6	$10	$9	$16
Throughput per unit	$9	$11	$9	$9
Machine hours per unit	0.1	0.2	0.3	0.2
Throughput per machine hour	$90	$55	$30	$45
Priority for manufacture	1st	2nd	4th	3rd

In the 750 hours available, the company should make 1,000 units of A (100 hours), then 500 units of B (100 hours), then 1,000 units of D (200 hours) leaving 350 hours available to make 1,166 units of Product C.

45   The correct answers are:

- Labour costs are a relatively minor proportion of total costs
- Overheads vary with many different measures of activity

That overheads are difficult to predict, and cost drivers difficult to identify, are not reasons to prefer ABC.

46   **This question appeared in the December 2017 exam**

The correct answer is: 12,000 units

First of all, the target cost needs to be calculated; the market price is $120 and the company has a target mark-up of 25% therefore the target cost is $120/125% = $96.

Of this target cost $46 is variable, leaving $50 which can be fixed.

The current budgeted fixed cost is $600,000 (10,000 units × $60) so if these are to be absorbed at $50/unit then the minimum production must be 12,000 units.

Selecting '11,778 units' meant that the target cost was calculated based on a 25% margin rather than a mark-up ie $120 × 75% = $90. The total costs were calculated to be $1,060,000 ($106 × 10,000 units) and then divided by the $90 so the variable costs were not removed from the $90 either.

Selecting '13,636 units' meant that the target cost was also calculated based on a 25% margin but the variable costs were deducted which left an incorrect fixed cost of $44. The total fixed costs were calculated correctly at $600,000 but were divided by $44.

Selecting '11,042 units' calculated the target cost correctly at $96 but did not adjust for the variable costs. The total costs of $1,060,000 were then divided by the $96.

OTQ bank – Specialist cost and management accounting techniques

47   The correct answer is: 2 only

Financial returns can be improved over the life cycle of a product by minimising the breakeven time, minimising the time to get a new product to market and maximising the length of the product life cycle.

48   The correct answers are:

- Unless output capacity is greater than sales demand, there will always be a binding constraint

- The production capacity of a bottleneck resource should determine the production schedule for the organisation as a whole

Output from a binding constraint should be used immediately, not built up as inventory, because it is the factor that constrains output and sales. Some inventory may build up before the binding constraint, but the general principle in throughput accounting is that any inventory is undesirable.

The production capacity of a bottleneck resource should determine the production schedule for the organisation as a whole. This means inevitably that there will be idle time in other parts of production where capacity is greater.

49   The correct answer is: $50.95

Variable costs	$
Year 1: $(30 + 6 + 4) × 25,000	1,000,000
Year 2: $(25 + 5 + 3) × 100,000	3,300,000
Year 3: $(20 + 4 + 2) × 75,000	1,950,000
R&D costs	940,000
Other fixed costs	3,000,000
Total life cycle costs	10,190,000
Total units made and sold	200,000
Average life cycle cost per unit	$50.95

50   The correct answers are: 'Target costing may be applied to services that are provided free of charge to customers' is false and the others are true.

Cost reduction measures may reduce the perceived value of a product to customers, so that the target selling price becomes unachievable for the sales volume required. The projected cost of a new product may be reduced by simplifying the design (such as using more standard components, fewer components in total and removing design features that do not add value), but simplification of the design should not reduce the value of the product for customers.

Overhead costs are usually a large proportion of total costs; therefore it is important to have reliable estimates of sales demand at a given target sales price in order to establish a target cost. Target costing is dependent on identifying a target selling price for an item, so it is not appropriate for costing services provided free of charge. Call centre costs, for example, should be managed using other methods of cost control.

51   The correct answer is: Output flows

Flow cost accounting divides the material flows into three categories: material, system and delivery and disposal.

52 The correct answers are:

- An important use of life cycle costing is to decide whether to go ahead with the development of a new product

- Life cycle costing encourages management to find a suitable balance between investment costs and operating expenses

A product is usually most profitable during the maturity phase of its life cycle. Life cycle costing is not particularly useful for deciding the selling price for a product, because the appropriate selling price changes over the life of a product.

By looking at the costs over the entire life cycle of a product, and comparing these with expected sales revenues, a decision can be taken at an early stage, before too much cost has been committed, about whether to go ahead with developing a new product. Life cycle costing also helps management to consider the merits of investing more money at the design stage for a new product if this will reduce operating costs over the product life cycle.

53 The correct answer is: Both 1 and 2

Factory labour costs are always treated as a part of the factory cost/conversion cost of a product. Throughput accounting does not make a distinction between direct and indirect costs. It is also assumed that labour costs are a fixed cost, so if machine time is the bottleneck resource, nothing is gained by improving labour efficiency, because this will not increase throughput.

54 The correct answer is: $362.50

Required return: $500,000 × 30% = $150,000
Total sales revenue: $550 × 800 units = $440,000
Therefore total cost = $440,000 – $150,000 = $290,000
Unit cost = $290,000/800 = $362.50

55 **This question appeared in the September 2017 exam.**

The correct answer is: 1, 2 and 3

Environmental failure costs are costs incurred as a result of environmental issues being created either internally or outside the company. These can be financial or societal costs. Compensation, penalties and air pollution are all environmental failure costs.

56 The correct answer is: $92.00

	Year 1 $'000	Year 2 $'000	Year 3 $'000	Year 4 $'000	Total $'000
R&D costs	900	300			1,200
Marketing	300	300	100	100	800
Production	400	400	750	300	1,850
Customer services	100	150	250	50	550
Disposal				200	200
Total					4,600
Units					50,000
Life cycle cost per unit					$92.00

57 The correct answer is: $80.00

The return per factory hour is measured using the bottleneck resource as a measure of factory hours. Return = Throughput

Return per machine hour = $(30 – 10)/0.25 hours = $80.00.

58 The correct answer is: 2.4

Throughput per unit of Product X = $(50 − 14) = $36.

Throughput per bottleneck hour = $36/0.05 hours = $720

Factory costs per year = $1,620,000 + (18,000 × $10) = $1,800,000

Factory cost per bottleneck hour = $1,800,000/6,000 hours = $300

Throughput accounting ratio = $720/$300 = 2.40.

59 The correct answers are:

- ABC recognises the complexity of modern manufacturing by the use of multiple cost drivers

- ABC establishes separate cost pools for support activities

Reapportionment of service centre costs is not done via ABC specifically. It would instead be done via the direct, step or reciprocal method under traditional absorption costing. If ABC is used to allocate costs it uses the cost driver approach, where costs are allocated to a cost pool and a cost driver is used to allocate to a product.

ABC is an appropriate system if overheads are high relative to prime costs and when there is significant diversity in the product range. If overheads could be allocated based solely on production time then traditional AC would be fine.

60 The correct answer is: Method 1 and Method 2

The aim should be to improve the output capacity of the binding constraint. This can be done by achieving more output per unit of binding resource (improving efficiency) or obtaining more of the resource that is the binding constraint.

By increasing output through the binding constraint, a point will eventually be reached where it ceases to be the binding constraint, and another resource becomes the binding constraint.

61 The correct answers are:

- Set up costs
- Raw material handling costs

These two costs are likely to increase, as batch sizes get smaller.

Remember, the whole aim of JIT is to hold no inventory. Thus raw material storage costs should fall, not rise. Customer order costs will not be changed by the introduction of JIT.

Brick by Brick

62 The correct answer is: $3,000

Overhead absorption rate is calculated as $400,000/40,000hrs = $10/hr

A GC takes 300 labour hours to complete.

300 × $10/hr = $3,000

63 The correct answer is: GC: $180

Supervisor costs of the **GC using ABC**.

1 **Cost drivers**

	Costs	Number of drivers	Cost per driver
	$		$
Supervisor	90,000	500	180

2 **Cost per product**

	Supervisor
Cost per driver (W1)	$180
GC	180 × 1 = 180

64   The correct answer is: EX: $1,400

Planning costs of the **EX using ABC.**

1   **Cost drivers**

	Costs	Number of drivers	Cost per driver
	$		$
Planning	70,000	250	280

2   **Cost per product**

	Planning
Cost per driver (W1)	$280
EX	280 × 5 = 1,400

65   The correct answer is: 'Changing to a system of ABC costing should lead to a more competitive price being charged for the GC' is **true**. 'Using ABC would cause total overhead costs to increase' is **false**.

ABC leads to more competitive pricing of the GC because it is allocated a fairer proportion of the total overheads. This will reflect the reality of the overheads that the GC is actually generating. Traditional absorption costing is more arbitrary which can lead to uncompetitive pricing.

Total overhead costs will be the same no matter which method of allocation is used, therefore 'Using ABC would cause total overhead costs to increase' is false.

66   The correct answer is: ABC improves pricing decisions.

It is ABC which gives a better indication of where cost savings can be made. BBB uses cost-plus pricing and so more accurate costs will lead to better pricing decisions.

ABC is expensive to implement and BBB currently has an absorption costing system set up.

ABC does not eliminate the need for cost apportionment. It may still be required at the cost pool stage for shared items such as rent.

Midhurst Co

67   The correct answers are: At the introduction stage, further capital expenditure will be needed as production capacity will need to increase to meet demand and The majority of a product's life-cycle costs are determined by decisions which are made at the design and development stage.

These statements are correct as capital expenditure is likely to increase at the introduction stage and the majority of a product's costs are determined at the outset.

'The maturity stage occurs when the market has reached 'saturation point' and bought enough of the product' defines the decline stage of the product lifecycle and ' The growth stage, when sales will have reached their peak and become stable, will be the most profitable stage' defines the maturity stage.

68   The correct answer is: $90,735

To calculate a cost per unit using life-cycle costing, the first step is to calculate the total cost over the full life-cycle of the product.

The total cost of the new product (in $000s) is $6,200 + $33,450 + $177,685 + ($42 x 10,000) + $98,470 +($9 x 10,000) + $10,300 + ($4 x 10,000) + $7,790 + $23,450 = $907,345

To calculate the cost per unit, divide the total cost by the number of units to be produced over the life-cycle of the product. $907,345,000/10,000 = $90,735.

69 The correct answer is: $6,940

Current variable material cost per unit = 20% × $42,000 = $8,400 Revised variable material cost per unit = (85% × ($8,400 - $2,000)) + (75% × $2,000) = $6,940.

70 The correct answer is: Maturity.

Normally product development occurs at the maturity phase in order to extend the profitable stage of the life-cycle. This is usually done by adding enhancements or new features.

71 The correct answer is: 1, 2 and 4 only.

Statements 1, 2 and 4 are correct. Statement 3 is an advantage of target costing and not life-cycle costing.

Jola Publishing Co

72 The correct answer is: $2.57 per unit

Number of units produced per year = 1,000,000 + (12 × 10,000) = 1,120,000 units

Overhead absorption rate is calculated as $2,880,000/1,120,000 units = $2.57/unit

73 The correct answer is:

Correct order	
Step 1	Identify major activities within each department which creates cost.
Step 2	Create a cost centre/cost pool for each activity – the 'activity cost pool'.
Step 3	Determine what causes the cost of each activity – the 'cost driver'.
Step 4	Calculate the absorption rate for each 'cost driver'.
Step 5	Calculate the overhead cost per unit of CB and TJ.

74 The correct answer is: $1,800,000

Production of CB takes a total of 100,000 hours at **$18 per machine hour**

Cost per driver

Cost pool	Cost $'000	Quantity of cost drivers	Rate per cost driver $	
Production costs	2,160	120,000*	18	per machine hour

* Number of machine hours

CB
1,000,000 units × 6 mins/60 = 100,000 hours

TJ
(10,000 × 12) units × 10 mins/60 = 20,000 hours

75 The correct answer is: $66,800

Quality control of the TJ : $3,340 per inspection × 20 inspections

Cost per driver

Cost pool	Cost $'000	Quantity of cost drivers	Rate per cost driver $	
Quality control	668	180 + 20 = 200	3,340	per inspection

BPP
LEARNING
MEDIA

76   The correct answer is: More accurate costs per unit.

Distracters:

- There will not be a reduction in overhead costs as a result of the adoption of ABC. However, management of Jola Publishing Co may benefit from improved decision-making regarding cost control, if they understand the cost drivers better.

- ABC tends to be a more expensive approach to absorption costing.

- ABC is a more complex form of costing.

Corrie

77   The correct answer is: $360,000.

Profit per day = throughput contribution − conversion cost

= [($80 × 6,000) + ($80 × 4,500) + ($200 × 1,200)] − $720,000 = $360,000

78   The correct answer is: 125%.

Product	Minutes in alpha per unit	Minutes in alpha per day
X	60/1,200 = 0.05	6,000 × 0.05 = 300
Y	60/1,500 = 0.04	4,500 × 0.04 = 180
Z	60/600 = 0.10	1,200 × 0.10 = 120
		600

Total hours = 600 minutes ÷ 60 = 10 hours

Hours available = 8, hours produced = 10, ∴ **Efficiency** = 10/8 × 100% = 125%

79   The correct answer is: $90,000

Conversion cost per factory hour = $720,000/8 = $90,000

80   The correct answer is:

X 1.2

Y 1.5

Z 1.5

TA ratio = throughput contribution per factory hour/conversion cost per factory hour

Product	Throughput contribution per factory hour	Cost per factory hour	TA ratio
X	$80 × (60 ÷ 0.05 mins) = $96,000	$80,000	1.2
Y	$80 × (60 ÷ 0.04 mins) = $120,000	$80,000	1.5
Z	$200 × (60 ÷ 0.10 mins) = $120,000	$80,000	1.5

81   The correct answers are:

- TA assumes that labour costs are largely fixed
- TA assumes that material costs can be controlled in the short term

There is a technical article on ACCA's website called 'Throughput accounting and the theory of constraints' which explains this.

'The TA ratio for each product should be less than 1' is incorrect. The TA ratio should be greater than 1.

'Corrie Co's priority, using TA, should be given to products with the highest throughput contribution per unit' is incorrect. Priority should be given to products with the highest throughput contribution per unit of bottleneck resource.

A Co

82   The correct answers are:

   B1 Department 1   40 units
   B1 Department 2   42 units
   B2 Department 1   30 units
   B2 Department 2   56 units

	Maximum number of B1 units	*Maximum number of B2 units*
Department 1	480/12 = 40	480/16 = 30
Department 2	840/20 = 42	840/15 = 56

83   The correct answer is: $1.93.

   The question requires us to use **traditional contribution analysis:**

   We need to calculate the contribution (sales less direct materials, labour and variable overheads) per unit of the bottleneck resource, which is time in Department 1. The contribution maximising output is found by dividing contribution per unit by the time in minutes required in Department 1.

		B1
	$	$
Sales price		50.00
Less variable costs		
Direct materials	10.00	
Direct labour	10.40	
Variable overheads	6.40	
		(26.80)
Contribution		23.20

   Contribution per unit of limiting factor $\dfrac{\$23.20}{12} = \$1.933$

84   The correct answer is: $3.13

   The **throughput approach** is based on throughput maximisation. Throughput is defined as **sales less direct materials**.

	B2
	$
Sales price	65
Less direct materials	(15)
	50

   Throughput per minute of bottleneck resource is:

	B2
	$
	50/16 = 3.125

85   The correct answer is: The throughput accounting approach is more suitable for short-term decision-making than limiting factor analysis

   The fundamental belief in throughput accounting is that all costs except direct material costs are largely fixed; therefore to work on the basis of maximising contribution is flawed because to do so is to take into account costs that cannot be controlled in the short term anyway. In most businesses, it is simply not possible to hire workers on a daily basis and lay workers off if they are not busy.

   Distracters:

   • In throughput accounting idle time must be accepted. To do otherwise can lead to non-bottleneck activities being falsely identified as bottleneck activities, and possibly obsolescence if products need to be stored for a period of time

- Bottlenecks cannot be eliminated, only the activity identified as the bottleneck can change
- A certain amount of buffer material may need to be held in order to maximise throughput through the bottleneck activity

86   The correct answer is:

Correct order	
Step 1	Identify A Co's bottlenecks.
Step 2	Decide how to exploit the system's bottlenecks.
Step 3	Subordinate everything else to the decisions made about exploiting the bottlenecks.
Step 4	Elevate the system's bottlenecks.

Step 1   Identify A Co's bottlenecks

Before any other work can be carried out, the bottleneck must first be identified.

Step 2   Decide how to exploit the system's bottlenecks

This involves making sure that the bottleneck resource is actively being used as much as possible and is producing as many units as possible.

Step 3   Subordinate everything else to the decisions made about exploiting the bottlenecks

The production capacity of the bottleneck resource should determine the production schedule for the organisation as a whole

Step 4   Elevate the system's bottlenecks

It is important that an organisation does not ignore Step 2 and jump straight to Step 4, which often happens. This ensures that no unnecessary capital investment occurs.

Cam Co

87   The correct answer is: $130

Target selling price per unit $200
Profit margin   35%
Target cost $200 − ($200 × 35%) = $130

88   The correct answer is: $21.60

Direct material cost

Parts to be replaced by standard parts = $40 × 80% = $32
New cost of standard parts at 45% (100% − 55%) = $14.40
Unique irreplaceable parts (original cost) = $40 × 20% = $8
New cost = $8 × 90% = $7.20
Revised direct material cost = $14.40 + $7.20 = $21.60

89   The correct answer is: $10.98.

Direct labour

$Y = ax^b$

$b = -0.152$ (given in question)

The question states that a learning curve of 90% is expected to occur until the 100th unit has been completed.

Total labour time for first 100 units

$x = 100$

The question states that the first unit is expected to take 45 minutes (a = 45)

$Y = 45 \times 100^{-0.152}$
    $= 45 \times (1/2.0137)$
    $= 22.3469$ minutes

Therefore, labour time for 100 units = 22.3469 × 100 = 2,234.69 minutes

Labour time for the 100th unit

Time for 99 units

$Y = 45 \times 99^{-0.152}$
    $= 45 \times (1/2.01065)$
    $= 22.38082$ minutes

Therefore, labour time for 99 units = 22.38082 × 99 = 2,215.70 minutes

Therefore, time for 100th unit = 2,234.69 − 2,215.70 = 18.99 minutes, say 19 minutes

Labour time for remaining 49,900 units × 19 = 948,100 minutes
Total labour time for 50,000 units = 2,234.69 + 948,100 = 950,334.69 minutes

Therefore, total labour cost = (950,334.69/60) × $34.67 per hour = $549,135
Average labour cost per unit = $549,135/50,000 = $10.98

90   The correct answer is: Both statements are false.

Cam Co's target costing system may take product development costs into consideration, but recovery of product design and development costs is associated more with life cycle costing. Even with life cycle costing, recovery of design and development costs is not assured: much depends on whether customers will buy enough webcams at the target price.

In target costing, a cost gap is the difference between the current estimate of the cost per webcam and the target cost that Cam Co wants to achieve.

91   The correct answer is: Use cheaper labour

Changes to selling price will have no effect upon target cost. The remaining options (employ more specialist staff; increase the number of bespoke components) would serve to increase the target cost gap rather than decrease it. Using cheaper labour (assuming this does not affect quality) would be a method of reducing the cost gap.

Yam Co

92   The correct answer is:

Product A: 450,000 metres
Product B: 450,000 metres
Product C: 562,500 metres

Output capacity for each process

Total processing hours for the factory = 225,000

	Product A Metres	Product B Metres	Product C Metres
Pressing	225,000/0.50 = 450,000	225,000/0.50 = 450,000	225,000/0.40 = 562,500

93   The correct answer is: $90

Conversion cost   = Labour costs + factory costs
                   = (225,000 hours × $10) + $18,000,000
                   = $20,250,000

Conversion cost per factory hour = $20,250,000/225,000 hours = $90

94   The correct answer is: $115

Return per factory hour = Sales − direct costs/usage of bottleneck resource in hours

	Product B $
Selling price per metre	60.00
Raw material cost per metre	2.50
Return	57.50
Usage of bottleneck resource in hours	0.50
Return per factory hour	115.00

95   The correct answer is: 1.41

Throughput accounting ratios

TPAR = Return per factory hour/total conversion cost per factory hour

Return per factory hour = Sales − direct costs/usage of bottleneck resource in hours

	Product A $
Return per factory hour	134.00
Conversion cost per factory hour	95.00
TPAR	1.41

96   The correct answer is: Both statements are true.

The theory of constraints is based on the view that the focus should be on elevating a bottleneck resource to the level where it ceases to be a bottleneck, and at this time a new bottleneck will 'take over'. The throughput accounting ratio is the ratio of return per factory hour divided by cost per factory hour. If this ratio is less than 1, the commercial viability of Yam Co's product should be questioned.

Ivey Co

97   The correct answer is: $24.54 per unit

Total component costs ($12.00 × 5,000) + ($10.00 × 7,500) = $135,000

Total labour costs ($14.00 × 5,000) + ($12.00 × 7,500) = $160,000

Fixed production costs = $5,000 + $4,500 = $9,500

Fixed selling and distribution costs = $1,000 + $1,200 = $2,200

Total costs = $135,000 + $160,000 + $9,500 + $2,200 = $306,700

Total units = 5,000 + 7,500 = 12,500 units

Cost per unit = $306,700/12,500 units = $24.54 (to two decimal places)

98   The correct answers are:

Scales concept design costs	INCLUDED
Scales testing costs	INCLUDED
Scales production costs	INCLUDED
Scales distribution costs	INCLUDED

Life cycle costs are incurred from design through to withdrawal from the market so all of the costs would be included.

99   The correct answers are:

- • LCC aims to ensure that a profit is generated over the entire life of the Diam
- • LCC ensures that the price set for the Diam is based on better knowledge of costs

LCC tracks and accumulates all costs and revenues relating to the Diam over its life and therefore helps to ensure that a profit is generated. Because the total profitability can be determined, this gives Ivey Co better information on which to base the price of the Diam.

'LCC focuses on the short-term by identifying costs at the beginning of the Diam's life cycle' is not correct. LCC looks at the entire life of a product or service and therefore considers the long term.

'LCC writes off costs to each stage of the Diam's life cycle' is not correct. The life cycle cost is the total cost of all stages of the life of the product or service.

100   The correct answer is: Statement 1 is true and Statement 2 is false

The main disadvantages of LCC are that it is costly and time consuming to operate.

101   The correct answer is: At the design and development stage

Research has shown that, for organisations operating within an advanced manufacturing technology environment, as Ivey Co does, approximately 90% of a product's life-cycle cost is determined by decisions made early within the life cycle. In such an environment there is therefore a need to ensure that the tightest cost controls are at the design stage, because the majority of costs are committed at this point.

Part C answers

OTQ bank – Decision-making techniques

102 The correct answer is: 2 only.

The decision options are given expected values, not the various different possible outcomes from each decision option. Each possible outcome is given a value, but not an expected value (EV).

103 The correct answer is: Z3 1st   Z2 2nd   Z1 3rd

	Z1	Z2	Z3
Materials per unit	7 kg	4 kg	2 kg
	$	$	$
Profit per unit	40	35	30
Add back fixed overheads	30	25	20
Contribution per unit	70	60	50
Contribution per kg	10	15	25
Ranking	3rd	2nd	1st

104 The correct answer is: 2 only

A price in excess of full cost per unit will not necessarily ensure that a company will cover all its costs and make a profit. Making a profit with cost plus pricing also depends on working at a sufficient capacity level, so that all fixed costs are covered by sales revenue.

Cost plus pricing is an appropriate pricing strategy when there is no comparable market price for the product or service.

105 The correct answer is: 200%

Breakeven point = $20,000 = 500 × (selling price – $20)

$20,000/500 = $40

$40 = selling price – $20

$60 = selling price

Profit mark up on marginal cost = ($60 – $20) / $20 × 100% = 200%

Note. Fixed overheads ($40) are omitted, as only marginal costs are included in the calculation of the profit or 'contribution' to the recovery in the fixed costs of $20,000.

106 **This question appeared in the December 2017 exam.**

The correct answer is: 44%

In order to calculate the margin of safety, the break-even point must first be calculated. The break-even point is calculated by dividing fixed costs by the contribution per unit. In this example fixed costs are budgeted to be $150,000 (10,000 units × $15 per unit) and the contribution per unit is $27 ($60 - $12 - $15 - $3 - $3) which would give a break-even point of 5,556 units.

Note. in the contribution calculation includes the deduction of the 5% sales commission as this is a variable cost related to the sales price. The margin of safety % is then calculated by (budgeted sales units – break even sales units)/budgeted sales units therefore in this example (10,000 – 5,556)/10,000 = 44%.

Selecting 80% would have been based on calculating the margin of safety as a % of the BEP units ie 4,444/5,556.

Selecting 50% meant that the sales commission had been missed in the calculation of the contribution per unit.

Selecting option 55% meant that both the variable production overhead and the sales commission had been missed in the calculation of the contribution per unit.

107 **This question appeared in the June 2017 exam.**

The correct answer is: $75

The relevant cost of diverting labour away from existing production when the resource is being used at full capacity is the variable cost of a labour hour + opportunity cost. The opportunity cost in this case would be the contribution of product P lost for every hour diverted away from its production. As each unit of P takes one labour hour the opportunity cost per labour hour is $25 and the cost per labour hour must be $30 (from the cost card). Therefore the relevant cost of labour is $55. Note that the question asks for the total relevant cost of labour and variable overheads. As these overheads are variable they are incurred when production happens and so are relevant and the variable overheads cost per hour is $20 (from the cost card). The total relevant cost of labour and variable overheads is $75

108 The correct answer is: $2,802,000

When sales revenue is $1.5 million, total contribution is 45% × $1.5 million = $675,000.

This leaves a further $625,000 of fixed costs to cover. To achieve breakeven, sales in excess of $1.5 million need to be $625,000/0.48 = $1.302 million.

Total sales to achieve breakeven = $1.5 million + $1.302 million = $2.802 million.

109 The correct answer is: Opportunity cost

The question provides a definition of opportunity cost. An opportunity cost is a relevant cost for the purpose of decision-making, but the definition in the question is too narrow to fit the term 'relevant cost'.

110 The correct answer is: $2,750

	FP1	FP2	Total
Input to further processing (kg)	5,500	4,000	
Finished output (kg)	4,950	3,800	
	$	$	$
Revenue from sales of FP1/FP2	44,550	34,200	
Relevant further processing costs	(11,000)	(12,000)	
Revenue from sales of CP1/CP2	(33,000)	(20,000)	
	550	2,200	2,750

111 The correct answer is: Choice 4

EV of Choice 1 = $9,500
EV of Choice 2 = (0.3 × 14,000) + (0.3 × 10,000) + (0.4 × 5,000) = $9,200
EV of Choice 3 = (0.4 × 10,000) + (0.6 × 9,000) = $9,400
EV of Choice 4 = (0.7 × 8,000) + (0.3 × 14,000) = $9,800

112 The correct answer is: Simulation modelling

A unique feature of simulation modelling using the Monte Carlo method is the use of random numbers to determine the value of input variables to the model.

113 **This question appeared in the June 2019 exam.**

The correct answer is: 1 only

If a resource constraint does not pass through the optimum point on the graph then its shadow price is zero, as adding another unit of that resource will not change the optimum solution nor the contribution earned.

The shadow price is the maximum extra a company would pay for one more unit of scarce resource on top of its existing cost.

The slope or gradient of the objective function depends on the contribution earned by each product.

BPP
LEARNING
MEDIA

ANSWERS

114 The correct answer is: Up to but not including $12.50

The shadow price of a limiting resource is the amount above the normal variable cost that will be added to the objective function (total contribution) if one extra unit of the resource is made available. This means that the company would increase contribution by paying up to $(8 + 4.50) = $12.50 per hour for additional labour time. However, it would not pay exactly $12.50, as this would leave it no better and no worse off than if it did not have the extra labour hour.

115 The correct answers are:

- The final sales value of the joint product
- The further processing cost of the joint product

When deciding whether or not to process further a joint product, the final sales value of the joint product is deducted from the sum of the further processing cost of the joint product and the opportunity cost of further processing (ie the sales value of the joint product at the separation point).

116 The correct answer is: $1.50 per hour for the next 38,000 direct labour hours

If one extra direct labour hour is available, the optimal solution will change to the point where:

(1): sales demand for X	x	=	10,000
(2): direct labour	5x + 4y	=	60,001
Multiply (1) by 5			
(3)	5x	=	50,000
Subtract (3) from (2)	4y	=	10,001
	y	=	2,500.25

Total contribution = $(10,000 × $8) + $(2,500.25 × $6) = $80,000 + $15,001.15 = $95,001.50

Total contribution in original solution = $(10,000 × $8) + $(2,500 × $6) = $95,000

The shadow price per direct labour hour is therefore $1.50

The solution is changing because each additional labour hour allows the company to produce an additional 0.25 units of Product Y, to increase total contribution by $1.50.

This shadow price will cease to apply when the direct labour hours constraint is replaced in the optimal solution by the sales demand for Product Y constraint. At this level of output, total labour hours would be (10,000 units of X at 5 hours) + (12,000 units of Y at 4 hours) = 98,000 hours.

The shadow price of $1.50 per hour therefore applies for an additional 38,000 hours above the current limit.

OTQ bank – Decision-making techniques

117 The correct answer is: Total revenue will fall and profit will fall.

If demand is price-inelastic, a reduction in price will result in a fall in total sales revenue. At the lower price, there will be some increase in sales demand, so total costs will increase. With falling revenue and increasing costs, profits will fall.

118 The correct answer is: 1 only.

In circumstances of inelastic demand, prices should be increased because revenues will increase and total costs will reduce (because quantities sold will reduce).

Price elasticity of demand is measured as the amount of change in quantity demanded (measured as a percentage of the current sales volume) divided by the amount of change in sales price (measured as a percentage of the current sales price).

$$\frac{\text{The change in quantity demanded, as a \% of demand}}{\text{The change in price, as a \% of the price}}$$

119 The correct answer is: W, Y, X then Z

Product	W	X	Y	Z
Extra cost of external purchase	$1	$2.1	$2	$1
Direct labour hours per unit	0.1	0.3	0.25	0.2
Extra cost per hour saved by purchasing	$10	$7	$8	$5
Priority for external purchasing	4th	2nd	3rd	1st
Priority for making in-house	1st	3rd	2nd	4th

120 The correct answer is: Price discrimination

Price discrimination involves charging different prices in two or more different markets. This is only effective when the markets can be kept entirely separate – such as charging different prices for different age groups (children and old age pensioners), or charging a different price for a product or service at different times of the day or week.

121 **This question appeared in the Mar/Jun 2021 exam.**

The correct answers are:

Joint costs are relevant in decisions about whether to sell a joint product at the split-off (separation) point or after further processing.		**FALSE**
The relevant costs and revenues in decisions relating to the operating of internal service departments or the use of external services, are the differential costs between the two options.	**TRUE**	

Examination team comments

Joint costs are not relevant in decisions about whether to sell a joint product at the split-off point or after further processing. When making a decision about further processing, the relevant costs are the incremental revenues from selling after further processing and the incremental costs of further processing. Where the incremental revenues exceed the incremental costs, then further processing is financially worthwhile.

The relevant costs and revenues in decisions relating to the operating of internal service departments or the use of external services are the differential costs between the two options.

122 The correct answer is: $7,500

EV of Project 1 = (0.1 × 70,000) + (0.4 × 10,000) – (0.5 × 7,000) = $7,500
EV of Project 2 = (0.1 × 25,000) + (0.4 × 12,000) + (0.5 × 5,000) = $9,800
EV of Project 3 = (0.1 × 50,000) + (0.4 × 20,000) – (0.5 × 6,000) = $10,000

Project 3 would be chosen on the basis of EV without perfect information. With perfect information, this decision would be changed to Project 1 if market research indicates strong demand and Project 2 if market research indicates weak demand.

EV with perfect information: (0.1 × 70,000) + (0.4 × 20,000) + (0.5 × 5,000) = $17,500

Value of perfect information = $(17,500 – 10,000) = $7,500 – ignoring the cost of obtaining the information.

123 The correct answer is: $376

	$
Additional purchases (5 tonnes × $50)	250
Relevant cost of material M already held:	
higher of $126 and (3 × $35)	126
Relevant cost total	376

124 The correct answer is: There are two breakeven points: $5.64 million and $6.36 million

Note that because there are two levels of fixed costs, there must be two breakeven points.

	$
Total cost at sales of $6.8 million	6,560,000
Deduct step increase in fixed costs	(400,000)
Total cost excluding step cost increase	6,160,000
Total cost at sales of $5.2 million	5,440,000
Therefore variable cost of sales of $1.6 million	720,000

Variable cost = 720,000/1,600,000 = 45% of sales. Contribution/sales ratio is 55%.

	$
Total cost at sales of $6.8 million	6,560,000
Variable cost (45%)	(3,060,000)
Fixed cost	3,500,000

If fixed costs are $3.5 million at the higher sales level and $3.1 million at the lower sales level.

When fixed costs are $3.1 million, breakeven sales = $3.1 million/0.55 = $5.636 million

When fixed costs are $3.5 million, breakeven sales = $3.5 million/0.55 = $6.363 million

125 The correct answer is: P1

	Weekly contribution			
	Price P1	Price P2	Price P3	Price P4
	$	$	$	$
Best possible	30,000	31,500	32,000	31,500
Most likely	24,000	26,250	28,000	27,000
Worst possible	18,000	17,500	16,000	13,500

The maximin decision rule is to select the price offering the maximum possible benefit under the worst of circumstances. (It is similar to the minimax rule for decisions on minimising cost.) Price P1 will provide the biggest weekly contribution under the worst of circumstances, which is a contribution of $18,000 if the worst possible demand occurs. Only the bottom line of the above table needs to be calculated for your answer. The full table is shown here for the sake of completeness.

126 The correct answer is: $1.968 million

Breakeven sales = $(2.4 million – 400,000) = $2,000,000

Contribution at this level of sales = $360,000. Therefore contribution/sales ratio = 360,000/2,000,000 = 18%

Variable costs = 82% of sales. At a sales level of $2.4 million, variable costs = 82% × $2.4 million = $1.968 million

127 The correct answer is: 4,000 units of W and 4,000 units of Z

Material	W	X	Y	Z
	$	$	$	$
Extra cost per unit of external purchase	1	6	3	2
Total extra cost of external purchase	4,000	12,000	9,000	8,000
Fixed costs saved by not making in-house	(5,000)	(8,000)	(6,000)	(7,000)
Difference	(1,000)	4,000	3,000	1,000

It would save $1,000 in cash to buy Material W externally. If full production can be achieved for the other materials, only W would be purchased externally. However, there is insufficient capacity to produce all three materials in-house.

Only 8,000 units can be produced in-house. If all the requirement for W is purchased externally (4,000 units), at least 1,000 units of X, Y or Z must be purchased externally too. The additional cost of buying Z externally is the least of these three.

If in-house production of Material Z is reduced to 3,000 units, the additional cost of external purchase would be only $6,000, so that $1,000 would be saved by purchasing all of Z externally.

128 **This question appeared in the March 2019 exam.**

The correct answer is: $20,400

To determine the minimum revenue required to break even, ie the break-even revenue, the break-even point for each product needs to be calculated. To do that the contribution per unit for each product needs to be established.

	Product X	Product Y
Contribution per unit (C/S ratio ×selling price)	0.3 × $3.00 = $0.90	0.5 × $4.80 = $2.40
Break-even point (Fixed costs /contribution per unit)	$9,000/$0.90 = 10,000 units	$9,000/$2.40 = 3,750 units
Maximum demand	8,000 units	3,000 units

From the table above, either 10,000 units of Product X or 3,750 units of Product Y need to be produced to break-even. However, as there is a maximum demand for both products, the break-even sales units cannot be achieved on either product. If the break-even point cannot be achieved with only one of the products, then the combination of units of Products X and Y to be sold in order to break even needs to be determined.

To do this, the product with the highest contribution per unit would be produced first, up to its maximum demand, to cover the fixed costs as quickly as possible. Product Y contributes $2.40 per unit, so it will be produced first, up to its maximum demand of 3,000 units, giving a total contribution of (3,000 units x $2.40) $7,200. Therefore sales of Product Y would cover $7,200 of the fixed costs but there will be $1,800 of fixed costs remaining, which need to be covered by sales of Product X.

Production of Product X will therefore be (remaining fixed costs/contribution per unit of Product X - $1,800/$0.90) = 2,000 units.

As the question asks for the minimum revenue (break-even revenue), the last step would be to calculate the sales revenue from the production plan calculated above.

Product X sales revenue = 2,000 units × $3.00 = $6,000

Product Y sales revenue = 3,000 units × $ 4.80 = $14,400

The minimum sales revenue required to break even would therefore be $ 20,400

129 The correct answer is: Statements 1 and 2 only

When the price elasticity of demand is elastic, a reduction in price by x% will increase the quantity demanded by more than x% and as a result total sales revenue will increase. Without knowing about marginal costs, it is not possible to determine whether profits would increase or fall.

130 The correct answer is: $1,500

EV of Project 1 = (0.2 × 80,000) + (0.4 × 50,000) − (0.4 × 5,000) = $34,000
EV of Project 2 = (0.2 × 60,000) + (0.4 × 25,000) + (0.4 × 10,000) = $26,000

Project 1 would be chosen on the basis of EV without perfect information. With perfect information, this decision would be changed to Project 2 if market research indicates weak demand.

EV with perfect information: (0.2 × 80,000) + (0.4 × 50,000) + (0.4 × 10,000) = $40,000

Value of perfect information = $(40,000 − 34,000) − $4,500 cost = $1,500

131 The correct answer is: $5.188 million

Weighted average sales price per unit = [(20 × 2) + (18 × 3) + (24 × 5)]/(2 + 3 + 5) = $21.40
Weighted average variable cost per unit = [(11 × 2) + (12 × 3) + (18 × 5)]/(2 + 3 + 5) = $14.80
Therefore weighted average contribution per unit = $(21.40 − 14.80) = $6.60
Weighted average C/S ratio = 6.60/21.40 = 0.3084112

Sales required to achieve target contribution of $1.6 million = $1.6 million/0.3084112 = $5.188 million.

132 The correct answer is: To gain insight into which assumptions or variables in a situation are critical

Sensitivity analysis can be used to identify how much the outcome from a situation or decision would be different if the value of an input variable changes. In this way, the input variables that are most critical to the situation or decision can be identified. Sensitivity analysis can also be described as assessing how projected performance or outcome will be affected by changes in the assumptions that have been used.

133 The correct answer is: $96

An increase in price of $25 will result in a fall in demand quantity by 6,250 units. Each $1 change in price therefore results in a change in demand by 6,250/25 = 250 units.

Demand Q will be 0 when the price P is $145 + $(5,000/250) = $165
Demand function = 165 – Q/250 = 165 – 0.004Q
Marginal revenue = 165 – 0.008Q

Profit is maximised when marginal revenue equals marginal cost:

When 27 = 165 – 0.008Q, so Q = 138/0.008 = 17,250

Price = 165 – (17,250/250) = $96

134 **This question appeared in the June 2020 exam.**

The correct answer is: $35 million

Go through each of the figures in Division A and decide how they will be affected if the division is shut down.

Product	Division A $ million
Lost revenue	(1,000)
Saved variable costs	400
Saved divisional fixed costs	650
Saved allocated head office costs (50%)	25
Overall saving	75

The current total divisional net loss is $110m ($100m + $10m). If Division A is shut down there will be an overall saving of $75m, therefore the revised total divisional net loss will be $110m - $75m = $35m.

It is important to read the requirements of the question carefully. A common mistake was to give the answer as $75m, which showed that candidates did not fully read the requirements.

135 The correct answer is: $4.00

If one extra direct labour hour is available, the optimal solution will change to the point where:

(1): direct labour hours	2x + 4y	=	10,001
(2): materials	4x + 2y	=	14,000
Multiply (1) by 2			
(3)	4x + 8y	=	20,002
Subtract (2) from (3)	6y	=	6,002
	y	=	1,000.333
Substitute in (2)	4x + 2,000.667	=	14,000
	×	=	2,999.8333

Total contribution = $(2,999.833 × $12) + $(1,000.333 × $18) = $35,998 + $18,006 = $54,004

Total contribution in original solution = $(3,000 × $12) + $(1,000 × $18) = $54,000

The shadow price per direct labour hour is therefore $54,004 - $54,000 = $4

136 The correct answers are:

- If the aim is to minimise costs, the solution is where the total cost line touching the feasible area at a tangent is as close to the origin as possible.

- If the aim is to maximise profit, the solution is where the total contribution line touching the feasible area at a tangent is as far away from the origin as possible.

If the aim is to minimise costs, the solution is where the total cost line touching the feasible area at a tangent, is as close to the origin as possible as this will allow the company to make as little as possible given constraints. If the aim is to maximise profit, the solution is where the total contribution line touching the feasible area at a tangent, is as far away from the origin as possible as this will allow the company to make as much as possible given contraints.

All other statements are false.

Home Electrics Co

137 The correct answer is $17

From the scenario, it is stated that the limiting factor for Product T in the first quarter was direct materials. The calculation is therefore the contribution per kg of direct materials.

Selling price	$120
Variable cost ($15 + $35 + $18)	$68
Contribution ($120 − $68)	$52
Kgs of material required per unit	3
Contribution per kg of material ($52/3)	$17.33

The answer is to be provided to the nearest whole $, therefore $17.

138 The correct answer is $35,600

The constraint equations are given:

Materials 2B + 3T = 2,000 (1)

Skilled Labour 3B + 5T = 3,200 (2)

To solve the simultaneous equations, we must multiply the equations so that we end up with the value of Bs or the value of Ts the same. We could multiply equation (1) by 5 and (2) by 3 to give:

10B + 15T = 10,000 (3)

9B + 15T = 9,600 (4)

Now we can eliminate the Ts by deducting equation (4) from equation (3). This leaves us with

1B = 400.

We can calculate the value of T, by using B = 400 in any of the equations. Using equation (1):

(2 × 400) + 3T = 2,000

800 + 3T = 2,000

3T = 1,200

Therefore, T = 400

Now that we know the quantities of B and T, we can calculate the total contribution.

The contribution of B = ($80 − $10 − $21 − $12) = $37.

The contribution of T = ($120 − $15 − $35 − $18) = $52.

The total contribution is therefore (37 × 400) + (52 × 400) = $35,600

139   The correct answer is Neither statement is true

The first statement is incorrect. Linear programming identifies the optimum number of units of each product to produce, not the optimum selling price.

The second statement is incorrect. Slack occurs when less of the limited resource is required than is available. When slack occurs, there will be some of the resource left over after production after production of the optimum production pan.

140   The correct answer is: $0

It is possible that this question could have caught many candidates out, if they had not read the scenario carefully. There are three constraints for the Large Applicances division (labour hours, material and machine hours). It is stated in the scenario that labour and machine time have been identified as the binding constraints. This suggests that material is NOT a binding constraint, and therefore will have a shadow price of $0. Only binding constraints will have a shadow price.

141   The correct answer is: 1, 2 and 3.

Work through each statement and decide if it is true.

(1)   Product D has a slack value. At the optimum solution, the demand for product D is 250, while the output is 200. Product D has unfulfilled demand at the optimum solution, so it has a slack value. This statement is true.

(2)   Contribution of $76,000 will be earned from the optimum production plan. The optimum production plan is to produce 240 units of product F and 200 units of product D. The total contribution will be (240 x $150) + (200 x $200) = $76,000. This statement is true.

(3)   Labour and machine time intersect at the optimum point if shown on a graph. As labour and machine time are the binding constraints, they will be the vertex where the optimum point occurs on a linear programming graph. This statement is true.

Cuckoo Co

142   The correct answer is: 800 units

Breakeven units = Fixed overheads / Contribution per unit

= ($8 × 1,200 units) / ($27 − $15) = 800 units

143   The correct answer is: 1,384 units

Sales volume to achieve a target profit = (Fixed cost + Target profit) / Contribution per unit

= ($10,000 + $6,600) / ($27 − $15) = 1,384 (rounded up)

144   The correct answer is: $664,000

Weighted average C/S ratio

	Contribution		Revenue	
	Per unit	Total	Per unit	Total
	$	$'000	$	$'000
Product C (15,000 units)	18	270	30	450
Product S (20,000 units)	17	340	20	400
Product D (10,000 units)	18	180	37	370
		790		1,220

Weighted average C/S ratio = $790 / $1,220 = 0.647541

Fixed cost = ($10 × 15,000) + (9 × 20,000) + (10 × 10,000) = $430,000

Breakeven sales revenue = Fixed costs/C/S ratio = $430,000 / 0.647541 = $664,051 = $664,000 to the nearest $'000

145 The correct answers are:

Point X is the breakeven point.		FALSE
Product D is the most profitable product in terms of C/S ratio.	TRUE	
Point Y is the fixed cost amount	TRUE	

The breakeven point is the point where the solid line crosses the x axis.

A PV chart shows products from left to right in order of the size of their C/S ratio there Product D has the highest C/S ratio and Product S has the lowest C/S ratio.

Point Y is the fixed cost amount.

146 The correct answer is: The average profit which will be earned from sales of three products in this mix.

BDU Co

147 The correct answer is: $500

The **maximin** decision rule involves choosing the outcome that offers the **least unattractive worst outcome**, in this instance choosing the outcome which **maximises the minimum contribution**.

Demand/price	Minimum contribution
1,000/$425	$165,000
730/$500	$175,200
420/$600	$142,800

BDU would therefore set a price of **$500**.

148 The correct answer is: $425

The **minimax regret** decision rule involves choosing the **outcome that minimises the maximum regret** from making the wrong decision, in this instance choosing the outcome which **minimises the opportunity loss** from making the wrong decision.

We can draw up an **opportunity loss table.**

Variable cost		Price	
	$425	$500	$600
$170	–	$14,100	$74,400 (W1)
$210	–	$3,300	$51,200 (W2)
$260	$10,200	–	$32,400 (W3)
Minimax regret	$10,200	$14,100	$74,400

Minimax regret strategy (price of $425) is that which minimises the maximum regret ($10,200).

Workings

1   At a variable cost of $170 per day, the best strategy would be a price of $425. The opportunity loss from setting a price of $600 would be $(255,000 – 180,600) = $74,400.

2   At a variable cost of $210 per day, the best strategy would be a price of $425. The opportunity loss from setting a price of $600 would be $(215,000 – 163,800) = $51,200.

3   At a variable cost of $260 per day, the best strategy would be a price of $500. The opportunity loss from setting a price of $600 would be $(175,200 – 142,800) = $32,400.

149   The correct answer is: $425

Expected values calculations:

$425: (255,000 × 0.4) + (215,000 × 0.25) + (165,000 × 0.35) = $213,500

$500: (240,900 × 0.4) + (211,700 × 0.25) + (175,200 × 0.35) = $210,605

$600: (180,600 × 0.4) + (163,800 × 0.25) + (142,800 × 0.35) = $163,170

150   The correct answers are:

- Market research
- Focus groups

Market research is used to obtain data about customer/consumer attitudes and preferences to products or markets, and the quantitative or qualitative information obtained from market research can help to reduce uncertainty for some elements of decision-making, such as pricing and product design decisions.

Like market research, focus groups reduce uncertainty by providing information and the information will influence decisions such as pricing decisions.

151   The correct answer is: Statement 1 is correct and statement 2 is incorrect.

The first statement 1 is correct. Expected values are more valuable as a guide to decision-making where they refer to outcomes that will occur many times. They represent a long-run average. Statement 2 is incorrect. The average profit calculated may not correspond to any of the possible outcomes, and this is a limitation of expected value analysis.

Metallica Co

152   The correct answers are: Product P4 $70, Product P6 $100

	Product P4	Product P6
	$	$
Selling price	125	175
Opportunity cost		
Direct materials:		
M1	15	10
M2	10	20
Direct labour	20	30
Variable overhead	10	15
Total variable costs	55	75
Contribution/unit	70	100

153   The correct answer is: The contribution per limiting factor of P4 and P6 is $113.33 and $190 respectively, therefore P6 should be produced first.

The most profitable course of action can be determined by ranking the products and components according to **contribution per unit of the limiting factor**. Direct material M1 is the limiting factor in this case, therefore the highest rank will be given to the product/component with the greatest contribution per m^2 of this material.

Contribution/unit	85	95
m^2 of M1/unit	0.75	0.5
Contribution/m^2	$113.33	$190
Ranking	2	1

154   The correct answers are:

Selling price	YES	
Direct materials	YES	
Direct labour		NO

In throughput accounting, a very similar calculation to limiting factor analysis is performed. However, in throughput accounting, it is not contribution per unit of scarce resource which is calculated, but throughput return per unit of bottleneck resource. Throughput is calculated as 'selling price less direct material cost'. This is different from the calculation of 'contribution', in which both labour costs and variable overheads are also deducted from selling price.

155   The correct answers are:

Limited demand for P4 or P6	YES	
Limited M1 or M2	YES	
Limited labour	YES	

Firms face many constraints on their activities and have to plan accordingly.

156   The correct answer is:

Correct order	
Step 1	Calculate the contribution per unit for each product
Step 2	Calculate the contribution per unit of the scarce resource for each product
Step 3	Rank the products in order of the contribution per unit of the scarce resource
Step 4	Allocate resources using the ranking

T Co

157   The correct answer is: $500

One of the three engineers has spare capacity to complete the installation and their salary will be paid regardless of whether they work on the contract for Push Co. The relevant cost is therefore $Nil.

The other two engineers are currently fully utilised and earn a contribution of $200 per week each on Contract X. The engineers could be temporarily taken off of Contract X to work on the contract for Push Co. Work on Contract X would recommence in one week's time when there is no other scheduled work for the engineers.

Delaying the work on Contract X would result in T Co missing the contractual completion deadline and having to pay a one-off penalty of $500.

Relevant cost = $500

158   The correct answer is: $2,184

120 handsets would need to be supplied to Push Co. Though 80 handsets are already in inventory, the handsets are frequently requested by T Co's customers and so would need to be replaced if supplied to Push Co. The current cost of a handset is $18.20.

Relevant cost = $18.20 × 120 handsets = $2,184

159   The correct answer is: $7,600

The current market price of Swipe 2 is $10,800.

The original cost of Swipe 1 ($5,400) is a sunk cost and not relevant to the decision.

The current market price of Swipe 1 ($5,450) is also not relevant to the decision as T Co has no intention of replacing Swipe 1.

The company could sell Swipe 1 for $3,000 if it does not use it for this contract. This represents an opportunity cost.

In addition to the $3,000, Swipe 1 could be modified at a cost of $4,600, bringing the total cost of converting Swipe 1 to $7,600.

160   The correct answer is: Both statements are false

An opportunity cost is the benefit forgone taking one course of action instead of the next most profitable course of action.

The effect that the decision to accept the Push Co contract has on profit or cost is an important factor in decision-making, but non-financial factors should also be taken into consideration.

161   The correct answer is: Sunk cost

The cost of the demonstration has already been incurred and cannot be recovered. It is, therefore, a sunk cost and is not relevant to the decision about whether or not to accept the Push Co contract.

Rotanola Co

162   The correct answer is: $P = 210 - 0.005Q$

Find the price at which demand would be nil: Each price increase of $10 results in a fall in demand of 2,000 phones. For demand to be nil, the price needs to rise by as many times as there are 2,000 units in 20,000 units (20,000/2,000 = 10) ie to $110 + (10 × $10) = $210.

So a = 210 and b = change in price/change in quantity = 10/2,000 = 0.005

The demand equation is therefore $P = 210 - 0.005Q$

> **Alternatively**
> $P = a - bQ$
> $110 = a - (0.005 \times 20,000)$
> $a = 110 + 100 = 210$
> $P = 210 - 0.005Q$

163   The correct answer is: $TC = 460,000 + 62Q$

Cost behaviour can be modelled using equations. These equations can be highly complex but in this case are quite simple.

b = variable cost = 30 + 18 + 14 = $62
a = fixed cost = $23 × 20,000 = 460,000
TC = 460,000 + 62Q where Q = number of units

164   The correct answer is: 6,425

b = change in price/change in quantity = $1/5 = 0.2

a = $250 + ((12,000 / 5) × $1 = $2,650

MR = 2,650 − (2 × 0.2)Q = 2,650 − 0.4Q

Profits are maximised when MC = MR, ie when 80 = 2,650 − 0.4Q

Q = (2,650 - 80) / 0.4 = 6,425

Profit maximising demand = 6,425

165   The correct answers are:

Demand will remain constant despite price changes.		**FALSE**
If price increases by 5%, demand will fall by 10%.		**FALSE**
Total expenditure will remain constant despite price changes.	**TRUE**	

Price elasticity of demand is given by percentage change in demand divided by percentage change in price. If it equals one, the two percentages must be equal so the effects on total expenditure will cancel out.

166   The correct answer is: If demand is highly elastic.

If demand is highly elastic, it responds well to low prices.

If a product is new and different, market skimming would be more appropriate. Customers would be prepared to pay high prices so as to be one up on other people who do not own the product. Market skimming is also appropriate when the product has high development costs that need to be recovered quickly. Market penetration pricing is appropriate if there are significant economies of scale to be achieved from a high volume of output so that quick penetration into the market is desirable in order to gain unit cost reductions.

167 Health Nuts

Workbook reference. Cost volume profit analysis is covered in Chapter 8.

Top tips. There are easy marks available throughout this question so ensure you allocate enough time to each requirement. Make sure you refer to the numbers you have calculated in your explanations.

Easy marks. You should be able to score well in all parts of this question.

Marking scheme

			Marks
(a)	(i)	Calculation of breakeven point for the gym	2
		Calculation of margin of safety for the gym	1
	(ii)	Calculation of breakeven point for the cafe	1.5
		Calculation of margin of safety for the cafe	0.5
(b)		Explanation relating to the breakeven point calculations	1.5
		Explanation relating to the margins of safety	1.5
(c)		Calculation of the weighted average C/S ratio for the gym and creche	5.5
		Calculation of the budgeted profit for the gym and creche	0.5
(d)		Advice as to the viability of closing the café and opening the creche	6
			20

(a) (i) **Gym**

Breakeven point

	$	
Average sales revenue per customer		
Gym entry	8.40	
Car park expected value (0.8 × $1)	0.80	
	9.20	
Variable cost	1.20	
Contribution per customer	8.00	
Total fixed costs	48,000	
BEP (in customers)	6,000	($48,000 / $8)

Margin of safety

Total number of customers per day	330	(80 + 40 + 20 + 90)
Number of days in the month	30	
Total customers for June	9,900	
Margin of safety (in customers)	3,900	(9,900 − 6,000)
Margin of safety (%)	39.39%	(3,900 / 9,900)

(ii) **Cafe**

Breakeven point

	$	
Average contribution per customer		
Drinks	0.792	($2.20 × 60% × 60%)
Food	0.352	($2.20 × 40% × 40%)
	1.144	
Total fixed costs	3,600	
BEP (in customers)	3,147	($3,600 / $1.144)

Margin of safety

Total customers for June	4,950	
Margin of safety (in customers)	1,803	(4,950 − 3,147)
Margin of safety (%)	36.43%	(1,803 / 4,950)

(b) The gym needs 6,000 customers per month and the café needs 3,147 customers per month in order to cover its fixed costs.

Each $1 of contribution after this point generates profit.

Whether or not these figures are particularly high can be gauged by comparing them to the expected (or, in this case, actual) customers in one month and this is where the margin of safety is useful. Both the margin of safety for the gym and the café are quite similar, at approximately 39% and 36% respectively. This tells Health Nuts the extent to which it can feel confident about covering its fixed costs and making a profit. In this instance, its margin of safety is such that, even if its customer numbers went down by over one third it could still cover its fixed costs.

(c)

Total sales/contribution from gym

Original number of customers	330	
New customers	120	
Total number of customers per day	450	
Number of days in the month	30	
Total customers for the month (450 × 30)	13,500	

	$
Entry fee	8.40
Car park	0.80
	9.20
Total sales from gym entry/car park	124,200

Contribution per customer	$
Sales revenue	9.20
Less: variable cost	1.20
	8.00
Total contribution	108,000

Total sales/contribution from creche	
Total customers using the creche per day	120
Number of days in the month	30
Total customers for the month	3,600
Number of children per customer	2
Total number of children per month	7,200
	$
Price per child	4.00
Total sales from creche	28,800

Contribution per customer	$
Sales revenue	4.00
Less: variable cost	0.50
	3.50
Total contribution	25,200
Total contribution from gym and creche	133,200
Total sales from gym and creche	153,000
Weighted average C/S ratio	87.06%

Budgeted profit per month with creche	$
Total contribution from gym and creche	133,200
Less: total fixed costs	56,000
Budgeted profit	77,200

(d)

	$
Total contribution from gym	79,200
Total contribution from cafe	5,663
	84,863
Less total fixed costs	51,600
Profit for June	33,263

With the creche, profit will increase from $33,263 to $77,200 per month, an increase of $43,937. Therefore, from a purely financial point of view, the crèche would seem like a good idea.

However, there are various other factors that need to be taken into account:

Details of how much the conversion from the café to the creche will cost has not been provided. The investment would need to be appraised using a technique like NPV to assess its financial viability.

ANSWERS

The research for the revised customer numbers is only initial. Is this data realistic and can it be relied on? There is no information about how Health Nuts got this research.

The opening of a creche could put off other customers, who want to exercise in a child-free environment, from using the gym during the day. There is no indication that Health Nuts have taken this into account.

Similarly, closing the café could upset many other customers at all times of day and lead to the loss of their business.

The calculations so far performed are not therefore enough to make this decision.

168 Belton Park Resort

> **Workbook references.** Incremental costs and revenues are covered in Chapters 10 and 11.
>
> **Top tips.** In part (a), use a clear layout, read the information carefully and make sure you state which costs should be excluded (eg electricity $0) rather than not mentioning them at all. It's a good idea to practise answering numerical Section C questions like this on a spreadsheet. Don't forget to state whether the hotel and water park should stay open or not.
>
> In part (b) use your common sense to make sensible suggestions and don't be afraid to state the obvious.
>
> **Easy marks.** There are plenty of easy marks available for the calculations in part (a).
>
> **Examining team's comments.** Using the CBE software is key skill is passing Applied Skills exams.
>
> A common mistake in part (b) was to suggest that the resort should look at costs versus benefits, but this was done in part (a).

Marking scheme

			Marks	
(a)	(i)	Hotel revenue	1.5	
		Extras contribution	1	
		Staff costs	2.5	
		Maintenance cost	1	
		Gas variable cost	1	
		Water not security	0.5	
		Net cash flow	0.5	
		Conclusion: hotel	0.5	
				8.5
	(ii)	Admission revenue	1.5	
		Extras contribution	1	
		Staff costs	0.5	
		Maintenance costs	1	
		Gas variable costs	1	
		Water not security	0.5	
		Net cash flow	0.5	
		Conclusion: water park	0.5	
				6.5
(b)	Discussion		5	
				5
				20

(a) (i) **Hotel**

Incremental revenue and contribution

		$
Room revenue		
Number of rooms	120	
Number of nights	31	
Total room nights	3,720	
Occupancy rate	50%	
Total nights occupied	1,860	
Rate per night	$70	
Total room revenue		130,200
Extras' contribution		
Total nights occupied	1,860	
Contribution per night	$12.00	
Total 'extras' contribution		22,320
Total cash inflows		152,520
Incremental running costs		
Staff costs	$120,000	
Less: manager's salary	($2,500)	
Less: chef's salary	($2,000)	
	$115,500	
50% normal hours		57,750
50% at reduced hours × 50/90		32,083
Maintenance costs:		
If open	$14,600	
If closed	$4,000	
Incremental cost		10,600
Power costs:		
Electric	$0	
Gas – fixed charge	$0	
Gas – variable ($20,000 − $10,200) × 1·5		14,700
Security		0
Water		6,450
Total cash outflows		121,583
Total incremental cash flows		30,937

(ii) **Water park**

Incremental revenue and contribution

		$
Visitor revenue		
Number of visitors	5,760	
Admission cost	$16.80	
Admission revenue		96,768
Extras' contribution		
Number of visitors	5,760	
Contribution per visitor	$7.20	
Total contribution		41,472
Total cash inflows		138,240

		$
Incremental running costs		
Staff costs:		
Manager	$0	
Other staff ($75,600 − $2,000) × 48%		35,328
Maintenance costs:		
If open	$6,000	
If closed	($2,000)	
Incremental cost		4,000
Power costs:		
Electric	$0	
Gas – fixed charge	$0	
Gas – variable ($18,000 − $8,500) × 1.5		14,250
Security		0
Water		12,100
Total cash outflows		65,678
Total incremental cash flows		72,562

Conclusion

Based on these figures, both of them should stay open because the incremental cash flows are both positive.

(b) As regards the estimates calculated, these have been based on very limited data and should be approached with caution. The calculations are based on the first two months' of opening only and, consequently, it is difficult to say how accurate they are likely to be. In addition, the basis of estimating the revised occupancy rates for the hotel, for example, has not been given. If these estimates are too optimistic, the actual results could be far worse.

The figures suggest that both the water park and the hotel should stay open. Given that this is a new business and therefore it is still building up its customer base, this would seem like a wise decision anyway, even if the calculations had shown that the estimated incremental cash flows were not as positive as this.

Similarly, if Belton Park were to close either the hotel or the water park, they would invariably lose some valuable staff who might seek out other jobs after the closure. These staff might not be available again when the hotel and water park reopened in February.

The interdependency of the two sets of projections has not been taken into account in the calculations either. Since the incremental cash flows suggest that both the hotel and the water park should stay open, it is not a big problem. However, if they had shown, for example, that the water park alone should close, the effect that this could have on the number of hotel visitors would also need to be taken into account. Many visitors may be attracted to the hotel because it has a water park.

Tutorial note: There are many factors which could have been discussed here and would be given credit.

169 Robber Co

Marking scheme

		Marks
(a)	Incremental cost of buying in:	
	Direct materials	0.5
	Direct labour	0.5
	Heat and light	0.5
	Set-up costs	3
	Depreciation and insurance	1
	Total cost of making	0.5
	Total cost of buying	0.5
	Saving	0.5
	Conclusion	1
		8
	Method 2:	
	Direct materials	0.5
	Direct labour	0.5
	Heat and power	0.5
	Avoidable fixed costs	0.5
	Activity related costs	3
	Avoidable depreciation and insurance	0.5
	Total relevant manufacturing costs	0.5
	Relevant cost per unit	0.5
	Incremental cost of buying in	0.5
	Conclusion	1
		8

(b)   If 100,000 control panels made:

Variable cost of making per unit	1
Saving from making	1
Saving per labour hour	1
Ranking	1
Make 100,000 keypads	1
Make 66,666 display screens	1
Buy 33,334 display screens	<u>1</u>
	7

(c)   Non-financial factors:

1–2 marks per factor	Max <u>5</u>
	<u>20</u>

(a)   **Incremental costs of making in-house compared to cost of buying**

	Keypads (K) $	Display screens (D) $
Variable costs		
Materials:		
K = ($160k × 6/12) + ($160k × 1.05 × 6/12) : D = ($116k × 1.02)	164,000	118,320
Direct labour	40,000	60,000
Machine set-up costs:		
K = ($26k − $4k) × 500/400 : D = ($30k − $6k) × 500/400	<u>27,500</u>	<u>30,000</u>
	231,500	208,320
Attributable fixed costs		
Heat and power: K = ($64k − $20k) : D = ($88k − $30k)	44,000	58,000
Fixed machine costs	4,000	6,000
Depreciation and insurance: K = ($84k × 40%) : D = ($96k × 40%)	<u>33,600</u>	<u>38,400</u>
	81,600	102,400
Total incremental costs of making in-house	<u>313,100</u>	<u>310,720</u>
Cost of buying: K = (80,000 × $4.10) : D = (80,000 × $4.30)	328,000	344,000
Total saving from making	<u>14,900</u>	<u>33,280</u>

Robber Co should therefore make all of the keypads and display screens in-house.

Note. The above calculations assume that the fixed set-up costs only arise if production takes place.

Alternative approach (Relevant costs)

	Keypads (K) $	Display screens (D) $
Direct materials:		
K = ($160k/2) + ($160k/2 × 1.05) : D = $116k × 1.02	164,000	118,320
Direct labour	40,000	60,000
Heat and power		
K = $64K − (50% × $40K) : D = $88k − (50% × $60k)	44,000	58,000
Machine set-up costs:		
Avoidable fixed costs	4,000	6,000
Activity related costs (W1)	27,500	30,000
Avoidable depreciation and insurance costs:		
K = ($84k × 40%) : D = ($96k × 40%)	<u>33,600</u>	<u>38,400</u>

BPP LEARNING MEDIA

	Keypads (K) $	Display screens (D) $
Total relevant manufacturing costs	313,100	310,720
Relevant cost per unit	3.91375	3.884
Cost per unit of buying in	4.10	4.30
Incremental cost of buying in	0.18625	0.416

As each of the components is cheaper to make in-house than to buy in, the company should continue to manufacture both products in-house.

Working

Current no. of batches produced = 80,000/500 = 160
New no. of batches produced = 80,000/400 = 200
Current cost per batch for keypads = ($26,000 – $4,000)/160 = $137.50
Therefore new activity related batch cost = 200 × $137.50 = $27,500
Current cost per batch for display screens = ($30,000 – $6,000)/160 = $150
Therefore new activity related batch cost = 200 × $150 = $30,000

(b) **Note.** Attributable fixed costs are not included in the following calculation. Attributable fixed costs remain unaltered irrespective of the level of production of keypads and display screens, because as soon as one unit of either is made, the costs rise. We know that we will make at least one unit of each component as both are cheaper to make than buy. They are therefore an irrelevant common cost.

Plan to minimise costs

	Keypads (K) $	Display screens (D) $
Buy-in price	4.10	4.30
Variable cost of making:		
K = ($231,500 / 80,000): D = ($208,320 / 80,000)	2.89	2.60
Saving from making (per unit)	1.21	1.70
Labour hours per unit	0.50	0.75
Saving from making (per unit of limiting factor)	2.42	2.27
Priority of making	1	2

Total labour hours available = 100,000 hours

Make maximum keypads ie 100,000 using 50,000 labour hours (100,000 × 0.5 hours per unit)

Use remaining 50,000 labour hours to make 66,666 display screens (50,000/0.75 hours per unit)

Therefore buy in 33,334 display screens (100,000 – 66,666).

(c) Robber Co should consider the following non-financial factors when making a decision about outsourcing the manufacture of keypads and display screens.

Supplier performance

Robber Co would need to establish whether the supplier is reliable in meeting **delivery dates** and delivering components of a **high quality**.

If the components delivered are not of the required quality Robber risks damaging its **reputation** and losing sales as well as incurring **high repair costs** for control panels under warranty. This is particularly significant given that the supplier is based overseas – Robber therefore has less control over quality and continuity of supply than if it were dealing with a locally based supplier.

Information to support the supplier's record in meeting delivery dates may be hard to come by, especially as the supplier is a newly established company. Late delivery of components could disrupt Robber's production schedule and its ability to supply control panels to meet market demand.

New company

The potential supplier is a **newly formed company**. There is no guarantee the company will be able to operate at the level required to supply the desired level of components at the right quality.

Robber Co should consider whether there are any other potential suppliers of the components. This would enable Robber to compare prices and get the best deal. It could also provide the company with an **alternative supplier** should the new supplier go out of business.

Pricing

The new supplier has only guaranteed the current price for **two years**. After this, the supplier could increase prices significantly. Robber Co should negotiate **a price fix** for a longer period of time as part of the agreement or seek out **alternative suppliers** to ensure that the company is not forced to accept a significant increase in component prices at the end of the two-year period.

170 Gam Co

Workbook reference. Risk and uncertainty is covered in Chapter 12.

Top tips. Part (a) is straightforward provided you read the information carefully and use a clear layout and workings. Make sure you make a recommendation in your answer in part (b). Know the difference between maximin, minimax and maximax for part (c).

Examining team's comments. This was a very well answered question. Where mistakes were made it was through inaccurate reading of the question, incorrectly applying probabilities to profit figures (part (b)), or failure to recommend which option Gam Co would choose (part (b)). In part (c), some candidates mixed up maximin with minimax regret or maximax and consequently gave the wrong explanation and recommendation.

Marking scheme

		Marks	
(a)	Profit calculations:		
	Unit contribution up to 100,000 units	1	
	Unit contribution above 100,000 units	1	
	Each line of table for price of $30 (3 in total)	3	
	Each line of table for price of $35 (3 in total)	3	
			8
(b)	Expected values		
	Expected value for $30	1	
	Expected value for $35	1	
	Recommendation	1	
			3
(c)	Maximin		
	Explanation	2	
	Decision	1	
			3
(d)	Uncertainty		
	Each point made	1	
			6
			20

(a) Profit outcomes

			$30	$35
Price per unit			$30	$35
Contribution to 100,000 units ($30/$35 – $12)			$18	$23
Contribution above 100,000 units ($30/$35 – $12)			$19	$24

	1	2	3	4	5	6
	$	$	$	$	$	$
Sales price	30	30	30	35	35	35
Sales volume (units)	120,000	110,000	140,000	108,000	100,000	94,000
Unit contribution	19	19	19	24	23	23
Total contribution	2,280,000	2,090,000	2,660,000	2,592,000	2,300,000	2,162,000
Fixed costs	(450,000)	(450,000)	(450,000)	(450,000)	(450,000)	(450,000)
Advertising costs	(900,000)	(900,000)	(900,000)	(970,000)	(970,000)	(970,000)
Profit	930,000	740,000	1,310,000	1,172,000	880,000	742,000

(b) Expected values

	1	2	3	4	5	6
Sales price	$30	$30	$30	$35	$35	$35
Sales volume (units)	120,000	110,000	140,000	108,000	100,000	94,000
Profit	$930,000	$740,000	$1,310,000	$1,172,000	$880,000	$742,000
Probability	0.4	0.5	0.1	0.3	0.3	0.4
EV of profit ($)	$372,000	$370,000	$131,000	$351,600	$264,000	$296,800
Totals			$873,000			$912,400

Using the expected value of profit as the basis for decision, a sales price of $35 should be chosen as it gives the highest expected value.

(c) Maximin decision rule

The maximin decision rule involves choosing the outcome that offers the least unattractive worst outcome, in this instance choosing the outcome which maximises the minimum profit. Management would therefore choose a selling price of $35, which has a lowest possible profit of $742,000. This is better than the worst possible outcome from a selling price of $30, which would provide a profit $740,000.

(d) Reasons for uncertainty arising in the budgeting process

Uncertainty arises largely because of changes in the external environment over which a company will sometimes have little control. Reasons include:

- Customers may decide to buy more or less goods or services than originally forecast. For example, if a major customer goes into liquidation, this has a huge effect on a company and could also cause them to go into liquidation.

- Competitors may strengthen or emerge and take some business away from a company. On the other hand, a competitor's position may weaken leading to increased business for a particular company.

- Technological advances may take place which lead a company's products or services to become out-dated and therefore less desirable.

- The workforce may not perform as well as expected, perhaps because of time off due to illness or maybe simply because of lack of motivation.

- Materials may increase in price because of global changes in commodity prices.

Inflation can cause the price of all inputs to increase or decrease.

- If a company imports or exports goods or services, changes in exchange rates can cause prices to change.

- Machines may fail to meet production schedules because of breakdown.

- Social/political unrest could affect productivity, eg the workforce goes on strike.

Note. This list is not exhaustive, nor would candidates be expected to make all the points raised in order to score full marks.

171 Cardio Co

Workbook reference. Cost-volume-profit analysis is covered in Chapter 8.

Top tips. Parts (a) and (b) are fairly straightforward. Part (c) requires knowledge of breakeven charts but even if you think you can't remember how to do a breakeven chart, it is worth writing down some workings for yourself to see if they match the graph. Recognising the chart and knowing what the axes were was worth a mark so don't miss this easy point. For part (e) you needed to think of the assumptions of CVP analysis. Assumptions are often the limitations in accounting techniques.

Examining team's comments. In part (a) some students added the individual contribution/unit and divided by the sum of the individual selling prices. This does not give the correct weighting, which is why we have to multiply by volume first. Part (b) was well answered. Part (c) was not well answered with many answers giving a PV chart instead of breakeven chart. In part (d) most students did not pick up the 'explain' mark – that fixed costs would be covered quicker by the higher C/S ratio.

Marking scheme

			Marks
(a)	Weighted average C/S ratio:		
	Variable labour cost	1	
	Total revenue	1	
	Total contribution	1	
	WA C/S ratio	<u>1</u>	
			4
(b)	Margin of safety		
	Fixed costs	1	
	Breakeven sales	1	
	Margin of safety	<u>1</u>	
			3
(c)	Breakeven chart		
	Point A	0.5	
	Length B	1	
	Length C	1	
	Line D	0.5	
	Line E	1	
	Line F	0.5	
	Axis labels	1	
	Graph name (breakeven chart)	<u>0.5</u>	
			<u>6</u>

		Marks
(d)	Discussion	
	Each point made	1
		2
(e)	Limitations	
	Each point made	1-2
		5
		20

(a) **Weighted average C/S ratio**

Weighted average contribution to sales ratio (WA C/S ratio) = total contribution/total sales revenue.

Per unit	T		C		R	
	$	$	$	$	$	$
Selling price		1,600		1,800		1,400
Material	(430)		(500)		(360)	
Variable labour (40%)	(88)		(96)		(76)	
Variable overheads	(110)		(120)		(95)	
Total variable costs		(628)		(716)		(531)
Contribution		972		1,084		869
Sales units		420		400		380
Total sales revenue		$672,000		$720,000		$532,000
Total contribution		$408,240		$433,600		$330,220

WA C/S ratio = ($408,240 + $433,600 + $330,220)/($672,000 + $720,000 + $532,000)

= $1,172,060/$1,924,000 = 60.92%.

(b) **Margin of safety**

Margin of safety = budgeted sales − breakeven sales

Budgeted sales revenue = $1,924,000

Fixed labour costs = ((420 × $220) + (400 × $240) + (380 × $190)) × 0.6 = $156,360k.

Therefore total fixed costs = $156,360 + $55,000 = $211,360.

Breakeven sales revenue = fixed costs/weighted average C/S ratio

= $211,360/60.92% = $346,947

Therefore margin of safety = $1,924,000 − $346,947 = $1,577,053.

(c)   The chart is a multi-product breakeven chart

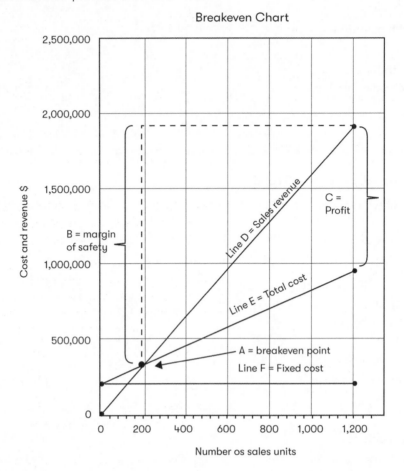

Breakeven Chart

(d)   **BEP if products sold in order of profitability**

If the more profitable products are sold first, this means that the company will cover its fixed costs more quickly. Consequently, the breakeven point will be reached earlier, ie fewer sales will need to be made in order to break even. So, the breakeven point will be lower.

(e)   The limitations of CVP analysis are the unrealistic assumptions required.

   (i)   It is assumed that fixed costs are the same in total and variable costs are the same per unit at all levels of output. This assumption is a great simplification.

       –   Fixed costs will change if output falls or increases substantially (most fixed costs are step costs).

       –   The variable cost per unit will decrease where economies of scale are made at higher output volumes, but the variable cost per unit will also eventually rise when diseconomies of scale begin to appear at even higher volumes of output (for example, the extra cost of labour in overtime working).

   The assumption is only correct within a normal range or relevant range of output. It is generally assumed that both the budgeted output and the breakeven point lie within this relevant range.

   (ii)   It is assumed that sales prices will be constant at all levels of activity. This may not be true, especially at higher volumes of output, where the price may have to be reduced to win the extra sales.

   (iii) Production and sales are assumed to be the same, so that the consequences of any increase in inventory levels or of 'de-stocking' are ignored.

   (iv)   Uncertainty in the estimates of fixed costs and unit variable costs is often ignored.

172 TR Co

Marking scheme

		Marks
(a)	Demand function	1.5
	Marginal cost/batch	2.5
	Labour 1,000th batch	3.5
	Establishing MR function	0.5
	Solve MR to find Q	1
	Use demand function and Q to find P	1
	Contribution based on P and Q	1
	Deduction of fixed costs	0.5
	Profit	0.5
		12
(b)	Penetration pricing	3
	Skimming pricing	3
	Other relevant comments/recommendation	2
		8
		20

(a)   **Step 1: Establish the demand function**

b = change in price/change in quantity

b = $2/5,000 units = 0·0004

The maximum demand for Parapain is 1,000,000 units, so where P = 0, Q = 1,000,000, so 'a' is established by substituting these values for P and Q into the demand function:

0 = a − (0·0004 × 1,000,000)

0 = a − 400

Therefore a = 400

Demand function is therefore: P = 400 − 0·0004Q

Step 2: Establish the marginal cost

		Total
		$
Material Z	500g × $0.10	50
Material Y	300g × $0.50	150
Labour	Working 1	6.6039
Machine running cost	(20/60 × $6.00	2
Total marginal cost per batch		208.6039

Note. Fixed overheads have been ignored as they are not part of the marginal cost.

The marginal cost will now be rounded down to $208·60 per batch.

Working 1: Labour

The labour cost of the 1,000th unit needs to be calculated as follows as this is the basis TR Co will determine the price for Parapain:

Learning curve formula: $Y = aX^b$

'a' is the cost for the first batch: 5 hours × $18 = $90

If X = 1,000 batches and b = –0.321928, then

Y = 90 × 1,000–0.321928 = 9.7377411

Total cost for 1,000 batches = $9,737.7411

If X = 999 batches, then

Y = 90 × 999–0.321928 = 9.7408781

Total cost for 999 batches = $9,731.1372

Therefore the cost of the 1,000 batches ($9,737·7411 – $9,731.1372) = $6.6039

Step 3: Establish the marginal revenue function: MR = a – 2bQ

Equate MC and MR and insert the values for 'a' and 'b' from the demand function in step 1.

208.60 = 400 – (2 × 0.0004 × Q)

Step 4: Solve the MR function to determine optimum quantity, Q

208.60 = 400 – 0.0008Q

0.0008Q = 191.4

Q = 239,250 batches

Step 5: Insert the value of Q from Step 4 into the demand function determined in Step 1 and calculate the optimum price

P = 400 – (0.0004 × 239,250)

P = $304.30

Step 6: Calculate profit

	$
Revenue (239,250 batches × $304.30)	73,803,775
Variable costs (239,250 batches × $208.60)	(49,907,550)
Fixed costs (250,000 batches × $2)	(500,000)
Profit	22,396,225

(b) **Market penetration pricing**

With penetration pricing, a low price would initially be charged for the anti-malaria drug. The ideology behind this is that the price will make the product accessible to a larger number of buyers and therefore the high sales will compensate for the lower prices being charged. The anti-malaria drug would rapidly become accepted as the only drug worth buying, ie it would gain rapid acceptance in the marketplace.

The circumstances which would favour a penetration pricing policy are:

- Highly elastic demand for the anti-malaria drug, ie the lower the price, the higher the demand. There is no evidence that this is the case.

- If significant economies of scale could be achieved by TR Co so that higher sales volumes would result in sizeable reductions in costs. It cannot be determined if this is the case here.

- If TR Co was actively trying to discourage new entrants into the market, however in this case, new entrants cannot enter the market anyway due to the patent.

- If TR Co wished to shorten the initial period of the drug's life-cycle so as to enter the growth and maturity stages quickly but there is no evidence the company wish to do this.

Market skimming pricing

With market skimming, high charges would initially be charged for the anti-malaria drug rather than low prices. This would enable TR Co to take advantage of the unique nature of the product. The most suitable conditions for this strategy are:

- The product has a short life cycle and high development costs which need to be recovered. There is no information about the drug's life cycle but development costs have been high.

- Since high prices attract competitors, there needs to be barriers to entry if competitors are to be deterred. In TR Co's case it has a patent for the drug and also the high development costs could act as a barrier.

- Where high prices in the early stages of a product's life cycle are expected to generate high initial cash flows, this will help TR Co recover the high development costs it has incurred.

Recommendation

Given the unique nature of the drug and the barriers to entry, a market skimming pricing strategy would appear to be the far more suitable pricing strategy. Also, whilst there is demand curve data, it is unknown how reliable this data is, in which case a skimming strategy may be the safer option.

173 The Alka Hotel

Workbook references. Cost volume profit analysis is covered in Chapter 8.

Top tips. Parts (a) and (b) are relatively straightforward. Part (c) requires some thought as to how to calculate the contribution. For part (d), take your time to study the graph carefully and remember that there are four marks available for calculations.

Easy marks. You should score well in parts (a) and (b).

Marking scheme

			Marks
(a)	Contribution	0.5	
	BEP	1.0	
	Total rooms available	1.0	
	Budgeted occupancy	0.5	
	Margin of safety %	1.0	
			4
(b)	Profit/loss	1.5	
	Recommendation	0.5	
	Explanation	2.0	
			4
(c)	C/S ratio	1.0	
	BEP $ revenue	0.5	
	Recommendation	0.5	
	Explanation	2.0	
			4
(d)	Calculations	4	
	Commentary	4	
			8
			20

(a) Breakeven point (in occupied room nights) = Fixed cost/contribution per room

$600,000/($180 − $60) = 5,000 occupied room nights

Margin of safety = (Budgeted room occupancy − breakeven room occupancy)/budgeted room occupancy

Total rooms available per annum: 365 days × 25 rooms = 9,125 rooms

Budgeted occupancy level: 9,125 × 70% = 6,387.5 rooms

Margin of safety: (6,387.5 − 5,000)/6,387·5 = 21.72%

(b) **Profit or loss for Q1**

	$
Contribution (900 rooms × $120)	108,000
Fixed costs (($600,000/12) × 3)	(150,000)
Loss	(42,000)

The Alka Hotel should not close in Q1. The fixed costs will still be incurred and closure would result in lost contribution of $108,000. This in turn would result in a decrease in annual profits of $108,000. In addition, the hotel could lose customers at other times of the year, particularly their regular business customers, who may perceive the hotel as being unreliable.

(c) **Contribution/sales ratio of Project 1**

	$
Sales value of two room nights (2 × $67·50)	135
Sales value of a pair of theatre tickets	100
	235
Variable cost of two room nights (2 × $60)	(120)
Variable cost of a pair of theatre tickets	(95)
Contribution	20
C/S ratio (20/235)	8.51%

Breakeven point in revenue ($20,000/0·0851) $235,000

Alternatively:

Contribution per theatre package sold	$20
Breakeven point in theatre packages ($20,000/$20)	1,000
Breakeven point in revenue (1,000 × $235)	$235,000

The unit contribution per theatre package is low and it requires a large number of sales to break even. Each theatre package would require two room nights to be sold which would mean 2,000 room nights needed in Q1 to break even. The available rooms for Q1 are only 2,281.25 (9,125/4) and the Alka Hotel has already sold 900 rooms, so there is insufficient capacity. Based on this, Project 1 is not viable at the quoted prices.

(d) Project 2 will cause the fixed costs of the hotel to rise from $600,000 per annum to $800,000 per annum for the hotel and restaurant combined. This is an annual increase of $200,000.

Revenue per occupied room will rise from $180 to $250 ($2,000,000/8,000 rooms) which reflects the extra guest expenditure in the restaurant.

The total cost predicted at a level of 8,000 occupied rooms is $1,560,000 which means the variable costs must be $760,000 ($1,560,000 − $800,000 fixed costs). This is a variable cost per occupied room of $95 which is an increase of $35. This reflects the variable costs of the restaurant.

As a result of these changes, the breakeven point has increased from 5,000 to 5,161 occupied rooms so the hotel needs to sell more room nights to cover costs.

However, budgeted occupancy is now 7,300 occupied room nights which gives 80% occupancy (7,300/9,125). This gives a margin of safety of 2,139 occupied room nights or 29%. This is an increase on the current position and the hotel's position appears safer. At 7,300 occupied room nights the Alka Hotel's budgeted profit is $331,500 (7,300 × ($250 − $95) − $800,000.

174 HMF Co

> **Workbook reference.** Risk and uncertainty techniques are covered in Chapter 12.
>
> **Top tips.** Part (a) involves a very straightforward compilation of a contribution table which should not cause too many problems. You should practise answering questions like this using a spreadsheet because it is likely that, for this type of question, you would be provided with a spreadsheet in the exam.
>
> The trickiest part of part (b) is dealing with the minimax regret decision rule. You do need to have a good understanding not only of how to do the calculations but also what they mean.
>
> Part (c) is straightforward application of knowledge but do make sure you apply it to this specific company.

(a)   Price

Variable cost	$400	$450	$500
$120	560,000 (W1)	577,500 (W3)	570,000
$160	480,000 (W2)	507,500	510,000
$210	380,000	420,000	435,000

Workings

1   (400 − 120) × 2,000 = $560,000
2   (400 − 160) × 2,000 = $480,000
3   (450 − 120) × 1,750 = $577,500

You will probably be provided with a spreadsheet for this type of question and so your formulae may look like this:

	A	B	C	D	E	F	G
1							
2	(a)					Price	
3							
4					400	450	500
5			Variable	120	=(E4-D5)*C11	=(F4-D5)*C12	=(G4-D5)*C13
6			cost	160	=(E4-D6)*C11	=(F4-D6)*C12	=(G4-D6)*C13
7				210	=(E4-D7)*C11	=(F4-D7)*C12	=(G4-D7)*C13
8							
9							
10							
11		Demand	2000				
12			1750				
13			1500				

(b)   **Maximax**

The maximax criterion looks at the best possible results. Maximax means 'maximise the maximum profit'. In this case, we need to maximise the maximum contribution.

Demand/price	Maximum contribution
2,000/$400	$560,000
1,750/$450	$577,500
1,500/$500	$570,000

HMF Co would therefore set a price of $450.

Note that we don't know what the probability of the demand will be.

Maximin

The maximin decision rule involves choosing the outcome that offers the least unattractive worst outcome, in this instance choosing the outcome which maximises the minimum contribution.

Demand/price	Minimum contribution
2,000/$400	$380,000
1,750/$450	$420,000
1,500/$500	$435,000

HMF Co would therefore set a price of $500.

Minimax regret

The minimax regret decision rule involves choosing the outcome that minimises the maximum regret from making the wrong decision, in this instance choosing the outcome which minimises the opportunity loss from making the wrong decision.

We can use the calculations performed in (a) to draw up an opportunity loss table.

Variable cost		Price	
	$400	$450	$500
$120	$17,500 (W1)	–	$7,500
$160	$30,000 (W2)	$2,500	–
$210	$55,000 (W3)	$15,000	–
Minimax regret	$55,000	$15,000	$7,500

Minimax regret strategy (price of $500) is that which minimises the maximum regret ($7,500).

Workings

1   At a variable cost of $120 per unit, the best strategy would be a price of $450. The opportunity loss from setting a price of $400 would be $(577,500 − 560,000) = $17,500.

2   At a variable cost of $160 per unit, the best strategy would be a price of $500. The opportunity loss from setting a price of $400 would be $(510,000 − 480,000) = $30,000.

3   At a variable cost of $210 per unit, the best strategy would be a price of $500. The opportunity loss from setting a price of $400 would be $(435,000 − 380,000) = $55,000.

Using a spreadsheet, your formulae for the minimax regret may look like this:

	A	B	C	D	E	F	G
1							
2	(a)					Price	
3							
4					400	450	500
5			Variable	120	=(E4-D5)*C11	=(F4-D5)*C12	=(G4-D5)*C13
6			cost	160	=(E4-D6)*C11	=(F4-D6)*C12	=(G4-D6)*C13
7				210	=(E4-D7)*C11	=(F4-D7)*C12	=(G4-D7)*C13
8							
9							
10							
11		Demand	2000				
12			1750				
13			1500				
14							
15							
16	(b)	Minimax regret					
17					Price		
18		Variable cost		=E4	=F4	=G4	
19		=D5		=F5-E5	=F5-F5	=F5-G5	
20		=D6		=G6-E6	=G6-F6	=G6-G6	
21		=D7		=G7-E7	=G7-F7	=G7-G7	
22							
23		Maximum regret		=D21	=E21	=F19	

(c) **Expected values**

Where probabilities are assigned to different outcomes we can evaluate the worth of a decision as the expected value, or weighted average, of these outcomes. The expected value is calculated as the probability of the outcome multiplied by the outcome. The principle is that when there are a number of alternative decisions, each with a range of possible outcomes, the optimum decision will be the one which gives the highest expected value. However, the expected value may never actually occur.

Expected values are more valuable as a guide to decision-making where they refer to outcomes which will occur many times over. Examples would include the probability that so many customers per day will buy a loaf of bread, the probability that a customer services assistant will receive so many phone calls per hour, and so on.

We have not been given information on probabilities of each demand occurring for HMF Co's scooters and it is unlikely that demand will be sufficiently predictable to use this technique successfully.

Note. Other valid points would be given credit, up to a maximum of three marks.

Sensitivity analysis

Sensitivity analysis can be used in any situation so long as the relationships between the key variables can be established. Typically this involves changing the value of a variable and seeing how the results are affected.

For example, HMF Co could use sensitivity analysis to estimate by how much costs and revenues would need to differ from their estimated values before the decision would change or to estimate whether a decision would change if estimated costs were x% higher than estimated, or estimated revenues y% lower than estimated.

Sensitivity analysis can help to concentrate management attention on the most important factors and can be particularly useful when launching a new product.

175 Cut and Stitch

Workbook reference. Linear programming is covered in Chapter 9.

Top tips. Remember to show all your workings in part (a) to maximise your score. Think carefully about the overtime rate in part (c). The premium is $4.50 – $1.50 = $3 (not just $4.50).

Easy marks. There are four marks available for calculating the optimal production mix and related contribution in part (a).

Examiner's comments. A good attempt at part (a) would have been to solve the two simultaneous equations for the critical constraints at point B, in order to arrive at the optimum quantity of W and L to be produced. Then, these numbers needed to be put into the objective function in order to find contribution. It is essential to show all workings. Where workings are not shown, full marks cannot be given.

Most answers to part (b) were poor and this is clearly an area that needs to be revisited. A common error was finding a total shadow price of $14 for fabric and tailor time jointly, rather than calculating them separately. Such answers scored poorly.

If part (b) was poorly answered, part (c) was really poorly answered! Many candidates could perform the calculations in part (b) but did not, on the whole, understand that the shadow price is the premium OVER AND ABOVE the normal price that could be paid for extra tailor time. Again, this area clearly needs revisiting.

It was surprising to see that candidates who completed part (a) correctly could not do part (d) as essentially, the technique required was the same.

		Marks
(a)	Optimal point calculation	4
	Contribution	2
		6
(b)	For each shadow price	3
		6
(c)	Rate discussion	3
	Other factors eg tiredness, negotiation	3
		6
(d)	Find optimum point	0.5
	Solve two equations	1
	Conclusion	0.5
		2
		20

(a) **The optimal production mix can be found by solving the constraint equations for F and T**

7W + 5L = 3,500 (1)
2W + 2L = 1,200 (2)

Multiply the second equation by 2.5 to yield a common value for L in each equation

7W + 5L = 3,500 (1)
5W + 5L = 3,000 (3)
2W = 500 (1) − (3)
W = 250

Substitute W = 250 into the fabric equation to calculate L

2 × 250 + 2L = 1,200
2L = 700
L = 350

Calculate the related contribution to the optimal production mix

C = 48W + 40L
C = (48 × 250) + (40 × 350)
C = 26,000

The contribution gained is $26,000

(b) **The shadow prices can be found by adding one unit to each constraint in turn.**

Shadow price of T

7W + 5L = 3,501 (1)
2W + 2L = 1,200 (2)

Multiply the second equation by 2.5 to yield a common value for L in each equation

7W + 5L = 3,501 (1)
5W + 5L = 3,000 (3)
2W = 501 (1) − (3)
W = 250.5

Substitute W = 250.5 into the fabric equation to calculate L

(2 × 250.5) + 2L = 1,200
2L = 1,200 − 501
L = 349.5

Contribution earned at this point would be = (48 × 250.5) + (40 × 349.5) = 26,004 (increase of $4).

The shadow price of T is $4 per hour.

Shadow price of F

7W + 5L = 3,500
2W + 2L = 1,201

Multiply the second equation by 2.5 to yield a common value for L in each equation

7W + 5L = 3,500.0
5W + 5L = 3,002.5
2W = 497.5
W = 248.75

Substitute W = 248.75 into the fabric equation to calculate L

(2 × 248.75) + 2L = 1,201
2L = 1,201 − 497.5
L = 351.75

Contribution earned at this point would be = (48 × 248.75) + (40 × 351.75) = 26,010 (increase of $10).

The shadow price of F is $10 per metre.

(c)   The **shadow price** is the increase in contribution created by the availability of an extra unit of a limited resource at its original cost.

In this instance, it represents the maximum **premium** above the normal rate that a business should be willing to pay for one more unit of a scarce resource.

The shadow price of labour is $4 per hour (as calculated in part (b)). The tailors are usually paid $1.50 per hour and have offered to work the extra time providing they are paid three times their normal rate ($4.50). This represents a premium of $3.00 per hour.

This is $1.00 per hour below the maximum premium and so the offer appears to be acceptable.

The company should consider negotiating with the tailors in order to reduce the premium further. Furthermore, there is a potential risk that the tailors may be tired from working the extra hours which could detract from the quality of the suits and have an adverse impact on the reputation of the Cut and Stitch brand.

(d)   If the maximum demand for W falls to 200 units, the constraint for W will move left to 200 on the X axis on the graph. The new optimum point will then be at the intersection of:

W = 200 and
2W + 2L = 1,200

Solving the equation simultaneously:

(2 × 200) + 2L = 1,200
L = 400

Therefore, the new production plan will be to make 400L and 200W.

Part D answers

OTQ bank – Budgeting and control

176   The correct answer is: 300 units

Trend value = 345.12 – (1.35 × 16) = 323.52

Forecast sales = trend + seasonal component

= 323.52 – 23.62

= 299.9

= 300 (to the nearest whole unit)

If you selected 247 units you reduced the trend figure by 23.62 per cent, instead of subtracting 23.62 as an absolute figure.

If you selected 324 units you forgot to adjust the trend for the seasonal variation.

If you selected 347 units you added the seasonal component instead of subtracting it..

177   The correct answers are:

- This standard makes allowances for expected wastage and inefficiencies.
- This standard should give employees a realistic, but challenging target of efficiency.

The least useful, and most rarely used, type of standard is the basic standard, which is kept unaltered over a long period of time and may be out of date. The standard that is based on perfect operating conditions is the ideal standard which makes no allowances for wastage or inefficiencies.

178   The correct answer is: 72% of the variation in sales revenue can be explained by the corresponding variation in advertising expenditure

Correlation coefficient, r = 0.85. Therefore the coefficient of determination, $r^2 = 0.85^2$ = 0.72.

The coefficient of determination tells us that 72% of the variation in sales revenue can be explained by the corresponding variation in advertising expenditure.

179   The correct answer is: $880

	Actual mix kg	Standard mix kg	Mix variance kg	Std price $	Mix variance $
P	820	750	70 (A)	3.0	210 (A)
Q	1,740	1,500	240 (A)	2.5	600 (A)
R	2,300	2,250	50 (A)	4.0	200 (A)
S	2,640	3,000	360 (F)	5.25	1,890 (F)
	7,500	7,500	0		880 (F)

180   The correct answer is: Both 1 and 2

Flexed budgets enable actual results to be compared with expected results for the same volume of activity, such as production and sales. To reconcile an original budgeted profit to actual profit with variances there must be a sales volume variance (measured in terms of either budgeted/standard contribution or profit, depending on the type of costing system used).

181   The correct answers are:

- For standard costing to be useful for control purposes, it requires a reasonably stable environment.

- The ethos behind a system of standard costing is that performance is satisfactory if it meets predetermined standards.

In a standard costing environment, products or processes must be standardised and repetitive, so that standards can be established for budgeting and control. In a TQM environment, the objective is continuous improvement, which may involve continuous changes in procedures, input quantities and prices. A stable standard is never achieved.

Standard costing assumes that there is a target level of performance and achieving that target represents success. With TQM the view is that performance can be improved continually. There is no 'target'.

182   **This question appeared in the December 2019 exam.**

The correct answer is: $1,610 favourable

	Standard quantity Standard mix Kg	Actual quantity Standard mix Kg	Variance Kg	Standard cost per kg $	Variance $
Z	4,960	4,800	160 (F)	5	800 (F)
Y	2,790	2,700	90 (F)	9	810 (F)
	7,750	7,500			1,610 (F)

Alternative.

7,500 kg should produce (÷ 125 x 100)	6,000 kg
They did produce	6,200 kg
Yield variance in units of output	200 kg (F)
Standard material cost ($805 /100)	$8.05
Yield variance in $	$1,610 (F)

183   **This question appeared in the June 2015 exam.**

The correct answer is: $3,720 F

	Actual sales units in std mix	Standard sales units in std mix	Difference in units	Standard contribution	Variance
Product A	16,020	15,840	180 F	$12	$2,160 F
Product B	10,680	10,560	120 F	$13	$1,560 F
					$3,720 F

184   The correct answer is: 2 only

Standard costing systems are not compatible with a Total Quality Management approach to operations. With standard costing, the aim is to achieve standard cost or, perhaps, obtain some favourable variances. With TQM, guiding principles are 'continuous improvement' and 'zero defects'. Existing standards and methods of operating are always unsatisfactory and improvements should always be sought. This is not compatible with a standard costing 'philosophy'.

Standard costing tends to be of little value in a rapidly changing environment, because products are not standardised for a sufficient length of time to make the preparation of standard costs worthwhile.

185 The correct answer is: $114,400

From the regression equation, variable cost per unit = $286. If production is 400 units, variable production cost is $286 × 400 = $114,400.

186 The correct answer is: When the trend is increasing or decreasing

When the trend is increasing or decreasing, additive seasonal components change in their importance relative to the trend whereas multiplicative components remain in the same proportion to the trend. The second option is therefore a circumstance in which the multiplicative model would be preferred to the additive model.

It would generally be agreed that non-numerate people find the multiplicative model more difficult to understand than the additive model, perhaps due to problems with percentages. The first option does not apply in this instance.

When the trend is steady an additive model is acceptable but when it is increasing or decreasing it is important to use the multiplicative model so that the seasonal components remain the same proportion of the trend. The third option does not apply in this instance.

Provided the additive model is appropriate, as it is when the trend is steady, it will give forecasts as accurate as those given by the multiplicative model. The fourth option does not apply in this instance.

187 The correct answers are:

- It can result in much reduced inventory holding costs
- It requires suppliers to operate sound quality control procedures

The aim of JIT is to increase efficiency of inventory control systems in order to reduce company costs, principally by minimising inventory levels and thus stockholding costs. This is achieved by using local, reliable suppliers who can deliver goods of the right quality in the right quantity at the right time. The burden of quality control is generally passed back to the supplier to cut costs of the company.

JIT works best when a tied supplier relationship is formed, where the orders form a large part, if not the entirety, of the supplier's business. This precludes the use of many different suppliers. In a JIT system, steps will also be taken to improve customer relations and communications, so that demand can be more accurately determined. This means that reorder levels, and thus safety inventories, can be minimised without necessarily increasing the risks (and thus costs) of stock outs.

188 **This question appeared in the June 2018 exam.**

The correct answer is: $700 favourable

In order to get to the answer, the relationship between variances needed to be considered. The total material cost variance ($4,900 adverse) = Material price variance ($4,800 adverse) + material usage variance. Therefore the material usage variance is the balancing figure of $100 adverse. The material usage variance = material mix variance + material yield variance. We now have to calculate the material mix variance (in order to replace in the equation above) from the information given in the question as shown in the table below:

Material	Std ratio	Actual quantity Std mix	Actual quantity Actual mix	Variance Litres	Standard cost $	Variance $
R	30%	1,800	1,900	100 (A)	63	6,300 (A)
S	50%	3,000	2,800	200 (F)	50	10,000 (F)
T	20%	1,200	1,300	100 (A)	45	4,500 (A)
		6,000	6,000			800 (A)

Therefore, the material mix variance is $800 adverse. As stated above, the material usage variance ($100 adverse) = material mix variance ($800 adverse) + material yield variance. Therefore the material yield is $700 Favourable (balancing figure)

Selecting '$800 adverse', $800 adverse is the material mix. This does not answer the question and hence this is not the correct answer.

Selecting '$800 favourable', $800 favourable is the material mix variance but the adverse variances were incorrectly recorded as favourable and vice versa.

Selecting '$900 adverse' meant if the material mix is incorrectly calculated as $800 favourable, then we would get the material yield as $900 Adverse. Hence, this is not the correct answer.

189   The correct answer is: Rolling budget

If it is difficult to forecast or plan costs and revenues accurately for more than three months ahead, it would be appropriate to prepare new annual budgets every three months, giving most emphasis to the budget for the next three-month period. The disadvantage is that this would require four annual budgets in every 12-month period.

190   The correct answer is: 1 and 3

When x = 20, we don't know anything about the relationship between x and y since the sample only goes up to x = 10. Forecasting within the sample range of 10 is called interpolation. Forecasting outside the range is called extrapolation and this is less reliable. Statement 1 is therefore true.

A correlation coefficient of 0.8 would be regarded as strong and so the estimate would be reliable. Statement 2 is therefore untrue.

A sample of only 6 pairs is very small and is therefore likely to reduce the reliability of the estimate. Therefore statement 3 is true.

OTQ bank– Budgeting and control

191   The correct answer is: $1,248

Standard yield from actual input of materials at standard cost: $19,552

Actual yield at standard materials cost: $20,800

Yield variance (19,552 – 20,800): $1,248 (F)

192   The correct answer is: a = 28, b = 2.6

The least squares method of linear regression analysis involves using the following formulae for a and b in y = a + bx

$$a = \frac{\Sigma y}{n} - \frac{b\Sigma x}{n}$$

$$b = \frac{n\Sigma xy - \Sigma x\Sigma y}{n\Sigma x^2 - (\Sigma x)^2}$$

$$b = \frac{(5 \times 8,104) - (100 \times 400)}{(5 \times 2,040) - 100^2} = \frac{40,520 - 40,000}{10,200 - 10,000} = \frac{520}{200} = 2.6$$

$$a = \frac{400}{5} - \frac{2.6 \times 100}{5} = 28$$

Note that the formulae are provided in your exam.

193 The correct answer is: $645 Adverse

When $Y = ax^b$, $b = \log 0.90/\log 2 = -0.0457575/0.30103 = -0.1520031$

Average labour time for first 49 batches $= 2{,}000 \times 49^{-0.1520031} = 2{,}000 \times 0.5534584 = 1{,}106.916731$ hours

Average labour time for first 50 batches $= 2{,}000 \times 50^{-0.1520031} = 2{,}000 \times 0.5517614 = 1{,}103.522743$

	Hours
Total labour time for first 50 units ($\times 1{,}103.522743$)	55,176.14
Total labour time for first 49 units ($\times 1{,}106.916731$)	54,238.92
Labour cost for the 50th batch	937.22

Standard time = 937 hours. Actual time = 980 hours.

Labour efficiency variance for this unit = 43 hours (A) $\times$ $15 = $645 (A).

194 The correct answer is: 0.63

$$r = \frac{n\Sigma xy - \Sigma x\Sigma y}{\sqrt{\left(n\Sigma x^2 - (\Sigma x)^2\right)\left(n\Sigma y^2 - (\Sigma y)^2\right)}}$$

$$r = \frac{(11 \times 13{,}467) - (440 \times 330)}{\sqrt{(11 \times 17{,}986 - 440^2) \times (11 \times 10{,}366 - 330^2)}} = \frac{2{,}937}{\sqrt{4{,}246 \times 5{,}126}} = 0.63$$

195 The correct answer is: –$1,475

Product	Actual sales Units	Actual sales in std mix Units	Sales mix variance Units	Std profit $	Sales mix variance $
X	700	750.0	50.0 (A)	10	500 (A)
Y	1,200	937.5	262.5 (F)	6	1,575 (F)
Z	350	562.5	212.5 (A)	12	2,550 (A)
	2,250	2,250.0	0		1,475 (A)

196 The correct answers are:

- There is a strong relationship between the level of car ownership and the number of road accidents

- 53% of the variation in the level of road accidents from one country to the next can be explained by the corresponding variation in car ownership

High levels of correlation do not prove that there is cause and effect.

The coefficient of determination, r^2, explains the variation ($r^2 = 53\%$). Therefore 53% of the variation in the level of road accidents from one country to the next can be explained by the corresponding variation in car ownership.

197 The correct answer is: $40

	Kg
120 units of product should use ($\times 3.50$)	420
They did use	410
Operational usage variance in kg	10 (F)

Operational usage variance in $ ($\times$ Standard price per kg $4) = $40 (F)

198 The correct answer is: Neither 1 nor 2

Learning curves are more difficult to apply in teams with a high labour turnover, as it can affect efficiency and knowledge significantly. Learning rates are affected by time gaps between the production of additional units of a product, because acquired learning may be forgotten with the passage of time unless the work continues regularly.

199 The correct answers are:

- Control reports are provided too late
- Targets are not communicated

If targets are too easy, they cannot provide an incentive, but they cannot be a disincentive either.

If targets are set at high levels that cannot realistically be achieved, this can be demotivating. Demotivation can also occur if targets are imposed by senior management however this can be overcome if budgets are prepared on a bottom-up basis. Management will also be demotivated if control reports are provided late so that the manager responsible is unable to take prompt action to deal with problems that may arise.

200 The correct answer is: It is easier to put public sector activities into decision packages because they are more easily definable than in the private sector.

In an article in *Student Accountant* on incremental budgeting and zero-based budgeting, the ACCA examining team described two reasons why ZBB is often considered more suitable for public sector service organisations than for private sector companies. One is that ZBB is more suited to costs where there is a lot of discretionary spending, as in the public sector services. The second reason is that activities of public sector organisations are more easily definable and so can usually be put into decision packages. (For example, the activities of a local authority can be grouped into packages for local housing, local education, local refuse collection and waste disposal, and so on.)

201 The correct answers are: $400,000 and $450,000

For a multiplicative model, the seasonal variation is as follows:

TS = T × SV therefore T = TS/SV

Quarter 1 T = $520,000 / 1.3 = $400,000

Quarter 2 T = $630,000 / 1.4 = $450,000

202 The correct answer is:

- The quantity of work achievable at standard performance in an hour

This is the definition of a standard hour.

203 **This question appeared in the Sep/Dec 2020 exam.**

The correct answer is: $861,211

Examination team's comments

When using rolling budgets, two things happen at the end of an accounting period (month or quarter):

- The remaining budget for the year is updated based on the actual results and the up to date information available, and

- A further accounting period (month or quarter) is added. In this way there will always be a full year's budget available.

In this question, the total annual material purchases will be the sum of the next four quarters i.e. the remaining quarters of the current year (Y1 quarters 2, 3 and 4) plus the first quarter of the following year (Y2 quarter 1). The budgets for these quarters will have been updated based on the actual material purchases from quarter 1 ($210,000) and the predicted cost increase of 1%.

	Year 1 Quarter 1 Actual	Year 1 Quarter 2 Budget	Year 1 Quarter 3 Budget	Year 1 Quarter 4 Budget	Year 2 Quarter 2 Budget
Material purchases (increasing at 1% per quarter)	$210,000	$212,100	$214,221	$216,363	$218,527

The total annual material purchases figure in the updated rolling budget would therefore be $212,100 + $214,221 + $216,363 + $218,527 = $861,211

A common error in this question was to revise the budgets for quarters 2 – 4 as shown, but to state the annual budget as the sum of the actual for quarter 1 and the budgets for quarters 2 – 4. This showed a misunderstanding of the rolling budget technique.

Another common error was to state the answer as $212,100 which is the restated budget for quarter 2. This showed that the question requirements were not read carefully enough.

204 The correct answer is: A standard which can be attained if production is carried out efficiently, machines are operated properly and/or materials are used properly. Some allowance is made for waste and inefficiencies.

Attainable standards may provide an incentive to work harder as they represent a realistic but challenging target of efficiency.

205 The correct answer is: 326 units

The trend must be moved on from quarter 8 (fourth quarter of Year 2) to quarter 11 (third quarter of Year 3).

330.625 + (3 × 6) = 348.625 and this must be added to the seasonal variation of −22.5.

348.625 − 22.5 = 326.125

206 The correct answer is: A large sample used to calculate the regression equation.

A regression equation is worthless unless a sufficiently large sample is used to determine it. In practice, samples of ten or more are acceptable.

If you chose the second option, you forgot that forecasting for values of x outside the range of original data leads to unreliable estimates because there is no evidence that the same regression relationship holds for such values.

If you chose the third option, you didn't realise that working to a high number of decimal places gives spurious accuracy.

If you the fourth option, you obviously thought that a correlation coefficient close to 0 indicates a strong linear relationship between x and y. The coefficient must be close to +1 or −1 for such an indication, however.

207 The correct answer is: It is difficult to identify a standard item for costing

With road haulage and distribution, drivers' times on the road are measured automatically. Variable costs can be high (labour and fuel, for example). Standard costing is more common in manufacturing but in principle can be applied to service industries. The problem is to identify a standard item for which a cost can be measured and variances subsequently calculated. In road haulage, for example, a standard measure may be cost per tonne/kilometre delivered: this does not lend itself easily to variance analysis.

208   The correct answer is: Material usage operational variance

Material usage is within the control of a production manager, whereas material price variances are usually the responsibility of the purchasing manager. Line managers are responsible for operational variances, but planning variances are commonly assumed to be the responsibility of someone in senior management.

209   The correct answer is: 1.442 hours

$Y = ax^b$

$b = \log 0.75/\log 2 = -0.1249/0.3010 = -0.415$

When $x = 6$, $x^{-0.415} = 1/6^{-0.415} = 0.4754$

Average time for six jobs:

$Y = 5 \times 0.4754 = 2.377$ hours

Total time required for six jobs = 6×2.377 hours = 14.262 hours

Average time for five jobs: $5 \times 5^{-0.415} = 2.564$ hours

Total time required for five jobs = 5×2.564 hours = 12.820 hours

Time required to perform the 6th job = Total time required for six jobs – Total time required for five jobs.

Therefore, time required to perform the 6th job = 14.262 hours – 12.820 hours = 1.442 hours

210   The correct answer is: 2 only.

Mix variances should only be calculated when a product contains two or more materials that can be mixed together in different proportions. For example, calculating a mix variance for the production of a bicycle out of its component parts would be meaningless. It is important to be aware of the interdependence between variances: a favourable mix variance – meaning a cheaper mix of materials in a product – may result in adverse total output of the product (adverse yield).

211   The correct answer is: Managers should be held accountable only for costs and revenues over which they have some influence or control.

This should be a fundamental principle of management control, but it is not always applied in practice.

212   The correct answer is: 0.98

$$r = \frac{n\Sigma xy - \Sigma x\Sigma y}{\sqrt{\left(n\Sigma x^2 - (\Sigma x)^2\right)\left(n\Sigma y^2 - (\Sigma y)^2\right)}}$$

$$r = \frac{10 \times 4,208 - 210 \times 187}{\sqrt{(10 \times 4,634 - 210^2) \times (10 \times 3,865 - 187^2)}} = \frac{2,810}{\sqrt{2,240 \times 3,681}} = \frac{2,810}{2,871.49} = 0.98$$

213   The correct answer is: Current standard.

Budgeted capacity is associated with current standards. Budgeted capacity is not associated with basic standards. Practical capacity is associated with attainable standards.

Full capacity is associated with ideal standards.

214   The correct answer is: 0.8

As this is a multiplicative model, the seasonal variations should sum (in this case) to 4 as there are four quarters.

Let x = seasonal variation in quarter 4.

$1.3 + 1.4 + 0.5 + x = 4$

Therefore $x = 4 - 1.3 - 1.4 \times 0.5 = 0.8$

215   The correct answers are:

- There is often no measurable output from service functions
- The activities of many service functions are of a non-standard nature

The output of services functions is not as easily measurable as it is with goods which are physically manufactured. This makes it difficult to establish standard unit rates, because there are no easily available standard times or usages.

216   The correct answers are:

Employees will focus on eliminating wasteful expenditure.	**TRUE**
Short-term benefits could be emphasised over long-term benefits.	**TRUE**

Zero-based budgeting begins by looking at the minimum budgeted expenditure, and building a budget from this zero base. This encourages employees to focus on wasteful and unnecessary spending.

However the focus is on short-term savings and may give insufficient consideration to longer-term benefits of current spending.

217   The correct answer is: An underlying long-term movement over time in the values of the data recorded

The first option describes a cyclical variation.

The third option describes a seasonal variation.

The fourth option describes a random variation.

218   The correct answers are:

Extrapolation is inherently risky.	**TRUE**	
The pattern of trend is expected to continue into the future.	**TRUE**	
The nearer in the future the forecast is for, the more unreliable it is.		**FALSE**

Extrapolation means forecasting outside of the range that was used to create the forecast. Interpolation means forecasting within the range. Extrapolation is far riskier than interpolation.

The pattern of trend is expected to continue into the future is true and this is one of the limitations of regression analysis. The past may not be a good predictor of the future.

The further in the future the forecast is for, the more unreliable it is.

219   The correct answer is: $59,000

	$
Total cost at 1,200 units	66,600
Deduct step increase in fixed costs	(6,000)
Total cost at 1,200 units excluding step cost increase	60,600
Total cost of 900 units	58,200
Therefore variable cost of 300 units	2,400

Variable cost per unit = $8

	$
Total cost of 900 units	58,200
Variable cost of 900 units (at eight each)	7,200
Therefore fixed costs at this level of output	51,000

Total costs of 1,000 units = $51,000 + $(8 × 1,000) = $59,000

220   The correct answer is: Sales mix variance

The loss of the advertising campaign means that sales of Product Y will be less than budgeted, which should lead us to expect adverse sales volume variance for Y and an adverse sales quantity variance for both products together. The price discounting for Product Y should lead us to expect an adverse sales price variance. The increase in the proportion of Product X units sold in the total sales mix should lead us to expect a favourable sales mix variance, because Product X has a bigger standard contribution, both per unit and per $1 of standard sales price, than Product Y.

Crush Co

221   The correct answer is: 565.6 hours

Cumulative average time per batch for the first 64 batches

$Y = ax^b$

Where Y = the cumulative average time per unit to produce × units
          x = the cumulative number of units
          a = the time taken for the first unit of output
          b = the index of learning (logLR/log2)

The cumulative average time per batch, with a learning curve of 85%, is therefore

$Y = aX^{-0.2345}$

where a = the time for the first batch (1,500 hours) and X is the number of the batch. For the 64th batch, $X = 64$.

$Y = 1,500 \times 64^{-0.2345}$

   $= 1,500 \times 0.37709 = 565.6$

The cumulative average time per batch for the first 64 batches is 565.6 hours.

222   The correct answer is: 78%

Batches	Total time	Average time/unit
1	1,500	1,500
2		$1,500 \times r$
4		$1,500 \times r^2$
8		$1,500 \times r^3$
16	9,000	$1,500 \times r^4$

$9,000 = 16 \times 1,500\ r^4$

$9,000/(16 \times 1,500) = r^4$

$r = 0.78$ or 78%

223   The correct answer is: 1 only

Decisions about allocating resources and costing of the new product should be based on the time taken to produce the 64th batch because this is when the learning effect stops. After this point, the product will reach a point of steady state production. Using information regarding labour costs from a point prior to steady state level will result in too high a price being assigned to labour costs. The learning process starts when the first batch comes off the production line.

224 The correct answer is: Both statements are true

The first statement is one of the main assumptions of the learning effect. Employees must have some motivation to improve and learn, otherwise the learning effect will not appear. The second statement is also true.

225 The correct answer is: All of the above.

They are all conditions which allow the learning curve to flourish.

BBB Co

226 The correct answer is: 330.75 hours

Cumulative average time per batch for the first 71 batches

$Y = ax^b$

Where
- Y = the cumulative average time per unit to produce x units
- x = the cumulative number of units
- a = the time taken for the first unit of output
- b = the index of learning (logLR/log2)

The cumulative average time per batch, with a learning curve of 90%, is therefore

$Y = aX^{-0.152}$

where a = the time for the first batch (750 hours) and X is the number of the batch. For the 71st batch, $X = 71$.

$Y = 750 \times 71^{-0.152}$
$= 750 \times 0.5231 = 392.35$

The cumulative average time per batch for the first 71 batches is 392.35 hours.

Time taken for the 71st batch

The cumulative average time per batch for the first 70 batches is Y $= 750 \times 70^{-0.152}$
$= 750 \times 0.5243 = 393.23$

	Hours
Total time for 1st 71 batches (71 × 392.35)	27,856.85
Total time for 1st 70 batches (70 × 393.23)	27,526.10
Time for the 71st batch	330.75

227 The correct answer is: 92%

Batches	Total time	Average time/unit
1	750	750
2		$750 \times r$
4		$750 \times r^2$
8		$750 \times r^3$
16	8,500	$750 \times r^4$

$8,500 = 16 \times 750\, r^4$
$8,500/(16 \times 750) = r^4$
$r = 0.92$ or 92%

228 The correct answer is: Neither 1 nor 2

The learning curve will eventually come to an end in all cases.

The use of the learning curve is not restricted to the manufacturing industries that it is traditionally associated with. It is also used in other less-traditional sectors, such as professional practice, financial services, publishing and travel.

229 The correct answer is: Lower labour costs

The learning effect leads to a reduction in labour hours per batch, which therefore lowers the labour costs. The other factors are not affected by the learning rate.

230 The correct answer is: Increasing the level of staff training

Increasing staff training could lead to an extension of the learning curve as the higher skilled employees should demonstrate an even greater improvement than if they were not trained.

Mistletoe Co

231 The correct answer is: $116,699

The revised budget should incorporate a 3% growth rate per quarter starting with Quarter 1's actual sales.

Q1: $110,000
Q2: $110,000 × 1.03 = $113,300
Q3: $113,300 × 1.03 = $116,699.

232 The correct answer is: $77,000

The cost of sales in the original budget was 70% of sales.

$56,000/$80,000 × 100% = 70%
$57,120/$81,600 × 100% = 70%
$58,262/$83,232 × 100% = 70%

Therefore the revised cost of sales budget for Quarter 1 = $110,000 × 70% = $77,000

233 The correct answers are:

They reduce the element of uncertainty in budgeting

There is always a budget which extends for several months ahead

They are more realistic

If a high rate of inflation or major changes in market conditions or any other change is likely which cannot be quantified with accuracy, rolling budgets concentrate detailed planning and control on short-term prospects where the degree of uncertainty is much smaller. For example, if rolling budgets are prepared quarterly, there will always be a budget extending for the next 9 to 12 months. This is not the case when fixed annual budgets are used.

Planning and control will be based on a recent plan instead of a fixed annual budget that might have been made many months ago and which is no longer realistic. The regular revisions mean that rolling budgets are more time consuming and expensive to prepare than the current fixed annual budget approach.

234 The correct answers are:

It compounds budgetary slack.	**TRUE**	
It discourages efforts to improve performance.	**TRUE**	
It involves more time and effort than other methods.		**FALSE**

One of the main benefits of incremental budgeting is that it is quick and cheap to implement. Incremental budgeting compounds budgetary slack because any slack that has been built into the budget will be increased when the budgetary allowance is increased in subsequent periods.

Incremental budgeting can discourage efforts to improve performance because no attempt is made to scrutinise existing expenditure once it is included in the budget.

235 The correct answers are:

Probabilistic budgeting

Sensitivity analysis

These methods are suitable when the degree of uncertainty is quantifiable from the start of the budget period and actual results are not expected to go outside the range of these expectations.

Birch Co

236 The correct answer is: $3,750 Adverse

The sales volume planning variance compares the revised budget with the original budget. It may be called a market size variance.

Revised sales volume	17,500 units
Original budgeted sales volume	20,000 units
Sales volume planning variance in units of sales	2,500 units (A)
× standard contribution per unit	$1.5
Sales volume planning variance in $	3,750 (A)

237 The correct answer is: $2,250 Adverse

The operational variance is calculated in a similar way to the planning variance, except that actual results are compared with the revised standard or budget.

Actual sales volume	16,000 units
Revised sales volume	17,500 units
Operational sales volume variance in units	1,500 units (A)
× standard contribution per unit	$1.5
Operational sales volume variance in $ contribution	2,250 (A)

238 The correct answer is: $440 Adverse

Fixed production overhead total variance:
Units produced × standard fixed costs per unit − actual cost

[18,000 × ($3,000/17,500 units)] − $3,500
[18,000 × ($3,000/17,500 units)] − $3,500
[18,000 × 0.17] − $3,500
$3,060 − $3,500 = $440 (A)

239 The correct answer is: An improvement in technology led to an international reduction in sales price of Product X.

The improvement in technology is outside the control of the managers in Birch Co, and would therefore give rise to a planning variance. All of the other distracters are examples of operational issues.

240 The correct answer is: The sales volume operational variance

A sales volume operational variance, or market share variance, is caused by the difference between actual sales volume and the sales volume in the revised budget.

Organic Bread Co

241 The correct answer is: $3.30

Usage variance

	Std usage for actual output 950 units 'Should have used' kg	Actual usage 'Did use' kg	Variance kg	Standard cost per kg $	Variance $
White flour	427.50	408.50	19.00 (F)	1.80	34.20 (F)
Wholegrain flour	142.50	152.00	9.50 (A)	2.20	20.90 (A)
Yeast	9.50	10.00	0.50 (A)	20.00	10.00 (A)
	579.50	570.50			3.30 (F)

242 The correct answer is: $16.51 Adverse

Mix variance

	Actual usage kg	Actual usage in std mix (W1) kg	Mix Variance kg	Standard cost per kg $	Mix variance $
White flour	408.50	420.86	12.36 (F)	1.80	22.25 (F)
Wholegrain flour	152	140.29	11.71 (A)	2.20	25.76 (A)
Yeast	10	9.35	0.65 (A)	20.00	13.00 (A)
	570.50	570.50			16.51 (A)

Workings

$$\frac{450}{610} \times 570.50 = 420.86$$

$$\frac{150}{610} \times 570.50 = 140.29$$

$$\frac{10}{610} \times 570.50 = 9.35$$

243 The correct answer is: $19.77 Favourable

Yield variance

	Units
570.50 kg should produce (÷ 0.610)	935.25
They did produce	950.00
Yield variance in units of output	14.75 (F)
Standard material cost per unit	$1.34
Yield variance in $	$19.77 (F)

244 The correct answers are:

Not fully removing the mix out of the machine, leaving some behind.	**YES**	
Errors in the mix causing sub-standard loaves and rejections by the quality inspector.	**YES**	
An unexpected increase in the cost of flour introduced by the supplier.		**NO**

A material yield variance arises because there is a difference between what the input should have been for the output achieved and the actual input. Therefore an increase in the price of flour will not affect the yield; it would affect the material price variance.

245 The correct answers are:

The production manager in Organic Bread Co deviates from the standard mix.	**YES**	
The selling price of the Mixed Bloomer changes.		**NO**
An inferior quality of flour or yeast is used unknowingly.		**NO**

A change in the selling price of the Mixed Bloomer may influence the behaviour of the production manager, eg if the price has to be lowered, and cost savings made, so the mix may be reviewed. However, it will not lead directly to a mix variance.

An inferior quality of flour or yeast used unknowingly may lead to a yield variance, however, it will not lead to a mix variance.

Elm Co

246 The correct answer is: $44,000

Planning (selling price) variance

	$ per unit
Original budgeted sales price	8
Revised budgeted sales price	10
Sales price planning variance	2 (F)
× actual units sold	22,000
Planning variance for sales price	44,000 (F)

247 The correct answer is: $22,000

Operational (selling price) variance

	$
Actual sales revenue	198,000
Should have sold for (× $10)	220,000
Operational (selling price) variance	**22,000 (A)**

248   The correct answer is: $13,000

Labour rate variance

	$
4,000 hours should have cost (× $15)	60,000
But did cost	73,000
Labour rate variance	**13,000 (A)**

249   The correct answer is: 'The sales manager of Elm Co should be held responsible if an unfavourable planning sales price variance is found' is **false** and 'It is possible for the revised price to be manipulated and revised to a level whereby a favourable operational sales price could be found' is **true**.

The first statement is false because operational variances are the only variances within the control of the managers, so performance must be assessed with only operational variances in mind.

The second statement is true. One might question the validity of the revised price. The person responsible for the revised price should have sufficient evidence to support setting the revised price at that level to ensure that there is no manipulation of figures.

250   The correct answer is: Both statements are false.

An operational manager cannot appraise variances in isolation from each other. A favourable material price variance from using lower quality material may result in a much larger adverse usage variance, reaching the overall conclusion that the performance is poor.

Statement 2 is false because a change in the economic circumstances in Sealand is clearly outside of the control of the managers of Elm Co and will therefore not result in operational variances.

Maple Co

The original standard cost was 2.5 kg × $4 = $10. The revised standard cost is 4kg × $5.50 = $22.

251   The correct answer is: $22,000 (A)

Material price planning variance

This is the difference between the original standard price for Material X and the revised standard price.

	$ per kg
Original standard price	4
Revised standard price	5
Material price planning variance	1 (A)
× Actual quantity of material used (22,000 kg)	$22,000 (A)

252   The correct answer is: $13,000 (A)

Material price operational variance

This compares the actual price per kg of material with the revised standard price. It is calculated using the actual quantity of materials used.

	$
22,000 kg of Material X should cost (revised standard $5)	110,000
They did cost	123,000
Material price operational variance	13,000 (A)

253 The correct answer is: $8,000 (A)

Material usage operational variance

This variance is calculated by comparing the actual material usage with the standard usage in the revised standard, but is then converted into a monetary value by applying the original standard price for the materials, not the revised standard price.

	kg of X
8,000 units of Bark should use (× 2.5kg)	20,000
They did use	22,000
Material usage (operational) variance in kg of X	2,000 (A)
Original standard price per kg of Material X	$4
Material usage (operational) variance in $	$8,000 (A)

254 The correct answer is: 'Maple Co failed to order a sufficient amount of Material X for production from the main supplier. They sourced the rest of the material from another supplier at a higher price to make up for this' is **invalid** and 'There was a disruption to the supply of Material X to the market' is **valid**.

Statement 1 is an example of a controllable variance, and would therefore give rise to an operational variance. The second statement is outside the control of management and is therefore a planning variance.

255 The correct answer is: 'Any operational variances arising should be a realistic measure of what the causes of the variances have cost Maple Co' is **true** and 'The causes of the planning variances should be investigated immediately by the operational manager in Maple Co' is **false**.

Operational variances compare actual performance with a realistic standard cost or budget, and so should provide a realistic reflection of what the causes of the variances have cost Maple Co.

Planning variances are not the responsibility of operational managers, therefore there is no need for operational managers to immediately investigate their causes. However, their causes could be investigated by someone in Maple Co, since lessons may be learned for the future.

Pine Co

256 The correct answer is: $24,300 (F)

Labour rate planning variance

This is the difference between the original standard rate per hour and the revised standard rate per hour.

	$ per hour
Original standard rate	15
Revised standard rate	14
Labour rate planning variance	1 (F)
× actual no of hours worked	24,300
	24,300 (F)

257 The correct answer is: $180,000 (A)

Labour efficiency planning variance

This is the difference between the original standard time per unit and the revised standard time for the quantity of units produced.

	Hours
8,000 units of product should take: original standard ($\times$ 3)	24,000
8,000 units of product should take: revised standard ($\times$ 4.5)	36,000
Labour efficiency planning variance in hours	12,000 (A)
Original standard rate per hour	$15
Labour efficiency planning variance in $	$180,000 (A)

258 The correct answer is: $12,150 (A)

Labour rate operational variance

This is calculated using the actual number of hours worked and paid for.

	$
24,300 hours should cost (revised standard $14)	340,200
They did cost	352,350
Labour rate operational variance	12,150 (A)

259 The correct answer is: $175,500 (F)

Labour efficiency operational variance

	Hours
8,000 units of product should take ($\times$ 4.5 hours)	36,000
They did take	24,300
Labour efficiency (operational variance in hours)	11,700 (F)
Original standard rate per hour	$15
Labour efficiency (operational variance in $)	$175,500 (F)

260 The correct answers are: 'Production management's motivation is likely to increase if they know they will not be held responsible for poor planning and faulty standard setting' is **true** and 'Planning variances will provide a more realistic and fair reflection of actual performance' is **false**.

The second statement is false because it is operational variances which provide a more realistic and fair reflection of actual performance, since these are within the control of management.

Kiss Co

261 The correct answer is: 552 hours

Time taken for the 24th batch

Cumulative average time per batch for the first 24 batches

$Y = ax^b$

Where
- Y = the cumulative average time per unit to produce x units
- x = the cumulative number of units
- a = the time taken for the first unit of output
- b = the index of learning (logLR/log2)

The cumulative average time per batch, with a learning curve of 75%, is therefore

$Y = aX^{-0.415}$

where a = the time for the first batch (3,500 hours) and X is the number of the batch. For the 24th batch,

$$X = 24.$$
$$Y = 3,500 \times 24^{-0.415}$$
$$= 3,500 \times 0.2674 = 936$$

The cumulative average time per batch for the first 24 batches is 936 hours.

The cumulative average time per batch for the first 23 batches is $Y = 3,500 \times 23^{-0.415} = 3,500 \times 0.2722 = 952.7$

	Hours
Total time for 1st 24 batches (24 × 936)	22,464.0
Total time for 1st 23 batches (23 × 952.7)	21,912.1
Time for the 24th batch	551.9

262   The correct answer is: 79%

Batches		Hours
1		3,500
2	Doubled once	
4	Doubled twice	
8	Doubled three times	
16	Doubled four times	22,000

Cumulative average time per batch = 22,000 / 16 = 1,375
$$1,375 = 3,500 \, r^4$$
r = 0.79 or 79%

263   The correct answer is: $37,500 (F)

Labour efficiency planning variance

	Hours
10,000 batches of product should take: original standard (× 0.75)	7,500
10,000 batches of product should take: revised standard (× 0.5)	5,000
Labour efficiency planning variance in hours	2,500 (F)
Original standard rate per hour	$15
Labour efficiency planning variance in $	$37,500 (F)

264   The correct answer is: Both statements are true.

The learning effect has the effect of reducing the labour time per unit. Therefore, the labour efficiency planning variance will always be favourable.

Standards should be as accurate as possible. Therefore, it is not advisable to set standards before 'steady state' production is reached. However, it is possible to combine standard costing with the learning curve to calculate planning and operational variances.

265   The correct answer is: Provide workers with training

Training may help employees to improve their efficiency in a job. Overtime working should increase output, but there is no reason why it should improve efficiency (output per hour worked). Extra inspection and testing may reduce efficiency by taking up more time: they will not improve efficiency, because they do not test efficiency, only quality. Output capacity relates to potential output volume, not efficiency of working: for example, output capacity may be increased by hiring extra workers, but this does not affect productivity.

Hollie Hotels Co

266   The correct answer is: $240,492

The incremental budget is based on the previous year's actual results.

Budgeted contribution per room per night for 20X1 = $110 − ($40 × 105%) = $68

	20X1 budget $
Contribution (360 days × 20 rooms × 77% occupancy × $68)	376,992
Fixed costs ($130,000 × 105%)	(136,500)
Profit	240,492

267   The correct answer is:

	Correct order
Step 1	Identification of decision packages – base level
Step 2	Identification of decision packages – incremental packages
Step 3	Evaluation and ranking of each activity
Step 4	Allocation of resources

268   The correct answer is:

ZBB is particularly useful for cost reduction exercises.	**TRUE**
ZBB is particularly useful for cost structures such as Hollie Hotels Co's.	**TRUE**

Hollie Hotels Co were aiming to cut costs in order to achieve greater profitability and ZBB is particularly useful when making rationalisation decisions as it is possible to identify and remove inefficient or obsolete operations. Therefore, Statement 1 is true.

ZBB is particularly suitable for service industries such as hotels where variable expenses make up a large proportion of total expenditures. Alternative levels of provision for each activity, such as breakfast selection, are possible and cost and benefits are separately identifiable. Therefore, Statement 2 is true.

269   The correct answers are:

- Short term benefits may be to the detriment of long term benefits
- ZBB is more time consuming than incremental budgeting

Short-term benefits such as cost reduction may be emphasised to the detriment of long-term benefits. This is particularly significant in the luxury hotel market where customers have high expectations and reputation is easily lost.

The major problem associated with ZBB is the amount of management time and paperwork involved. Each hotel manager would have to spend considerably more time and effort on budgeting and may actively resist the process.

A usual problem cited with regards to ZBB is that individual managers may not have the necessary skills to construct decision packages and undertake the ranking process. However, in this case, we know that managers have been producing their own budgets each year and that online training is available. Therefore this argument is not valid.

Another potential problem with ZBB is that information systems may not be capable of providing suitable information and costly investment may be needed. However, in this case, the system is new and easy to use and so this argument does not hold.

270   The correct answer is: Hotel Northeast: Forecast profits are poor and control action is taken in advance.

Feedforward control is based on **forecast** results, ie, if the forecast is poor then control action is taken in advance of actual results.

Hotel Southwest: Fixed costs have deviated from plan and must be brought back on course – this describes negative feedback. **Results** must be brought back on course as they are deviating from the plan.

Hotel Southeast: Revenues and costs are going according to plan and no corrective action is necessary – this describes positive feedback.

Hotel Midwest: Variable costs are more than budget and must be reduced as they are deviating from plan – this describes negative feedback. **Results** must be brought back on course as they are deviating from the plan.

271 Mic Co

Workbook reference. The learning curve is covered in Chapter 14 of the BPP Workbook.

Top tips. There are quite a few calculations in this question, so you need to organise your presentation clearly and in a way that helps you to prepare your answer. Remember that every time output doubles, the cumulative average time per unit falls to the learning curve percentage figure of what the cumulative average time per unit was previously. You don't need the learning curve factor of −0.1844245 for most of your calculations.

The potential trick in the question is that the learning curve no longer applies in November, when the average time per batch is the same as the time required to produce the eighth batch in October. To calculate this time per batch, you need to calculate the average and total times for the seventh and eighth batches. The time for the 8th batch is the difference between the total times for the first seven and the first eight batches.

Easy marks. There are some easy marks to be won if you remember that every time output doubles the cumulative average time per unit is x% of what it was previously, where x is the learning curve percentage. If you can type your points reasonably quickly, there should be easy marks in the answer to part (b) too.

Marking scheme

			Marks
(a)	Cost each month: July and August (1.5 mark per month)	3	
	Cost each month: September and October (1.5 marks per month)	3	
	Cost in November	3	
			9
(b)	**End of learning period**		
	Each point discussed –maximum	2	Max 4
(c)	**Advantages and disadvantages**		
	Each advantage	1	
	Each disadvantage	1	Max 7
			20

(a) Every time output doubles, the average time per batch is 88% of what it was previously. The learning curve effect ends in October and does not apply in November, when the average time per unit is the same as the time required to make the eighth batch in October.

Month	Cumulative batches	Average time per batch	Total time	Incremental time in the month	Labour cost per month at $12 per hour
		Hours	Hours	Hours	$
July	1	200.00	200.00	200.00	2,400
August	2	176.00	352.00	152.00	1,824
September	4	154.88	619.52	267.52	3,210
October	8	136.294	1,090.35	470.83	5,650

Average time to produce first 7 batches = $200 \times 7^{-0.1844245} = 200 \times 1/1.4317157 = 139.6925$ hours

Total time for first 7 batches = $7 \times 139.6925 = 977.85$ hours

Average time to produce first 8 batches = $200 \times 8^{-0.1844245} = 200 \times 1/1.4674115 = 136.2944$ hours

Total time for first 8 batches = $8 \times 136.2944 = 1,090.35$ hours

Time to make the 8th batch = $1,090.35 - 977.85 = 112.50$ hours

Total labour cost in November = 8 batches × 112.50 per batch × $12 per hour = $10,800.

(b) The company sets selling prices on a cost plus basis, but in the first few months the cost per unit falls due to the 88% learning curve effect. The average time per batch was 200 hours for the first batch in July, but falls to 112.5 hours per batch from November onwards.

If cost plus pricing is used, and if the company wants to charge a stable price for its product, it should consider a cost plus price based on the longer-term unit cost from November onwards.

The company appears to have used actual cost plus to set the selling price on its initial batches, with the result that the price was high. This probably explains the disappointing initial sales.

Budgeting for labour time and labour costs should also take the learning curve into effect, because of the reduction in incremental labour time per batch in the months July – October.

(c) Involving senior staff at Mic Co in the budget-setting process

Advantages

- Since they are based on information from staff who are most familiar with the department, they are more likely to improve the accuracy of the budget. In Mic Co's case, the selling price could have been set more accurately and sales may have been higher if the production manager had been consulted.

- Staff are more likely to be motivated to achieve any targets as it is 'their' budget and they therefore have a sense of ownership and commitment. The production manager at Mic Co seems resigned to the fact that they are not consulted on budgetary matters.

- Morale amongst staff is likely to improve as they feel that their experience and opinions are valued.

- Knowledge from a spread of several levels of management is pooled.

- Co-ordination is improved due to the number of departments involved in the budget-setting process.

Disadvantages

- The whole budgeting process is more time consuming and therefore costly.

- The budgeting process may have to be started earlier than a non-participative budget would need to start because of the length of time it takes to complete the process.

272 Yumi Co

Marking scheme

			Marks
(a)	(i)	Flexed budget:	
		Revenue	0.5
		Food and drink	0.5
		Staff	0.5
		Heat, light and power	0.5
		Rent and rates	0.5
		Profit	0.5
			3
	(ii)	Weaknesses	4
(b)		Discussion	6
(c)		Definition of participative budgeting	1
		Advantages and disadvantages	6
			20

(a) (i) Flexed budget for Cowly restaurant

	Original budget	Flexed budget	Actual	Variance
Number of customers	1,500	1,800	1,800	
	$	$	$	$
Revenue	75,000	90,000	87,300	2,700 A
Food and drink costs	(22,500)	(27,000)	(26,100)	900 F
Staff costs	(31,500)	(37,800)	(38,250)	450 A
Heat, light and power	(7,500)	(9,000)	(8,100)	900 F
Rent, rates and other overheads	(12,000)	(12,000)	(12,600)	600 A
Profit	1,500	4,200	2,250	1,950 A

Notes:

Revenue: $75,000/1,500 = $50 per customer: $50 × 1,800 = $90,000

Food and drink: $22,500/1,500 = $15 per customer: $15 × 1,800 = $27,000

Staff costs: $31,500/1,500 = $21 per customer: $21 × 1,800 = $37,800

Heat, light and power: $7,500/1,500 = $5 per customer: $5 × 1,800 = $9,000

(ii) The most significant weakness in the current performance report is that the original budget is not flexed to adjust for the actual numbers of customers served.

The existing report shows that the Cowly restaurant has overspent on all its costs which could be a concern given the importance of cost control in Yumi Co. However, the main reason for the revenue variance and the costs variances is the fact that the number of customers the restaurant served was 20% higher than budgeted (1,800 v 1,500).

If the budget is flexed for the actual number of customers, this allows a more meaningful assessment of the restaurant's performance to be made.

Once the flexed budget is prepared, it can be seen that revenues were actually lower than would have been expected, given the number of customers served with average spend per head being $48·50 instead of $50. Food and drink costs were also less than budget. Taken together with the reduction in average customer spending, this might suggest that some of the items on the menu had been changed since the budget was originally set.

Another weakness in Yumi Co's budgetary control report is the fact that staff costs and heat, light and power costs are assumed to be purely variable costs – dependent on the number of customers. However, although the restaurant may recruit some temporary staff in busy periods, it is likely that at least some of the staff will be permanent, meaning that it would be more appropriate to treat staff costs as semi-variable rather than variable.

Similarly, it seems likely that there will be a significant fixed element within heat, light and power costs, so treating these as wholly variable costs does not seem appropriate.

(b) Under an incremental budgeting approach, the current year's budget and results are taken as the starting point for preparing the next year's budget. The budget is then adjusted for any expected changes, such as the impact of inflation on costs and prices, and sales growth or decline.

The main advantage of the incremental approach is that it is a relatively straightforward way of preparing a budget, appropriate for organisations which are operating in relatively stable environments. The locations of Yumi Co's restaurants, away from significant competition, suggest that the operating environment is relatively stable, meaning incremental budgeting is appropriate.

Similarly, the fact that Yumi Co appears to have a relatively well-established brand and customer base suggests that using an incremental approach to budgeting future revenues appears reasonable, even if it is difficult to identify some changes which need to be adjusted for in the next year's budget. However, one of the major disadvantages of incremental budgeting is that it does not provide any incentive to make operations more efficient or economical. If the current year figures include slack or inefficiencies, then using them as the start-point for the next year's figures means that inefficiency is automatically perpetuated into the next year.

Such an approach seems somewhat inconsistent with the focus on cost control within Yumi Co. If the company is worried about its relatively low margins, then an approach to budgeting which challenges costs more critically (such as zero-based budgeting or activity-based budgeting) might be more suitable for helping to drive down costs. For example, the highest cost is staff wages which could be analysed and Yumi Co could investigate making changes to its staffing model to reduce costs and/or improve efficiency.

As mentioned in part (a), whether labour costs and heat, light and power vary proportionately with the number of customers appears debatable. If Yumi Co's incremental budgets ignore the relationship between activities and costs, then ultimately the budgets will provide Yumi Co's management with little relevant information for managing costs. This could become an increasingly important issue if competition in Yumi Co's markets intensifies.

(c) The current budget process is a centralised, top-down process, meaning that the managers from Yumi Co's restaurants do not have any opportunity to influence the budgets for their restaurants.

By contrast, in a participative approach, the managers of each restaurant would be able to influence the figures for their restaurant, rather than having budget targets simply imposed on them.

Involving the managers in the budgeting process should help to make the budgets more effective and realistic. The local managers should have a greater understanding of the environmental factors and operational constraints which will influence the performance of their restaurants. For example, the manager of the Cowly restaurant will have a better understanding of their customers and market conditions and thus provide a greater insight into the potential impact of the new restaurant than a member of the finance team at Yumi Co's head office would have. Similarly, managers are more likely to be committed to achieving a budget if they have been involved in creating it – not least because their involvement in the preparing the budget should help to ensure that they feel the budget figures are realistic.

However, involving the restaurant managers in the budgeting process is likely to make it more time-consuming. For example, instead of running their restaurants, managers will have to spend time in meetings with head office staff planning and preparing their budgets. In this respect, it may be more appropriate for Yumi Co to maintain the current, top-down process for restaurants which are operating in a stable environment (and where the insights from local managers will add little value), but introduce a more participative approach for restaurants like Cowly which are facing a period of change.

Another potential disadvantage of participative budgeting is that managers may try to influence the budgets so that their targets can be achieved easily. By doing this, a restaurant's performance, compared to budget, will appear to improve, but this would actually be an illusion. One of the main issues Yumi Co could face in this respect is that, given the range of different locations of its restaurants, it will be difficult for head office staff to know whether individual managers are setting targets which are easy or challenging. If the restaurants were all similar, or in similar locations, it would be easier to compare the figures suggested by individual managers to assess how challenging, or not, they are.

Similarly, managers are more likely to highlight issues which will lead to a reduction in their budget targets, rather than ones which increase their targets. For example, the manager at Cowly has highlighted that the new competitor will make it more difficult for them to achieve budget. However, the manager does not appear to have made a corresponding acknowledgement that the increased numbers of visitors to Cowly could support an increased revenue target. There is a danger that the managers' participation in the budgets could lead to the targets becoming less challenging, which in turn could affect Yumi Co's competitiveness and profitability.

273 Crumbly Cakes

Workbook references. Variance analysis is covered in Chapters 16 and 17.

Top tips. You may find part (a) quite tricky. You need to plan a structured answer using the headings suggested by the question. Make some sensible, common sense suggestions and if you run out of ideas, move on to parts (b) and (c) where easier marks are available. Read the information very carefully and layout your workings clearly.

Easy marks. There are some easy variance calculations in parts (b) and (c) as well as some trickier mix and yield variances.

Examining team's comments. Many candidates completely missed the point in part (a). If a business fundamentally changes its business process without altering the standard costs of the process, it renders the variances that are produced meaningless. Some candidates tried to discuss each variance in turn rather than carry out a performance assessment of each manager. This is not as effective a method. Motivation is a complex topic and credit was given for any sensible comments.

Part (b) was well done with many candidates scoring good marks.

		Marks
(a)	Production manager assessment	2
	Sales manager assessment	2
	Bonus scheme comment	3
		7
(b)	Price variance	3
	Mix variance	3
	Yield variance	3
		9
(c)	Planning variance and comment	2
	Operational variance and comment	2
		4
		20

(a) **Production manager**

The production manager instigated the new organic cake production approach and this has **fundamentally changed** the nature of the business. Before the new system started, there were **favourable material variances** for price and yield and the production manager would have received a bonus as a result.

Organic ingredients are **more expensive** and this results in **adverse** material price and mix variances in March. The **material yield** variance is favourable but not by enough to compensate for the adverse variances. This means that the production manager would not receive a bonus under the current scheme.

Sales of the cakes have improved significantly so customers presumably appreciate the new flavour and mix of ingredients. The production manager does not receive any credit for the favourable sales variances and that does not seem fair.

Sales manager

In contrast, the **sales variances** that the sales manager is responsible for have moved from adverse in February to favourable in March. The new organic approach has, therefore, been a **success** with customers. The sales manager will have had to sell the new organic cakes to customers and is therefore **partly responsible** for the improvement, but the original impetus came from the production manager.

Bonus scheme

The bonus scheme does not seem to be fair as it will **not reward** the two managers fairly for their efforts. They are both responsible for the improved sales but it is very difficult to **fairly allocate responsibility** in this situation. Some form of **sharing** of responsibility and reward is required.

The **standards** that the variances are based on need to be changed to reflect the new approach that the business is taking. For example, the standard price of the materials needs to be increased.

(b) **Material price variances**

	$
5,700 kg of flour should have cost (× $0.12)	684
but did cost	741
Material price variance	57 (A)

		$
6,600 kg of eggs should have cost (× $0.70)		4,620
but did cost		5,610
Material price variance		990 (A)

		$
6,600 kg of butter should have cost (× $1.70)		11,220
but did cost		11,880
Material price variance		660 (A)

		$
4,578 kg of sugar should have cost (× $0.50)		2,289
but did cost		2,747
Material price variance		458 (A)

		$
Total material price variance		2,165 (A)

Material mix variances

Total quantity used = 5,700 + 6,600 + 6,600 + 4,578 = 23,478 kg
Standard mix of actual use of each ingredient is in equal proportions = 23,478/4 = 5,869.5 kg

	Actual quantity Actual mix	Actual quantity Standard mix	Variance	Standard cost per kg	Variance
	Kg	Kg	Kg	$	$
Flour	5,700	5869.5	169.5 (F)	0.12	20.34 (F)
Eggs	6,600	5869.5	730.5 (A)	0.70	511.35 (A)
Butter	6,600	5869.5	730.5 (A)	1.70	1,241.85 (A)
Sugar	4,578	5869.5	1,291.5 (F)	0.50	645.75 (F)
	23,478	23,478			1,087.11 (A)

Material yield variance

Standard cost of a cake

		$
Flour	0.1 kg × $0.12	0.012
Eggs	0.1 kg × $0.70	0.070
Butter	0.1 kg × $1.70	0.170
Sugar	0.1 kg × $0.50	0.050
		0.302

	Cakes
The actual quantity of inputs are expected to yield (23,478/0.4)	58,695
Actual output	60,000
Yield variance in cakes	1,305 (F)
× standard cost per cake ($0.302)	$394.11 (F)

Alternative method

	Standard quantity Standard mix Kg	Actual quantity Standard mix Kg	Variance Kg	Standard cost per kg $	Variance $
Flour	6,000	5869.5	130.5	0.12	15.66
Eggs	6,000	5869.5	130.5	0.70	91.35
Butter	6,000	5869.5	130.5	1.70	221.85
Sugar	6,000	5869.5	130.5	0.50	65.25
	24,000	23,478			394.11 (F)

(c) **Total operational variance**

	$
Revised standard cost of actual production (60,000 × $0.40)	24,000
Actual cost	20,978
Total operational variance	3,022 (F)

The variance is **favourable** because the actual cost was lower than the expected cost using the revised basis.

Total planning variance

	$
Revised standard cost (60,000 × $0.40)	24,000
Original standard cost (60,000 × $0.302)	18,120
Total planning variance	5,880 (A)

The planning variance reveals the extent to which the original standard was at fault. It is an **adverse variance** because the original standard was too optimistic, overestimating the expected profits by understating the standard cost. More simply, it is adverse because the revised standard cost is much higher than the original standard cost.

274 Medical Temp Co

Workbook reference. Planning and operational variances are covered in Chapter 17.

Top tips. Part (a) should not cause any problems as it's a pure knowledge and doesn't require application to the scenario.

In part (b) you must remember to clearly state whether the variance is adverse or favourable. The examining team state that there are different ways to calculate variances and it does not matter which technique you use. This answer shows the ACCA answer and then the BPP approach in the spreadsheet.

Part (c) has two requirements - 'discuss the actions' and 'how this has impacted on the variances' so it's useful to use a heading for each of these parts to make sure you cover them both.

Easy marks. Part (a) should be an easy four marks and there are easy marks available in part (b) for calculating the variances. Just remember that sales volume in this case is the number of staff.

Examining team's comments. In part (b) many students missed out the calculation of the total market size and share variances, which is probably the easiest part of the question. The most common mistake made was to use revenue instead of contribution. The key messages are:

1 Read the requirements carefully

2 Use the software to your advantage

3 Practise questions

		Marks
(a)	Market size and share variances are breakdown of sales volume variance/need to consider change in size of market	1
	Description of market size/market share variances/reference to controllability	3
		4
(b)	Original budget (1 mark each doctors and nurses)	2
	Revised budget (1 mark each doctors and nurses)	2
	Actual sales volume at standard contribution (0.5 each doctors and nurses)	1
	Market size variance - doctors	1
	Market size variance - nurses	1
	Total market size variance	0.5
	Market share variance - doctors	1
	Market share variance - nurses	1
	Total market share variance	0.5
		10
(c)	Discussion - up to 2 for each well discussed point. Must address both parts of the requirement	
		6
		20

(a) **Market size and market share variances**

The market size and market share variances are a breakdown of the sales volume variance. The sales volume variance shows the effect on profit of the actual sales level being different from the budgeted sales level. However, without considering how the market itself has changed, it is difficult to draw conclusions about performance from the sales volume variance. Therefore, the sales volume variance is broken down into its two components. By doing this, it is possible to assess the extent to which changes in profit are as a result of:

(i) A change in the size of the market as a whole, which is beyond the control of the sales manager; and

(ii) A change in the share of the market which the company holds, which is deemed to be within the control of the sales manager. Consequently, the variances become far more meaningful for performance management as businesses can identify external and internal factors which can influence the results and what was controllable and uncontrollable.

(b) **Variances**

Quarter 2 original budgeted sales volumes and contribution

	Nurses	Doctors
National Q1 sales volume (no. of weekly contracts)	14,000	4,000
Percentage of market	30%	40%
Budgeted sales volume	4,200	1,600
	S'000	S'000
Budgeted revenue for MTC	4,200	3,200
Standard contribution	80%	80%
Budgeted standard contribution	3,360	2,560

Quarter 2 revised budgeted sales volumes and contribution

	Nurses	Doctors
National Q2 sales volume (no. of weekly contracts)	18,900	4,100
Percentage of market	30%	40%
Revised sales volume	5,670	1,640
	S'000	S'000
Budgeted revenue for MTC	5,670	3,280
Standard contribution	80%	80%
Revised standard contribution	4,536	2,624

Quarter 2 actual results

	S'000	S'000
Actual revenue in quarter 2	5,300	3,600
Standard contribution	80%	80%
Actual sales volume at standard contribution	4,240	2,880

Market size variance (planning)
(Budget v revised contribution)

	S'000	S'000
Budgeted contribution for MTC	3,360	2,560
Revised budget contribution for MTC	4,536	2,624
Variance	1,176 F	64 F

Total market size variance = $1,176,000 + $64,000 = $1,240,000 F

Market share variance (operational)
(Revised contribution v actual)

	S'000	S'000
Revised budget contribution for MTC	4,536	2,624
Actual sales volume at standard contribution	4,240	2,880
Variance	(296) A	256 F

Total market share variance = $(296,000) + $256,000 = $(40,000) A

On a spreadsheet, your answer may have looked like this:

	A	B	C	D	E	F	G	H
1								
2	b)	**Market size variance**	Nurses		Doctors		Total	
3			$		$		$	
4		Revised sales volume	5,670		1,640			
5		Original budgeted sales volume	4,200		1,600			
6		Sales volume planning variance in number of staff	1,470	F	40	F		
7		x standard conribution	800		1,600			
8		Market size/Sales volume planning variance	1,176,000	F	64,000	F	1,240,000	F
9								
10								
11		**Market share variance**	Nurses		Doctors		Total	
12			$		$		$	
13		Actual sales volume	5,300		1,800			
14		Revised sales volume	5,670		1,640			
15		Operational sales volume variance in number of staff	- 370	A	160	F		
16		x standard conribution	800		1,600			
17		Market share/Operational sales volume variance	- 296,000	A	256,000	F	- 40,000	A

The formulae behind the figures are:

	A	B	C	D	E	F	G	H
1								
2	b)	**Market size variance**	Nurses		Doctors		Total	
3			$		$		$	
4		Revised sales volume	=(18900000/1000)*30%		=(8200000/2000)*40%			
5		Original budgeted sales volume	=(14000000/1000)*30%		=(8000000/2000)*40%			
6		Sales volume planning variance in number of staff	=C4-C5	F	=E4-E5	F		
7		x standard conribution	=1000*80%		=2000*80%			
8		Market size/Sales volume planning variance	=C6*C7	F	=E6*E7	F	=C8+E8	F
9								
10								
11		**Market share variance**	Nurses		Doctors		Total	
12			$		$		$	
13		Actual sales volume	=5300000/1000		=3600000/2000			
14		Revised sales volume	=C4		=E4			
15		Operational sales volume variance in number of staff	=C13-C14	A	=E13-E14	F		
16		x standard conribution	=C7		=E7			
17		Market share/Operational sales volume variance	=C15*C16	A	=E15*E16	F	=C17+E17	A

(c)   **Cheat Co**

The sales director at Cheat Co has deliberately manipulated the market size figures to make the market for doctors and nurses look smaller. Now, instead of being the actual market size of 18,900 weekly contracts ($18·9m/$1,000) and 4,100 weekly contracts ($8·2m/$2,000), they will be much lower at 13,230 and 2,870 respectively. This means that the revised budgeted sales volume figures used to calculate Cheat Co's variances were far lower. This behaviour is unethical and may well lead to the sales director getting a bonus which he does not deserve.

As a consequence of this, the market size variances are highly adverse, so it looks like Cheat Co's original budgets are very wrong. The sales director will not care about this since he will not be held accountable for that variance; instead he will be responsible for the favourable market share variance of over $2m. This makes the sales director's performance look really good, but the reality is that it only looks this high because the budgeted sales figures include revenue for maternity units and the revised budgeted figures do not. This does not reflect the sales director's real performance for the quarter.

275 Clear Co

Marking scheme

			Marks
(a)	(i)	Calculation of sales mix contribution variance	4
	(ii)	Calculation of sales quantity contribution variance	4
(b)		Explanation of what sales mix contribution variance measures	1
		Explanation of what sales quantity contribution variance measures	1
(c)		Calculations	4
		Discussion of sales performance	6
			20

(a) **Total sales mix variance**

	Actual total sales in standard mix (W1)	Actual total sales in actual mix	Sales mix variance in units	× Standard contribution (W2)	Variance $
RLE	3,764.79 units	4,130 units	365.21 (F)	× $2,400	876,504 (F)
ICL	1,325.21 units	960 units	365.21 (A)	× $2,500	913,025 (A)
	5,090 units	5,090 units			36,521 (A)

Total sales quantity variance

Budgeted total sales units (3,750 + 1,320)	5,070
Actual total sales units	5,090
Total sales quantity variance in units	20 (F)
Average standard contribution per unit (W3)	$2,426.04
Total sales quantity variance	$48,521 (F)

Workings

1   Actual sales quantity in standard mix

Product	Actual quantity in standard mix
RLE: 5,090 × (3,750/5,070) =	3,764.79
ICL: 5,090 × (1,320/5,070) =	1,325.21
	5,090.00

2   Standard contribution per unit

RLE: $3,000 - $600 = $2,400

ICL: $3,650 - $1,150 = $2,500

3   Average standard contribution per unit

Total budgeted contribution = (3,750 × $2,400) + (1,320 × $2,500) = $12,300,000

Budgeted total sales quantity = 3,750 + 1,320 = 5,070 units

Weighted average = $12,300,000 / 5,070 units = $2,426,04

Alternative sales quantity variance calculation

	Standard sales in standard mix Units	Actual total sales in standard mix (W1) Units	Sales mix variance in units	× Standard contribution (W2)	Variance $
RLE	3,750	3,764.79	14.79 (F)	× $2,400	35,496 (F)
ICL	1,320	1,325.21	5.21 (F)	× $2,500	13,025 (F)
	5,070	5,090			48,521 (F)

(b) The sales mix contribution variance measures the effect on contribution of changing the mix of actual sales from the budgeted sales mix.

The sales quantity contribution variance measures the effect on contribution of selling a different total quantity from the budgeted total quantity.

(c) Possible additional calculations

Actual compared to budgeted revenue	RLE	ICL	Total	
	$	$	$	
Actual sales revenue	11,977,000	3,264,000	15,241,000	
Budgeted sales revenue	11,250,000	4,818,000	16,068,000	
Difference in revenue	727,000	−1,554,000	−827,000	
Percentage terms	6.46%	−32.25%	−5.15%	
Sales volume variance (Actual qty − budgeted qty) × std contribution	$ 912,000 (F)	$ 900,000 (A)	$ 12,000 (F)	
Selling price variance (Actual price − Selling price) × actual qty	413,000 (A)	900,000 (A)	12,000 (F)	
Total sales variance	9,499,000	2,160,000	11,659,000	Actually received
(Actual price − std var cost) × actual qty	9,000,000	3,300,000	12,300,000	Expect to receive
	499,000 (F)	1,140,000 (A)	641,000 (A)	

Sales performance

When comparing budgeted revenues to actual revenues, it can be seen that ICL has under-performed this year, with revenues being 32.25% lower than budgeted. This is a result of both lower sales volumes and a lower selling price for ICL, which has resulted in an adverse sales volume variance of $900,000 and an adverse sales price variance of $240,000. The main reason for this is probably the merger that took place during the year, which resulted in Clear Co's now biggest competitor subsequently reducing prices for ICL and presumably capturing a bigger slice of the market as a result. Even though Clear Co's actual price for ICL was $250 less than budgeted, its sales volumes still fell by 27% so it was apparently unable to match the competition.

Looking at the mix of sales between RLE and ICL at Clear Co, there is an adverse mix variance of $36,521. This is because, whilst the sales of ICL were lower than budgeted, the sales of RLE were higher than budgeted. Since RLE has a lower standard contribution than ICL, this produced an adverse mix variance. This shift in sales mix could be partly attributable to the fact that the RLE procedure is for people aged over 40 and there is an increasingly ageing population in Zeeland. Clear Co has had to lower its price to make these sales of RLE but again, this is probably due to increased pressure to reduce prices resulting from the merger.

Another factor which it is not possible to quantify from the information provided, but which will invariably have had an impact on sales of lens treatments overall, is the increased availability of laser treatments to customers. Given that 90% of customers are now eligible for the less complex laser treatment, this side of the business may well have grown at Clear Co.

Overall, the sales volume variance is favourable for Clear Co because of the increased sales of RLE. However, to achieve this, prices have been reduced, resulting in a significant adverse sales price variance of $653,000. These results are disappointing and Clear Co may have to rethink its strategy moving forwards.

276 Truffle Co

Workbook references. Basic variances are covered in Chapter 16. Planning and operational variances are covered in Chapter 17.

Top tips. You should find part (a) relatively straightforward. Labour rate and efficiency variances are assumed knowledge from MA.

Part (b) contains some of the trickier variances stated on the PM syllabus. As a check, the sum of all variances in part (b) should equal the sum of the labour rate variance and the labour efficiency variance calculated in part (a). Ensure you leave enough time to assess the performance of the production manager, based on your calculations (part (c)).

Easy marks. There are easy marks available in part (a) for calculating the labour rate and efficiency variances.

Marking scheme

			Marks
(a)	Rate and efficiency variances:		
	Rate variance	2	
	Efficiency variance	2	
			4
(b)	Planning and operational variances:		
	Labour rate planning variance	2	
	Labour rate operational variance	2	
	Labour efficiency planning variance	2	
	Labour efficiency operational variance	2	
			8
(c)	Discussion:		
	Only operational variances controllable	1	
	No labour rate operating variance	1	
	Planning variance down to company, not manager	2	
	Labour efficiency total variance looks bad	2	
	Manager has performed well as regards efficiency	2	
	Standard for labour time was to blame	2	
	Conclusion	2	
			Max 8
			20

(a) **Labour variances**

Standard cost per labour hour = $6.00 / 0.5 = $12.00

Labour rate variance

	$
12,000 hours of work should have cost (× $12 per hr)	144,000
but did cost	136,800
Labour rate variance	7,200 (F)

Labour efficiency variance

20,500 batches should have taken (× 0.5 hrs)	10,250 hrs
but did take	12,000 hrs
Efficiency variance in hours	1,750 hrs (A)
× standard rate per hour	× $12
Efficiency variance	$21,000 (A)

(b) **Planning and operational variances**

Labour rate planning variance

	$
Standard rate	12.00
Revised rate ($12 × 0.95)	11.40
Variance	0.60 (F)
× actual hours paid (12,000)	× 12,000
Labour rate planning variance	$7,200 (F)

Labour rate operational variance

	$
Revised cost of actual hours (12,000 × $12 × 95%)	136,800
Actual cost of actual hours	136,800
Labour rate operational variance	$nil

Labour efficiency planning variance

Standard hours for actual production (20,500 × 0.5 hrs per batch)	10,250 hrs
Revised hours for actual production (20,500 batches × 0.5 hrs per batch × 1.2)	12,300 hrs
Variance	2,050 hrs (A)
× original standard rate per hour	× $12
Labour efficiency planning variance	$24,600 (A)

Labour efficiency operational variance

20,500 batches should have taken (20,500 × 0.5 × 1.2)	12,300 hrs
but did take	12,000 hrs
Variance	300 hrs (F)
× original standard rate per hour	× $12
Labour efficiency operational variance	$3,600 (F)

Alternative solution

The following solution, calculating the **labour efficiency operational variance** using the **revised standard rate per hour**, and the **labour rate planning variance** based on **revised hours for actual production** also scored full marks.

Note that while this approach does not reconcile to the labour rate and efficiency variances calculated in part (a), it does **reconcile to the total labour variance ($13,800 adverse).**

Labour rate planning variance	$
Standard rate	12.00
Revised rate ($12 × 0.95)	11.40
Variance	0.60 (F)
× revised hours for actual production (12,300)	× 12,300
Labour rate planning variance	$7,380 (F)

Labour rate operational variance	$
Revised cost of actual hours (12,000 × $12 × 95%)	136,800
Actual cost of actual hours	136,800
Labour rate operational variance	$nil

Labour efficiency planning variance	
Standard hours for actual production (20,500 × 0.5 hrs per batch)	10,250 hrs
Revised hours for actual production (20,500 batches × 0.5 hrs per batch × 1.2)	12,300 hrs
Variance	2,050 hrs (A)
× standard rate per hour	× $12
Labour efficiency planning variance	$24,600 (A

Labour efficiency operational variance	
20,500 batches should have taken (20,500 × 0.5 × 1.2)	12,300 hrs
but did take	12,000 hrs
Variance	300 hrs (F)
× revised standard rate per hour	× $11.40
Labour efficiency operational variance	$3,420 (F)

(c) **Performance of the production manager for the month of November**

The total labour rate variance calculated in part (a) suggests that the production manager has managed to secure **labour at a lower rate** than budgeted (favourable variance of $7,200). However, the total labour efficiency variance (adverse variance of $21,000) would appear to indicate that they have been extremely poor at controlling their **staff's efficiency**.

These variances should be split into **planning and operational variances** to give a truer indication of performance. Planning variances arise due to **inaccurate** planning and/or faulty standards (factors that are outside the control of the production manager). Therefore, the production manager should only be assessed on operational variances.

Labour rate

The labour rate operational variance was $nil. This means that the workforce were paid the **agreed reduced rate** of $11.40 per hour. It is unlikely that the production manager paid anyone for overtime, as this would have increased the hourly rate.

The production manager cannot take credit for the favourable total labour rate variance. The labour rate planning variance of $7,200 indicates that the reduced labour rate was beyond the production manager's control and was **secured by the company**.

Labour efficiency

The total labour efficiency variance is $21,000 adverse.

The planning variance is **$24,600 adverse**. This is because the standard labour time per batch was not updated in November to reflect the fact that it would take **longer to produce the truffles** as a result of the retailer requesting the truffles to be made slightly softer. The production manager cannot be held responsible for this variance.

ANSWERS

In contrast, the operational variance is **$3,600 favourable**. When the truffle recipe changed in November, it was expected that the production process would take 20% longer for the first month, as the workers became used to working with the **new ingredient mix**. The workers actually took less than the 20% extra time predicted, yielding a **favourable operational variance**. The production manager can take credit for this variance.

In summary, the production manager **performed well** in the month of November.

277 Block Co

Workbook reference. Sales mix and quantity variances are covered in Chapter 16 of the BPP Workbook. Sales planning and operational variances are covered in Chapter 17.

Top tips. You may have been surprised that this question focussed on sales variances rather than cost variances, but the principles are very similar. In part (a), the planning and operational variances for Commodity 1 and 2 have already been calculated and the information is available to calculate the variances for both commodities, so you can check your logic as you calculate the variances for Commodity 3.

The use of a proforma layout in part (b) is essential for clarity of presentation.

Easy marks. There are easy marks available in part (c) providing you understand what the variances you have calculated in parts (a) and (b) mean for the business and refer to the scenario throughout your answer.

Examining team's comments. Part (a) was really well answered with the majority of candidates scoring the full marks. Part (b) tested the sales mix and sales quantity variances. This was well answered by some candidates, but the main error that did arise was the failure to realise that the company was using absorption costing, which meant that the variances should have been based on the profit margins of each product rather than the contribution margins. Quite a few candidates had calculated their variances using selling prices rather than profit margins.

Finally, another common error was to calculate the sales volume variance rather than the sales quantity variance. This is an error in understanding, since the sales volume variance is the total variance, which breaks down into its two component parts of sales mix and sales quantity.

Marking scheme

			Marks
(a)	Planning and operational variances:		
	Operational variance	2	
	Planning variance	2	
			4
(b)	Mix and quantity variances:		
	Standard profit per unit	4	
	Mix variance	4	
	Quantity variance	3	
			11
(c)	Discussion:		
	1 mark per valid comment		Max 5
			20

(a)   **Sales price operational variance for Commodity 3**

	$
Actual sales (25,600 units × $40.40)	1,034,240
Revised budget at market price (25,600 units × $39.10)	1,000,960
Sales price operational variance	33,280 (F)

Sales price planning variance for Commodity 3

	$
Revised 'standard' sales price budget	39.10
Original standard sales price	41.60
Sales price planning variance per unit	2.50 (A)
Units sold	25,600
Sales price planning variance in total	$64,000 (A)

(b)   **Total sales mix variance**

	Actual total sales in actual mix	Actual total sales in standard mix (W1)	Sales mix variance in units	× Standard profit margin (W2)	Variance $
Commodity 1	29,800 units	30,643 units	843 (A)	× $11.20	9,442 (F)
Commodity 2	30,400 units	28,600 units	1,800 (F)	× $4.20	7,560 (A)
Commodity 3	25,600 units	26,557 units	957 (A)	× $12.00	11,484 (A)
	85,800 units	85,800 units			13,366 (A)

Total sales quantity variance

Budgeted total sales units (30,000 + 28,000 + 26,000)	84,000
Actual total sales units	85,800
Total sales quantity variance in units	1,800 (F)
Average standard profit per unit (W3)	$9.11
Total sales quantity variance	$16,406 (F)

Workings

1   Actual sales quantity in standard mix

Product	Actual quantity in standard mix
Commodity 1: 85,800 × 30/84 =	30,643
Commodity 2: 85,800 × 28/84 =	28,600
Commodity 3: 85,800 × 26/84 =	26,557
	85,800

2   Standard profit margins per unit

$$\text{Overhead absorption rate (OAR)} = \frac{\$174,400}{\left[(0.2 \times 30,000) + (0.6 \times 28,000) + (0.8 \times 26,000)\right]} =$$

$4 per hour

Product	Commodity 1 $	Commodity 2 $	Commodity 3 $
Standard selling price	30.00	35.00	41.60
Variable production costs	(18.00)	(28.40)	(26.40)
Fixed production overheads ($4 per hr)	(0.80)	(2.40)	(3.20)
Standard profit margin	11.20	4.20	12.00

3 Average standard profit per unit

	Budgeted sales units	Standard profit per unit $	Budgeted profit $
Commodity 1	30,000	11.20	336,000
Commodity 2	28,000	4.20	117,600
Commodity 3	26,000	12.00	312,000
	84,000		765,600

Budgeted average profit per unit = $765,600/84,000 = $9.11

(c) The calculations above have shown that, as regards the sales price, there is a $23,360 favourable operational variance and a $54,680 adverse planning variance. In total, these net off to a sales price variance of $31,320 adverse. The sales manager can only be responsible for a variance to the extent that they control it. Since the standard selling prices are set by a consultant, rather than the sales manager, the sales manager can only be held responsible for the operational variance. Given that this was a favourable variance of $23,360, it appears that they have performed well, achieving sales prices which, on average, were higher than the market prices at the time. The consultant's predictions, however, were rather inaccurate, and it is these that have caused an adverse variance to occur overall in relation to sales price.

As regards sales volumes, the mix variance is $13,366 adverse and the quantity variance is $16,406 favourable, meaning that the total volume variance is $3,040 favourable. This is because total sales volumes were higher than expected, although it is apparent that the increased sales related to the lower margin Commodity 2, with sales of Commodity 1 and Commodity 3 actually being lower than budget.

The total variance relating to sales is $28,280 adverse. This looks poor but, as identified above, it is due to the inaccuracy of the sales price forecasts made by the consultant. We know that Block Co is facing tough market conditions because of the economic recession and therefore it is not that surprising that market prices were actually a bit lower than originally anticipated. This could be due to the recession hitting even harder in this quarter than in previous ones.

278 Newtown School

Workbook reference. Budgetary systems are covered in Chapter 13 of the BPP Workbook.

Top tips. This is a relatively straightforward question with a number of easy marks available, provided that you can work reasonably quickly.

Remember to clearly show all workings to part (a) and relate each point back to the scenario in part (d).

Easy marks. There are easy marks available for straightforward knowledge in parts (b) and (d).

Examining team's comments. In part (a) the calculations were quite straightforward and most candidates scored decent marks on this part of the question. The main error that arose was in relation to the salaries' cost. Many candidates were unable to split the year into two halves, deduct one staff member's cost and then apply the pay rise to only half of the year.

But, even if they had managed to do that, many candidates then went on to erroneously inflate the resultant cost of $599,940 by the rate given in the question, even though the pay rise was the relevant increment, not the rate of inflation.

Marks

(a) Budgeted costs:
Budgeted income   2.0
Repairs and maintenance   1.0
Teachers' salaries   1.5
Capital expenditure   1.0
Deficit   0.5
                                                                    6

(b) Advantages and disadvantages:
Two advantages   2.0
Two disadvantages   2.0
                                                                    4

(c) Zero-based budgeting:
Explanation of ZBB process   Max 4.0
Relevance to the school: one mark for each point made   Max 4.0
Total for part (c)   Max 6

(d) Use of ZBB to Newtown School
Each point made   1.0   Max 4
                                                                   20

(a) **Budgeted income** $
Income from pupils registered on 1 June Year 1 (given in question)   724,500
Expected income from new joiners (W1)   26,100
Total expected income   750,600

Budgeted expenditure
Repairs and maintenance ($30,000 × 1.03)   30,900
Salaries (W2)   599,940
Expected capital expenditure [(0.7 × $145,000) + (0.3 × $80,000)]   125,500
Total expected expenditure   756,340
Budget deficit   5,740

Workings

1   **Expected income from new joiners**

Expected number of new joiners = $(0.2 \times 50) + (0.3 \times 20) + (0.5 \times 26) = 29$

$900 income from each new joiner × 29 = $26,100

2   **Salaries**

$[(\$620,000 - \$26,000)/2] + [(\$620,000 - \$26,000 \times 1.02)/2]$

$= \$297,000 + \$302,940 = \$599,940$

(b) Incremental budgeting bases the budget on the results for the current period plus an amount for estimated growth or inflation in the next period. It is therefore suitable for organisations that operate in a **stable environment** where historical figures are a reliable guide to the future.

Advantages

Incremental budgeting is very **quick** compared to other methods of budgeting such as zero-based budgeting.

The information required to prepare a budget under this approach is also **readily available**.

For the above reasons, incremental budgeting is very **easy to perform**. This makes it possible for an employee with little accounting training to prepare a budget.

Disadvantages

Incremental budgeting is a reasonable procedure if current operations are as **effective, efficient and economical** as they can be. In general, however, it is an inefficient form of budgeting as it encourages **slack** and **wasteful spending** to creep into budgets. Past inefficiencies are perpetuated because cost levels are rarely subjected to close scrutiny.

There is also a risk that **errors** from one year are carried to the next, since the previous year's figures are not questioned.

(c) **Zero-based budgeting**

The three main steps involved in preparing a zero-based budget are as follows:

(1) Activities are identified by managers. Managers are then forced to consider different ways of performing the activities.

These activities are then described in what is called a 'decision package', which:

– Analyses the cost of the activity

– States its purpose

– Identifies alternative methods of achieving the same purpose

– Establishes performance measures for the activity

– Assesses the consequence of not performing the activity at all or of performing it at different levels

As regards this last point, the decision package may be prepared at the base level, representing the minimum level of service or support needed to achieve the organisation's objectives. Further incremental packages may then be prepared to reflect a higher level of service or support.

(2) Management will then rank all the packages in the order of decreasing benefits to the organisation. This will help management decide what to spend and where to spend it. This ranking of the decision packages happens at numerous levels of the organisation.

(3) The resources are then allocated, based on order of priority up to the spending level.

(d) The principle behind **zero-based budgeting** is that the budget for each cost centre should be prepared from 'scratch' or zero. Every item of expenditure must be justified, to be included in the budget for the forthcoming period.

The ZBB process involves identifying decision packages, which are activities or items of expenditure about which a decision should be made about cost. There are two types of decision package.

Mutually exclusive packages are alternative ways of getting the same job done. The best option among the packages must be selected by comparing costs and benefits and the other packages are then discarded.

Incremental packages analyse an activity into different levels of effort. The 'base' package will describe the minimum amount of work that must be done to carry out the activity and the other incremental packages describe what additional work could be done, at what cost and for what benefits.

Packages are ranked in order of priority, and given a limited budget (limited cash and other resources); the preferred mutually exclusive and incremental packages are selected for the budget.

Use of ZBB at Newtown School

Implementing ZBB would enable the school to distinguish between **necessary** and **discretionary expenditure**, and allocate resources accordingly.

For example, although some level of sports education is needed, the extent of the different activities offered is discretionary. As a bare minimum, it is essential that children have somewhere safe and secure to exercise. ZBB could be used to put together **decision packages** which reflect the **different levels of sports facilities** available to the children. For example, the most basic level could be to continue to hold all sports classes inside in the existing gym. The next level would be to offer a combination of indoor and outdoor sports classes which would require the sports field to be maintained. Finally, the highest level would be a state-of-the-art gym and sports pitches. At Newtown School the sports staff could **prepare the decision packages** and they would be decided upon by the head teacher, who would **rank them accordingly**.

ZBB can take a long time to implement however, and would **not be appropriate for all categories of expenditure** at the school. Incremental budgeting could still be **used as a basis for essential expenditure** such as repairs and maintenance, since the costs of the checks and repairs needed to comply with health and safety standards seem to stay largely the same year on year, with an inflationary increase.

279 Bedco

Workbook reference. Planning and operational variances are covered in Chapter 17 of the BPP Workbook.

Top tips. To answer this question within the allocated time, you need to be familiar with planning and operational variances. You should identify that the planning variance for material usage applies to pillow cases only.

Remember that when calculating an operational variance for usage, the standard cost to apply is the standard cost per unit of material in the original standard cost.

If you have time, comment on the usage operational variances for bed sheets and pillow cases separately.

Part (b) of the question is worth eight marks, so make sure that you allocate the right amount of time to this part of your answer.

Easy marks. When answering a question on planning and operational variances, calculate the original standard cost and the revised standard cost. This should indicate what the planning variances are, per unit or price or usage. Having done this, the task is then to convert the planning variance as a price per unit of material or a quantity used of material into a total variance.

Marking scheme

			Marks
(a)	For each variance: 3 marks		12
(b)	Each valid point	2	
			8
			20

(a)

Original standard cost		
Sheets	2m² × \$5 per m²	\$10 per unit
Pillow cases	0.5m² × \$5 per m²	\$2.50 per unit
Revised standard cost		
Sheets	2m² × \$6 per m²	\$12 per unit
Pillow cases	0.55m² × \$6 per m²	\$3.30 per unit

(i) **Material price planning variance**

	$
Original standard price of materials per m²	5.0
Revised standard price	6.0
Material price planning variance per m²	1.0 (A)
Actual quantity used/purchased (248,000 + 95,000)	343,000
Material price planning variance in $	$343,000 (A)

(ii) **Material price operational variance**

	$
Revised standard price of materials per m²	6.0
Actual price paid	5.8
Material price operational variance per m²	0.2 (F)
Actual quantity used/purchased (248,000 + 95,000)	343,000
Material price operational variance in $	$68,600 (F)

(iii) **Material usage planning variance**

This applies to pillow cases only

	m²
180,000 pillow cases should use: original standard (× 0.5)	90,000
180,000 pillow cases should use: revised standard (× 0.55)	99,000
Material usage planning variance in m²	9,000 (A)
Original standard price per m²	$5
Material usage planning variance in $	$45,000 (A)

(iv) **Material usage operational variance**

This applies to pillow cases only

	m²
180,000 pillow cases should use: revised standard (× 0.55)	99,000
120,000 sheets should use (× 2)	240,000
Together they should use	339,000
They did use	343,000
Material usage operational variance in m²	4,000 (A)
Original standard price per m²	$5
Material usage operational variance in $	$20,000 (A)

Check:	$	$
Actual cost of materials: 343,000 m² × $5.80		1,989,400
Original standard cost: (120,000 sheets × $10) + (180 pillow cases × $2.50)		1,650,000
Total materials cost variance		339,400 (A)
Variances:		
Price planning	343,000 (A)	
Usage planning	45,000 (A)	
Price operational	68,600 (F)	
Usage operational	20,000 (A)	
		339,400 (A)

(b) The production manager is not responsible for setting the standard costs and is therefore not responsible for any planning variances. They are responsible, however, for the operational variances (including the price variance, since they have responsibility for materials purchasing).

The manager is also not responsible for the production shortfall of 10,000 pillow cases in the month, since this was caused by the change in customer requirements. However, this did not affect the materials variances. (It is much more likely to have affected labour efficiency or idle time variances in the month.)

Assessing performance on operational variances only, it would appear that the production manager has performed well. Although the expected material price rose to $6 per m², they were able to purchase materials at $5.80 per m², which 'saved' $68,600 in purchase costs.

The materials usage operational variance was adverse in total, by 4,000 m². The usage of materials on bed sheets (248,000m²) was more than the expected 240,000 m² for 120,000 sheets produced (120,000 × 2). On the other hand, materials usage for pillow cases (95,000m²) was 4,000 m² less than the expected usage of 99,000 m² for the 180,000 pillow cases produced (180,000 × 0.55). The production manager should therefore be asked to explain the adverse usage of materials in producing the bed sheets.

The large favourable variance for materials usage on pillow cases should also be explained, to make sure that the pillow cases are being made properly to the new standard requirement.

280 Valet Co

Marking scheme

			Marks
(a)	Calculations		
	Sales mix contribution variance		4
	Sales quantity contribution variance		4
(b)	Description		
	One mark per description		2
(c)	Discussion on sales performance		
	Calculations – each one 0.5, max 2	2	
	Maximum for each point made	2	10
			20

(a) **Variances**

(i) **Sales mix contribution variance**

	Should mix Actual qty Std mix	Did mix Actual qty Actual mix	Difference	Std contribution $	Variance $
Full	5,130 (W1)	4,000	1,130 (A)	22.30 (W2)	25,199 (A)
Mini	2,850 (W1)	3,980	1,130 (F)	16.50 (W2)	18,645 (F)
	7,980	7,980	0		6,554 (A)

Workings

1   **Actual sales quantity in standard mix**

Full	7,980	× (3,600/5,600)	=	5,130
Mini	7,980	× (2,000/5,600)	=	2,850

2   **Standard contributions per valet**

Full	$50	× 44.6%	=	$22.30 per valet
Mini	$30	× 55%	=	$16.50 per valet

(ii)   **Sales quantity contribution variance**

	Should mix Actual qty Std mix	Budgeted Std qty Std mix	Difference	Std contribution $	Variance $
Full	5,130 (W1)	3,600	1,530 (F)	22.30 (W2)	34,119 (F)
Mini	2,850 (W1)	2,000	850 (F)	16.50 (W2)	14,025 (F)
	7,980	5,600	2,380		48,144 (F)

(b)   **Description**

The sales mix variance occurs when the proportions of the various products sold are different from those in the budget.

The sales quantity variance shows the difference in contribution/profit because of a change in sales volume from the budgeted volume of sales.

(c)   **Sales performance of the business**

The sales performance of the business has been very good over the last year, as shown by the favourable sales quantity variance of $48,144. Overall, total sales revenue is 33% higher than budgeted (($319,400 – $240,000)/$240,000). This is because of a higher total number of valets being performed. When you look at where the difference in sales quantity actually is, you can see from the data provided in the question that it is the number of mini valets which is substantially higher. This number is 99% ((3,980 – 2,000)/2,000) higher than budgeted, whereas the number of full valets is only 11% ((4,000 –3,600)/3,600) higher. Even 11% is still positive, however.

The fact that the number of mini valets is so much higher, combined with the fact that they generate a lower contribution per unit than the full valet, led to an adverse sales mix variance of $6,554 in the year. This cannot be looked at in isolation as a sign of poor performance; it is simply reflective of the changes which have occurred in Strappia. We are told that disposable incomes in Strappia have decreased by 30% over the last year. This means that people have less money to spend on non-essential expenditure – such as car valeting. Consequently, they are opting for the cheaper mini valet rather than the more expensive full valet. At the same time, we are also told that people are keeping their cars for an average of five years now, as opposed to three years. This may be leading them to take more care of them and get them valeted regularly, because they know that the car has to be kept for a longer period. Thus, the total quantity of valets is higher than budgeted, particularly the mini valets.

Also, there is now one less competitor for Valet Co than there was a year ago, so Valet Co may have gained some of the old competitor's business. Together, all of these factors would explain the higher number of total valets being performed and, in particular, of the less-expensive type of valet.

Note. Other valid points will be given full credit.

281 Glove Co

Marking scheme

			Marks
(a)	Basic variances		
	Each variance	1	2
(b)	Operational and planning variances		
	Labour rate planning	1.5	
	Labour rate operational	1.5	
	Labour efficiency planning	1.5	
	Labour efficiency operational	1.5	
			6
(c)	Explanation of controllability principle		4
	Performance		
	Only operational variances	1	
	Adverse operational variance	2	
	Failure to update the standard	1	
	Overtime rate impacted	2	
	Favourable efficiency variance	2	
	Good overall	1	
		Max	8
			20

(a) Basic variances

Labour rate variance

Standard cost of labour per hour = $42/3 = $14 per hour

	$
37,000 hours should have cost (× $14)	518,000
but did cost	531,930
Rate variance	13,930 (A)

Labour efficiency variance

12,600 units should have taken (× 3 hrs)	37,800 hrs
but did take	37,000 hrs
Efficiency variance in hours	800 (F)
× standard rate per hour	× $14
Efficiency variance in $	$11,200 (F)

(b) **Planning and operational variances**

Labour rate planning variance

	$ per hour
Original standard rate	14.00
Revised standard rate (14 × 1.02)	14.28
Labour rate planning variance	0.28 (A)

Labour rate planning variance = 37,000 hours × $0.28 (A) = $10,360 (A).

Labour efficiency planning variance

	Hours
12,600 units of product should take: original standard (× 3.00)	37,800
12,600 units of product should take: revised standard (× 3.25)	40,950
Labour efficiency planning variance in hours	3,150 (A)
Original standard rate per hour	$14
Labour efficiency planning variance in $	$44,100 (A)

Labour rate operational variance

	$
37,000 hours should cost (revised standard $14.28)	528,360
They did cost	531,930
Labour rate operational variance	3,570 (A)

Labour efficiency operational variance

	Hours
12,600 units of product should take (× 3.25 hours)	40,950
They did take	37,000
Labour efficiency (operational variance in hours)	3,950 (F)
Original standard rate per hour	$14
Labour efficiency (operational variance in $)	$55,300 (F)

(c) **Controllability principle**

The **controllability principle** is that managers of responsibility centres should only be held accountable for costs over which they have some influence. From a **motivation** point of view, this is important because it can be very demoralising for managers who feel that their performance is being judged on the basis of something over which they have no influence. It is also important from a **control** point of view in that control reports should ensure that information on costs is reported to the manager who is able to take action to control them.

The controllability principle can be **implemented** either by removing the uncontrollable items from the areas that managers are accountable for, or producing reports which calculate and distinguish between controllable and uncontrollable items.

For example, the controllability principle means that operational managers should only be held responsible for **excess** idle time, above that which is expected, based on realistic forecasts.

Analysis of performance

At a first glance, performance looks mixed because the total labour rate variance is adverse and the total labour efficiency variance is favourable. However, the operational and planning variances provide a lot more detail on how these variances have occurred.

The production manager should only be held accountable for variances which they can control. This means that they should only be held accountable for the operational variances. When these operational variances are looked at, it can be seen that the labour rate operational variance is $3,570 A. This means that the production manager did have to pay for some overtime in order to meet demand but the majority of the total labour rate variance is driven by the failure to update the standard for the pay rise that was applied at the start of the last quarter. The overtime rate would also have been impacted by that pay increase.

Then, when the labour efficiency operational variance is looked at, it is actually $55,300 F. This shows that the production manager has managed their department well, with workers completing production more quickly than would have been expected when the new design change is taken into account. The total operating variances are therefore $51,730 F and so overall performance is good.

The adverse planning variances of $10,360 and $44,100 do not reflect on the performance of the production manager and can, therefore, be ignored here.

282 SU Co

Workbook reference. Planning and operational variances are covered in Chapter 17.

Top tips. Variance questions are frequently examined in PM so it is worthwhile learning how to do the calculations. If you know how to calculate planning and operational variances then parts (a) and (b) should be straightforward.

Easy marks. Easy marks could be gained for explaining that the materials usage and labour efficiency planning variances were due to the change in design and therefore not controllable, and the materials price planning variance was due to GPST's decision to change the material – again, not controllable.

Examining team's comments. This was a fairly typical variances question but unfortunately students found it difficult. The question didn't say which material variances were required and this was one of the key skills being tested. The main reason why scores were low was that only the basic variances were calculated. It is worth noting that the most common error when calculating variances of this type is to use budgeted production, instead of the actual production, to calculate standard usage.

Marking scheme

		Marks
(a)	Standard price	1
	Standard quantity	0.5
	Standard quantity actual price	0.5
	Revised quantity actual price	0.5
	Price planning variance	1.5
	Usage planning variance	1.5
	Usage operational variance	1.5
		7
(b)	Actual hours	1
	Standard hours actual price	0.5
	Revised hours actual price	0.5
	Planning variance	1.5
	Operational variance	1.5
		5
(c)	Controllability principle	1
	Variances/performance	6
	Other/conclusion	1
		8
		20

BPP
LEARNING
MEDIA

(a)   **Material price planning variance**

	$
Original standard price of materials per m ($2.85/0.95)	3.00
Revised standard price	2.85
Material price planning variance per m	0.15 (F)
Actual quantity used/purchased	54,560
Material price planning variance in $	8,184 (F)

Material price operational variance

	$
54,560m should cost (× $2.85)	155,496
Did cost	155,496
Material price operational variance	0

Total price variance = $8,184 (F) + $0 = $8,184 (F)

Material usage planning variance

	m
24,000 dresses should use: original standard (× 2.2m/1.1)	48,000
24,000 dresses should use: revised standard (× 2.2m)	52,800
Material usage planning variance in m	4,800 (A)
Original standard price per m	$3
Material usage planning variance in $	$14,400 (A)

Material usage operational variance

	m
24,000 dresses should use: revised standard (× 2.2m)	52,800
They did use	54,560
Material usage operational variance in m	1,760 (A)
Original standard price per m	$3
Material usage operational variance in $	$5,280 (A)

Total usage variance = $14,400 (A) + $5,280 (A) = $19,680 (A)

Total material variance = $8,184 (F) + $19,680 (A) = $11,496 (A)

(b)   **Labour efficiency planning variance**

	Hours
24,000 dresses should take: original standard (× 8/60)	3,200
24,000 dresses should take: revised standard (× 10/60)	4,000
Labour efficiency planning variance in hours	800 (A)
Original standard rate per hour	$12
Labour efficiency planning variance in $	$9,600 (A)

Labour efficiency operational variance

	Hours
24,000 dresses should take (× 10/60 hours)	4,000
They did take (24 staff × 160 hours)	3,840
Labour efficiency (operational variance in hours)	160 (F)
Original standard rate per hour	$12
Labour efficiency (operational variance in $)	$1,920 (F)

Total labour efficiency variance = $9.600 (A) + $1,920 (F) = $7,680 (A)

(c)   The production manager did not have any control over the change in the design of the dress as this change was requested by the client. Similarly, it was not their fault that the company accountant responsible for updating standard costs was off sick and therefore unable to update the standards. Therefore, the production manager should be judged only by those variances over which they have control, which are the operational variances.

Materials

No operational variance arose in relation to materials price, since the actual price paid was the same as the revised price. A planning variance of $8,184F does arise but the production manager cannot take the credit for this, as the material chosen by GPST for the new dresses just happens to be cheaper.

As regards usage, an adverse variance of $5,280 arose. This suggests that, even with the revised quantity of material being taken into account, staff still used more than 2.2 metres on average to produce each dress. This is probably because they had to learn a new sewing technique and they probably made some mistakes, resulting in some wastage. The manager is responsible for this as it may have been caused by insufficient training. However, the labour efficiency variances below shed some more light on this.

Labour

The labour efficiency operational variance was favourable, which suggests good performance by the production manager. Staff took less than the expected revised 10 minutes per dress. However, when looked at in combination with the material usage operational variance above, it could be inferred that staff may have rushed a little and consequently used more material than necessary.

When both of the operational variances are looked at together, the adverse materials usage $5,280 far outweighs the favourable labour efficiency variance of $1,920. Consequently, it could be concluded that, overall, the manager's performance was somewhat disappointing.

283 Kappa Co

Workbook reference. Mix and yield variances are covered in Chapter 16.

Top tips. This question is a gift! Part (a)(i) asks for the usage variance for each ingredient as well as the total so make sure you show these. You would probably be given a spreadsheet in the exam for part (a) so it is worth practising setting up your variances on a spreadsheet so that you know exactly how to lay out a variances question in the exam. Use the formulae on the spreadsheet for your calculations to help avoid errors, and always, always label your variances. Remember also to state whether the variances are adverse or favourable.

For part (b) you will probably be given a Word document. The important thing for part (b) is to read and re-read the scenario and pick out the relevant points. Use the point from the scenario to answer the question.

(a)   **Material usage variance**

	Std usage for actual output Kg (W1)	Actual usage kg	Variance kg	Standard cost per kg $	Variance $
Alpha	1,840	2,200	360 (A)	2	720 (A)
Beta	2,760	2,500	260 (F)	5	1,300 (F)
Gamma	920	920	0	1	0
	5,520	5,620			580 (F)

Material mix variance

	Actual usage/mix kg	Standard Mix (W2) kg	Mix variance kg	Standard cost $ per kg	Mix variance $
Alpha	2,200	1,873	327 (A)	2	654 (A)
Beta	2,500	2,810	310 (F)	5	1,550 (F)
Gamma	920	937	17 (F)	1	17 (F)
	5,620	5,620	0		913 (F)

Workings

1   Alpha   40/100 × 4,600 = 1,840

     Beta   60/100 × 4,600 = 2,760

     Gamma   20/100 × 4,600 = 920

2   5,620 kg in standard mix:

     Alpha   40/120 × 5,620 = 1,873

     Beta   60/120 × 5,620 = 2,810

     Gamma   20/120 × 5,620 = 937

Material yield variance

	Std usage for actual output	Actual usage in standard mix	Variance	Standard cost per kg	Variance
	kg	kg	kg	$	$
Alpha	1,840	1,873	33 (A)	2	66 (A)
Beta	2,760	2,810	50 (A)	5	250 (A)
Gamma	920	937	17 (A)	1	17 (A)
	5,520	5,620			333 (A)

Alternative yield calculation

		kg
5,620 kg should yield	@ (100/120)	4,683
Did yield		4,600
Difference		83
Valued at standard cost per kg	($400/100)	$4
		$333 (A)

Your formulae in a spreadsheet might look like this:

	A	B	C	D	E	F	G	H
1	i) Material usage variance							
2			4,600 kg	But	Variance	Std	$	
3			should	did		cost/kg		
4			use	use				
5			Kg		Kg			
6		Alpha	=4600*(40/100)	2200	=C6-D6	2	=E6*F6	Adverse
7		Beta	=4600*(60/100)	2500	=C7-D7	5	=E7*F7	Favourable
8		Gamma	=4600*(20/100)	920	=C8-D8	1	=E8*F8	-
9			=SUM(C6:C8)	=SUM(D6:D8)			=SUM(G6:G8)	Favourable
10								
11								
12	ii) Material mix variance							
13			Actual	Actual	Variance	Std	$	
14			usage	usage in		cost/kg		
15				std mix				
16			Kg	Kg	Kg			
17		Alpha	=D6	=(40/120)*C20	=C17-D17	2	=E17*F17	Adverse
18		Beta	=D7	=(60/120)*C20	=C18-D18	5	=E18*F18	Favourable
19		Gamma	=D8	=(20/120)*C20	=C19-D19	1	=E19*F19	Favourable
20			=SUM(C17:C19)	=SUM(D17:D19)			=SUM(G17:G19)	Favourable
21								
29	iii) Material yield variance							
30								
31			4,600 kg	Actual	Variance	Std	$	
32			should	usage in		cost/kg		
33			use	std mix				
34			Kg	Kg	Kg			
35		Alpha	=C6	=D17	=C35-D35	2	=E35*F35	Adverse
36		Beta	=C7	=D18	=C36-D36	5	=E36*F36	Adverse
37		Gamma	=C8	=D19	=C37-D37	1	=E37*F37	Adverse
38			=SUM(C35:C37)	=SUM(D35:D37)			=SUM(G35:G37)	Adverse

Remember that the mix variance + the yield variance = the usage variance.

$913F – $333A = $580F

(b)   The raw material price variances included in the report are probably outside the production manager's control, and are more the responsibility of the purchasing manager. Furthermore, the production manager has no participation in setting the standard mix. Holding managers accountable for variances they cannot control is demotivating.

There appears to be no use of planning variances. Prices and quality of the three materials are volatile and using ex ante prices and usage standards can give a distorted view of mix and yield variances. Failing to isolate non-controllable planning variances can be demotivating.

The standard mix for the product has not changed in five years despite changes in the quality and price of ingredients. It can also lead the production manager to attempt control action based on variances which are calculated based on standards which are out of date.

As Kappa Co does not currently give feedback or commentary, a true picture is lacking as to the production manager's performance. There is also no follow up on the variances calculated. As Kappa Co does not appear to place much importance on the variances, the production manager will not be motivated to control costs and could become complacent which could adversely impact Kappa Co overall.

This can be illustrated by looking at the overall usage variance reported which shows a $580 favourable variance, so the production manager could assume good performance. However, if the usage variance is considered in more detail, through the mix and yield calculations, it can be seen that it was driven by a change in the mix. There is a direct relationship between the materials mix variance and the materials yield variance and by using a mix of materials which was different from standard, it has resulted in a saving of $913.33; however, it has led to a significantly lower yield than Kappa Co would have got had the standard mix of materials been adhered to. Also changing the mix could impact quality and as a result sales and there is no information about this.

Part E answers

OTQ bank – Performance measurement and control

284 The correct answer is: Both 1 and 2

Internal transfers should be preferred to external purchases because the company will have better control over output quality from Division A and the scheduling of production and deliveries. Transfer prices determine how total profit will be shared between the divisions.

285 The correct answer is: $15

The minimum transfer price is a price that should be sufficient to make the manager of Division A wiling to transfer units of Component X to Division B. This is the marginal cost of manufacture plus the opportunity cost of not being able to sell the component in the external market.

This is $8 + $(16 – 8 – 1) = $15.

286 The correct answer is: Neither 1 nor 2

Not-for-profit organisations do have financial objectives, which may sometimes be described as financial constraints. For example, a charity organisation may want to maximise its funding and a government department may seek to carry out its activities within the spending budget for the department.

The outputs produced by commercial organisations can be measured simply by profit, which is a measure of the value created by the organisation in a period. Outputs of not-for-profit organisations cannot be measured as easily because they often have many different objectives, each measured in different ways.

287 The correct answer is: Profit before interest and tax

Gross profit ignores other expenses other than cost of sales. Profit before tax and profit after tax are after deducting items that do not relate to divisional performance (costs of interest on company debt and tax charges). Profit before interest and tax is the most appropriate measure of the four, and it will often be the same as operating profit.

288 The correct answers are:

- Percentage of repeat customers
- Number of warranty claims

Dividend yield and profit margin are shareholder measures.

289 The correct answer is: Average waiting time at the hospital

Adherence to appointment times means starting an appointment at the scheduled time. One suitable measure might be the percentage of appointments that begin later than a certain amount of time, say 15 minutes. Of the performance measurements in the question, average waiting time on the appointment date would be the most appropriate.

290 The correct answer is: Sales revenue from new products as a percentage of total revenue

R&D expenditure on its own is not a measure of performance, and costs in the previous year will not relate to all four products introduced to the market in the past two years.

The most appropriate of these measures as an indication of innovation within the organisation is revenue from new products as a percentage of total revenue. (This is more meaningful for comparison purposes than simply measuring average revenue per new product.)

291 The correct answer is: Number of patients treated per $1 spent on the state hospital service

Number of patients treated per $1 spent relates outputs to inputs, and is a measure of efficiency. Reducing a departmental budget is a measure of economy. A crime clear-up rate and an examination pass rate are measures of effectiveness for the police force and the state-owned college, respectively.

292 **This question appeared in the Mar/Jun 2021 exam.**

The correct answers are: Opportunity cost and Market price

Examination team comments

In setting a transfer price, the organisation should be aiming for a price which will result in the best outcome for the division and for the organisation as a whole.

With the opportunity cost method, the transfer price is the variable cost plus the opportunity cost. Where the selling division can sell externally, the opportunity cost will be the contribution lost from selling internally rather than externally. This transfer price ensures that anything in excess of this will incentivise the seller to sell. The buyer's maximum price is the lower of divisional net revenue and market price. Anything lower than this will incentivise the buyer to buy.

With the market-based method, the transfer price is equal to the market price. With this transfer price, neither the seller or the buyer will end up paying more or selling for less than they would if an external sale or purchase took place. In reality the transfer price might be slightly less than the market price as savings can be made from reduced distribution or packaging costs internally.

Actual cost methods, using either marginal cost or full cost, could result in inefficiencies being passed from the seller to the buyer. This would incentivise the seller but not the buyer. The buyer may buy externally when it is in fact more goal congruent to buy internally.

Standard full cost plus would incentivise the seller, depending on the mark up assigned. However, it is likely that the resulting transfer price may be too high, and the buyer may buy externally, when this is in fact a dysfunctional decision and would not result in the best outcome for the organisation as a whole.

293 **This question appeared in the Sep/Dec 2020 exam.**

The correct answer is: $32.5 million

Sales forecast adjusted for inflation only: 30.9 x 1.02/1.03 = 30.6 $61.8 million would have included inflation of 3%, so adjusting that for the actual 2% inflation, 61.6 x 1.02/1.03 = 61.2 Market growth = 65/61.2 = 1.0621 Therefore, a fair sales figure to aim for would be: 30.6 x 1.0621 = 32.5.

294 The correct answer is: Percentage of customers making repeat orders

Making repeat orders is possibly a measure of customer satisfaction, and so might be used as a measure of performance from a customer perspective in a balanced scorecard. The growth in the product range is more relevant to innovation, and speed of order processing and orders per sales representative are measures of operational efficiency and effectiveness, rather than customer attitudes to the organisation and its products.

295 The correct answer is: Neither 1 nor 2

Providing value for money (VFM) means providing a service that is economical, efficient and effective. 'Economical' means getting the best price, but this does not necessarily mean 'cheap'. Measuring the percentage of collected refuse that is recycled is a measure of effectiveness, if recycling refuse is an objective of the service. ('Efficiency' measures an amount of output or benefit per unit of resource input.)

296 The correct answer is: 2 only

When divisional performance is measured by residual income, a fair comparison of divisional performances is not possible, because the divisional residual incomes are not related to the size and asset value of each division. For example, residual income of $50,000 when divisional assets are $10 million is not as impressive as residual income of $50,000 when divisional assets are only $100,000.

When a transfer price is based on cost, the size of the profit mark-up is a matter for negotiation, and one of the divisional managers (or even both of them) are likely to consider the agreed transfer price as 'unfair', favouring the other division.

297 **This question appeared in the December 2018 exam.**

The correct answer is: 0.64

The quick ratio = (current assets − inventory)/current liabilities. To be able to calculate this ratio, the value of inventory, current assets and current liabilities need to be established.

To determine the value of inventory, the cost of sales value and the inventory turnover period need to be used. First the cost of sales has to be calculated based on the mark-up on cost of 50%. The cost of sales will be 100/150 x $960,000 = $640,000. On that basis, the inventory value can be calculated using the inventory turnover period as 90 days/360 days x $640,000 = $160,000.

The current ratio = current assets/current liabilities. In Binny Co, the current ratio is 3.2:1 and the only current assets are inventory and cash balances as all sales are on cash basis.

From the above information, the current liabilities can be calculated.

- Current assets = $160,000 (inventory) + $40,000 (cash balance) = $200,000
- Rearranging the formula for current ratio, the current liabilities = $200,000/3.2 = $62,500

Now we have the inventory value, current assets and current liabilities, the quick ratio can be calculated = ($200,000 - $160,000)/$62,500 = 0.64. Alternatively the quick ratio could have been calculated by taking the cash balance only of $40,000 and dividing by the current liabilities.

298 The correct answer is: Competitiveness

In the Fitzgerald and Moon model there are six dimensions of performance. Two of these reflect past results and achievements: financial performance and competitiveness. The other four dimensions of performance are determinants of future performance: flexibility, innovation, quality and resource utilisation.

OTQ bank – Performance measurement and control

299 The correct answer is: Minimum transfer price $8, maximum transfer price $16

The minimum transfer price is the marginal cost of production in Division A, because any transfer price in excess of this amount will add to the division's contribution and profit. The maximum transfer price is the external market price of Component X, because any price in excess of this amount will lead to Division B sourcing Product X externally.

300 The correct answer is: Innovation

Fitzgerald and Moon identified six dimensions or aspects of performance in a service business: financial performance, competitiveness, quality, resource utilisation, flexibility and innovation.

301 The correct answers are:

- Granting credit to customers
- Inventory carrying decisions

The investment centre manager would have power to make decisions over granting credit to customers and the level of inventory carried. This affects the investment centre's level of working capital and hence is the responsibility of the investment centre manager.

302 The correct answer is: 23.2%

Capital employed at start of 20X2 = $2 million + $0.2 million + $0.8 million + $0.1 million = $3.1 million

Capital employed at the end of 20X2 is the capital employed at the beginning of the year, minus depreciation of $0.4 million on the 'old' assets and $0.2 million on the 'new' asset.

Capital employed at end of 20X2 = $1.6 million + $0.2 million + $0.6 million + $0.1 million = $2.5 million

Mid-year capital employed = $(3.1 m + 2.5m)/2 = $2.8 million

Profit = $0.5 million + $0.35 million − depreciation $0.2 million = $0.65 million

ROI = 0.65/2.8 = 0.232 = 23.2%

303   The correct answer is: $5,000

	$'000	$'000
Sales (7,000 units × $154)		1,078
Variable costs in Division B (7,000 × $33)	231	
Costs of transfers (14,000 × $43)	602	
		833
		245
Fixed costs		160
Operating profit		85
Notional interest (16% × $500,000)		80
Residual income		5

304   The correct answer is: Standard cost plus a profit margin equal to a percentage of cost

Transfers should not be at actual cost, because there is no incentive for the transferring division to control the costs of the transferred item. A transfer price based on actual cost plus would be even worse, since the transferring division (Division A) would make a profit on any overspending that it incurs. Standard cost plus is preferable to standard cost because the profit margin provides an incentive for Division A to make and transfer the item.

305   The correct answer is: 30.9%

	Profit $	Capital employed $
Original forecast	65,000	210,000
Effect of machine sale	(2,500)	(6,000)
Effect of machine purchase	5,200	15,000
	67,700	219,000

Revised ROI = 67,700/219,000 = 30.9%

306   The correct answer is: Goal congruence in decision-making

There is a risk of dysfunctional decision-making and a lack of goal congruence with divisionalisation. Divisional managers may base investment decisions on whether they will improve ROI, which is inappropriate. Transfer pricing disputes, too, may lead to bad decisions by divisional managers. However, the risk can be avoided or minimised if divisional management and head office management are aware of the potential problem.

Authority is delegated to divisional managers; therefore there is some loss of head office control over operations, but decision-making at 'local' operational level should be faster, since the decision does not have to be referred to head office for a decision. There is likely to be some duplication of costs, since each division will have its own administration activities.

307 The correct answers are:

- Volume of customer complaints – Quantitative
- Employee revenue – Quantitative
- Defective products per batch – Quantitative
- Customer needs – Qualitative
- Employee morale – Qualitative
- Brand recognition – Qualitative
- Customer satisfaction – Qualitative
- Repeat business – Quantitative

Quantitative performance measures are something that can be actually measured and a value assigned.

Volume of customer complaints, employee revenue, defective products per batch and repeat business are all performance measures which can be regularly monitored, values assigned and benchmarks made.

Qualitative performance measures are more difficult to measure and are based on judgement. It is only possible to gain an opinion as opposed to a concrete value. They are still important as many decisions are swayed by the strength of the qualitative arguments rather than the cold facts presented as part of qualitative analysis.

Customer needs, customer satisfaction, employee morale and brand recognition are all examples of qualitative performance measures. They are very difficult to measure accurately and their rating tends to be based on judgement.

There are still ways to devise quantitative measures for these areas. For example, volume of repeat business may give an indication of customer satisfaction. Additionally, surveying a sample of customers may help to devise some measure of satisfaction.

308 The correct answer is: Internal business perspective

The innovation and learning perspective is concerned with: 'Can we continue to improve and create value?'

The internal business perspective is concerned with operational efficiency and excellence.

309 The correct answers are:

- Efficiency
- Effectiveness
- Economy

Effectiveness is the relationship between an organisation's outputs and its objectives (ie getting done what was supposed to be done). Efficiency is the relationship between inputs and outputs (ie getting out as much as possible for what goes in).

Economy is attaining the appropriate quantity and quality of inputs at lowest cost (ie spending money frugally). Enterprise, efficacy, expediency and endurance although perhaps relevant are all red herrings in this context.

310 **This question appeared in the June 2015 exam.**

The correct answer is: $162,000

Divisional profit before depreciation = $2.7m × 15% = $405,000 per year.
Less depreciation = $2.7m × 1/50 = $54,000 per year
Divisional profit after depreciation = $351,000
Imputed interest = $2.7m × 7% = $189,000
Residual income = $162,000

311 The correct answer is: Both 1 and 2

When an organisation is structured into divisions, there will almost inevitably be some transfer of goods or services between divisions, for which transfer prices are required.

Statement 2 is one of the guiding rules for identifying the optimal transfer price.

312 The correct answer is: Cost of the local fire service per member of the local population

The cost of resources (inputs) per member of the local community is a measure of the resources spent on the fire service, without providing any measure of outputs obtained from the resources. A measure of the cost of the service provides an indication of the resources committed to it, but does not measure the value or benefits obtained from them

313 **This question appeared in the June 2018 exam.**

The correct answer is: 1 and 2 only

Statement 1: holding on to heavily depreciated assets gives a low figure for 'capital employed' which, in turn, gives a higher figure for ROI which could lead to bonuses for divisional managers. However, there are likely to be higher running costs for an old machine, making the organisation less profitable than it might be. Low depreciation charges may also hide this but cash flow would be affected.

Statement 2: when a manufacturing division uses absorption costing, building high inventory levels will result in a large proportion of production overheads being carried from one period to the next in inventory. This increases the return figure benefiting the divisional managers if these are linked to bonuses but would only benefit the company if those units of inventory can be sold in the following period.

Statement 3: this is useful for the organisation as whole - by setting a relative target on market share when the market increases, then more sales are expected in absolute terms. This adds controllability to the organisation, since the sales manager could not be held responsible for a rise (or a fall) in the overall market. Since this target is outside of the control of the divisional managers, it is more likely to benefit the organisation rather than the divisional managers.

Cherry Co

314 The correct answer is: $30

Division A has available capacity of 15,000 units. Division A does not want to lose its contribution margin of $7 per unit, and therefore the minimum price it would now accept is $30 as shown below.

$30 (variable cost) + $0 (opportunity cost) = $30

In this case Division A and B should negotiate a transfer price within the range of $30 and $35 (cost from outside supplier).

315 The correct answer is: $37

Division A charges $37 and derives a contribution margin of $7 per unit of Product X. Division A has no spare capacity.

Therefore, Division A must receive from Division B a payment that will at least cover its variable cost per unit plus its lost contribution margin per unit (the opportunity cost). If Division A cannot cover that amount (the minimum transfer price), it should not sell units of Product X to Division B.

The minimum transfer price that would be acceptable to Division A is $37, as shown below.

$30 (variable cost) + $7 (opportunity cost) = $37

316   The correct answer is: Full cost

Under this approach, the full cost (including fixed overheads absorbed) incurred by the supplying division in making the 'intermediate' product is charged to the receiving division. It can be used when there is no external marker for the product being transferred, or if an imperfect market exists.

317   The correct answers are:

Cherry Co's transfer pricing system should seek to establish a transfer price for X that will provide an incentive for the managers of A and B to make and sell quantities of products that will maximise sales of Product Y.		FALSE
The manager of division B is likely to be more motivated if she is given freedom in which to operate and is able to purchase from outside suppliers if prices are cheaper.	TRUE	

Statement 1 is false. Cherry Co's transfer pricing system should seek to establish a transfer price for X that will provide an incentive for the managers of A and B to make and sell quantities of products that will maximise the company's total profit. Statement 2 is true.

318   The correct answers are:

The performance of the managers of A and B will be easier to assess in an environment in which managers are able to control greater elements of the business.	TRUE	
In a competitive market, it is likely that suppliers will offer product X to Division B significantly cheaper than Division A can, for a sustained period of time.		FALSE

Statement 1 is true. Statement 2 is false because Division A is likely to save money on selling and distribution expenses if they can sell product X to Division B.

Jamair

319   The correct answer is: Financial

The financial perspective considers whether the management in Jamair meets the expectations of its shareholders and how it creates value for them.

This perspective focuses on traditional measures such as growth, profitability and cost reduction.

320   The correct answer is: Customer perspective

The customer perspective considers how new and existing customers view Jamair. The objective is to ensure that flights land on time.

321   The correct answer is: Internal business perspective

The internal business perspective makes Jamair consider what processes it must excel at in order to achieve financial and customer objectives. The measure may be: Reduction in 'on the ground' time from 50 minutes.

322   The correct answer is: Financial perspective

The measure could be 'Revenue per available passenger mile'. The financial perspective considers whether the management in Jamair meets the expectations of its shareholders and how it creates value for them.

323 The correct answers are:

When performance is not quantified, it is difficult to target and monitor.	**TRUE**	
Jamair is more likely to have a reliable and comprehensive system for collecting data about qualitative aspects of performance than a well-established system for measuring quantitative data.		**FALSE**

Statement 1 is true. By its very nature, qualitative data is not quantified. At best, qualitative measures are converted into quantitative measures using a subjective scoring system.

Statement 2 is false. An organisation is much more likely to have a well-established system for measuring quantitative data, especially in the areas of accounting and sales statistics.

Stickleback Co

324 The correct answer is: Before investment: 20%, After investment 19.3%.

	Before investment $	After investment $
Divisional profit	30,000	31,900
Capital employed	150,000	165,000
ROI	20%	19.3%

325 The correct answer is: Before investment: $7,500, after investment $7,150.

	Before investment $	After investment $
Divisional profit	30,000	31,900
Imputed interest (15% of $150,000)	(22,500)	
Imputed interest (15% of $165,000)		(24,750)
Residual income	7,500	7,150

326 The correct answer is: 2 only.

Statement 1 is false because, if a manager's performance is being evaluated, only those assets which can be traced directly to the division and are controllable by the manager should be included.

The second statement is true. Short-termism is when there is a bias towards short-term rather than long-term performance. It is often due to the fact that a manager's performance is measured on short-term results such as ROI.

327 The correct answers are:

- Increase payables
- Keep Kingfisher's old machinery

One of the problems with using ROI as a performance measure is that it can be manipulated. Allowing non-current assets to depreciate (giving a lower NBV) and delaying payments to suppliers, both reduce the capital employed and therefore increase the ROI.

Accepting all projects with a positive NPV may not necessarily increase the ROI. Projects may have lower ROIs than Kingfisher's current ROI and this could cause Kingfisher's overall ROI to reduce.

ROI is calculated using profit before interest and so interest makes no difference to the ROI.

328 The correct answer is: 1 only

Statement 1 is a danger of decentralisation. Managers may make dysfunctional decisions.

Statement 2 is false. The divisional organisation frees top management from detailed involvement in day-to-day operations and allows them to devote more time to strategic planning.

Squarize

329 The correct answer is: Internal business perspective

This is measuring the effectiveness of improving the broadband service (an internal process) and is therefore part of the internal business perspective.

330 The correct answer is: Customer perspective

The performance objective associated with this measure would be to 'Increase number of new customers'.
It measures whether customers are willing to pay the individual prices for each service.

331 The correct answer is: Sales revenue from new standalone service as a percentage of total revenue

The most appropriate of these measures as an indication of innovation within the organisation is revenue from new standalone services as a percentage of total revenue. (This is more meaningful for comparison purposes than simply measuring average revenue per new standalone service.)

332 The correct answer is: Percentage of customers renewing their subscription or making repeat orders

Renewing subscription or making repeat orders is possibly a measure of customer satisfaction, and so might be used as a measure of performance from a customer perspective in a balanced scorecard.

The growth in the product range is more relevant to innovation, and speed of order processing and orders per sales representative are measures of operational efficiency and effectiveness rather than customer attitudes to the organisation and its products.

333 The correct answer is: Innovation

Innovation is an element of the 'Dimensions of performance' building block, but it is not included as a standalone building block.

The three building blocks are:

- Dimensions of performance
- Standards
- Rewards

Alder Co

334 The correct answer is: Before investment 27%, after investment 25%.

	Before investment $	After investment $
Controllable divisional profit	200,000	220,000
Capital employed	750,000	875,000
ROI	27%	25%

335 The correct answer is: Before investment: $87,500. After investment $88,750.

	Before investment $	After investment $
Divisional profit	200,000	220,000
Imputed interest		
(750,000 × 0.15)	(112,500)	
(875,000 × 0.15)		(131,250)
Residual income	87,500	88,750

336 The correct answer is: 'The authority to act to improve performance motivates the divisional managers in Alder Co, more so than if the company was centralised' is **true** and 'Alder Co's top management must have involvement in the day-to-day operations of Alder Co' is **false**.

Statement 1 is said to be one of the key advantages of a divisionalised structure.

Statement 2 is false because the divisional organisation frees top management from detailed involvement in day-to-day operations and allows them to devote more time to strategic planning.

337 The correct answer is: Both statements are false.

Statement 1 is false because, if a manager's performance is being evaluated, only those assets which can be traced directly to the division and are controllable by the manager should be included.

Statement 2 is false because an investment centre could not operate without the support of head office assets and administrative backup.

338 The correct answer is: Both statements are true.

The first statement is true and is a key exam focus point that should be remembered for your exam.

The second statement is true, and it is a risk associated with the use of ROI. If the bonus of a manager in Alder Co depends on ROI being met, the manager may feel pressure to massage the measure.

Apple Co

339 The correct answer is: 30%

	Investment $
Divisional profit	24,000
Capital employed (20,000 + 60,000)	80,000
ROI	30%

340 The correct answer is: $23,000.

	Investment $
Divisional profit	35,000
Imputed interest (100,000 × 12%)	(12,000)
Residual income	23,000

341 The correct answer is: Both statements are true.

Statement 1 is a key advantage of working with RI.
Statement 2 is a key disadvantage of working with RI.

342 The correct answer is: 'The market price acts as an incentive to use up any spare capacity in the selling division of Apple Co' is **false** and 'Using the market price as the transfer price encourages selling and buying decisions which appear to be in the best interests of the division's performance. This leads to the company as a whole achieving optimal results as each division optimises its performance' is **true**.

Statement 1 is false. The market price can act as a disincentive to use up any spare capacity in the selling division of Apple Co, particularly if the market price does not provide a significant mark-up. A price based on incremental cost, in contrast, might provide an incentive to use up the spare resources in order to provide a marginal contribution to profit.

Statement 2 is true and is a key advantage of using market price as a basis for transfer pricing.

343 The correct answer is: Both statements are true

Both statements are examples of the conditions under which market-based transfer prices are not suitable, and therefore a cost-based approach would be preferable.

Box Co

344   The correct answers are: Before investment: 21%, after investment 20.4%.

	Before investment $	After investment $
Divisional profit	20,000	21,400
Capital employed	95,000	105,000
ROI	21.1%	20.4%

345   The correct answers are: Without investment: $8,600, with investment $8,800.

	Before investment $	After investment $
Divisional profit	20,000	21,400
Imputed interest (12% of $95,000)	(11,400)	
Imputed interest (12% of $105,000)		(12,600)
Residual income	8,600	8,800

346   The correct answer is: Both statements are true.

Both statements are reasons for the growing emphasis on NFPIs.

Traditional responsibility accounting systems fail to provide information on the quality of products, and therefore statement 1 is true.

Financial performance indicators tend to focus on the short term. They can give a positive impression of what is happening now but problems may be looming. Therefore statement 2 is true.

347   The correct answer is: Keep managers informed about the short-term budget targets

The other options are all methods to encourage managers to take a long-term view, so that the 'ideal' decisions are taken.

Providing sufficient management information to allow managers to see what trade-offs they are making is a method of encouraging managers to take a long-term view. Managers must be kept aware of the long-term aims as well as shorter-term (budget) targets.

348   The correct answer is: 'There is a danger that managers in Box Co may use their decision-making freedom to make decisions that are not in the best interests of the overall company' is **true** and 'A good performance measure for the divisional managers in Box Co should include a portion of head office costs in the calculations' is **false**.

Statement 1 is a danger of divisionalised structures. Managers may make dysfunctional decisions.

Statement 2 is false. Only factors for which the manager can be held accountable should be included in calculations, and therefore head office costs would not be included.

Willow Co

349   The answer is: Before investment: 17%, after investment 16%.

	Before investment $	After investment $
Divisional profit	100,000	123,000
Capital employed	600,000	750,000
ROI	17%	16%

350   The answer is: Before investment: $22,000, after investment $25,500.

	Before investment $	After investment $
Divisional profit	100,000	123,000
Imputed interest		
(600,000 × 0.13)	78,000	
(750,000 × 0.13)		97,500
Residual income	22,000	25,500

351   The correct answer is: Investment centre

Distracters:

- Profit centre. The manager's area of responsibility is: 'Decisions over costs and revenues', and a typical financial performance measure is 'Controllable profit'.

- Responsibility centre. This is the overall name of the categories of centre or accounting unit that can exist within a divisionalised company.

- Cost centre. The manager's area of responsibility is: 'Decisions over costs', and a typical financial performance measure is 'Standard cost variances'.

352   The correct answer is: ROI is a relative measure, therefore small investments with a high rate of return may appear preferable to a larger investment with lower ROI. However, the larger investment may be worth more in absolute terms.

The distracters are all examples of limitations which are common to both ROI and RI.

353   The correct answer is: Manager 1 will show a higher RI because of the size of the division rather than superior managerial performance.

The first two distracters are examples of limitations which are common to both ROI and RI. Distracter 3 is false, RI ties in with NPV.

354 Biscuits and Cakes

> **Workbook reference.** Return on investment and residual income are covered in Chapter 20.
>
> **Top tips.** Parts (a) and (b) ask you to calculate the **annualised** return on investment and residual income. Remember to multiply the monthly net profit figure by 12, to reflect that there are 12 months in a year.
>
> Part (c) asks you to conclude as to whether the two divisions have performed well, using additional calculations as necessary. In order to fairly assess performance, take time to recalculate ROI and/or RI using controllable profit.
>
> **Easy marks.** There are five marks up for grabs in parts (a) and (b) for calculating the annualised ROI and RI.
>
> **Examining team's comments.** This was a straightforward performance measurement question in a divisional context. Parts (a) and (b) were relatively straightforward.
>
> In part (c), stronger candidates realised that, in order to discuss the performance of the divisions well, they needed to recalculate the ROI and/or RI using controllable profit. Where candidates did this, they generally accompanied it with some good discussion and scored full marks.
>
> Weaker answers performed other calculations on the two divisions and gave some general commentary, even though the question asked for a discussion 'using both ROI and RI'.
>
> In part (e) candidates were supposed to identify the fact that changing the basis for calculating ROI and using this for performance measurement without changing the target ROI would cause managers to be demotivated. Many candidates answered this well, although some simply discussed the general problems encountered when using ROI, which were relevant to a degree but shouldn't have been the sole answer.

Marks

(a) ROI/RI calculations:
ROI for B 1
ROI for C .... <u>1</u>
.... 2

(b) ROI/RI discussion:
RI for B 1.5
RI for C .... <u>1.5</u>
.... 3

(c) Discussion:
ROI discussion 2
RI discussion 2
Extra ROI calculation under old method 1
Valid conclusion drawn .... <u>1</u>
.... 6

(d) ROI/RI after investment:
ROI calculation 2
RI calculation 1
Comments and conclusion .... <u>2</u>
.... 5

(e) Behavioural issues:
ROI of investment – mark per valid point .... Max <u>4</u>
.... <u><u>20</u></u>

(a) **Annualised return on investment (ROI)**

ROI = (Net profit / Net assets) × 100%

Division B

Net profit = $311,000 × 12 months = $3,732,000
ROI = ($3,732,000 / $23,200,000) × 100%
= 16.09%

Division C

Net profit = $292,000 × 12 months = $3,504,000
ROI = ($3,504,000 / $22,600,000) × 100%
= 15.5%

(b) **Annualised residual income (RI)**

	Division B $'000	Division C $'000
Net profit (part (a))	3,732	3,504
Less: imputed interest charge:		
$23.2m × 10%	(2,320)	nil
$22.6m × 10%	nil	(2,260)
	1,412	1,244

(c) **Performance based on ROI**

The ROIs calculated for each division in part (a) are both significantly below the company's **target ROI** (20%). This would suggest that both divisions are performing poorly.

However, both divisions are now required to deduct a share of **head office costs** in their respective operating statements before arriving at 'net profit' which is then used to calculate ROI. The company's target ROI has not been reduced to take account of these **uncontrollable costs**.

Using the old method (prior to head office costs being recharged to divisions), ROI for both divisions would have **exceeded the 20% target**, and increased on ROIs for the last three months (Division B: 22% pa, Division C: 23% pa) – showing that both divisions have actually **improved their performance**.

ROI using the old method

Division B net profit = ($311,000 + $155,000) × 12 = $5,592,000

Division B ROI = $5,592,000 / $23,200,000 × 100% = **24.1%**

Division C net profit = ($292,000 + $180,000) × 12 = $5,664,000

Division C ROI = $5,664,000 / $22,600,000 × 100% = **25.06%**

Performance based on RI

Division B and Division C both have healthy RI figures of $1.4 million and $1.2 million respectively. These figures are impressive when you consider that they are based on **net profits** as opposed to **controllable profits**.

However, the company's cost of capital of 10% is significantly lower than the target return on investment (20%). This makes the residual income figure show a more **positive position**.

(d) **Division B's revised annualised net profit and opening net assets after investment**

Depreciation = ($2,120,000 – $200,000) / 48 months = $40,000 per month

Net profit for July = $311,000 + ($600,000 × 8.5%) – $40,000 = $322,000

Annualised net profit = $322,000 × 12 = $3,864,000

Opening net assets after investment = $23,200,000 + $2,120,000 = $25,320,000

Division B ROI

ROI = (Net profit / Net assets) × 100%

= $3,864,000 / $25,320,000 × 100% = 15.26%

Division B will not proceed with the investment as it will cause a decrease in ROI.

Division B RI

	$'000
Net profit	3,864
Less: imputed interest charge:	
$25.32m × 10%	(2,532)
Residual income	1,332

Based on the above calculation, it is clear that RI is lower with the investment. This would suggest that the company should not proceed with the investment and shows that the use of ROI as a performance measure is likely to result in the manager of Division B making a decision that is **in the best interests** of the company as a whole.

(e) **Behavioural problems**

Staff in both divisions are used to exceeding the target ROI of 20% and being rewarded for doing so. As a result of including head office costs in the calculation of net profit, staff will see that their respective divisions are **no longer meeting the target ROI,** despite performance actually improving.

The target ROI should be revised to take account of the these **uncontrollable allocated costs**.

Staff are likely to become **demotivated** by the fact that they are no longer meeting the target ROI despite continuing to operate at the same level as before. They may feel that management have deliberately altered how performance is measured in order to **avoid paying staff bonuses** for exceeding targets.

Staff may deliberately work slowly and refuse to work overtime to show their opposition to the new system. The company should resolve the situation as soon as possible to avoid a decrease in **production output** and **product quality.**

355 Hammer

Workbook reference. Transfer pricing is covered in Chapter 20.

Top tips. Do not forget to exclude fixed costs from your calculations in part (a). The question states that the current pricing policy is variable cost plus 30%.

Easy marks. Six marks are available in part (d) for discussing factors to consider when purchasing from outside suppliers.

Examining team's comments. The numerical parts to the question were quite well answered by most candidates. However, a disappointing number of answers included the fixed costs within part (a) and part (b) which defied the purpose of the whole question really. That having been said, most answers were good.

The quality of answers to part (c) was really poor. The question was looking for a couple of key points, for example, that including fixed costs guarantees a profit for the seller but invites manipulation of overheads and passes on inefficiencies from one part of the business to another. Also, that this strategy causes fixed costs of one division to be turned into a variable cost for another division.

Similarly, part (d) rarely produced answers scoring full marks. It asked whether retail stores should be allowed to buy in from outside suppliers. Key points in any answer should have been that the overall profitability of the company is key, as is goal congruence; these points were rarely made. Thankfully, many candidates did spot the more obvious points such as the fact that the quality and reliability of any external supplier would need to be assessed.

Marking scheme

			Marks
(a)	Steel	1	
	Other material	1	
	Labour	1	
	Variable overhead	1	
	Delivery	1	
	Margin	1	
			6
(b)	Fixed cost	2	
	Margin	2	
			4
(c)	Covers all cost	1	
	Risk	1	
	Fixed cost accounting	1	
	Converts a FC to VC	2	
			Max 4

		Marks
(d)	Market price may be temporary	1
	Brand	1
	Profitability	1
	Flexibility	1
	Control	1
	Motivation	1
	Performance assessment	<u>1</u>
		Max <u>6</u>
		<u><u>20</u></u>

(a) **Price Nail would charge under existing policy (cost plus 30%)**

	$
Steel (0.4kg/0.95 (5% steel loss)) × $4.00	1.68
Other materials ($3.00 × 0.9 × 0.1)	0.27
Labour ($10 × 0.25)	2.50
Variable overhead ($15 × 0.25)	3.75
Delivery	<u>0.50</u>
Total variable cost	8.70
Mark-up (30%)	<u>2.61</u>
Transfer price	<u>11.31</u>

(b) **Price Nail would charged under total cost plus 10%**

	$
Total variable cost from part (a)	8.70
Extra fixed cost (0.25 × $15 × 0.8)	<u>3.00</u>
Total cost	11.70
Mark up (10%)	<u>1.17</u>
Transfer price	<u>12.87</u>

The increase in price if the pricing policy switches to total cost plus 10% is $1.56 per unit ($12.87 – $11.31).

(c) Fixed costs can be accounted for in a number of ways. As such, including the fixed cost within the transfer price could lead to **manipulation of overhead treatment**. For example, employing absorption costing or activity-based costing.

Including the fixed costs in the transfer price will benefit the manufacturer, who can ensure that **all costs** incurred during the manufacturing process are **covered**. Assuming the fixed overhead absorption calculations are accurate, the manufacturing division should be **guaranteed a profit**.

The main **problem** with this pricing strategy is **fixed costs** are **effectively treated as variable costs** from the perspective of the stores, as they are included within the variable buy-in price. This could lead to **poor decision-making** from a **group perspective**.

(d) Managers of the retail stores are likely to be more **motivated** if they are given **freedom** in which to **operate** and are able to purchase from outside suppliers if prices are cheaper.

In addition, the performance of **store managers will be easier to assess** in an environment in which managers are able to control greater elements of the business.

Price differences are perhaps to be expected, given that products are rarely identical. There is a **risk** that store managers purchase cheaper shears of **inferior quality** to those produced internally (whilst claiming they are comparable) in order to achieve a greater margin. Such scenarios jeopardise the **reputation** of the brand for the benefit of individual stores.

Allowing store managers to purchase from cheaper suppliers could result in Hammer **losing control** of its business as retail stores could potentially stock different shears and other products from a range of different suppliers. On the other hand, **flexibility is increased** and profits could increase as store managers find bargain prices.

In a competitive market, it is unlikely that suppliers will offer products significantly cheaper to Hammer for a sustained period of time. Any cheap prices accessed by store managers are likely to be the result of a sale or special promotion. If this is the case, it would not be advisable for Hammer to grant store managers the power to purchase from cheaper external suppliers in the long term.

Overall profitability of the company is key. The retail stores and Nail should be working in a way that is best for the company overall. This is known as **goal congruence**.

356 Tonford School

Workbook reference. Performance measurement is covered in Chapter 19.

Top tips. Take your time on this question and use your common sense to make sensible suggestions.

Easy marks. Part (a) provides easy marks.

Marking scheme

		Marks
(a)	Explain the problems for not-for-profit organisations	4
(b)	Performance assessment of Tonford School	12
(c)	Explanation of difficulties in qualitative objectives	4
		20

(a) The primary objective of commercial organisations is to maximise the wealth they generate for their owners (shareholders). In contrast, the objectives of NFPO's are often non-financial and reflect the interests which the various stakeholders have in an organisation. These stakeholders often have varying interests in the organisation, meaning that the organisation will also have a number of different objectives.

These conflicts may make it difficult to set clear objectives on which all stakeholders agree. Consequently, the organisation's management will face a dilemma when trying to decide which objectives are most important and therefore prioritised in the course of strategic planning and decision-making. This can be a particular problem when different objectives make different demands on resources or require different courses of action.

Another problem is that these organisations often do not generate revenue but simply have a fixed budget for spending which they have to keep to and are often subject to strong external influences which will influence the setting of objectives, eg political factors.

(b) **Note:** This solution is longer than one which candidates would need to produce to score the marks available. However, it is intended to illustrate the range of relevant points candidates could have identified from the scenario, and therefore the number of marks potentially available in this question.

Objective 1 – Strive for continuous improvement in performance standards.

The percentage of pupils achieving the target grades is not only below the national target, it is also lower than Tonford School achieved five years ago. As such, the school's does not appear to be achieving continuous improvement.

However, exam results alone are not necessarily an accurate indicator of a school's performance. For example, exam results will reflect the underlying ability of the pupils, as well as the quality of the teaching they receive.

There is a danger that if Tonford School focuses only on exam results it will become 'selective' and will only accept the most academically gifted pupils. However, such an approach would contradict the objective to provide 'all children' with access to high quality education, regardless of their background.

Pupil progress may be a more valuable measure than exam results, because the extent to which pupils' performance improves provides an indication of the value added by the school, rather than pupils' inherent ability.

Given the typical range of scores, Tonford School's performance in this respect (+0.4) is significantly above the national target (+0.25) and is at the upper end of the range.

The fact that pupil numbers have increased seems likely to suggest that the school is becoming more popular with parents. Given that parents can choose which school to select for their children, the increase in pupil numbers is likely to reflect a perception among parents that the school is performing well.

The results of the recent inspection visit would seem likely to reinforce this perception.

Note: An alternative interpretation could be that all the other schools in the area are already full, and Tonford has spare capacity, which is why its pupil numbers increased. However, such an explanation seems less likely given the context of the other performance indicators.

Objective 2 – Provide a supportive learning environment, which encourages a high standard of pupil achievement

The 'pupil progress' score suggests the school is providing children with a high quality education and a learning environment which encourages a high standard of pupil achievement. The fact that Tonford School's 20X7 score is higher than its 20X2 score also suggests an improvement in the learning environment (although here again, to some extent the scores may reflect pupils' aptitude for learning as well as the efforts of the school).

The school's inspection grade is higher than five years ago, and is above the national target, which suggests the school is improving, and is performing relatively well. Although there is no indication that the DoE gives any more weighting to any single aspect of the performance data compared to other areas, the inspection grades could potentially be the most important indicator of how well as school is performing.

However, although Tonford School's grading is 'Very good' this suggests there is still room for further improvement, because the school did not achieve the top grade: 'Excellent'.

Tonford School's teacher/pupil ratio has remained essentially the same over the last five years – at 19 pupils per teacher, which is favourable compared to the national target of 22 pupils per teacher.

20X7: 662 pupils/35 members of teaching staff =18.9 pupils per member of staff

20X2: 627 pupils/33 members of teaching staff = 19 pupils per member of staff

Having a low teacher pupil ratio is likely to be beneficial because it will allow teachers to give more time to each pupil, thereby providing a supportive learning environment.

Given that the school is funded by the DoE, it seems likely that the DoE would have had to authorise the budget needed to recruit the additional teachers. On this basis, the fact that Tonford School has been able to increase the number of teachers it employs suggests that the DoE is pleased with the way it is performing, and therefore authorised the additional budget.

ANSWERS

> **Objective 3 – Ensure pupils are prepared for adult life and have the skills and character necessary to contribute to society and the economy**
>
> The inspector has highlighted Tonford School's 'strong sense of community values and citizenship'. This suggests the school is performing well in relation to the objective of preparing students for adult life, and developing their social skills.
>
> Exam results and the 'pupil progress' scores in compulsory subjects indicate that the school is making a significant contribution in providing pupils with core knowledge and skills necessary for adulthood.

> **Objective 4 – Provide all children with access to high quality education, regardless of their location or background**
>
> The inspector's report has highlighted that pupils at Tonford School come from diverse backgrounds' and awarded the school an improved grading over the last five years. Coupled with 'pupil progress' scores, this indicates that the school is fulfilling the objective to provide children which access to high quality education, regardless of their background.

(c) In order to assess any organisation's performance against its objectives, performance information needs to be available, and, in many cases, this information is obtained by measuring aspects of performance relevant to the objectives .

Difficulties of measurement

However, one of the inherent difficulties with qualitative objectives compared to quantifiable objectives is how to measure them.

For example, exam success rate (% of pupils achieving 5 grades A-C) is quantifiable, and relatively easy to measure, using exam results data. However, trying to measure the overall quality of education in a school or whether a school provides a 'supportive learning environment' is potentially much more difficult, because there aren't any specific outputs (eg results) which can be measured.

So, while exam results and pupil progress metrics are indicators of pupil achievement in schools – which can be measured – assessing them only provides a partial assessment of whether schools are providing children with 'access to high quality education' or whether they are providing 'supportive learning environment which encourages a high standard of pupil achievement.'

A related problem is that the aspects of performance which are monitored end up being the ones where performance can most easily be measured, rather than those which are most important in ensuring that the objectives are achieved.

The DoE has recognised these issues though and acknowledged the need for inspectors to visit schools on a regular basis, to gain an insight into the aspects of performance which cannot be reflected in statistical measures.

Subjectivity

Another major problem with assessing qualitative aspects of performance is that they tend to be subjective. For example, people are likely to have different expectations of what constitutes a high quality of education, a supportive learning environment, or the extent to which students are prepared for adult life.

In this respect, one of the key things the DoE has to ensure is that its inspectors are consistent in their grading of schools. For example, if one inspector rates a school as 'Good', but another inspector would have rated the same school as 'Excellent', this inconsistency would significantly reduce the validity of the performance data which is produced.

357 Ties Only Co

Marking scheme

			Marks
(a)	Sales	2	
	Gross profit	2	
	Website development	2	
	Administration	2	
	Distribution	1	
	Launch marketing	2	
	Overall comment	2	
			Max 10
(b)	Future profits comment		3
(c)	Number of tie sales	1	
	Tie price calculation	2	
	On-time delivery	2	
	Returns	2	
	System downtime	1	
	Summary comment	1	
			Max 7
			20

(a) Financial performance

Sales growth

Ties Only Co appears to have made an excellent start with initial sales of $420,000 growing by 62% ((680,000 − 420,000)/420,000 × 100%) to Quarter 2. This is particularly impressive given the acknowledged competitiveness of this business sector.

Gross profit

The gross profit margin in Quarter 1 was 52% (218,400/420,000 × 100%) and 50% (339,320/680,000 × 100%) in Quarter 2. The level of margin may be as expected for this business sector but we would need industry average data for comparison.

However, a **fall in margin** needs to be investigated. It could be that Ties Only was initially able to source cheaper ties but the rapid growth meant that alternative, more expensive, suppliers had to be found. Alternatively, competitors quickly responded to this new entrant and lowered their prices in response. This pressure could have forced Ties Only to lower their prices.

Website development

All website development costs are being **written off as incurred** so we would expect costs to be higher in the initial quarters. The website costs are over a third of total expenses, so the initial loss is mostly explained by this write-off and does not therefore give any major cause for concern.

Administration costs

Although administration costs have risen in absolute terms, as a **percentage of sales** they have **fallen** from 23.9% (100,500/420,000 × 100%) to 22.2% (150,640/680,000 × 100%). Administration costs are the second biggest expense so very important to control.

This could indicate that administration costs are being **effectively controlled** which is good news. It could also be because fixed overheads are being **spread over a larger volume** and this will continue to improve as the business grows.

Distribution costs

These costs form the **smallest proportion** of total expenses (about 6%) and the proportion of distribution costs to sales has **remained constant** at 4.9% (20,763/420,000 × 100%). These costs will be subject to external influences, such as a general rise in postage costs.

Launch marketing

This is similar to the website costs as it is expected to fall once the business is established. Ties Only will need to **continue to market** its website but this is likely to be cheaper than the initial big launch marketing campaign. The negative impact on profitability will therefore reduce over time.

Other variable expenses

These have again increased in line with the sales volume and are 11.9% of sales (50,000/420,000 × 100%).

(b) **Current and future profits**

An initial look at the accounts would identify a worrying total loss of $188,303 in the first two quarters.

However, much of this loss is due to the website development costs which will not be incurred again. Websites do need to be maintained and continually improved, but this cost will be much lower. Launch marketing is another initial cost which will fall rapidly. If we deduct these expenses, the business made an **underlying profit** of $47,137 in Quarter 1 and $75,360 in Quarter 2, an encouraging **upward trend**.

The initial impact of the business has been very good. There is a threat from falling margins to consider but cost control looks effective so the future is promising.

These figures illustrate that a short-term view of a new business is not necessarily a good indicator of future performance.

(c) **Non-financial performance indicators**

Average price of ties

Quarter 1: $420,000/27,631 = $15.20
Quarter 2: $680,000/38,857 = $17.50

In part (a) it was suggested that **the fall in gross profit margin** might be due to a price reduction. This data provides evidence that this is **not** the case. There must therefore be an alternative explanation.

On-time delivery

This has dropped significantly from 95% to 89% and this is worrying. The service provided to customers is a **key differentiator**, especially if the company is competing on quality, not price. Customers will go elsewhere if their expectations are not met. Action will need to be taken to remedy this problem.

Sales returns

This is again a key indicator of **quality** and whether **customers' expectations** are being met. Returns have risen from 12% to 18% and are now above the industry average of 13%. Returns are to be expected on internet sales where the product may look different in reality, but a higher than average rate means that the internet is **not adequately describing and illustrating** the products. Again, quality may be less than customers expect.

Alternatively, the **pressure to dispatch orders** may be resulting in **errors** or packaging problems. Either of these reasons does not bode well for the business and action must be taken to remedy the problem.

System downtime

Customers who use shopping websites are usually **time-pressured** individuals who will not react well to delays in loading pages. It is all too easy to immediately switch to a competitor's website so it is essential that system downtime is kept to an absolute minimum to **avoid lost sales**.

It would be useful to compare the figures with an **industry average** but the important point is that system downtime has **doubled**. This could be due to **pressure on the website** as a result of the volume of demand. As the website development has been such a costly and important part of the business set-up, the owners of Ties Only should have an urgent discussion with the website developers to come up with a solution.

Conclusion

Ties Only is doing well in terms of sales growth and potential profitability for a brand new business. However the owners need to focus their attention on the accuracy of order delivery, website reliability and the quality of the product. Further investigation needs to be made of the fall in gross profit margin.

358 Best Night Co

ANSWERS

Workbook reference. Performance measurement is covered in Chapter 19.

Top tips. At first glance, you may not know where to begin with this question! Look carefully at the scenario and decide on some headings for your answer – for example, revenue, discounts, operating profit. You'll need to perform some calculations (worth five marks) and then you'll have something to talk about.

Be sure to explain what your calculations mean for Best Night Co specifically, to add depth to your answer. Do not forget to comment on non-financial performance indicators.

Easy marks. There are easy marks available throughout this question.

Examining team's comments. This type of question has been tested many times before in the Performance Management (PM) examination and shares many similarities with recent questions published on ACCA's website'''. This particular question comprised of one 20-mark requirement which can appear daunting at first but this can be overcome by applying good exam technique. A key skill is the ability to break the requirement down into manageable parts and tackle each in turn. The first point to note about this requirement is that there is already some guidance about how the 20 marks are broken down – five marks for calculations and 15 marks for discussion. In this type of performance measurement question, each correct calculation is worth 0·5 marks so candidates should aim to be performing ten relevant and correct calculations to score all of the five marks. There were in excess of 30 relevant calculations which could have been performed from the data provided in the scenario, so these five calculation marks should have been relatively simple to score. Unfortunately, some candidates did not perform as well as they could have on this question because they did not perform enough calculations.

	Marks
Calculations	5
Revenue	4
Operating profit	2
ROCE	2
Customer satisfaction	3
Other valid points	4
	20

Gross room revenue – Best Night's 'gross' room revenue based on standard room rates has increased by 6·6% in 20X7, which reflects the higher occupancy rates (74% v 72%) and the increase in standard room rates ($140 v $135 per night)'.

However, this gives a rather misleading impression of how well the hotels have performed in the year to 20X7.

Revenue after discounts – Revenue from room sales, adjusted for discounts or rate reductions offered, has actually only increased 1·8%, and that reflects the significant 45% increase in discounts or reductions offered:

	20X7 $'000	20X6 $'000	% change $'000
Standard revenue	111,890	104,976	6·6%
Discounts/reductions	16,783	11,540	45·4%
Room revenue net of discounts	95,107	93,436	1·8%

Faced with the declining number of business customers, and consequently the prospect of lower occupancy rates, managers may have decided to offer lower room rates to try to retain as many of their existing business customers as possible, or to try to attract additional leisure customers.

Although occupancy rates increased by 2·8% (from 72% to 74% which now exceeds the budgeted level), revenue, net of discounts, only increased by 1·8%. This means that revenue per room per night after discounts in 20X7 was lower than in 20X6, despite the standard rate being higher ($140 v $135).

In the context of tough market conditions, the decision to increase the standard room rate for 20X7 appears rather optimistic. Although the hotel managers have managed to achieve occupancy rates higher than budget, they have only managed to do so by reducing room rates.

Additional revenue – One of the potential benefits of increased occupancy rates, even if guests are paying less per room per night, is that they will generate additional revenue from food and drink sales. This appears to be the case because additional revenues have increased by approximately 5%.

Total revenue – In total, revenue (net of discounts) has increased 2·4% in 20X7 v 20X6. Given the tough competitive environment, Best Night Co could view any increase in revenues as positive. Moreover, provided the revenue achieved from selling the room is greater than the variable cost of providing it, then increasing occupancy levels should increase the hotels' contribution to profit.

Operating profit – However, despite the increase in revenue, operating profits have fallen by $0·3m (1·3%) between 20X7 and 20X6, due to a sizeable increase in operating costs.

There is no detail about Best Night Co's operating costs, for example, the split between fixed and variable costs. However, in an increasingly competitive market, cost control is likely to be very important. As such, the $3 million (3·3%) increase in operating costs between 20X6 and 20X7 is potentially a cause for concern, and the reasons for the increase should be investigated further.

However, when looking to reduce costs, it will be very important to do so in a way which does not compromise customer satisfaction. More generally, Best Night Co needs to avoid cutting expenditure in areas which will have a detrimental impact on customer satisfaction ratings, for example, not replacing mattresses even though they are becoming uncomfortable to sleep on.

Operating profit margin – The increase in costs has also led to a fall in operating profit margin from 20·8% to 20·0%.

It is perhaps more instructive to look at the margin based on standard room rates per night, thereby reflecting the impact of the discounts offered as well as the increase in costs. On this basis, the margin falls slightly more: from 18·9% to 17·6%.

	20X7	20X6
	$'000	$'000
Total revenue	119,377	116,621
Discounts offered	16,783	11,430
Gross revenue	136,160	128,051
Operating profit	23,915	4,242
Operating profit margin	17·6%	18·9%

ROCE – This reduced profitability is also reflected in the company's return on capital employed which has fallen slightly from 62% ($24·2m/$39·1m) to 60·5% ($23·9m/$39·5m). This suggests that the value which Best Night Co is generating from its assets is falling. The decline in ROCE could be a particular concern given the relative lack of capital investment in the hotels recently. Capital investment will increase the cost of Best Night Co's non-current assets, thereby reducing ROCE for any given level of profit.

Customer satisfaction scores

Although the reduction in profitability should be a concern for Best Night Co, the reduction in customer satisfaction scores should potentially be seen as a greater cause for concern. The scores suggest that, in the space of one year, Best Night Co hotels have gone from being in the top 10% of hotels to only just being in the top 25%. This is a significant decline in one year, and one which Best Night Co cannot afford to continue.

Best Night Co prides itself on the comfort of its rooms and the level of service it offers its guests. Both of these factors are likely to be important considerations for people when considering whether or not to stay in a Best Night Co hotel. Therefore, falling customer satisfactions levels could be seen as an indication that fewer existing customers will stay at a Best Night Co hotel in future – thereby threatening occupancy rates, and prices, in future.

Moreover, the scores suggest that the decision to defer the refurbishment programme is likely to have a detrimental impact on future performance.

359 Jump

Workbook reference. Performance measurement is covered in Chapter 19.

Top tips. Ensure that your answer to part (b) supports both arguments. Use headings in your answer, one for each target.

Easy marks. Part (c) is relatively straightforward and is worth five marks.

Examining team's comments. Answers to part (a) were good on the whole. For a narrative requirement, part (b) was fairly well answered overall. Part (c) asked for a description of ways in which the manager could manipulate the situation in order to make sure they get their bonus.

Again, there were some good answers here, with only a minority of candidates talking about manipulating profits, which wasn't relevant to a business where profit-based targets weren't being used.

Marks

(a)	Per target	2
		6
(b)	For each target – supporting controllability	1.5
	For each target – denying controllability	1.5
		9
(c)	For each idea of manipulation	2.5
		5
		20

(a) Bonus calculation

	Qtr to 30 June 20X9	Qtr to 30 September 20X9	Qtr to 31 December 20X9	Qtr to 31 March 20Y0	Bonus hits
Staff on time?					
On-time %	95.5% (430/450)	94.2% (452/480)	94.0% (442/470)	95.8% (460/480)	
Bonus earned?	Yes	No	No	Yes	2

	Qtr to 30 June 20X9	Qtr to 30 September 20X9	Qtr to 31 December 20X9	Qtr to 31 March 20Y0	Bonus hits
Member visits					
Target visits	21,600 (60% × 3,000 × 12)	23,040 (60% × 3,200 ×12)	23,760 (60% × 3,300 × 12)	24,480 (60% × 3,400 × 12)	
Actual visits	20,000	24,000	26,000	24,000	
Bonus earned?	No	Yes	Yes	No	2

	Qtr to 30 June 20X9	Qtr to 30 September 20X9	Qtr to 31 December 20X9	Qtr to 31 March 20Y0	Bonus hits
Personal training					
Target visits	300 (10% × 3,000)	320 (10% × 3,200)	330 (10% × 3,300)	340 (10% × 3,400)	
Actual visits	310	325	310	339	
Bonus earned?	Yes	Yes	No	No	2

Total number of bonus hits from table above = 6

The bonus earned by the manager is 6 × $400 = $2,400. This represents 50% of the total bonus available.

(b) It is essential that the targets set are based on elements of the job that the local managers are able to control. Targets that are based on elements that local managers are unable to influence will be seen as pointless and unrealistic and could **demotivate staff** at the local manager level.

Staff on time

Individual members of staff may be late for work as a result of external factors, including home pressures or delayed public transport. Such factors cannot be controlled by the local manager. However if such problems occur on a regular basis to certain members of staff, the local manager does have the power **to amend their contract of employment**.

The way in which the local manager manages staff will impact upon how **motivated** they are to work and to arrive on time. The **local manager** has the power to **devise shift patterns** that best suit their team and can **reward** them accordingly, through their ability to amend employment contracts.

In summary, **lateness** to work **can be controlled** by the local manager.

Personal training sessions

The local manager has control over prices charged to customers. If demand for personal training sessions falls they can reduce prices or make special offers in a bid to increase customer numbers.

A number of potential customers may view personal training sessions as a luxury, particularly in the current economic climate. Also, the personal training market is particularly competitive, which may make it difficult for the local managers to increase sales. Local managers can take steps to improve the service offered by the sports club but any significant expenditure requires approval at Board level.

In summary, the local manager can only **partly control** the number of **personal training sessions** that are booked.

Member use of facilities

The local manager controls the staff and hence the level of customer service. It is likely that a **high level of customer service** could encourage some **members to use** the facilities **more often**. The local manager also has the ability to influence member numbers by **adjusting membership prices**.

However, external factors such as **work pressures** and level of **health** may prevent some members from visiting the club as often as they would like.

In summary, the local manager can only **partly control** the **number of member visits**.

(c) **Reduce prices**

The targets are largely volume-driven and local managers have the power to **adjust membership fees** and **prices for personal training sessions**. Local managers could therefore reduce prices to ensure that they meet the targets and therefore obtain their bonus. Such a scenario would **harm** Jump's **overall profitability**.

Recording of transactions

A local manager with access to the accounting records could deliberately record visits to the club in the **incorrect period** in order to ensure that they achieve a bonus. For example, in Q2 the target for personal training sessions was not met by five sessions. The manager could record the first five transactions of Q3 in Q2 to ensure that they obtain an extra $400 bonus.

360 Bridgewater Co

Workbook reference. Performance measurement is covered in Chapter 19.

Top tips. The key to success in this type of question is reading the information in the question very carefully and making full use of it. When the ACCA examining team asks for 'comment', an opinion is required, not simply a re-statement of the proposals.

Easy marks. For half marks in part (a) all that was expected was a statement (with simple supporting calculations) of whether or not the manager would meet each of the targets.

Examining team's comments. Candidates must be able to assess performance, which means interpret financial and other data and make sensible comments on it. Few candidates realised that the division's improving performance in Quarters 3 and 4 came too late for the promotion at the end of Quarter 2. Many only commented on the profits of the division and ignored all the other targets. Many also assessed the performance more generally, calculating among other things % margins and ignored the targets altogether. This was very disappointing.

Part (b) was also poorly performed and misreading the question was common. Candidates must learn to read performance management questions more carefully.

For Part (c) candidates answers primarily consisted of a re-statement of the different steps being proposed with little or no comment at all. A comment requires opinion and anything sensible scored marks.

Candidates should prepare themselves to assess the performance of a business, both financially and non-financially, if they want to pass.

Marking scheme

		Marks	
(a)	Per target discussed	2	
			8
(b)	Revised forecasts		
	Voucher sales effect	1	
	Vista sales effect	2	
	Extra trainer cost	1	
	Extra room hire cost	1	
	Staff training increase	0.5	
	Software cost	0.5	
	Overall revised profit calculation	1	
			Max 6
(c)	Per idea commented on	2	
			Max 6
			20

(a) **Each quarter, sales should grow and annual sales should exceed budget**

In the Northwest division, sales are forecasted to fall by 10% (4/40 × 100%) from Quarter 1 to Quarter 2 but then start to grow. Average growth per quarter over the year is 14.5% $(\sqrt[3]{(60/40)}-1)$. Annual sales are forecast to exceed the sales budget by $6,000 (186 – 180).

It would therefore appear that the annual **target will be met**. However, the promotion decision is to be taken in Quarter 3 and the **slow start** to the year may not reflect well on the manager of the Northwest division.

Trainer costs should not exceed $180 per teaching day

The manager is paying $200 (8,000/40) per teaching day in trainer costs, which **exceeds the target**. They believe in quality and therefore appear to be paying more to attract better teaching staff. This may well improve sales in the long term as the reputation for quality delivery becomes known, but it is at the expense of increased costs in the short term.

Room hire costs should not exceed $90 per teaching day

The manager of this division is also **spending more** on room hire costs than the target. They are spending $100 per teaching day rather than $90. This could be again part of their quality improvement policy as they are hiring better facilities, but it could also be due to poor negotiation and buying strategy.

Each division should meet its budget for profit per quarter and annually

The achievement of this target suffers from the same problem as the sales target. The manager will meet the target for the year by $2,500, but is **below target** in the first two quarters.

This again will impact on their promotion prospects which, overall, are not looking good. They are failing to meet any of the targets in the first two quarters and will have to hope that the senior managers agree with their **long-term** rather than **short-term** approach.

(b) **Revised forecasts**

	Q1 $'000	Q2 $'000	Q3 $'000	Q4 $'000	Total $'000
Existing sales	40.0	36.0	50.0	60.0	186.0
Voucher sales ($125 × 80/4)	2.5	2.5	2.5	2.5	10.0
Software training			10.0	12.0	22.0
	42.5	38.5	62.5	74.5	218.0
Less:					
Existing trainer costs	8.0	7.2	10.0	12.0	37.2
Additional training costs ($200 × teaching days)			2.0	2.4	4.4
Room hire	4.0	3.6	5.0	6.0	18.6
Additional room hire ($100 × teaching days)			1.0	1.2	2.2
Staff training	1.0	1.0	1.0	1.0	4.0
Additional staff training	0.5	0.5			1
Other costs	3.0	1.7	6.0	7.0	17.7
Software	1.8				1.8
Forecast net profit	24.2	24.5	37.5	44.9	131.1
Original budget profit	25.0	26.0	27.0	28.0	106.0

(c) **Voucher scheme**

The voucher scheme looks like a good idea as the manager is confident that the take-up would be good and customers would follow their advice to attend one session per quarter. This will **increase revenue** without incurring additional costs, as customers would attend existing planned courses. However, some additional unforeseen costs may still be incurred.

The additional revenue and profit will help, but targets for Quarters 1 and 2 will still not be met so the voucher scheme will not necessarily improve the manager's promotion prospects.

There is always the danger with offering a discount that **existing customers** will be disgruntled, particularly if they have already paid a higher price for a course that is now being offered at a discount. The vouchers are, however, only being offered to **new** customers so the manager should be able to offer this promotion without upsetting existing customers.

Software upgrade

It is essential that a software training company uses the **latest software technology** on its courses. The investment in software and staff training is therefore a **necessity** and cannot be avoided.

The courses will generate **extra revenue** but not until Quarters 3 and 4. This software upgrade will therefore further damage the achievement of targets in Quarters 1 and 2, as costs will rise but the extra revenue will be too late for the promotion assessment.

It is to be hoped that the senior managers will recognise the essential long-term planning being undertaken.

BPP LEARNING MEDIA

Delaying payments to trainers

This is not a good idea. None of the performance targets will be affected, as the plan will not affect costs or profits. The only positive impact will be on **cash flow**. The worrying aspect is the negative impact it may have on **relationships with trainers**. Software training is a competitive market and good trainers will be in demand by a number of training providers. If the company is to offer quality training, it must have the best trainers and this is not the way to retain them.

In conclusion, if all the proposals were taken together, they will **not improve** the manager's chance of promotion as any benefits will accrue after Quarter 2.

361 One Stop Car Co

Marking scheme

		Marks	
(a)	Calculations	6	
	Justification of PI	3	
	Discussion of performance under the dimensions	<u>7</u>	
			16
(b)	Explanation	<u>4</u>	
			<u>4</u>
			<u><u>20</u></u>

(a) **Competitiveness**

	MSC	OSC Average
Percentage of website hits converted into orders		
$(9,506/14,000) \times 100$	67·9%	
$(11,870/18,260) \times 100$		65%

This ratio indicates whether MSC's services are attractive compared to its competitors, which is important if it is going to survive in such a competitive market.

It has performed substantially better than other OSC service centres on average, having converted 67·9% of website hits into jobs, compared to the 65% converted by other service centres. This is a good result.

Financial performance

	MSC	OSC Average
Gross profit margin		
($304,200/$760,500) × 100	40%	
($328,146/$890,365) × 100		36·9%

Gross profit margin is the preferred measure for financial performance from the data presented. It shows the percentage of revenue which exceeds the cost of goods sold.

MSC's gross profit margin is almost three percentage points higher than the average, which is a good result. This could be partly because they did relatively well on their new service pack sales (note 4) but it is also likely to be because their ratio of senior mechanics to junior mechanics is lower than the average, and junior mechanics will invariably be paid less than senior ones.

Quality of service

	MSC	OSC Average
Percentage of jobs from repeat customers		
(1,500/9,506) × 100	15.78%	
(1,660/11,870) × 100		13.98%

Quality is a key element of MSC's service to customers and if it is poor, customers will not return.

Again, MSC has outperformed the other service centres on average by 1·8 percentage points. This could be because it has a higher ratio of senior mechanics to junior mechanics than other service centres, so the quality of work is probably better, hence the higher level of repeat customers.

Flexibility

	MSC	OSC Average
Time taken per job		
(23,100/9,506)	2·43 hours	
(24,800/11,870)		2·09 hours

The time taken to complete each job is important as many customers will use MSC because they can sit and wait for the work to be done, rather than having to hire a rental car for the day, for example.

The comparison shows that MSC takes longer to complete a job than the OSC average. This is not really a good thing and is probably because they have slightly less experienced staff on the whole, but it could also be that they do a more thorough job than other service centres. Given the fact that they have a higher level of return customers than the average and they are graded 9 or 10 by their customers (10 percentage points higher than the average), this is presumably not viewed negatively by customers.

Resource utilisation

	MSC	OSC Average
Sales per mechanic		
$760,500/12	$63,375	
$890,365/13		$68,490

The key resource in a service company is its staff and so these indicators measure how this resource is being utilised.

MSC's utilisation of its staff is lower than that of the other service centres by $5,115 per mechanic. This clearly ties in with the fact that the average time to complete a job is longer at MSC than other service centres. However, given that they use a slightly less experienced staff on average than other centres and the fact that their gross margin is higher than average, this should not be viewed too negatively.

BPP
LEARNING
MEDIA

Innovation

	MSC	OSC Average
Percentage revenue generated from new service packs [($66,000 + $58,000 + $54,000)/$760,500]	23·4%	

MSC wants to offer a wide variety of service packs to its customers and needs to be innovative in packaging services up.

The 23·4% indicates that MSC is indeed innovative in their approach to their customers' needs, offering an innovative mix of services. MSC has really outperformed other service centres on this front, generating a far larger part of its revenue by the introduction of new service packs, which must have attracted customers. This is a really strong performance.

(b) The standards block sets the target for the performance indicators chosen for each of the dimensions. The targets must meet three criteria – they must be achievable, fair and encourage employees to take ownership. If the targets set do not meet these criteria, then the performance of the organisation could suffer.".

The rewards block ensures that employees are motivated to achieve the standards. It also considers the properties of good reward schemes which are that they should be clear, motivating and based on controllable factors.

If standards and rewards are set appropriately, the staff will be engaged and motivated and it is then more likely that the goals, ie dimensions, of the organisation will be achieved.

362 Web Co

> **Workbook reference.** Performance measurement is covered in Chapter 19.
>
> **Top tips.** This question may look daunting at first glance, given the 20 marks available for a single requirement. Use the information in the scenario as a framework when structuring your answer and address each performance indicator under a separate heading. Don't forget to highlight any instances where further information is required.

Marking scheme

	Marks
Calculations	4
Missing info	3
Discussion and further analysis (2–3 marks per point)	18
Conclusion	2
	Max 20

Total sales revenue

Web Co's total **sales revenue has increased 25%** (W1) on Quarter 1 (Q1), from $2.2m to $2.75m. This is impressive given the decision to give a $10 discount to all customers who spend over $100. It is not possible to attribute the increase to any particular change or incentive without analysing the **performance indicators** below.

Net profit margin

The net profit margin has decreased from 25% to 16.7%. Net profit was $550,000 in Q1 and $459,250 in Q2 (W2). If the profit margin remained at 25%, net profit for Q2 would have been $687,500. Net profit for Q2 is therefore $228,250 **lower** than it would have been.

This significant decrease is largely due to the fee of $200,000 paid for an advert on **the webpage of a well known fashion magazine**. A further $20,000 is attributable to the fee paid to the **website consultant**.

The remaining $8,250 could be the costs of providing the **free 'Fast Track' delivery service**. Alternatively it could be the cost of offering a $10 discount to all customers who spent more than $100. More information would be required on **how the discounts are accounted for** (whether they are included in cost of sales or netted off against sales revenue). Further detail of the **costs of providing the 'Fast Track' service** would also be useful.

Number of orders from customers/customers spending over $100

The number of orders received from customers has increased by 22%, from 40,636 in Q1 to 49,600 in Q2 (W3). This 22% increase is **in line with the 25% increase in sales revenue**.

The number of customers spending more than $100 per visit has increased by 37%, from 4,650 in Q1 to 6,390 in Q2. This increase is likely to explain the 3% increase in sales revenue that is not due to increased order numbers, depending on **how the discounts are accounted for**.

Number of visits to website

The number of visits to the website has also increased significantly, from 101,589 to 141,714 (39.5% (W4)). Of this increase, 28,201 (W5) can be attributed to visitors coming through the **fashion magazine's website**. The remainder of the increase is likely to be due to the work of the website consultant.

It is clear that both changes have been effective in increasing the number of visitors to Web Co's online store. At a cost of $20,000, the work of the web consultant represents excellent **value for money**. However Web Co's sales are not really high enough to justify an outlay of $200,000 for the web magazine advert, hence the **significant fall in net profit margin** (detailed above).

Conversion rate – visitor to purchaser

The conversion rate has decreased by five percentage points, from 40% to 35%. This is to be expected, given the substantial increase in visitors to the website as a result of the **web magazine advert and search engine optimisation**.

Readers of the fashion magazine may have clicked on the advert link out of curiosity and may return to the site and purchase products at a **later date**.

Further information is required to confirm the above. For example, the total number of 'visitors to purchasers' split into (i) visitors who visited the site through the link on the online magazine, and (ii) visitors who did not.

Website availability

Website availability has remained at 95%. This indicates that the changes made by the IT department **have not corrected the problem(s).**

Lack of availability **may have lost Web Co a significant number of sales**. Further information is required to quantify the impact. For example, the number of **aborted purchases** due to the website becoming unavailable.

Subscribers to online newsletter

The number of subscribers has increased by 159%, from 4,600 to 11,900 (W6). This huge increase is most likely due to the **free 'Fast Track' delivery service** offered to all subscribers.

As the fall in net profit has already been accounted for above, it appears that Web Co has managed to offer this service **without incurring any extra cost**.

Further information is required to establish whether the company's view of subscribers is correct (that subscribers become customers who place further orders). For example, **has the number of repeat customers increased?**

Conclusion

In summary, **Web Co performed well in Q2**. With the exception of the work performed by the IT department to make the website more available, all other changes have increased sales and/or increased subscribers to the online newsletter.

Though further information is required in a number of areas, it is clear that the business has **responded well to the changes and incentives introduced**.

The cost of the web advert ($200,000) was so high that **profits have decreased substantially despite the incentives** and changes detailed above.

Workings

1   **Increase in sales revenue**

   $2.75m – $2.2m/$2.2m = 25% increase

2   **Net profit**

   Quarter 1 = $2.2m × 25% = $550,000

   Quarter 2 = $2.75m × 16.7% = $459,250

3   **Increase in orders**

   49,600 – 40,636/40,636 = 22%

4   **Increase in number of visits to website**

   141,714 – 101,589/101,589 = 39.5%

5   **Customers accessing website through magazine advert**

   141,714 × 19.9% = 28,201

6   **Increase in subscribers to newsletter**

   11,900 – 4,600/4,600 = 159%

363 PAF Co

Workbook reference. Performance measurement is covered in Chapter 19 of the BPP Workbook.

Top tips. This question allows you to analyse performance as much as you can within the available time. For every ratio or other performance measure that you calculate, be ready to comment on its significance. Even if a ratio does not seem significant, you can say so.

Some ratios for measuring performance might seem easy to identify, but remember to use the information given in the question. There are five items in particular you could use.

(1)   The aim five years ago was to become the market leader in Sista.

(2)   Division S left its prices for products and services unchanged in 20X3 rather than increasing them in line with its competitors – so increases in sales volume are down to sales volume entirely.

(3)   Skilled staff are in short supply – so it is worth looking at labour costs.

(4)   In Sista, fire safety regulations were introduced; this could have an impact on the requirement for labour.

(5)   In addition, the property tax has affected rental costs, so these should be looked at too.

And where possible, compare the relative performance of the two divisions.

There is a lot you could discuss – but remember to keep your time discipline and do not exceed your allocated time for the question.

Easy marks. The question enables you to make as many ratio calculations as you can, and you should be able to calculate some quite easily – such as the increase in sales revenue and profit in each division, and the change in the ratio of operating profit to sales from one year to the next. However, there are twice as many marks available for discussion of performance as for calculation of ratios, so make sure that you comment on the measures you have calculated.

	Marks	
0.5 marks per calculation	Max	7
Per comment – two marks per point		13
		20

Workings

	Division S Year on year	Division C Year on year
Increase in sales revenue	44%	9%
Increase in material costs	36%	25%
Increase in payroll costs	70%	15%
Increase in property costs	78%	6%
Gross profit margin in 20X3	56%	65%
Gross profit margin in 20X2	61%	67%
Increase in D&M costs	38%	18%
Increase in administration costs	6%	0%
Net profit margin in 20X3	11%	21%
Net profit margin in 20X2	9%	22%
Revenue per employee in 20X3	$102,224	$104,917
Revenue per employee in 20X2	$111,772	$104,828
Payroll cost per employee in 20X3	$27,000	$21,000
Payroll cost per employee in 20X2	$25,020	$20,000
Total market size ($ revenue) in 20X3 (w1)	$129.48m	$80.12m
Total market size ($ revenue) in 20X2 (w1)	$107.75m	$77.61m

Working 1 for market size

Division S 20X3: $38,845m/30% = $129.48m   Division C 20X3: $44,065m/55% = $80.12m

Division S 20X2: $26,937/25% = $107,75m   Division C 20X2: $40,359m/52% = $77.61m

Note. Percentages have been calculated to the nearest 1%

Commentary

General overview

Overall, Division S has performed well in 20X3, although it has not managed to meet its objective of becoming market leader despite its $2m advertising campaign. Since it has 30% of the market in 20X3 and there are only two competitors holding 70% of the market between them, at least one of those competitors must hold 35% or more of the market.

Revenue and market share

This has increased by a huge 44% in the last year. This compares to an increase of only 9% in Division C. However, part of the reason that this has been achieved is because the changes in fire safety laws introduced by the government at the end of 20X2 have caused the market for fire products and services to increase from $107.75m to $129.48m. Part of Division S's success is therefore down to increased opportunity. However, Division S has also increased its market share by a further five percentage points compared to 20X2. Division C has only managed a 3 percentage point increase in its market share, so this is a good result by Division S. One can assume that this is at least partly as a result of the advertising campaign carried out by Division S. However, this did cost a large amount, $2m, and it did not quite enable the Division to achieve its aim of becoming market leader.

Materials costs

The increase in materials costs is 36%, compared to an increase in revenue of 44%. It is difficult to say whether this is good or bad since the increase in revenue includes revenue from services, for which no materials costs would be expected to arise. Further information is needed on the split of revenue between products and services.

Payroll costs, revenue per employee and cost per employee

Payroll costs have increased by a massive 70% and far more than Division C's 15% increase. This is largely due to the fact that Division S's employee numbers increased from 241 in 20X2 to 380 in 20X3. This is a really big increase in employee numbers and has been accompanied by a fall in revenue per employee from $111,772 in 20X2 to $102,224 in 20X3. It is possible that Division S over-recruited, as it hoped to secure a greater level of business than it did through its advertising campaign. Division S's payroll cost per employee also increased from $25,020 in 20X2 to $27,000 in 20X3. Presumably, this is because of the fact that there is high demand for staff skilled in this area and Division S has probably had to increase pay in order to attract the calibre of staff which it needs.

Increase in property costs

In percentage terms, the biggest increase in costs which Division S has suffered is in relation to its property costs. They have increased by 78%, compared to Division C's 6% increase. It would appear that this increase is due to the increased rent charged by Division S's landlords on its business premises, which in turn has risen because of the increased tax charges. However, it is not possible to quantify this precisely without further information on rent increases.

Gross profit margin

This has actually fallen from 61% to 56%. Division C has also seen a fall in its GPM, but only a two percentage point fall as opposed to Division S's five percentage point fall. The reasons for Division S's lower GPM are the higher material, payroll and property costs. Also, Division S did not try to pass on any of its increased costs to its customers in the form of higher prices.

Distribution and marketing costs

These have increased by 38% compared to Division C's 18%. However, when you take out the advertising costs in both years' figures and work out the cost increase without them ($8.522m − $7.102m/$7.102m), it leaves an increase of only 20%. This increase would be expected given the 20% increase in world fuel prices which occurred. Division S has to deliver to a wider geographical spread of customers than Division C, so it would be expected to feel the full brunt of fuel price increases.

Administrative costs

These have increased by 6% compared to Division C's less than 1% increase (0% when rounded down to the nearest percent).

Further information is needed about the items included in these cost figures to explain why this increase has arisen.

Net profit margin

Despite challenging cost increases in all categories, Division S has still managed to increase its NPM from 9% to 11%. However, this is substantially lower than the NPM in Division C, which has fallen slightly but is still 21%, almost twice that in Division S. As we have seen, Division S's GPM is lower than Division C's anyway and, on top of that, Division C has not suffered a big increase in advertising costs like Division S; nor have administrative costs risen inexplicably.

Head Office

There is no information given about Head Office. If the Calana Division is also the Head Office, there could be Head Office costs included in Calana's figures, which would affect the comparisons being made. Further information is required here.

364 CIM Co

(a) **Division F**

Controllable profit = $2,645k.

Total assets less trade payables = $9,760k + $2,480k − $2,960k = $9,280k. ROI = 28.5%.

Division N

Controllable profit = $1,970k.

Total assets less trade payables = $14,980k + $3,260k − $1,400k = $16,840k. ROI = 11.7%.

In both calculations, controllable profit has been used to reflect profit, rather than net profit. This is because the managers do not have any control over the Head Office costs; responsibility accounting deems that managers should only be held responsible for costs which they control. The same principle is being applied in the choice of assets figures being used. The current assets and current liabilities figures have been taken into account in the calculation because of the fact that the managers have full control over both of these.

(b) **Bonus**

Bonus to be paid for each percentage point = $120,000 × 2% = $2,400. Maximum bonus = $120,000 × 0.3 = $36,000.

Division F: ROI = 28.5% = 18 whole percentage points above minimum ROI of 10%.

18 × $2,400 = $43,200.

Therefore manager will be paid the maximum bonus of $36,000.

Division N: ROI = 11.7% = 1 whole percentage point above minimum.

Therefore bonus = $2,400.

(c) Discussion

- The manager of Division N will be paid a far smaller bonus than the manager of Division F. This is because of the large asset base on which the ROI figure has been calculated. Total assets of Division N are almost double the total assets of Division F. This is largely attributable to the fact that Division N invested $6.8m in new equipment during the year. If this investment had not been made, net assets would have been only $10.04m and the ROI for Division N would have been 19.62%. This would have led to the payment of a $21,600 bonus (9 × $2,400) rather than the $2,400 bonus. Consequently, Division N's manager is being penalised for making decisions which are in the best interests of their division. It is very surprising that they did decide to invest, given that they knew that they would receive a lower bonus as a result. They have acted totally in the best interests of the company. Division F's manager, on the other hand, has benefitted from the fact that they have made no investment – even though it is badly needed. This is an example of sub-optimal decision-making.

- Division F's trade payables figure is much higher than Division N's. This also plays a part in reducing the net assets figure on which the ROI has been based. Division F's trade payables are over double those of Division N. In part, one would expect this because sales are over 50% higher (no purchases figure is given). However, it is clear that it is also because of low cash levels at Division F. The fact that the manager of Division F is then being rewarded for this, even though relationships with suppliers may be adversely affected, is again an example of sub-optimal decision-making.

- If the controllable profit margin is calculated, it is 18.24% for Division F and 22.64% for Division N. Therefore, if capital employed is ignored, it can be seen that Division N is performing better. ROI is simply making the division's performance look worse because of its investment in assets. Division N's manager is likely to feel extremely demotivated by their comparatively small bonus and, in the future, they may choose to postpone investment in order to increase their bonus. Managers not investing in new equipment and technology will mean that the company will not keep up with industry changes and affect its overall future competitiveness.

- To summarise, the use of ROI is leading to sub-optimal decision-making and a lack of goal congruence, as what is good for the managers is not good for the company and vice versa. Luckily, the manager at Division N still appears to be acting for the benefit of the company but the other manager is not. The fact that one manager is receiving a much bigger bonus than the other is totally unfair here and may lead to conflict in the long run. This is not good for the company, particularly if there comes a time when the divisions need to work together.

(d) Steps that could be taken to encourage managers to take a **long-term view**, so that the 'ideal' decisions are taken, include the following.

    (i) **Making short-term targets realistic**. If budget targets are unrealistically tough, a manager will be forced to make trade-offs between the short and long term.

    (ii) **Providing sufficient management information** to allow managers to see what trade-offs they are making. Managers must be kept aware of long-term aims as well as shorter-term (budget) targets.

    (iii) **Evaluating managers' performance** in terms of contribution to long-term as well as short-term objectives.

    (iv) **Link managers' rewards to share price.** This may encourage goal congruence.

    (v) **Set quality-based targets** as well as financial targets. Multiple targets can be used.

365 Man Co

> **Workbook reference.** Transfer pricing is covered in Chapter 20 of the BPP Workbook.
>
> **Top tips.** Part (a) is fairly straightforward, so don't fall into the trap of thinking that's more complicated than it is. It's only worth three marks. Make sure that you read the question again carefully before attempting part (c).
>
> **Easy marks.** Part (d) is pure knowledge covered in the Workbook and provides easy marks.
>
> **Examining team's comments.** Most students got part (a) wrong, perhaps because they expected it to be more difficult than it was. Part (b) was attempted by most students. In part (c) some students failed to notice that the divisions had autonomy.

(a) **Maximising group profit**

Division L has enough capacity to supply both Division M and its external customers with component L.

Therefore, incremental cost of Division M buying externally is as follows:

Cost per unit of component L when bought from external supplier: $37

Cost per unit for Division L of making component L: $20.

Therefore incremental cost to group of each unit of component L being bought in by Division M rather than transferred internally: $17 ($37 – 20).

From the group's point of view, the most profitable course of action is therefore that all 120,000 units of component L should be transferred internally.

(b) **Calculating total group profit**

Total group profits will be as follows:

Division L:

Contribution earned per transferred component = $40 – $20 = $20
Profit earned per component sold externally = $40 – $24 = $16

	$
120,000 × $20	2,400,000
160,000 × $16	2,560,000
	4,960,000
Less fixed costs	(500,000)
Profit	4,460,000

Division M:

Profit earned per component sold externally = $27 – $1 = $26

	$
120,000 × $26	3,120,000
Less fixed costs	(200,000)
Profit	2,920,000
Total profit	7,380,000

(c) **Problems with current transfer price and suggested alternative**

The problem is that the current transfer price of $40 per unit is now too high. While this has not been a problem before, since external suppliers were charging $42 per unit, it is a problem now that Division M has been offered component L for $37 per unit. If Division M now acts in its own interests rather than the interests of the group as a whole, it will buy component L from the external supplier rather than from Division L. This will mean that the profits of the group will fall substantially and Division L will have significant unused capacity.

Consequently, Division L needs to reduce its price. The current price does not reflect the fact that there are no selling and distribution costs associated with transferring internally, ie the cost of selling internally is $4 less for Division L than selling externally. So, it could reduce the price to $36 and still make the same profit on these sales as on its external sales. This would therefore be the suggested transfer price, so that Division M is still saving $1 per unit compared to the external price. A transfer price of $37 would also presumably be acceptable to Division M since this is the same as the external supplier is offering.

(d) (i) Divisionalisation can **improve** the **quality of decisions** made because divisional managers (those taking the decisions) know local conditions and are able to make more informed judgements. Moreover, with the personal incentive to improve the division's performance, they ought to take decisions in the division's best interests.

(ii) **Decisions should be taken more quickly** because information does not have to pass along the chain of command to and from top management. Decisions can be made on the spot by those who are familiar with the product lines and production processes and who are able to react to changes in local conditions quickly and efficiently.

(iii) The authority to act to improve performance should **motivate divisional managers**.

(iv)   Divisional organisation **frees top management** from detailed involvement in day-to-day operations and allows them to devote more time to strategic planning.

(v)   Divisions provide **valuable training grounds for future members of top management** by giving them experience of managerial skills in a less complex environment than that faced by top management.

(vi)   In a large business organisation, the **central head office will not have the management resources or skills to direct operations closely enough itself**. Some authority must be delegated to local operational managers.

Note that you would probably need to have discussed three of the above points to get five marks.

366 Rotech group

Workbook references. Performance measurement is covered in Chapters 19 and 20.

Top tips. Use a clear layout for your calculations and headings to give a structure to your discussions and explanations. Each part of the question can be answered separately, so if you get stuck or are unsure what is required, move on.

Easy marks. The calculations are straightforward and there are plenty of marks available for common sense explanations.

Examining team's comments. The calculations in the first part of the question were done quite well, although a common mistake was to combine the two divisions of W Co and calculate the ratios for W Co as a whole. This was presumably caused by insufficient reading of the requirement. Students had difficulty dealing with the discussion that followed the calculations, with candidates failing to identify the difficulty comparing a design business to a manufacturing business.

Marking scheme

		Marks
(a)	Ratios	
	Calculating ROCE	1.5
	Calculating asset turnover	1.5
	Calculating operating profit margin	1.5
	Marks per valid comment (max 5.5)	5.5
		10
(b)	Transfer pricing	
	Each valid comment/calculation	1.5
		10
		20

(a)   **Financial ratios**

		W Co Design	W Co Gearbox	C Co
Return on capital employed	$\dfrac{\text{Profit before interest and tax}}{\text{Capital employed}}$ %	$6,000/$23,540 = 25.49%	$3,875/$32,320 = 11.99%	$7,010/$82,975 = 8.45%
Asset turnover	$\dfrac{\text{Sales}}{\text{Capital employed}}$	$14,300/$23,540 = 0.61 times	$25,535/$32,320 = 0.79 times	$15,560/$82,975 = 0.19 times
Operating profit margin	$\dfrac{\text{Profit before interest and tax}}{\text{Sales}}$ %	$6,000/$14,300 = 41.96%	$3,875/$25,535 = 15.18%	$7,010/$15,560 = 45.05%

Return on capital employed

ROCE shows how much profit has been made in relation to the amount of resources invested. C Co and both divisions of W Co are profitable. The Design division of W Co has the highest ROCE, at over 25%, while the Gearbox division and C Co are significantly lower at 11.99% and 8.45% respectively. This is primarily due to the nature of the design business which derives its profits from personnel rather than physical assets. Employees generate profits by designing products, rather than by using expensive machinery. Therefore the Design division's capital employed (asset) figure is significantly lower.

C Co has the largest asset base, and this is reflected in a relatively low ROCE. The Gearbox division is closer to this than to the Design division, but this is as a result of similarities in the nature of the business rather than division performance alone.

Asset turnover

Asset turnover is a measure of how well the assets of a business are being used to generate sales. The Gearbox division has the highest level at 79%, while C Co has the lowest at 19%. This is probably due in part to the fact that the Gearbox division buys from C Co, therefore C Co must hold a large asset base to produce the relevant components. Both divisions of W Co do not have the same requirement and this is reflected in the higher asset turnover figures.

Operating profit margin

C Co comes out on top in the final profitability measure, which is the operating profit margin at just over 45%, while the Gearbox division is the lowest at 15.18%. The Design division performs well at 41.96%, as it did in asset turnover. This was to be expected from the ROCE of 25%, which is a combination of the other two ratios. The Design division has both high unit profitability and generates sales at a high level compared to its asset base.

There are limitations to these types of comparisons due to the differing nature of the businesses. It would be more useful to compare each business unit to an industry average for similar businesses, as well as comparing year-on-year figures to monitor the units on an ongoing basis.

(b) **Transfer prices**

From C Co's perspective

C Co transfers components to the Gearbox division at the same price as it sells components to the external market. However, if C Co were not making internal sales then, given that it already satisfies 60% of external demand, it would not be able to sell all of its current production to the external market. External sales are $8,010,000, therefore unsatisfied external demand is ([$8,010,000/0.6] – $8,010,000) = $5,340,000.

From C Co's perspective, of the current internal sales of $7,550,000, $5,340,000 could be sold externally if they were not sold to the Gearbox division. Therefore, in order for C Co not to be any worse off from selling internally, these sales should be made at the current price of $5,340,000, less any reduction in costs which C Co saves from not having to sell outside the group (perhaps lower administrative and distribution costs).

As regards the remaining internal sales of $2,210,000 ($7,550,000 – $5,340,000), C Co effectively has spare capacity to meet these sales. Therefore, the minimum transfer price should be the marginal cost of producing these goods. Given that variable costs represent 40% of revenue, this means that the marginal cost for these sales is $884,000. This is therefore the minimum price which C Co should charge for these sales.

In total, therefore, C Co will want to charge at least $6,224,000 for its sales to the Gearbox division.

From the Gearbox division's perspective

The Gearbox division will not want to pay more for the components than it could purchase them for externally. Given that it can purchase them all for 95% of the current price, this means a maximum purchase price of $7,172,500.

Overall

Taking into account all of the above, the transfer price for the sales should be somewhere between $6,224,000 and $7,172,500.

367 Bus Co

Marking scheme

			Marks
(a)	Calculations		2
(b)	Accuracy of statement		
	First part untrue, Express higher percentage	1	
	Correct re what customers value	1	
	Correct re punctuality	1	
	Incorrect re leader	1	
			4
(c)	Efficiency and effectiveness:		
	Definition of efficiency	1	
	Performance measure for efficiency	1	
	Definition of effectiveness	1	
	Performance measure for effectiveness	1	
			4
(d)	Balanced scorecard approach:		
	Stating what it is	2	
	Financial perspective	2	
	Customer perspective	2	
	Internal perspective	2	
	Innovation and learning perspective	2	
			10
			20

(a) Calculations

Bus: $(0.4 \times 0.67) + (0.32 \times 0.8) + (0.28 \times 0.82) = 75.36\%$
Prime: $(0.4 \times 0.58) + (0.32 \times 0.76) + (0.28 \times 0.83) = 70.76\%$
Express: $(0.4 \times 0.67) + (0.32 \times 0.76) + (0.28 \times 0.89) = 76.04\%$

(b) Accuracy of statement

The MD's statement says that Bus Co's customers are the most satisfied of any national bus operator. However, this is not quite the case since, when the 'overall satisfaction' levels are calculated, Express's level is 76.04% compared to Bus Co's 75.36%. So, the first part of the MD's statement is untrue.

The MD then goes on to say that Bus Co is leading the way on what matters most to customers – value for money and punctuality. Given the weightings attached to these two criteria, it appears true to say that these are the factors which matter most to customers. Similarly, it is true to say that Bus Co is leading as regards punctuality, being four percentage points ahead of Prime and Express on this criterion. However, given that Express also has the same level of satisfaction as regards offering value for money, Bus Co is only leading ahead of Prime on this criterion, not ahead of Express. Therefore, while it can say that it is the leader on punctuality, it can only say that it is the joint leader on value for money.

(c)   **VFM**

'Efficiency' focuses on the relationship between inputs and outputs, considering whether the maximum output is being achieved for the resources used.

Performance measure:

Occupancy rate of buses

Utilisation rate for buses (utilisation rate = hours on the road/total hours available)

Utilisation rate for drivers

(Many others could be given too, but only one was asked for.)

'Effectiveness' focuses on the relationship between an organisation's objectives and outputs, considering whether the objectives are being met.

Possible performance measures:

Percentage of customers satisfied with cleanliness of buses

Percentage of carbon emissions relative to target set

(Many others could be given too, but only one was asked for.)

(d)   **Balanced scorecard**

The **balanced scorecard** approach to performance measurement emphasises the need to provide management with a set of information which covers all relevant areas of performance in an objective and unbiased fashion.

The information provided may be both financial and non-financial and cover areas such as profitability, customer satisfaction, internal efficiency and innovation.

The balanced scorecard focuses on **four different perspectives**, as follows.

Customer perspective

The customer perspective considers how new and existing customers view the organisation. This perspective should identify targets that matter to customers, such as cost, quality, delivery, inspection and so on.

The customer perspective is linked to revenue/profit objectives in the financial perspective. If customer objectives are achieved, it is likely that revenue/profit objectives will also be achieved.

Performance measure: number of repeat trips to measure customer retention.

Internal perspective

The internal perspective makes an organisation consider what processes it must excel at in order to achieve financial and customer objectives.

The perspective aims to improve internal processes and decision-making.

Performance measure: costs saved after reassessing internal processes.

Innovation and learning perspective

The innovation and learning perspective requires the organisation to consider how it can continue to improve and create value.

BPP LEARNING MEDIA

Organisations must seek to acquire new skills and develop new products in order to maintain a competitive position in their respective market(s) and provide a basis from which the other perspectives of the balanced scorecard can be accomplished.

Performance measure: revenue generated from new routes introduced.

Financial perspective

The financial perspective considers whether the organisation meets the expectations of its shareholders and how it creates value for them.

This perspective focuses on traditional measures, such as growth, profitability and cost reduction.

Performance measure: increase in market share compared to Prime and Express.

368 People's Bank

Workbook references. The balanced scorecard approach to performance measurement is covered in Chapter 19.

Top tips. Part (a) is fairly straightforward but make sure you use the information in the scenario to help you answer the question. For part (b), make sure you structure your answer using the four headings of the balanced scorecard. This question requires you to analyse the information given and spot how factors affect one another. Don't forget to finish with a brief conclusion.

Easy marks. You should score highly in part (b) providing your answer covers all four perspectives of the balanced scorecard and picks out information from the scenario. There is not a great deal of technical knowledge required.

Examining team's comments. Performance on this question was reasonably strong, although poor exam technique in addressing the specific requirement did let some students down. A key skill in these questions is to identify linkages between measures – cause and effect relationships. For example, new lending to SMEs was down on target and this is not in line with the bank's third value (financial perspective). The drop in new lending is due to the fact that fewer colleagues have been trained to provide advice to SMEs (innovation and learning perspective).

Marking scheme

			Marks
(a)	Discussion		4
(b)	Financial	4	
	Customer	4	
	Internal	4	
	Innovation and learning	4	
			16
			20

(a) The balanced scorecard approach looks not only at the financial performance but also non-financial performance. In order to maintain a competitive edge, organisations have to be very aware of the changing needs of their customers. In the case of The People's Bank, this has involved identifying specific categories of customers which have particular needs, like SMEs in a commercial context, or like the disabled or visually impaired in a non-commercial context. This permits these needs to be addressed.

The People's Bank has a vision and strategy which goes far beyond just making money. They want to help the community and disadvantaged people and give something back to customers also. Hence, by using the balanced scorecard, performance measures which address whether the Bank is being successful in pursuing their vision can be incorporated.

In addition, from a purely business perspective, if employees and customers are valued and internal processes are efficient, an organisation should have more chance of achieving long-term success anyway. So, even putting aside the social objectives The People's Bank has, the balanced scorecard can be useful to The People's Bank to measure these other aspects of future success too.

(b)   The performance of the bank will be considered under each of the headings used in the balanced scorecard:

Financial perspective

The People's Bank has had a year of mixed success when looking at the extent to which it has met its financial targets. Its return on capital employed (ROCE) shows how efficiently it has used its assets to generate profit for the business. The target for the year was 12% but it has only achieved an 11% return. The People's Bank's interest income, however, was in fact $0.5m higher than its target, which is good. This may have been achieved by offering slightly better interest rates to customers than competing banks, as the interest margin The People's Bank achieved is slightly lower than target. The most likely reason for the under target ROCE is therefore probably the investment which The People's Bank has made in IT security and facilities for the disabled and visually impaired. Whilst this may have reduced ROCE, this investment is essentially a good idea as it helps The People's Bank pursue its vision and will keep customers happy. It will also, in the case of the IT security investment, prevent the bank and its customers from losing money from fraud in the future.

The other performance measure, the amount of new lending to SMEs, is a little bit disappointing, given The People's Bank's stated value of making a difference to communities. The failure to meet this target may well be linked to the fact that an insufficient number of staff were trained to provide advice to SMEs and consequently, fewer of them may have been successful in securing additional finance.

Customer perspective

With regard to its customers, The People's Bank has performed well in the year. It has exceeded its target to provide mortgages to new homeowners by 6,000. This is helping The People's Bank pursue its vision of helping new homeowners. It has also managed to beat the target for customer complaints such that there are only 1.5 complaints for every 1,000 customers, well below the target of 2. This may be as a result of improved processes at the bank or improved security. It is not clear what the precise reason is but it is definitely good for The People's Bank's reputation.

The bank has also exceeded both of its targets to help the disabled and visually impaired, which is good for its reputation and its stated value of making services more accessible.

Internal processes

The number of processes simplified within the bank has exceeded the target, which is good, and the success of which may well be reflected in the lower customer complaints levels. Similarly, the investment to improve IT systems has been a success, with only three incidences of fraud per 1,000 customers compared to the target of 10. However, perhaps because of the focus on this part of the business, only two new services have been made available via mobile banking, instead of the target of five, which is disappointing. Similarly, it is possible that some of the new systems have prevented the business from keeping its CO_2 emissions to their target level.

Innovation and learning

The People's Bank has succeeded in helping the community, exceeding both of its targets relating to hours of paid volunteer work and number of community organisations supported by volunteers or funding. These additional costs could have contributed to the fact that the bank did not quite meet its target for ROCE.

However, the bank has not quite met its targets for helping small businesses and helping the disadvantaged. As mentioned earlier, the shortfall in training of employees to give advice to SMEs may have had an impact on The People's Bank's failure to meet its target lending to SMEs. As regards the percentage of trainee positions, the target was only just missed and this may well have been because the number of candidates applying from these areas was not as high as planned and the bank has no control over this.

Overall, the bank has had a fairly successful year, meeting many of its targets. However, it still has some work to do in order to meet its stated values and continue to pursue its vision.

369 Sports Co

Workbook reference. Return on investment (ROI) is covered in Chapter 20

Top tips. Questions on return on investment are often unpopular with students. One of the key things that you need to realise, is that ROI should be calculated using 'controllable' figures only. So the formula for ROI is controllable profit / controllable net assets. So part (a)(i) requires you to calculate the controllable profit first and then divide it by the **average** controllable net assets. Make sure you show your workings so that marker can clearly see 'what' you have divided by 'what'! For part (a)(ii) this is your chance to show off what you know about the relationship between ROI, investment in assets and depreciation. Make sure you refer to the scenario when you make a point. Part (b)(i) is a calculation involving controllable profit again so make sure you use the same profit figure that you calculated in (a).

Easy marks. Part (b)(ii) is a gift. You should know the advantages and disadvantages of residual income.

(a) (i) Return on investment = controllable profit/average divisional net assets

Controllable profit

	Division C	Division E
	$'000	$'000
Net profit	1,455	3,950
Add back depreciation on non-controllable assets	49.5	138
Add back Head Office costs	620	700
Controllable profit	2,124.5	4,788

Average divisional net assets

	Division C	Division E
	$'000	$'000
Opening assets	13,000	24,000
Closing assets	9,000	30,000
Average assets	11,000	27,000
ROI	19.3%	17.7%

(ii) Whilst Division C has exceeded the target ROI, Division E has not. If controllable profit in relation to revenue is considered, Division C's margin is 56% compared to Division E's margin of 57%, so Division E is actually performing slightly better. However, Division E has a larger asset base than Division C too, hence the fact that Division C has a higher ROI.

Since Division E appears to be a much larger division and is involved in sports equipment manufacturing, then it could be expected to have more assets. Division E's assets have gone up partly because it made substantial additions to plant and machinery. This means that as well as increasing the average assets figure, the additions will have been depreciated during the year, thus leading to lower profits. This may potentially have had a large impact on profits since Division E uses the reducing balance method of depreciation, meaning that more depreciation is charged in the early years.

Based on the ROI results, the manager of Division C will get a bonus and the manager of Division E will not. This will have a negative impact on the motivation level of the manager of Division E and may discourage him from making future investments, unless a change in the performance measure used is adopted.

(b) (i)

	Division C	Division E
	$'000	$'000
Controllable profit	2,124.5	4,788
Less: imputed charge on assets at 12%	(1,320)	(3,240)
Residual income	804.5	1,548

From the residual income results, it can clearly be seen that both divisions have performed well, with healthy RI figures of between $0·8m and $1·55m. The cost of capital of Sports Co is significantly lower than the target return on investment which the company seeks, making the residual income figure show a more positive position.

(ii) **Advantages**

The use of RI should encourage managers to make new investments, if the investment adds to the RI figure. A new investment can add to RI but reduce ROI and in such a situation measuring performance with RI would not result in the dysfunctional behaviour which has already been seen at Sports Co. Instead, RI will lead to decisions which are in the best interests of the company as a whole being made.

Since an imputed interest charge is deducted from profits when measuring the performance of the division, managers are made more aware of the cost of assets under their control. This is a benefit as it can discourage wasteful spending.

BPP
LEARNING
MEDIA

Alternative costs of capital can be applied to divisions and investments to account for different levels of risk. This can allow more informed decision-making.

Disadvantages

RI does not facilitate comparisons between divisions since the RI is driven by the size of divisions and their investments. This can clearly be seen in Sports Co where the RI of Division E is almost twice that of Division C, which will be related to Division E being a much larger division.

RI is also based on accounting measures of profit and capital employed which may be subject to manipulation so as, for example, to obtain a bonus payment. In this way it suffers from the same problems as ROI.

370 Portable Garage Co

Workbook reference. Transfer pricing is covered in Chapter 20.

Top tips. This question tests transfer pricing principles without being overly complicated. If you are well prepared you should score highly in part (a). Part (b) asks you to explain something which may be intuitive to you. Part (c) is probably the hardest part of the question and requires you to remember that when there is no spare capacity, the transfer price is marginal cost + opportunity cost.

Easy marks. You should pick up plenty of easy marks in parts (a) and (b).

Marking scheme

		Marks	
(a)	External sales - A/B	1	
	Internal sales - A	0.5	
	External materials - A/B	1	
	Internal costs - B	0.5	
	Labour costs - A/B	1	
	Other costs - A	1	
	Fixed costs	0.5	
	Profit - A/B	1	
	PGC Co figures	2.5	
			9
(b)	External cont of $7 - A	1	
	Incremental cost of $6	1	
	External sales first - A	1	
	150,000 from A/30,000 externally	1	
	Approach	2	6
(c)	Minimum transfer price (marginal cost + opportunity cost)	1	
	Opportunity cost - lost contribution $7	1	
	Add marginal cost for transfer price of $14	1	
	Approach	2	5
			20

(a) **Profit statement for current position:**

	Division B $'000	Division A $'000	PGC CO $'000
Sales revenue:			
External sales (150,000 × $180,000/200,000 × $15)	27,000	3,000	30,000
Internal transferred sales (150,000 × $13)		1,950	
Total revenue	27,000	4,950	30,000
Variable costs:			
External material costs	6,750	1,050	7,800
Internal transferred costs	1,950		
Labour costs	5,250	1,400	6,650
Other costs of external sales		200	200
Total variable costs	13,950	2,650	14,650
Contribution	13,050	2,300	15,350
Less fixed costs	5,460	2,200	7,660
Profit	7,590	100	7,690

(b) If Division B can buy adaptors from outside the group at $13 per unit, then the optimum position is for Division A to sell as many adaptors as possible to external customers at $15 each and then sell the remainder to Division B at a price to be agreed between them.

This would mean that Division A continues to sell Division B 150,000 adaptors but Division B then buys the remaining 30,000 adaptors from an external supplier. This is because the contribution per unit for Division A's external sales is $7 ($15 – $3 – $4 – $1). This means that for every external sale it loses, it forfeits $7 for the group. However, the incremental cost for the group of Division B buying adaptors from outside the group is only $6 ($13 external cost less the $7 cost of making them in-house). So, it makes sense for Division A to satisfy its external sales first before selling internally.

(c) In order for Division A to supply Division B with 180,000 adaptors, it would have to reduce its external sales from 200,000 units to 170,000. This is because it only has enough spare capacity to supply Division B with 150,000 units at present after it has supplied adaptors to its external customers.

The minimum transfer price in situations where there is no spare capacity is marginal cost plus opportunity cost. In this case, contribution is lost by not selling 30,000 units to the external customers. As the marginal cost for Division A's internal sales is $7 ($4 + $3) and the contribution per unit for external sales is $7 per unit ($15 – $3 – $4 – $1), the transfer price for the additional 30,000 units would need to be $14.

371 Robinholt University

Workbook reference. Performance measurement in covered in Chapter 19 although this question does not require much textbook knowledge.

Top tips. Use headed paragraphs to discuss each of the strategic aims. Much of your discussion should be based on common sense and information given in the scenario. Remember there are only four marks for calculations so quickly calculate the percentage differences between the two years so that have some numbers to discuss. When you discuss a number, try to bring in some information given in the scenario that might explain **why** the number has increased or decreased.

Easy marks. There are easy marks available for percentage change calculations and for saying whether or not each of the five strategic aims has been met.

Marks

Calculations 4

Strategic aims discussion 16

20

(1) **To provide education which promotes intellectual initiative and produces confident and ambitious graduates who have reached the highest academic standards to prepare them for success in life and the workplace.**

There are various performance indicators which can be looked at to ascertain whether RU is meeting this strategic aim. First, question 1 of the survey shows that 83% of students think that the course is intellectually stimulating and the quality of teaching is high. This has gone down by three percentage points since 20X5, which is not good.

In the NOS survey, the percentage of graduates agreeing that the course has developed them as a person has increased from 80% in 20X5 to 82% in 20X6. This would indicate that RU is indeed developing confident and ambitious graduates.

However, the number of graduates achieving first class degrees in 20X6 has fallen vastly from 28% to 20%. Given that the entry requirements were only relaxed in 20X6, this should not have had any impact on results. This infers that the quality of teaching may have declined and the ratio of students to academic staff has increased from 35:1 to 40:1. It appears that, although many new students were recruited in 20X6, there were not enough new academic staff recruited to deal with the influx of students. This is shown by the fact that student numbers increased by 13% but academic staff costs only increased by 6%.

As there was presumably a pay rise in the year too, it is clear that a proportionate amount of new staff were not recruited. This failing is also reflected by the fall in the answer to question 2 from 86% to 82%, with students being less satisfied in 20X6 with the advice and support they have received. Also, the staff retention rate has gone down in 20X6, meaning that staff are less familiar with RU and therefore more likely to provide a fragmented service.

However, in 20X5 74% of employers were happy with the graduates they recruited, in 20X6 this dropped to 72%. In addition, in 20X5 only 65% of students have managed to obtain graduate jobs within a year compared to previous years. Given that RU has relaxed the entry requirements for students in 20X6, this may mean that its 20X6 recruits are not as well qualified as its 20X5. This could mean that in the future the number of graduates obtaining graduate jobs within a year and the satisfaction percentages of employers could fall further. This decision has meant that there has been a 23% increase in fee income, but it compromises RU's ability to meet its first strategic aim.

(2) **To provide an organised, efficient learning environment with access to cutting edge technology and facilities.**

As regards premises, the money spent on maintaining these has decreased by 10% in 20X6, despite the increased student numbers. In the NOS survey, the percentage of students satisfied with these facilities has gone down nine percentage points from 92% to 83%. This suggests that this particular strategic aim has been neglected. Students seem far less satisfied with the way that the courses are run and administered now, with a fall of nine percentage points in answers to question 4. Administration staff costs have only increased by 5% despite a 13% increase in student numbers and, presumably, a pay rise during the year. It can be inferred that staff are under increasing pressure and unable to cope with the increased numbers. This is again reflected by the fall in the staff retention rate from 90% in 20X5 to 75% in 20X6.

(3) **To be a leader in sustainable business practices which protect the environment and support local people**

As with the above strategic aim, this one also seems to have been a little forgotten in 20X6. In 20X5, RU won an environmental award for its campuses. It also took part in a food sharing initiative which helped the local community. It has now got rid of its recycling bins and ceased to be involved in the food share project. RU's spending on sustainability and community assistance has actually halved in 20X6. This decline in activity is partly attributable to staff shortages. All in all, this is not very good as RU is now failing to meet one of its main strategic aims.

(4) **To provide attractive, innovative conference and event facilities, attracting clients both nationally and internationally**

Conference and event income has gone up by 13% in 20X6, which is a good increase for RU. It has managed to control its costs relating to these events well too, since these have only increased by 4%. RU has also won an award for its conference facility and attracted a number of new clients. RU therefore appears to be focusing well on this strategic aim.

(5) **To be recognised both nationally and internationally for the scope and relevance of their research**

Income from research at RU has actually gone down by 13% this year, as have the associated costs. Whilst a local university has won an award for their contribution to research, RU has not been successful in this regard. The suggestion is that this aim has not been focused on in 20X6.

Overall satisfaction

In addition to the above, it should be considered that the overall satisfaction percentage for students has decreased from 83% to 81%. This could have serious implications for RU as it is the main performance indicator used both internally and externally to assess how RU is performing. As well as meaning that RU may well now attract fewer students, it will also have an impact on the fees which can be charged to students in future years. The university needs to consider how it can improve the service it is providing in order to improve overall satisfaction.

Calculations

	2016 $m	2015 $m	%age Increase/decrease
Income			
Tuition fees	148	135.6	9%
Research grants	3.5	4.5	(22%)
Conferences and other events	18	16	13%
Total income	169.5	156.1	9%
Expenditure			
Academic staff costs	80.8	76.2	6%
Administration staff costs	50.4	48	5%
Premises, facilities and technology costs	7.6	8.4	(10%)
Event and conference costs	8.3	8	4%
Research grants	3.1	4	(23%)
Sustainability and community assistance	1.2	2.4	(50%)
Total expenditure	151.4	147	3%
Surplus	18.1	9.1	99%
Student numbers	27,000	24,000	13%

372 Hammocks Co

Marking scheme

				Marks
(a)		Discuss the performance of Hammocks		8
(b)	(i)	Two advantages of using the Balanced Scorecard	3	
		One goal, two performance measures for:		
	(ii)	Internal business processes	4.5	
	(iii)	Innovation and learning	4.5	
				12
				20

(a) **To make a profit long-term**

In order to make a profit the long term revenues need to be higher than the long term costs.

The weekly revenue per guest is $2,000 in the 20X7 budget, the 20X7 actual results and the 20X6 actual results which is not in line with inflation. This means that revenues per guest are falling in real terms.

However all staff costs have increased by 2% which is caused by inflation.

Overall this means that the profit per guest, based on the limited figures available is falling.

The repair costs, allowing for inflation have been set at the same level as 20X6. The actual for 20X7 appears to be better than budget, but as repairs are likely to be incurred on an ad hoc basis, this does not necessarily indicate an improvement. The 20X6 repair costs are higher than the competitor's but it is difficult to compare because Hammocks Co have more rooms so we are not comparing like with like. On a repair per room basis Hammocks has slightly lower cost at $163 per room compared to the competition's $164 per room.

Due to the secure long-term contracts which Hammocks Co offers its staff, staff costs are fixed costs in the management accounts. This means that in order to be profitable, these costs need to be covered by the contribution per guest. Although there is not the data to calculate the contribution per guest per week, the higher level of guest occupancy level in 20X7 (both budgeted and actual) is a positive indication. Hammocks' occupancy level per room was 81% compared to the competitor's 77% (all based on double occupancy) indicating that performance is good.

To create customer loyalty

There are a number of indicators to show that Hammocks Co have created a loyal customer base.

Firstly compared to their main competitor Hammocks Co receive more revenue, charge a higher price per guest per week and have better occupancy rates. This indicates good customer satisfaction.

Secondly the ratio of staff to guest is higher than the competition; 1.5 compared to 1.3 in 20X6 (actual in 20X7 is slightly higher due to a lower occupancy rate than budgeted and the fact that staff numbers are fixed). As this is a seasonal business this is may simply be a blip.

Finally, the comments on TripEvent are very positive about the level of service and standard of cleanliness and maintenance. However it should be noted that the entire customer experience is not positive. Complaints like the administrative errors and unchanging menus could be a warning sign of possible erosion of customer loyalty.

(b)   (i)   A balanced scorecard approach to performance management is important to Hammocks Co because it will provide management with a set of information which covers all relevant areas of business performance. At present Hammocks Co considers performance from a financial and customer perspective. These perspectives are important but they do not allow a wide enough consideration of all of the factors that should be considered in this business.

Introducing the balanced scorecard will:

Ensure that all internal systems and processes support the customer and financial objectives. For example, in decision-making there is little point in buying a new IT system that does not either improve customer experience or reduce processing costs.

Encourage full integration between all departments. Errors in invoicing or sending specific requirements are system or internal process errors. While a customer might not choose a holiday resort for its excellent administration, they may refuse to use a company again if they receive poor service. Thus neglecting one aspect of the scorecard can impact on customer satisfaction and longer term financial performance.

Make sure important elements are assessed and expected performance levels quantified and/or qualified. This means that performance can be measured, explained, compared and where necessary, control action can be taken. The errors that occur at Hammocks Co are spoiling the company's reputation, but there is no evidence that any action is being taken.

Note: Only TWO were required.

(ii)   **Internal business process**

Goal: To have an effective and efficient administration.

The feedback on TripEvent indicates that the only guest complaints relate to administrative issues prior to the guest arrival and not operational issues at the resort. In fact the actions of the resort staff with the speedy resolution of bedding issues and the organising of a complimentary transfer seems to have diverted trouble. Therefore measures need to be focused on the weaker area which is the administration.

Measures:

(1)   Number of times that a guest request is not received at resort prior to their arrival/number of requests made.

This will measure the number of times the guest experience is not seamless from booking to arrival.

(2)   Average number of corrections to booking due to an administrative error.

This measures inefficient use of staff time and potentially increased customer frustration.

Innovation and Learning

Goal: To match leading competitor's facilities

The comment on TripEvent shows that even loyal customers are noticing that rivals are including more innovative facilities at their resorts. Although the true strength of

Hammocks Co lies in the quality of the service it is important that the facilities' appliances and service offerings are updated to compare favourably with that of its rivals.

Measures:

(1) Number of in-room appliances offered by rivals but not by Hammocks Co.

The measure will ensure that Hammocks Co consider what is included within the guest rooms by comparing to external factors.

(2) Number of new items offered on the menu each month.

This should ensure that the chefs consider the latest trends in fine dining and do not ever appear stagnant from the point of view of the customer.

373 Medcomp

Workbook reference. Performance measurement and the balanced scorecard are covered in Chapter 19.

Top tips. Balanced scorecard questions are often not answered well which is probably why the four perspectives were given in the question, along with the critical success factors. You need to note down the correct critical success factor from the scenario, suggest an appropriate KPI that links to the CSF and then discuss the performance using the KPI and any relevant calculations. Remember to think about reasons for the results you have calculated.

Easy marks. There are easy marks available for using the information given in the scenario and also for part (b), which was pure knowledge. Note that part (b) asked for balanced scorecard benefits only.

Examining team comments. In part (a) some students suggested KPIs of absolute numbers such as 'the number of successful treatments' rather than 'percentage of successful treatments' but absolute numbers don't mean much on their own. Part (b) was answered less well than part (a) with some students describing the balanced scorecard and this was not required. Although a template was given showing the four scorecard perspectives, this will not always be provided and being able to structure an answer appropriately is a key skill for PM.

		Marks
(a)	Identification of CSF for each perspective (0.5 each)	2
	Identification of KPI for each perspective (1 each)	4
	Analysis of performance using the KPIs (max 4 for any perspective)	10
(b)	Benefits of balanced scorecard - up to 2 for each well discussed point	4
		20

(a) The balanced scorecard uses four perspectives: financial, customer, innovation and learning and internal business process.

Financial	CSF: The critical success factor identified for this perspective is most likely to be positive cash flow.
	KPI: The most appropriate performance indicator is total donations less operating costs.
	Performance analysis: Total donations in 20X8, 20X7 and 20X6 are $1,710,000, $1,605,000 and $1,475,000 respectively and when the operating costs are deducted, the net cash flows are $(20,000), $55,000 and $45,000 respectively. This shows that for the current year Medcomp is not achieving a positive cash flow. However, this is a relatively small cash deficit for the year and does not suggest that the charity has any real problems. The size of the donations has risen considerably over the years and the number of businesses donating has fallen. This could indicate that the fundraisers have focused their efforts on a smaller number of more affluent businesses.
Customer	CSF: The critical success factor identified for this perspective is most likely to be medical effectiveness.
	KPI: The best performance indicator for this perspective is the percentage of successful treatments.
	Performance analysis: For the years 20X8, 20X7 and 20X6 these are 77%, 86% and 87% respectively. As treatment for cataracts is a relatively simple procedure, a high success rate would be expected but the results in 20X8 show a significant deterioration. The reasons for the recent fall in effectiveness could be the result of factors outside the control of Medcomp, such as variations in the disease or the advanced condition of the disease when presented. However, it could be also linked to the lack of efficiency of the new treatments.
Internal business process	CSF: The critical success factor identified for this perspective is most likely to be functional efficiency.
	KPI: The performance indicator for this perspective could be: 'average number of days to deliver drugs and equipment to treatment centres'.
	Performance analysis: This has remained at seven days since 20X6 and in some ways this can be expected as the 12 treatment centres have been at the same location for many years and the logistics of the delivery well established. It should be noted that this measure is an average lead time and will also vary on location. However, as Medcomp rarely experiences shortages at the treatment centres, it can be surmised that transport costs are managed as efficiently as possible and this means an average seven-day lead time.

ANSWERS

Innovation and learning	**CSF:** The critical success factor identified for this perspective is most likely to be innovation.
	KPI: The performance indicator for this perspective is the new procedures as a percentage of total procedures from the table.
	Performance analysis: It is clear that Medcomp has made several changes to the existing protocol in 20X8. One in five procedures administered are new and have been introduced within the past 12 months. This is a clear improvement on 20X7 and 20X6 as the CSF is for new treatments. However, the new treatments have not improved the efficiency of the treatment, as evidenced by the percentage of successful treatments, and this will need to be monitored.

(b)   The benefits to an organisation of using the balanced scorecard to assess performance instead of relying solely on financial measures are as follows:

Not all organisations have profit or financial return as the main objective. In an altruistic not-for-profit charity such as Medcomp, the objectives are based on delivering a service which can be measured in benefit to people who are unable to pay for the service. Therefore, it is necessary to have measures which are not purely financial to reflect the different emphasis of the mission and supporting objectives.

Financial performance indicators are 'lagging' indicators. This means that the events and decisions which caused these indicators occurred long ago. The balanced scorecard includes 'leading' indicators. For example, the innovation and learning perspective may encourage spending on training or techniques which will depress profits or increase costs in the short term, but will have much greater benefits in the future.

The balanced scorecard helps to align key performance measures with strategy at all levels. This means that all employees will be able to link their individual goals to those of the organisation as a whole. The benefit of this is that it ensures that what gets measured is important to the organisation.

Financial measures used in isolation are relatively easy to manipulate in the short term. For example, a high return on investment figure may be considered an indicator of good performance whereas it may have been caused by a manager delaying the purchase of a necessary asset. The balanced scorecard provided a range of indicators which makes this type of manipulation more difficult to conceal.

OTQ mixed bank

374   The correct answer is: Penetration pricing in market A and price skimming in market B

Charging low prices initially to gain a large market share is market penetration pricing. Charging high prices in order to maximise unit profits is market skimming. Market penetration pricing is most effective when demand for the product is elastic (sensitive to price) and market skimming can maximise profitability when demand is inelastic (fairly insensitive to price).

Price elasticity of demand can be reduced by trying to persuade customers to buy products for reasons other than price, such as quality or design features. Advertising and sales promotion can also have the effect of reducing price elasticity.

375   The correct answer is: 15,000

Sales = $62,500

Breakeven sales = $13,000/0.40 = $32,500

Margin of safety (sales revenue) = $62,500 – $32,500 = $30,000

Margin of safety (units) $30,000/$2 = 15,000 units

376   **This question appeared in the June 2017 exam.**

The correct answer is: There is no inventory of work in progress or finished goods held

Holding no inventory of work in progress or finished goods is **not** consistent with the theory of constraints as the theory of constraints specifies that a small amount of buffer inventory should be maintained prior to the bottleneck activity so that the bottleneck never has to be slowed down or delayed. The other three statements are all consistent with the theory of constraints.

377   The correct answer is:

The costs of implementation may outweigh the benefits.	**TRUE**	
Employees will always welcome any new system which improves planning and control within the organisation.		**FALSE**

The costs of introducing a new system may exceed the benefits. Employees are often inclined to resist change, even though the planned changes may improve planning and control within the organisation.

378   The correct answer is: 13.16%

Opening capital employed: $6m + $0.5m = $6.5m
Closing capital employed: $8m + ($0.5m + $0.2m) = $8.7m
Average capital employed: ($6.5m + $8.7m)/2 = $7.6m
Profit after depreciation: $1.6m − $0.6m = $1m
Therefore ROI = $1m/$7.6m = 13.16%.

379   **This question appeared in the September 2017 exam.**

The correct answer is: $204,500

To calculate breakeven revenue in a multi-product situation requires the annual fixed costs to be divided by the weighted average contribution to sales ratio. To do this firstly the selling price of both products need to be determined.

The selling price of a table is calculated as the variable cost divided by one − the C/S ratio: $120/(1 − 0.4) = $200. The selling price of a chair is $16/(1 − 0.6) = $40. Once the selling prices are determined the contribution of each product can be calculated. For a table this will be $200 × 0.4 = $80 and for a chair this will be $40 × 0.6 = $24. Now we have the selling price and contribution for both products we can calculate the weighted average C/S ratio.

Sales revenue based on the sales mix will be (1 × $200) + (4 × $40) = $360 and contribution will be (1 × $80) + (4 × $24) = $176; this gives a C/S ratio of 0.489. Therefore the breakeven revenue is $100,000/0.489 = $204,499 and to the nearest hundred dollars is $204,500.

380   The correct answer is: All of the above

Material flow cost accounting (MFCA) and input-output analysis are environmental management accounting techniques. Life cycle costing is concerned with analysing costs of a product over its entire life cycle from initial development to eventual withdrawal from the market. However, as long as you are aware that activity-based costing is a management accounting technique, the answer to this question is straightforward.

381   **This question appeared in the June 15 exam.**

The correct answer is: It identifies the market price of a product and then subtracts a desired profit margin to arrive at the target cost

A target cost is arrived at by identifying the market price of a product and then subtracting a desired profit margin from it.

382 **This question appeared in the June 15 exam.**

The correct answers are:

Contribution will be increased by $2 for each additional kg of material B purchased at the current market price.	**TRUE**	
The maximum price which should be paid for an additional kg of material B is $2.		**FALSE**
Contribution will be increased by $1.20 for each additional kg of material B purchased at the current market price		**FALSE**
The maximum price which should be paid for an additional kg of material B is $2.80	**TRUE**	

Statement 2 is wrong as it reflects the common misconception that the shadow price is the maximum price which should be paid, rather than the maximum extra over the current purchase price.

Statement 3 is wrong but could be thought to be correct if two was wrongly assumed to be correct.

383 The correct answer is: Substitute current raw materials with cheaper versions

Reducing the target cost gap should focus on ways of reducing the direct or variable costs of the product. This can be achieved by using a substitute cheaper raw material, but without affecting product quality. Reducing fixed overhead costs is not a way of reducing the gap. Using overtime is likely to increase costs and the target cost gap. Raising the selling price does not affect the cost gap directly, although it may lead to a reassessment of the target cost.

384 The correct answer is: ROI: No   RI: Yes

Current ROI 360/1,600 = 22.5% Residual income (in $'000) = 360 − (18% × 1,600) = $72 ie $72,000

The new project: ROI = 25,000/130,000 = 19.2%. This is less than 22.5%; therefore ROI will fall.

New project RI = 25,000 − (18% × 130,000) = + $1,600. RI would increase.

385 The correct answer is: (3) only Simulation model

Sensitivity analysis is a term used to describe any technique whereby decision options are tested for their vulnerability to changes in any 'variable' such as expected sales volume, sales price per unit, material costs or labour costs. It can be used in any situation so long as the relationships between the key variables can be established.

Simulation models can be used to deal with decision problems involving a large number of uncertain variables, when the relationship between the variables is uncertain or unpredictable. In practice, simulation modelling is carried out using a computer model.

386 **This question appeared in the September 2015 exam**

The correct answer is: $110

Relevant cost = contribution lost + labour cost
                        = $4 + $7
                        = $11 per hour
$11 × 10 hours = $110

387 **This question appeared in the March 2017 exam.**

The correct answer is: Both ROI and RI will favour the older division.

ROI is calculated as (divisional profit/capital employed) × 100%

RI is calculated as divisional profit − (capital employed × cost of capital)

To see how ROI and RI would treat each division, it's a fair assumption to assume they're both generating the same profit (as they're virtually identical).

Both divisions have the same assets – however the older division will have suffered more depreciation, as it is three years older – reducing its capital employed.

Looking at both calculations, the smaller capital employed will give the older division an artificially high ROI compared to the newer division.

Likewise, the 'imputed interest' (capital employed × cost of capital) for the older division will be smaller. Both divisions use the overall company's cost of capital, thus giving the older division a higher RI than the newer division.

If in doubt with questions like this, make up some numbers. If they both generate profits of $100k, but the older division's assets have a NBV of $500k compared to the newer division's $2,000k (for example), this gives ROI of 20% and 5% respectively. Similarly, if you use a cost of capital of 10% (keeping the numbers simple), this gives RI of $50k and ($100k) – both clearly favouring the older division.

388 **This question appeared in the March 2018 exam.**

The correct answer is: $12.50

The account runs for four years:
Year 1 1,000 new customers
Year 2 1,000 new customers 500 from Year 1
Year 3 1,000 new customers 500 from Year 2
Year 4 1,000 new customers 500 from Year 3
                               500 from Year 4

Total 4,000   2,000

From the above, since customers are joining every year for the four years there will be a total of 4000 customers that will cost the bank $400 per customer in the first year and 2000 customers in total that will cost $50 per customer in the second year. Calculation of profit over the life cycle will be as follows:

First year	4000 × ($300 – $400)
Second year	2000 × ($300 – $50)
Less the development and advertising costs	($50,000)
Total profit	$50,000
Divided by 4,000 customers	

Lifecycle profit per customer $12.50

Selecting $8.33, the total profit of $50,000 is divided by 6000 customers = $8.33

Selecting $25.00, the development and advertising costs has been omitted-$100,000 divided by 4000 customers= $25.00

Selecting $16.67- combines both mistakes as above- $100,000 divided by 6000 customers = $16.67

ANSWERS

Mock exams

ACCA

Performance Management

Mock Exam 1

(September 2016 CBE)

Question Paper: 3 hours
ALL questions are compulsory and MUST be attempted

DO NOT OPEN THIS PAPER UNTIL YOU ARE READY TO START
UNDER EXAMINATION CONDITIONS

Section A – ALL FIFTEEN questions are compulsory and MUST be attempted

Each question is worth 2 marks.

1   A manufacturing company which produces a range of products has developed a budget for the life cycle of a new product, P. The information in the following table relates exclusively to product P:

	Lifetime total	Per unit
Design costs	$800,000	
Direct manufacturing costs		$20
Depreciation costs	$500,000	
Decommissioning costs	$20,000	
Machine hours		4
Production and sales units	300,000	

The company's total fixed production overheads are budgeted to be $72 million each year and total machine hours are budgeted to be 96 million hours. The company absorbs overheads on a machine hour basis.

What is the budgeted life-cycle cost per unit for product P?

O $24.40

O $25.73

O $27.40

O $22.73

---

2   A company makes and sells product X and product Y. Twice as many units of product Y are made and sold as that of product X. Each unit of product X makes a contribution of $10 and each unit of product Y makes a contribution of $4. Fixed costs are $90,000.

What is the total number of units which must be made and sold to make a profit of $45,000 (to the nearest whole unit)?

[   ] units

---

3   Product GX consists of a mix of three materials, J, K and L. The standard material cost of a unit of GX is as follows:

12,000

		$
Material J	5 kg at $4 per kg	20
Material K	2 kg at $12 per kg	24
Material L	3 kg at $8 per kg	24

During March, 3,000 units of GX were produced, and actual usage was:

Material J 13,200 kg
Material K 6,500 kg
Material L 9,300 kg

What was the favourable materials yield variance for March (to the nearest whole $)?

$ [   ]

BPP LEARNING MEDIA

Questions **323**

4   A manufacturer and retailer of kitchens introduces an enterprise resource planning system.

Which of the following is **NOT** likely to be a potential benefit of introducing this system?

O   Schedules of labour are prepared for manufacturing

O   Inventory records are updated automatically

O   Sales are recorded into the financial ledgers

O   Critical strategic information can be summarised

---

5   Different management accounting techniques can be used to account for environmental costs.

One of these techniques involves analysing costs under three distinct categories: material, system, and delivery and disposal.

What is this technique known as?

O   Activity-based costing

O   Life-cycle costing

O   Input-output analysis

O   Flow cost accounting

---

6   A government is trying to assess schools by using a range of financial and non-financial factors. One of the chosen methods is the percentage of students passing five exams or more.

Which of the three Es in the value-for-money framework is being measured here?

O   Economy

O   Efficiency

O   Effectiveness

O   Expertise

---

7   Which of the following techniques is **NOT** relevant to target costing?

O   Value analysis

O   Variance analysis

O   Functional analysis

O   Activity analysis

---

8   A government department generates information which should not be disclosed to anyone who works outside of the department. There are many other government departments working within the same building.

Which of the following would **NOT** be an effective control procedure for the generation and distribution of the information within the government department?

○   If working from home, departmental employees must use a memory stick to transfer data, as laptop computers are not allowed to leave the department.

○   All departmental employees must enter non-disclosed and regularly updated passwords to access their computers.

○   All authorised employees must swipe an officially issued, personal identity card at the entrance to the department before they can gain access.

○   All hard copies of confidential information must be shredded at the end of each day or locked overnight in a safe if needed again.

---

9   A jewellery company makes rings (R) and necklaces (N).

The resources available to the company have been analysed and two constraints have been identified:

Labour time $3R + 2N \le 2,400$ hours

Machine time $0.5R + 0.4N \le 410$ hours

The management accountant has used linear programming to determine that R = 500 and N = 400.

Indicate, by clicking on the relevant boxes in the table below, whether each of the following is a slack resource.

	Slack resource	
	Yes	No
Labour time available	○	○
Machine time available	○	○

---

10   At the end of 20X1, an investment centre has net assets of $1m and annual operating profits of $190,000. However, the bookkeeper forgot to account for the following:

A machine with a carrying value of $40,000 was sold at the start of the year for $50,000 and replaced with a machine costing $250,000. Both the purchase and sale are cash transactions. No depreciation is charged in the year of purchase or disposal. The investment centre calculates return on investment (ROI) based on closing net assets.

Assuming no other changes to profit or net assets, what is the return on investment (ROI) for the year?

○   18.8%

○   19.8%

○   15.1%

○   15.9%

---

11   A manufacturing company uses three processes to make its two products, X and Y. The time available on the three processes is reduced because of the need for preventative maintenance and rest breaks.

The table below details the process times per product and daily time available:

Process	Hours available per day	Hours required to make one unit of product X	Hours required to make one unit of product Y
1	22	1.00	0.75
2	22	0.75	1.00
3	18	1.00	0.50

Daily demand for product X and product Y is 10 units and 16 units respectively.

Which of the following will improve throughput?

O   Increasing the efficiency of the maintenance routine for Process 2

O   Increasing the demand for both products

O   Reducing the time taken for rest breaks on Process 3

O   Reducing the time product X requires for Process 1

---

12   PlasBas Co uses recycled plastic to manufacture shopping baskets for local retailers. The standard price of the recycled plastic is $0.50 per kg and standard usage of recycled plastic is 0.2 kg for each basket. The budgeted production was 80,000 baskets.

Due to recent government incentives to encourage recycling, the standard price of recycled plastic was expected to reduce to $0.40 per kg. The actual price paid by the company was $0.42 per kg and 100,000 baskets were manufactured using 20,000 kg of recycled plastic.

What is the materials operational price variance?

O $2,000 Favourable

O $1,600 Favourable

O $400 Adverse

O $320 Adverse

---

13 A profit centre manager claims that the poor performance of her division is entirely due to factors outside her control.

She has submitted the following table along with notes from a market expert, which she believes explains the cause of the poor performance:

Category	Budget this year	Actual this year	Actual last year	Market expert notes
Sales volume (units)	500	300	400	The entire market has decreased by 25%
Sales revenue	$50,000	$28,500	$40,000	Rivalry in the market saw selling prices fall by 10%
Total material cost	$10,000	$6,500	$8,000	As demand for the raw materials is decreasing, suppliers lowered their prices by 5%

After adjusting for the external factors outside the manager's control, in which category/categories is there evidence of poor performance?

O   Material cost only

O   Sales volume and sales price

O   Sales price and material cost

O   Sales price only

---

14 Indicate, by clicking on the relevant boxes in the table below, whether each of the following statements regarding market penetration as a pricing strategy are correct or incorrect.

	Correct	Incorrect
It is useful if significant economies of scale can be achieved	O	O
It is useful if demand for a product is highly elastic	O	O

---

15 A company makes two products using the same type of materials and skilled workers. The following information is available:

	Product A	Product B
Budgeted volume (units)	1,000	2,000
Material per unit ($)	10	20
Labour per unit ($)	5	20

Fixed costs relating to material handling amount to $100,000. The cost driver for these costs is the volume of material purchased.

General fixed costs, absorbed on the basis of labour hours, amount to $180,000. Using activity-based costing, what is the total fixed overhead amount to be absorbed into each unit of product B (to the nearest whole $)?

$ [   ]

Section B – All FIFTEEN questions are compulsory and MUST be attempted

Mylo

The following scenario relates to questions 16–20.

Mylo runs a cafeteria situated on the ground floor of a large corporate office block. Each of the five floors of the building are occupied and there are in total 1,240 employees.

Mylo sells lunches and snacks in the cafeteria. The lunch menu is freshly prepared each morning and Mylo has to decide how many meals to make each day. As the office block is located in the city centre, there are several other places situated around the building where staff can buy their lunch, so the level of demand for lunches in the cafeteria is uncertain.

Mylo has analysed daily sales over the previous six months and established four possible demand levels and their associated probabilities. He has produced the following payoff table to show the daily profits which could be earned from the lunch sales in the cafeteria:

		Supply level			
Demand level	Probability	450	620	775	960
		$	$	$	$
450	0.15	1,170	980	810	740
620	0.30	1,170	1,612	1,395	1,290
775	0.40	1,170	1,612	2,015	1,785
960	0.15	1,170	1,612	2,015	2,496

16   If Mylo adopts a maximin approach to decision making, which daily supply level will he choose?

> **450** lunches

17   If Mylo adopts a minimax regret approach to decision making, which daily supply level will he choose?

- O   450 lunches
- O   620 lunches
- O   775 lunches
- ◉   960 lunches

18   Which **TWO** of the following statements are true if Mylo chooses to use expected values to assist in his decision making regarding the number of lunches to be provided?

- ☐   Mylo would be considered to be taking a defensive and conservative approach to his decision.
- ☑   Expected values will ignore any variability which could occur across the range of possible outcomes.
- ☐   Expected values will not take into account the likelihood of the different outcomes occurring.
- ☑   Expected values can be applied by Mylo, as he is evaluating a decision which occurs many times over.

19 The human resources department has offered to undertake some research to help Mylo to predict the number of employees who will require lunch in the cafeteria each day. This information will allow Mylo to prepare an accurate number of lunches each day.

What is the maximum amount which Mylo would be willing to pay for this information (to the nearest whole $)?

○ $191

○ $359

○ $478

○ $175

---

20 Mylo is now considering investing in a speciality coffee machine. He has estimated the following daily results for the new machine:

	$
Sales (650 units)	1,300
Variable costs	(845)
Contribution	455
Incremental fixed costs	(70)
Profit	385

Indicate, by clicking on the relevant boxes in the table below, whether each of the following statements regarding the sensitivity of this investment are true or false.

	True	False
The investment is more sensitive to a change in sales volume than sales price	☐	☐
If the variable costs increase by 44% the investment will make a loss	☐	☐
The investment's sensitivity to incremental fixed costs is 550%	☐	☐
The margin of safety is 84.6%	☐	☐

Corfe Co

The following scenario relates to questions 21–25.

Corfe Co is a business which manufactures computer laptop batteries and it has developed a new battery which has a longer usage time than batteries currently available in laptops. The selling price of the battery is forecast to be $45.

The maximum production capacity of Corfe Co is 262,500 units. The company's management accountant is currently preparing an annual flexible budget and has collected the following information so far:

Production (units)	185,000	200,000	225,000
	$	$	$
Material costs	740,000	800,000	900,000
Labour costs	1,017,500	1,100,000	1,237,500
Fixed costs	750,000	750,000	750,000

In addition to the above costs, the management accountant estimates that for each increment of 50,000 units produced, one supervisor will need to be employed. A supervisor's annual salary is $35,000.

The production manager does not understand why the flexible budgets have been produced as they have always used a fixed budget previously.

21 Assuming the budgeted figures are correct, what would the flexed total production cost be if production is 80% of maximum capacity?

- O $2,735,000
- O $2,770,000
- O $2,885,000
- O $2,920,000

---

22 The management accountant has said that a machine maintenance cost was not included in the flexible budget but needs to be taken into account.

The new battery will be manufactured on a machine currently owned by Corfe Co, which was previously used for a product which has now been discontinued. The management accountant estimates that every 1,000 units will take 14 hours to produce. The annual machine hours and maintenance costs for the machine for the last four years have been as follows:

	Machine time (hours)	Maintenance costs ($'000)
Year 1	5,000	850
Year 2	4,400	735
Year 3	4,850	815
Year 4	1,800	450

What is the estimated maintenance cost if production of the battery is 80% of maximum capacity (to the nearest $'000)?

- O $575,000
- O $593,000
- O $500,000
- O $735,000

---

23 In the first month of production of the new battery, actual sales were 18,000 units and the sales revenue achieved was $702,000. The budgeted sales units were 17,300.

Based on this information, which of the following statements is true?

- O When the budget is flexed, the sales variance will include both the sales volume and sales price variances.
- O When the budget is flexed, the sales variance will only include the sales volume variance.
- O When the budget is flexed, the sales variance will only include the sales price variance.
- O When the budget is flexed, the sales variance will include the sales mix and quantity variances and the sales price variance.

24 Which of the following statements relating to the preparation of a flexible budget for the new battery are true?

(1) The budget could be time-consuming to produce as splitting out semi-variable costs may not be straightforward

(2) The range of output over which assumptions about how costs will behave could be difficult to determine

(3) The flexible budget will give managers more opportunity to include budgetary slack than a fixed budget

(4) The budget will encourage all activities and their value to the organisation to be reviewed and assessed

O 1 and 2 only

O 1, 2 and 3

O 1 and 4

O 2, 3 and 4

25 Which of the following is an alternative budgeting system that Corfe Co could use to allow for uncertainty?

O Incremental budget

O Zero based budget

O Activity based budget

O Rolling budget

Helot Co

The following scenario relates to questions 26–30.

Helot Co develops and sells computer games. It is well known for launching innovative and interactive role-playing games and its new releases are always eagerly anticipated by the gaming community. Customers value the technical excellence of the games and the durability of the product and packaging.

Helot Co has previously used a traditional absorption costing system and full cost plus pricing to cost and price its products. It has recently recruited a new finance director who believes the company would benefit from using target costing. They are keen to try this method on a new game concept called Spartan, which has been recently approved.

After discussion with the board, the finance director undertook some market research to find out customers' opinions on the new game concept and to assess potential new games offered by competitors. The results were used to establish a target selling price of $45 for Spartan and an estimated total sales volume of 350,000 units. Helot Co wants to achieve a target profit margin of 35%.

The finance director has also begun collecting cost data for the new game and has projected the following:

Production costs per unit	$
Direct material	3.00
Direct labour	2.50
Direct machining	5.05
Set up	0.45
Inspection and testing	4.30

Total non-production costs	$'000
Design (salaries and technology)	2,500
Marketing consultants	1,700
Distribution	1,400

26 Which **TWO** of the following statements would the finance director have used to explain to Helot Co's board what the benefits were of adopting a target costing approach so early in the game's life cycle?

☐ Costs will be split into material, system, and delivery and disposal categories for improved cost reduction analysis.

☐ Customer requirements for quality, cost and timescales are more likely to be included in decisions on product development.

☐ Its key concept is based on how to turn material into sales as quickly as possible in order to maximise net cash.

☐ The company will focus on designing out costs prior to production, rather than cost control during live production.

---

27 What is the forecast cost gap for the new game (to two decimal places)?

$ [   ]

---

28 The board of Helot Co has asked the finance director to explain what activities can be undertaken to close a cost gap on its computer games.

Which **TWO** of the following would be appropriate ways for Helot Co to close a cost gap?

☐ Buy cheaper, lower grade plastic for the game discs and cases

☐ Use standard components wherever possible in production

☐ Employ more trainee game designers on lower salaries

☐ Use the company's own online gaming websites for marketing

---

29 The direct labour cost per unit has been based on an expected learning rate of 90% but now the finance director has realised that a 95% learning rate should be applied.

Which of the following statements is true?

○ The target cost will decrease and the cost gap will increase

○ The target cost will increase and the cost gap will decrease

○ The target cost will remain the same and the cost gap will increase

○ The target cost will remain the same and the cost gap will decrease

---

30   Helot Co is thinking about expanding its business and introducing a new computer repair
      service for customers. The board has asked if target costing could be applied to this
      service.

      **Which of the following statements regarding services and the use of target costing
      within the service sector is true?**

      O   The purchase of a service transfers ownership to the customer.

      O   Labour resource usage is high in services relative to material requirements.

      O   A standard service cannot be produced and so target costing cannot be used.

      O   Service characteristics include uniformity, perishability and intangibility.

Section C – Both questions are compulsory and MUST be attempted

31 Jungle Co

Jungle Co is a very successful multinational retail company. It has been selling a large range of household and electronic goods for some years. One year ago, it began using new suppliers from the country of Slabak, where labour is very cheap, for many of its household goods. In 20X4, Jungle Co also became a major provider of 'cloud' computing services, investing heavily in cloud technology. These services provide customers with a way of storing and accessing data and programs over the internet rather than on their computers' hard drives.

All Jungle Co customers have the option to sign up for the company's 'Gold' membership service, which provides next day delivery on all orders, in return for an annual service fee of $40. In September 20X5, Jungle Co formed its own logistics company and took over the delivery of all of its parcels, instead of using the services of international delivery companies.

Over the last year, there has been worldwide growth in the electronic goods market of 20%. Average growth rates and gross profit margins for cloud computing service providers have been 50% and 80% respectively in the last year. Jungle Co's prices have remained stable year on year for all sectors of its business, with price competitiveness being crucial to its continuing success as the leading global electronic retailer.

The following information is available for Jungle Co for the last two financial years:

	Notes	31 August 20X6 $'000	31 August 20X5 $'000
Revenue	1	94,660	82,320
Cost of sales	2	(54,531)	(51,708)
Gross profit		40,129	30,612
Administration expenses	3	(2,760)	(1,720)
Distribution expenses		(13,420)	(13,180)
Other operating expenses		(140)	(110)
Net profit		23,809	15,602

Notes

1   Breakdown of revenue

	31 August 20X6 $'000	31 August 20X5 $'000
Household goods	38,990	41,160
Electronic goods	41,870	32,640
Cloud computing services	12,400	6,520
Gold membership fees	1,400	2,000
	94,660	82,320

2   Breakdown of cost of sales

	31 August 20X6 $'000	31 August 20X5 $'000
Household goods	23,394	28,812
Electronic goods	26,797	21,216
Cloud computing services	4,240	1,580
Gold membership fees	100	100
	54,531	51,708

3   Administration expenses

Included in these costs are the costs of running the customer service department ($860,000 in 20X5; $1,900,000 in 20X6). This department deals with customer complaints.

4   Non-financial data

	31 August 20X6 $'000	31 August 20X5 $'000
Percentage of orders delivered on time	74%	92%
No. of customer complaints	1,400,000	320,000
No. of customers	7,100,000	6,500,000
Percentage of late 'Gold' member deliveries	14.00%	2.00%

Required

Discuss the financial and non-financial performance of Jungle Co for the year ending 31 August 20X6.

Note. There are 7 marks available for calculations and 13 marks available for discussion.

(Total = 20 marks)

32 CSC Co

CSC Co is a health food company producing and selling three types of high-energy products – cakes, shakes and cookies – to gyms and health food shops. Shakes are the newest of the three products and were first launched three months ago. Each of the three products has two special ingredients, sourced from a remote part the world. The first of these, Singa, is a super-energising rare type of caffeine. The second, Betta, is derived from an unusual plant believed to have miraculous health benefits.

CSC Co's projected manufacture costs and selling prices for the three products are as follows:

	Cakes	Cookies	Shakes
Per unit	$	$	$
Selling price	5.40	4.90	6.00
Costs:			
Ingredients: Singa ($1.20 per gram)	0.30	0.60	1.20
Ingredients: Betta ($1.50 per gram)	0.75	0.30	1.50
Other ingredients	0.25	0.45	0.90
Labour ($10 per hour)	1.00	1.20	0.80
Variable overheads	0.50	0.60	0.40
Contribution	2.60	1.75	1.20

For each of the three products, the expected demand for the next month is 11,200 cakes, 9,800 cookies and 2,500 shakes.

The total fixed costs for the next month are $3,000.

CSC Co has just found out that the supply of Betta is going to be limited to 12,000 grams next month. Prior to this, CSC Co had signed a contract with a leading chain of gyms, Encompass Health, to supply it with 5,000 shakes each month, at a discounted price of $5.80 per shake, starting immediately. The order for the 5,000 shakes is not included in the expected demand levels above.

Required

(a)   Assuming that CSC Co keeps to its agreement with Encompass Health, calculate the shortage of Betta, the resulting optimum production plan and the total profit for next month.   **(6 marks)**

One month later, the supply of Betta is still limited and CSC Co is considering whether it should breach its contract with Encompass Health so that it can optimise its profits.

Required

(b) Discuss whether CSC Co should breach the agreement with Encompass Health.

   Note. No further calculations are required.   **(4 marks)**

Several months later, the demand for both cakes and cookies has increased significantly to 20,000 and 15,000 units per month respectively. However, CSC Co has lost the contract with Encompass Health and, after suffering from further shortages of supply of Betta, Singa and of its labour force, CSC Co has decided to stop making shakes at all. CSC Co now needs to use linear programming to work out the optimum production plan for cakes and cookies for the coming month. The variable 'x' is being used to represent cakes and the variable 'y' to represent cookies.

The following constraints have been formulated and a graph representing the new production problem has been drawn:

Singa: 0.25x + 0.5y ≤ 12,000

Betta: 0.5x + 0.2y ≤ 12,500

Labour: 0.1x + 0.12y ≤ 3,000

x ≤ 20,000

y ≤ 15,000

x, y ≥ 0

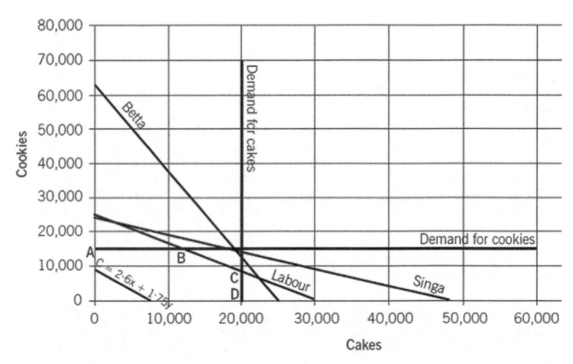

Required

(c) (i) Explain what the line labelled 'C = 2.6x + 1.75y' on the graph is, and what the area represented by the points OABCD means.   **(4 marks)**

   (ii) Explain how the optimum production plan will be found using the line labelled 'C = 2.6x + 1.75y' and identify the optimum point from the graph.   **(2 marks)**

   (iii) Explain what a slack value is and identify, from the graph, where slack will occur as a result of the optimum production plan.   **(4 marks)**

   Note. No calculations are needed for part (c).

                                                                    (Total = 20 marks)

Formulae sheet

Regression analysis

$y = a + bx$

$$a = \frac{\Sigma y}{n} - \frac{b\Sigma x}{n}$$

$$b = \frac{n\Sigma xy - \Sigma x\Sigma y}{n\Sigma x^2 - (\Sigma x)^2}$$

$$r = \frac{n\Sigma xy - \Sigma x\Sigma y}{\sqrt{\left(n\Sigma x^2 - (\Sigma x)^2\right)\left(n\Sigma y^2 - (\Sigma y)^2\right)}}$$

Learning curve

$Y = ax^b$

Where
- Y = cumulative average time per unit to produce x units
- a = the time taken for the first unit of output
- x = the cumulative number of units produced
- b = the index of learning (log LR/log2)
- LR = the learning rate as a decimal

Demand curve

$P = a - bQ$

$$b = \frac{\text{change in price}}{\text{change in quantity}}$$

a = price when $Q = 0$

$MR = a - 2bQ$

Answers

DO NOT TURN THIS PAGE UNTIL YOU HAVE
COMPLETED THE MOCK EXAM

A plan of attack

Managing your nerves

As you turn the pages to start this mock exam a number of thoughts are likely to cross your mind. At best, examinations cause anxiety so it is important to stay focused on your task for the next three hours! Developing an awareness of what is going on emotionally within you may help you manage your nerves. Remember, you are unlikely to banish the flow of adrenaline, but the key is to harness it to help you work steadily and quickly through your answers.

Working through this mock exam will help you develop the exam stamina you will need to keep going for three hours.

Managing your time

Planning and time management are two of the key skills which complement the technical knowledge you need to succeed. To keep yourself on time, do not be afraid to jot down your target completion times for each question, perhaps next to the title of the question on the exam. As all the questions are **compulsory**, you do not have to spend time wondering which question to answer!

Doing the exam

Actually doing the exam is a personal experience. There is not a single **right way**. As long as you submit complete answers to all questions after the three hours are up, then your approach obviously works.

Looking through the exam

Section A has 15 OTQs. This is the section of the exam where the ACCA examining team can test knowledge across the breadth of the syllabus. Make sure you read these questions carefully. The distractors are designed to present plausible, but incorrect, answers. Don't let them mislead you. If you really have no idea – guess. You may even be right.

Section B has three questions, each with a scenario and five objective test questions.

Section C has two longer questions:

- Question 31 is a traditional performance assessment question requiring a discussion on financial and non-financial performance of a business. There are plenty of easy marks available in this question. Make sure you lay out your percentage change calculations clearly and discuss possible reasons and implications for each one.

- Question 32 looks at limiting factors and linear programming. There is a lot to do on this question so make sure you don't over-run on time. You may want to start with part (c) first if linear programming is your strength.

Allocating your time

BPP's advice is to always allocate your time **according to the marks for the question**. However, **use common sense**. If you're doing a question but haven't a clue how to do part (b), you might be better off re-allocating your time and getting more marks on another question, where you can add something you didn't have time for earlier on. Make sure you leave time to recheck the OTQs and make sure you have answered them all.

Section A

Each question is worth 2 marks.

1   $27.40

    OAR for fixed production overheads ($72 million/96 million hours) = $0.75 per hour

    Total manufacturing costs (300,000 units × $20) = $6,000,000

    Total design, depreciation and decommissioning costs = $1,320,000

    Total fixed production overheads (300,000 units × 4 hours × $0.75) = $900,000

    Total life-cycle costs = $8,220,000

    Life-cycle cost per unit ($8,220,000/300,000 units) = $27.40

2   22,500

    Two units of Y and one unit of X would give total contribution of $18.

    Weighted average contribution per unit = $18/3 units = $6

    Sales units to achieve target profit = ($90,000 + $45,000)/$6 = 22,500

3   $6,800

    3,000 units should use 10 kg each (3,000 × 10) = 30,000 kg

    3,000 units did use = 29,000 kg

    Difference = 1,000 kg favourable

    Valued at $6.80 per kg ($68/10 kg)

    Variance = $6,800 favourable

4   Critical strategic information can be summarised

    The tracking and summarising of critical strategic information is done by an Executive Information System (EIS).

    The other three options are all likely to be potential benefits which would result from the introduction of an ERPS.

5   Flow cost accounting

    Under a system of flow cost accounting, material flows are divided into three categories – material, system, and delivery and disposal.

6   Effectiveness

    Exam success will be a given objective of a school, so it is a measure of effectiveness.

7   Variance analysis

    Variance analysis is not relevant to target costing as it is a technique used for cost control at the production phase of the product life cycle. It is a feedback control tool by nature and target costing is feedforward.

    Value analysis can be used to identify where small cost reductions can be applied to close a cost gap once production commences.

    Functional analysis can be used at the product design stage. It ensures that a cost gap is reached or to ensure that the product design is one which includes only features which customers want.

    Activity analysis identifies and describes activities in an organisation and evaluates their impact on operations to assess where improvements can be made.

8   If working from home, departmental employees must use a memory stick to transfer data, as laptop computers are not allowed to leave the department.

A memory stick is much more likely to get mislaid and compromise security than a password-protected laptop. It is likely that memory sticks could get lost or that information is left on home computers.

In the context of the scenario all the other options are good practice.

9   Labour time available   Yes

         Machine time available   No

If the values for R and N are substituted into the constraints:

Labour required = (3 × 500) + (2 × 400) = 2,300 hours which is less than what is available, so there is slack.

Machine time required = (0.5 × 500) + (0.4 × 400) = 410 hours which is exactly what is available, and so there is no slack.

10   19.8%

Revised annual profit = $190,000 + $10,000 profit on the sale of the asset = $200,000

Revised net assets = $1,000,000 − $40,000 NBV + $50,000 cash − $250,000 cash + $250,000 asset = $1,010,000

ROI = ($200,000/$1,010,000) × 100 = 19.8%

11   Increasing the efficiency of the maintenance routine for Process 2

Throughput is determined by the bottleneck resource. Process 2 is the bottleneck as it has insufficient time to meet demand.

The only option to improve Process 2 is to improve the efficiency of the maintenance routine. All the other three options either increase the time available on non-bottleneck resources or increase demand for an increase in supply which cannot be achieved.

12      $400 adverse

An operational variance compares revised price to actual price.

20,000 kg should cost $0.40 per kg at the revised price (20,000 kg × $0.40) = $8,000

20,000 kg did cost $0.42 per kg (20,000 kg × $0.42) = $8,400

Variance = $400 adverse

13   Material cost only

The material price when flexed is higher than budget while the external environment shows that prices are reducing. This indicates that although suppliers lowered their prices, the manager has still overspent which indicates poor performance.

When sales volumes and prices are flexed, it can be seen that the manager has performed better.

14   It is useful if significant economies of scale can be achieved   Correct

         It is useful if demand for a product is highly elastic   Correct

Penetration pricing involves setting a low price when a product is first launched in order to obtain strong demand.

It is particularly useful if significant economies of scale can be achieved from a high volume of output and if demand is highly elastic and so would respond well to low prices.

15    $120

Total material budget ((1,000 units × $10) + (2,000 units × $20)) = $50,000

Fixed costs related to material handling = $100,000

OAR = $2/$ of material

Product B = $2 × $20 = $40

Total labour budget ((1,000 units × $5) + (2,000 units × $20) = $45,000

General fixed costs = $180,000

OAR = $4/$ of labour

Product B = $4 × $20 = $80

Total fixed overhead cost per unit of Product B ($40 + $80) = $120

Section B

Each question is worth 2 marks.

16   450 lunches

The maximin rule selects the maximum of the minimum outcomes for each supply level.

For Mylo the minimum outcomes are:

450 lunches – $1,170

620 lunches – $980

775 lunches – $810

960 lunches – $740

The maximum of these is at a supply level of 450 lunches.

17   960 lunches

The minimax regret rule selects the minimum of the maximum regrets.

Demand level	Supply level			
	450	620	775	960
	$	$	$	$
450	–	190	360	430
620	442	–	217	322
775	845	403	–	230
960	1,326	884	481	–
Max regret	1,326	884	481	430

The minimum of the maximum regrets is $430, so suggests a supply level of 960 lunches.

18   Expected values will ignore any variability which could occur across the range of possible outcomes.

Expected values can be applied by Mylo as he is evaluating a decision which occurs many times over.

Expected values do not take into account the variability which could occur across a range of outcomes; a standard deviation would need to be calculated to assess that, so Statement 2 is correct.

Expected values are particularly useful for repeated decisions where the expected value will be the long-run average, so Statement 4 is correct.

Expected values are associated with risk-neutral decision makers. A defensive or conservative decision maker is risk averse, so Statement 1 is incorrect.

Expected values will take into account the likelihood of different outcomes occurring as this is part of the calculation, so Statement 3 is incorrect.

19    $191

This requires the calculation of the value of perfect information (VOPI).

Expected value with perfect information = (0.15 × $1,170) + (0.30 × $1,612) + (0.40 × $2,015) + (0.15 × $2,496) = $1,839.50

Expected value without perfect information would be the highest of the expected values for the supply levels = $1,648.25 (at a supply level of 775 lunches).

The value of perfect information is the difference between the expected value with perfect information and the expected value without perfect information = $1,839.50 – $1,648.25 = $191.25, therefore $191 to nearest whole $.

20	The investment is more sensitive to a change in sales volume than sales price	False
	If the variable costs increase by 44% the investment will make a loss	False
	The investment's sensitivity to incremental fixed costs is 550%	True
	The margin of safety is 84.6%	True

The investment's sensitivity to fixed costs is 550% ((385/70) × 100), so Statement 3 is correct.

The margin of safety is 84.6%. Budgeted sales are 650 units and BEP sales are 100 units (70/0.7), therefore the margin of safety is 550 units which equates to 84.6% of the budgeted sales, so Statement 4 is therefore correct.

The investment is more sensitive to a change in sales price of 29.6%, so Statement 1 is incorrect.

If variable costs increased by 44%, it would still make a very small profit, so Statement 2 is incorrect.

21 $2,920,000

An 80% activity level is 210,000 units.

Material and labour costs are both variable. Material is $4 per unit and labour is $5.50 per unit.

Total variable costs = $9.50 × 210,000 units = $1,995,000

Fixed costs = $750,000

Supervision = $175,000 as five supervisors will be required for a production level of 210,000 units.

Total annual budgeted cost allowance = $1,995,000 + $750,000 + $175,000 = $2,920,000

22 $593,000

Variable cost per hour ($850,000 − $450,000)/(5,000 hours − 1,800 hours) = $125 per hour

Fixed cost ($850,000 − (5,000 hours × $125)) = $225,000

Number of machine hours required for production = 210 batches × 14 hours = 2,940 hours

Total cost ($225,000 + (2,940 hours × $125)) = $592,500, therefore $593,000 to the nearest $'000.

23 When the budget is flexed, the sales variance will only include the sales price variance.

If the budget is flexed, then the effect on sales revenue of the difference between budgeted and actual sales volumes is removed, and the variance which is left is the sales price variance.

24 Statements 1 and 2

Flexible budgeting can be time-consuming to produce as splitting out semi-variable costs could be problematic, so Statement 1 is correct.

Estimating how costs behave over different levels of activity can be difficult to predict, so Statement 2 is correct.

A flexible budget will not encourage slack compared to a fixed budget, so Statement 3 is incorrect.

It is a zero-based budget, not a flexible budget, which assesses all activities for their value to the organisation, so Statement 4 is incorrect.

25   Rolling budget

Rolling budgets are a way of reducing the element of uncertainty in plans made because they are continuously updated throughout a financial year. This should help to keep plans more relevant and realistic.

26   Customer requirements for quality, cost and timescales are more likely to be included in decisions on product development.

The company will focus on designing out costs prior to production, rather than cost control during live production.

Target costing does encourage looking at customer requirements early on so that features valued by customers are included, so Statement 2 is correct. It will also force the company to closely assess the design and is likely to be successful if costs are designed out at this stage rather than later once production has started, so Statement 4 is correct.

Statement 1 explains a benefit of flow cost accounting. Statement 3 explains the concept of throughput accounting.

27     $2.05

Target price is $45 and the profit margin is 35% which results in a target cost of $29.25. The current estimated cost is $31.30 which results in a cost gap of $2.05.

28   Use standard components wherever possible in production, and use the company's own online gaming websites for marketing.

Using more standardised components and using its own websites for marketing will reduce processing and marketing costs.

Using cheaper materials and trainee designers will reduce costs but could impact the quality and customer perception of the product, which would impact the target price.

29   The target cost will remain the same and the cost gap will increase

The change in the learning rate will increase the current estimated cost, which will increase the cost gap.

The target cost will be unaffected, as this is based on the target selling price and profit margin; neither of which are changing.

30   Labour resource usage is high in services relative to material requirements.

Services do use more labour relative to materials.

The other three statements are incorrect as uniformity is not a characteristic of services, there is no transfer of ownership and although it is difficult to standardise a service due to the human influence, target costing can still be used.

ANSWERS

Section C

31 Jungle Co

> **Workbook reference.** Performance analysis is covered in Chapter 19.
>
> **Top tips.** You need to perform some calculations in order to have enough to discuss. Percentage change calculations are key. In your discussion, it is important to suggest why things have changed and how this might affect other parts of the business.
>
> **Easy marks.** The easy marks are for the percentage change calculations.
>
> **Examining team comments.** Marks are awarded for percentage change calculations but not for calculations of absolute change. Points such as 'Cost of sales have decreased by 18%. This is a good performance.' were common but, apart from the calculation, scored no marks. Answers which looked at why cost of sales might have decreased, or what impact that might have had, scored many more marks.

Marking scheme

	Marks
Sales volumes (up to 2 marks per revenue stream)	8
COS and gross margins	5
Administration expenses/customer complaints	3
Distribution costs/late deliveries	2
Net profit margin	20

Sales volumes

Since prices have remained stable year on year, it can be assumed that changes to revenue are as a result of increases or decreases in sales volumes. Overall, revenue has increased by 15%, which is a substantial increase. In order to understand what has happened in the business, it is necessary to consider sales by looking at each of the different categories.

Household goods

Although this was the largest category of sales for Jungle Co last year, this year it has decreased by 5% and has now been overtaken by electronic goods. The company changed suppliers for many of its household goods during the year, buying them instead from a country where labour was cheap. It may be that this has affected the quality of the goods, thus leading to decreased demand.

Electronic goods

Unlike household goods, demand for electronic goods from Jungle Co has increased dramatically by 28%. This is now Jungle Co's leading revenue generator. This is partly due to the fact that the electronic goods market has grown by 20% worldwide. However, Jungle Co has even outperformed this, meaning that it has secured a larger segment of the market.

Cloud computing service

This area of Jungle Co's business is growing rapidly, with the company seeing a 90% increase in this revenue stream in the last year. Once again, the company has outperformed the market, where the average growth rate is only 50%, suggesting that the investment in the cloud technology was worthwhile.

Gold membership fees

This area of the business is relatively small but has shrunk further, with a decrease in revenue of 30%. This may be because customers are dissatisfied with the service that they are receiving. The number of late deliveries for Gold members has increased from 2% to 14% since Jungle Co began using its own logistics company. This has probably been at least partly responsible for the massive increase in the number of customer complaints.

Gross profit margins

Overall, the company's gross profit margin (GPM) has increased from 37% to 42%. While the GPM for electronic goods has only increased by 1 percentage point, the margin for household goods has increased by 10 percentage points. This is therefore largely responsible for the increase in overall GPM. This has presumably occurred because Jungle Co is now sourcing these products from new, cheaper suppliers.

Gold membership fees constitute only a small part of Jungle Co's income, so their 2 percentage point fall in GPM has had little impact on the overall increase in GPM. Cloud computing services, on the other hand, now make up over $12m of Jungle Co's sales revenue. For some reason, the GPM on these sales has fallen from 76% to 66%. This is now 14 percentage points less than the market average gross profit margin of 80%. More information is needed to establish why this has happened. It has prevented the overall increase in GPM being higher than it otherwise would have been.

Administration expenses/customer complaints

These have increased by 60% from $1.72m to $2.76m. This is a substantial increase. The costs of the customer service department are in here. Given the number of late deliveries increased from 2% to 14%, and the corresponding increase in customer complaints from 5% to 20%, it is not surprising that the administration costs have increased. As well as being concerned about the impact on profit of this increase of over $1m, Jungle Co should be extremely worried about the effect on its reputation. Bad publicity about reliable delivery could affect future business.

Distribution costs

Despite an increase in sales volumes of 15%, distribution expenses have increased by less than 2 percentage points. They have gone down from $0.16 to $0.14 per $ of revenue. Although this means that Jungle Co has been successful in terms of saving costs, as discussed above, the damage which late deliveries are doing to the business cannot be ignored. The company needs to urgently address the issue of late deliveries.

Net profit margin

This has increased from 19% to 25%. This means that, all in all, Jungle Co has had a successful year, with net profit having increased from $15.6m to $23.8m. However, the business must address its delivery issues if its success is to continue.

Gross profit margins	31 August 20X6	31 August 20X5
Household goods	40.00%	30.00%
Electronic goods	36.00%	35.00%
Cloud computing services	65.81%	75.77%
Gold membership fees	92.86%	95.00%
Overall	42.39%	37.19%
Net profit margin	25.15%	18.95%
Increase/decrease in revenue		
Household goods	−5.27%	
Electronic goods	28.28%	
Cloud computing services	90.18%	
Gold membership fees	−30.00%	
Total revenue increase	14.99%	
Increase/decrease in cost of sales		
Household goods	−18.80%	
Electronic goods	26.31%	
Cloud computing services	168.35%	
Gold membership fees	0.00%	
Total cost of sales increase	5.46%	

	31 August 20X6	31 August 20X5
Increase in administration expenses	60.47%	
Increase in distribution expenses	1.82%	
Increase in other operating expenses	27.27%	
Increase in costs of customer service department ([$1,900,000 – $860,000]/$860,000)	120.93%	
Customer complaints as % customers	19.72%	4.92%
Delivery cost per $ of revenue	$0.14	$0.16

32 CSC Co

> **Workbook references.** Limiting factors and linear programming are covered in Chapter 9.
>
> **Top tips.** Part (a) is not particularly difficult but does require some care. Read the requirement carefully and ensure that you use quantities (not dollar values) to calculate your optimum production plan. Part (b) says that no further calculations are required so don't waste time performing any. Part (c) requires you to have a good understanding of how linear programming works.
>
> **Easy marks.** Part (a) has easy marks. There are also easy marks in part (b) for realising that breach of contract will have legal, reputational and unethical implications.
>
> **Examining team comments.** Responses to part (a) were poor, with students ignoring the fact that the company had entered into a contract and also omitting to calculate the material shortage. Part (b) was also disappointing as many students focused purely on financial factors. Part (c) was answered well overall. However, although most students identified the iso-contribution line and feasible region on the graph, few could explain what they meant.

Marking scheme

				Marks
(a)		Calculating shortage of Betta	1.5	
		Contribution per gram of Betta	1	
		Ranking	0.5	
		Optimum production plan	2	
		Profit	1	
				6
(b)		Each valid point	1	
				Max 4
(c)	(i)	Identification and explanation of the iso-contribution line	2	
		Identification and explanation of the feasible region	2	
				4
	(ii)	Explaining how to use line for identification of optimum point	1.5	
		Identification of optimum point	0.5	
				2
	(iii)	Explaining what slack values are	1	
		Identifying Betta as slack	1	
		Identifying Singa as slack	1	
		Identifying slack demand for cookies	1	
				4
				20

(a) **Step 1**   Calculate the shortage of Betta for the year

Total requirements in grams:

Cakes: grams used per cake	0.5
Expected demand	11,200
Total required:	5,600
Cookies: grams used per cookie	0.20
Expected demand	9,800
Total required:	1,960
Shakes: grams used per shake	1
Expected demand	7,500
Total required:	7,500
Overall total required:	15,060
Less available:	12,000
Shortage:	3,060

Step 2   Contribution per gram of Betta and ranking

	Cakes	Cookies	Shakes	Shakes (contract)
	$	$	$	$
Contribution per unit	2.60	1.75	1.20	1.00
Grams of Betta per unit	0.5	0.2	1	1
	$	$	$	$
Contribution per gram	5.20	8.75	1.20	1.00
Rank	2	1	3	4

Step 3   Optimum production plan

Product	Number to be produced	Grams per unit	Total grams per product	Cumulative grams	Contribution per unit	Total contribution
Shakes (contract)	5,000		5,000	5,000	1.00	5,000
Cookies	9,800	0.20	1,960	6,960	1.75	17,150
Cakes	10,080	0.5	5,040	12,000	2.60	26,208
Total contribution						48,358
Less: fixed costs						(3,000)
Profit						45,358

(b) **Breach of contract with Encompass Health (EH)**

It would be bad for business if CSC Co becomes known as a supplier which cannot be relied on to stick to the terms of its agreements. This could make future potential customers reluctant to deal with them.

Even more seriously, there could be legal consequences involved in breaching the contract with EH. This would be costly and also very damaging to CSC Co's reputation.

If CSC Co lets EH down and breaches the contract, EH may refuse to buy from them any more and future sales revenue would therefore be lost. Just as importantly, these sales to EH are currently helping to increase the marketability of CSC Co's shakes. This will be lost if these sales are no longer made.

Therefore, taking these factors into account, it would not be advisable to breach the contract.

BPP
LEARNING
MEDIA

(c) (i) This line is what is called the 'iso-contribution line' and it is plotted by finding two corresponding x and y values for the 'objective function'. At any point along this line, the mix of cakes and cookies will provide the same total contribution, 'C'.

Since each cake provides a contribution of $2.60 and each cookie provides a contribution of $1.75, the objective function has been defined as 'C = 2.6x + 1.75y'. This means that the total contribution will be however many cakes are made (represented by 'x') at $2.60 each plus however many cookies are made (represented by 'y') at $1.75 each.

The area OABCD is called the 'feasible region'. Any point within this region could be selected and would show a feasible mix of production of cakes and cookies. However, in order to maximise profit, the optimum production mix will be at a point on the edge of the feasible region, not within it.

(ii) The further the iso-contribution line is moved away from the origin, O, the greater the contribution generated will be. Therefore, a ruler will be laid along the line, making sure it stays at exactly the same angle as the line, and the ruler will then be moved outwards to the furthest vertex (intersection between two constraints) on the feasible region, as represented by either point A, B, C or D. In this case, the optimum point is 'C', the intersection of the 'labour' constraint and the 'demand for cakes' constraint.

(iii) A 'slack' value could arise either in relation to a resource or in relation to production of a product. It means that a resource is not being fully utilised or that there is unfulfilled demand of a product. Since the optimum point is the intersection of the labour and the demand for cakes lines, this means that there will be three slack values. First, there will be a slack value for cookies. This means that there will be unsatisfied demand for cookies, since the optimum point does not reach as far as the 'demand for cookies' line on the graph. Also, there will be slack values for Betta and Singa, which means that both of these materials are not actually the binding constraints, such that there will be more material available than is needed.

ACCA

Performance Management

Mock Exam 2

Specimen exam CBE

Question Paper: 3 hours
ALL FIVE questions are compulsory and MUST be attempted

DO NOT OPEN THIS PAPER UNTIL YOU ARE READY TO START
UNDER EXAMINATION CONDITIONS

BPP
LEARNING
MEDIA

$12/_{B_1} = 3$

$2005 - Q14-2$

2005   April May Jun = 14

2005   July Aug Sep = 15

2006   Oct Nov - Dec = 16

17

18

19

20

Section A – All FIFTEEN questions are compulsory and MUST be attempted

Each question is worth two marks.

1   A company manufactures two products, C and D, for which the following information is available:

	Product C	Product D	Total
Budgeted production (units)	1,000	4,000	5,000
Labour hours per unit/in total	8	10	48,000
Number of production runs required	13	15	28
Number of inspections during production	5	3	8
Total production set up costs	$140,000		
Total inspection costs	$80,000		
Other overhead costs	$96,000		

Other overhead costs are absorbed on a labour hour basis.

Using activity-based costing, what is the budgeted overhead cost per unit of Product D?

O $43.84

O $46.25

O $131.00

O $140.64

---

2   LPM Co has identified the trend line relating to its sales revenue as 2,000 + 25X.

X denotes the quarter number, with the first quarter of 20X5 being 13, the second quarter of 20X5 being 14, etc.

LPM Co uses the multiplicative model and has calculated the following seasonal variations:

Quarter 1: -0.20

Quarter 2: -0.08

Quarter 3: +0.04

Quarter 4: +0.24

What is LPM Co's seasonally adjusted sales revenue forecast for the second quarter of 20X7?

$ [   ]

---

3   P Co makes two products, P1 and P2. The budgeted details for each product are as follows:

	P1	P2
	$	$
Selling price	10.00	8.00
Cost per unit:		
Direct materials	3.50	4.00
Direct labour	1.50	1.00
Variable overhead	0.60	0.40
Fixed overhead	1.20	1.00
Profit per unit	3.20	1.60

Budgeted production and sales for the year ended 30 November 20X5 are:

Product P1	10,000 units
Product P2	12,500 units

The fixed overhead costs included in P1 relate to apportionment of general overhead costs only. However, P2 also included specific fixed overheads totalling $2,500.

If only product P1 were to be made, how many units would need to be sold in order to achieve a profit of $60,000 each year (to the nearest whole unit)?

⬚ units

---

4   Which TWO of the following statements regarding environmental cost accounting, are true?

☐ The majority of environmental costs are already captured within a typical organisation's accounting system. The difficulty lies in identifying them.

☐ Input/output analysis divides material flows within an organisation into three categories: material flows; system flows; and delivery and disposal flows.

☐ One of the cost categories used in environmental activity-based costing is environment-driven costs which is used for costs which can be directly traced to a cost centre.

☐ Environmental life cycle costing enables environmental costs from the design stage of the product right through to decommissioning at the end of its life to be considered.

---

5   To produce 19 litres of Product X, a standard input mix of eight litres of Chemical A and 12 litres of Chemical B is required.

Chemical A has a standard cost of $20 per litre and Chemical B has a standard cost of $25 per litre.

During September, the actual results showed that 1,850 litres of Product X were produced, using a total input of 900 litres of Chemical A and 1,100 litres of Chemical B.

The actual costs of Chemicals A and B were at the standard cost of $20 and $25 per litre respectively.

Based on the above information, which of the following statements is true?

⬚ ▼

Picklist:

Both variances were adverse.
Both variances were favourable.
The total mix variance was adverse and the total yield variance was favourable.
The total mix variance was favourable and the total yield variance was adverse.

---

6   A budget is a quantified plan of action for a forthcoming period. Budgets can be prepared using a variety of different approaches.

Match each of the following statements to the correct budgeting process.

Statements		Budgeting approach	
1 Builds in previous problems and inefficiencies		Beyond budgeting	**6**
2 Recognises different cost behaviour patterns		Incremental budgeting	**1**
3 Focuses employees on avoiding wasteful expenditure		Activity-based budgeting	**4**
4 Focuses on controlling the causes of costs		Rolling budgeting	**5**
5 Always extends the budget one year into the future		Flexible budgeting	**2**
6 Uses adaptive management processes		Zero-based budgeting	**3**

QUESTIONS

---

7   A leisure company owns a number of large health and fitness resorts, but one is suffering from declining sales and is predicted to make a loss in the next year. As a result management have identified a number of possible actions:

(1)   Shut down the resort and sell off the assets
(2)   Undertake a major upgrade to facilities, costing $4.5m
(3)   Undertake a minor upgrade to facilities, costing $2m

The upgrades are predicted to have variable results and the probability of good results after a major upgrade is 0.8, whereas the probability of good results after a minor upgrade is 0.7.

The company is risk neutral and has prepared the following decision tree.

BPP
LEARNING
MEDIA

Which decision should the company make?

- O Shutdown and sell
- O Undertake the major upgrade
- O Undertake the minor upgrade
- O Undertake the major upgrade if results are good

---

8 A company has the following production planned for the next four weeks. The figures reflect the full capacity level of operations. Planned output is equal to the maximum demand per product.

Product	A	B	C	D
	$ per unit	$ per unit	$ per unit	$ per unit
Selling price	160	214	100	140
Raw material cost	24	56	22	40
Direct labour cost	66	88	33	22
Variable overhead cost	24	18	24	18
Fixed overhead cost	16	10	8	12
Profit	30	42	13	48
Planned output	300	125	240	400
Direct labour hours per unit	6	8	3	2

It has now been identified that labour hours available in the next four weeks will be limited to 4,000 hours.

Rank the products in the order they should be manufactured, assuming that the company wants to maximise profits in the next four weeks.

Product
A
B
C
D

Ranking	
1st	
2nd	
3rd	
4th	

9   Def Co provides accounting services to government departments. On average, each staff member works six chargeable hours per day, with the rest of their working day being spent on non-chargeable administrative work. One of the company's main objectives is to produce a high level of quality and customer satisfaction.

Def Co has set its targets for the next year.

Match the correct value for money performance category to each of the following targets for Def Co.

Value for Money Performance Category		Performance targets
Economy		Increasing the number of chargeable hours handled by advisers to 6.2 per day
Efficiency		Obtaining a score of 4.7 or above on customer satisfaction surveys
Effectiveness		Cutting departmental expenditure by 5%

10   Different types of information systems provide the information which organisations need for strategic planning, management and operational control.

Match the following characteristics to the relevant information systems.

Characteristic	Management Information System	Transaction Processing System
Summarises internal data into periodic reports		
Can be set up with extranet links to customers and suppliers		

Characteristic	Executive Information System	Enterprise Resource Planning System
Utilises dashboard facilities and interactive graphics		
Facilitates the immediate processing of data		

11   Which **TWO** of the following are examples of direct data capture costs?

☐ Use of bar coding and scanners

☐ Payroll department processing time of personnel costs

☐ Use of chip readers to read data from chips on customers' bank cards when paying for goods

☐ Emails sent to staff on matters that do not relate to them

12   Which **TWO** of the following statements regarding life-cycle costing are correct?

☐   It can be applied not only to products but also to an organisation's customers.

☐   It includes any opportunity costs associated with production.

☐   The maturity phase is characterised by a rapid build-up in demand.

☐   Often between 70% to 90% of costs are determined early in the product life cycle.

---

13   A company manufactures a product which requires four hours per unit of machine time. Machine time is a bottleneck resource as there are only ten machines which are available for 12 hours per day, five days per week. The product has a selling price of $130 per unit, direct material costs of $50 per unit, labour costs of $40 per unit and factory overhead costs of $20 per unit. These costs are based on weekly production and sales of 150 units.

What is the throughput accounting ratio?

O   1.33

O   2.00

O   0.75

O   0.31

---

14   Ox Co has two divisions, A and B. Division A makes a component for air conditioning units which it can only sell to Division B. It has no other outlet for sales.

Current information relating to Division A is as follows:

Marginal cost per unit	$100
Transfer price of the component	$165
Total production and sales of the component each year	2,200 units
Specific fixed costs of Division A per year	$10,000

Cold Co has offered to sell the component to Division B for $140 per unit. If Division B accepts this offer, Division A will be closed.

If Division B accepts Cold Co's offer, what will be the impact on profits per year for the group as a whole?

O   Increase of $65,000

O   Decrease of $78,000

O   Decrease of $88,000

O   Increase of $55,000

15   Identify, by clicking on the relevant box in the table below, whether each of the following statements regarding Fitzgerald and Moon's Building Blocks model is true or false.

The determinants of performance are quality, innovation, resource utilisation and competitiveness	TRUE	FALSE
Standards are targets for performance and should be fair, achievable and controllable	TRUE	FALSE
Rewards encourage staff to work towards the standards and should be clear, motivating and controllable	TRUE	FALSE
It is a performance measurement framework suitable for service organisations	TRUE	FALSE

(Total = 30 marks)

Section B – All FIFTEEN questions are compulsory and MUST be attempted

Each question is worth two marks.

The following scenario relates to questions 16–20.

Glam Co is a hairdressing salon which provides both 'cuts' and 'treatments' to clients. All cuts and treatments at the salon are carried out by one of the salon's three senior stylists. The salon also has two salon assistants and two junior stylists.

Every client attending the salon is first seen by a salon assistant, who washes their hair; next, by a senior stylist, who cuts or treats their hair depending on which service the client wants; then finally, a junior stylist who dries their hair. The average length of time spent with each member of staff is as follows:

	Cut Hours	Treatment Hours
Assistant	0.1	0.3
Senior stylist	1.0	1.5
Junior stylist	0.6	0.5

The salon is open for eight hours each day for six days per week. It is only closed for two weeks each year. Staff salaries are $40,000 each year for each senior stylist, $28,000 each year for each junior stylist and $12,000 each year for each of the assistants. The cost of cleaning products applied when washing clients' hair is $1.50 per client. The cost of all additional products applied during a 'treatment' is $7.40 per client. Other salon costs (excluding labour and raw materials) amount to $106,400 each year.

Glam Co charges $60 for each cut and $110 for each treatment.

The senior stylists' time has been correctly identified as the bottleneck activity.

16   What is the annual capacity of the bottleneck activity?

     O   2,400 cuts or   1,600 treatments

     O   4,800 cuts or   4,800 treatments

     O   7,200 cuts or   4,800 treatments

     O   9,600 cuts or   9,600 treatments

---

17   The salon has calculated the cost per hour to be $42.56.

     Calculate the throughput accounting ratio (TPAR) for both services (to two decimal places).

Cuts	

Treatments	

---

18   Which **THREE** of the following activities could the salon use to improve the TPAR?

☐   Increase the time spent by the bottleneck activity on each service

☐   Identify ways to reduce the material costs for the services

☐   Increase the level of inventory to prevent stockouts

☐   Increase the productivity of the stage prior to the bottleneck

☐   Improve the control of the salon's total operating expenses

☐   Apply an increase to the selling price of the services

19   What would be the effect on the bottleneck if the salon employed another senior stylist?

○   The senior stylists' time will be a bottleneck for cuts only

○   The senior stylists' time will be a bottleneck for treatments only

○   The senior stylists' time will remain the bottleneck for both cuts and treatments

○   There will no longer be a bottleneck

20   Which of the following statements regarding the theory of constraints are correct?

(1)   It focuses on identifying stages of congestion in a process when production arrives more quickly than the next stage can handle

(2)   It is based on the concept that organisations manage three key factors – throughput, operating expenses and inventory

(3)   It uses a sequence of focusing steps to overcome a single bottleneck, at which point the improvement process is complete

(4)   It can be applied to the management of all limiting factors, both internal and external, which can affect an organisation

○   (1) and (2) only

○   (1), (2) and (3)

○   (2), (3) and (4)

○   (1), (3) and (4)

The following scenario relates to questions 21–25.

Chair Co has several new products in development. Information relating to three of these products is as follows:

Luxury car seat

The estimated labour time for the first unit is 12 hours but a learning curve of 75% is expected to apply for the first eight units produced. The cost of labour is $15 per hour.

The cost of materials and other variable overheads is expected to total $230 per unit. Chair Co plans on pricing the seat by adding a 50% mark up to the total variable cost per seat, with the labour cost being based on the incremental time taken to produce the eighth unit.

High chair

Another product which Chair Co has in development is a new design of high chair for feeding young children. Based on previous experience of producing similar products, Chair Co had assumed that a learning rate of 85% would apply to the manufacture of this new design but after the first phase of production had been completed, management realised that a learning rate of 80% had been achieved.

Office chair

Chair Co has also developed a new type of office chair and management is trying to formulate a budget for this product. They have decided to match the production level to demand, however, demand for this chair is uncertain.

Management have collected the following information:

	Demand Units	Probability
Worst possible outcome	10,000	0.3
Most likely outcome	22,000	0.5
Best possible outcome	35,000	0.2

The selling price per unit is $25. The variable cost per unit is $8 for any production level up to 25,000 units. If the production level is higher than 25,000 units then the variable cost per unit will decrease by 10% and this reduction will apply to all the units produced at that level.

Total fixed costs are estimated to be $75,000.

Chair Co uses cost-plus pricing when setting prices for its products.

21   In relation to the luxury car seat, what is the labour cost of the eighth unit?

    O $45.65

    O $75.94

    O $4.32

    O $3.04

---

22   The first phase of production has now been completed for the new car seat. The first unit actually took 12.5 hours to make and the total time for the first eight units was 34.3 hours, at which point the learning effect came to an end. Chair Co are planning on adjusting the price to reflect the actual time it took to complete the eighth unit.

What was the actual rate of learning which occurred (to two decimal places)?

[   ] %

---

23   In relation to the new design of high chair, which **THREE** of the following statements could explain why the actual rate of learning differed from the rate which was expected?

    ☐   Staffing levels were stable during the first manufacturing phase

    ☐   There were machine breakdowns during production

    ☐   Assembly of the chairs was manual and very repetitive

    ☐   There was high staff turnover during this period

    ☐   There were minimal stoppages in the production process

    ☐   The design of the chair was changed several times at this early phase

---

24   Using probabilistic budgeting, what is the expected budgeted contribution of the office chairs (to the nearest whole $)?

$ [   ]

---

25   Identify, by clicking on the table below, whether each of the statements regarding cost-plus pricing strategies is true or false.

Marginal cost plus pricing is easier where there is a readily identifiable variable cost	TRUE	FALSE
Full cost plus pricing requires the budgeted level of output to be determined at the outset	TRUE	FALSE
Cost plus pricing is a strategically focused approach as it accounts for external factors	TRUE	FALSE
Cost plus pricing requires that the profit mark-up applied by an organisation is fixed	TRUE	FALSE

(Total = 10 marks)

The following scenario relates to questions 26–30.

The Hi Life Co makes sofas. It has recently received a request from a customer to provide a one-off order of sofas, in excess of normal budgeted production. The order would need to be completed within two weeks.

The following cost estimate has already been prepared:

		Note	$
Direct materials:			
Fabric	200 m² at $17 per m²	1	3,400
Wood	50 m² at $8.20 per m²	2	410
Direct labour:			
Skilled	200 hours at $16 per hour	3	3,200
Semi-skilled	300 hours at $12 per hour	4	3,600
Factory overheads	500 hours at $3 per hour	5	1,500
Total production cost			12,110
General fixed overheads at 10% of total production cost			1,211
Total cost			13,321

Notes:

(1) The fabric is regularly used by Hi Life Co. There are currently 300 m² in inventory, which cost $17 per m². The current purchase price of the fabric is $17.50 per m².

(2) The wood is regularly used by Hi Life Co and usually costs $8.20 per m². However, the company's current supplier's earliest delivery time for the wood is in three weeks' time. An alternative supplier could deliver immediately but they would charge $8.50 per m². Hi Life Co already has 500 m² in inventory but 480 m² of this is needed to complete other existing orders in the next two weeks. The remaining 20 m² is not going to be needed until four weeks' time.

(3) The skilled labour force is employed under permanent contracts of employment under which they must be paid for 40 hours per week's labour, even if their time is idle due to absence of orders. Their rate of pay is $16 per hour, although any overtime is paid at time and a half. In the next two weeks, there is spare capacity of 150 labour hours.

(4) There is no spare capacity for semi-skilled workers. They are currently paid $12 per hour or time and a half for overtime. However, a local agency can provide additional semi-skilled workers for $14 per hour.

(5) Of the $3 per hour factory overheads costs, $1.50 per hour reflects the electricity costs of running the cutting machine which will be used to cut the fabric and wood for the sofas. The other $1.50 per hour reflects the cost of the factory supervisor's salary. The supervisor is paid an annual salary and is also paid $15 per hour for any overtime he works. The supervisor will need to work 20 hours' overtime if this order is accepted.

A quotation now needs to be prepared on a relevant cost basis so that Hi Life Co can offer as competitive a price as possible for the order.

26 What is the cost of the fabric and the wood which should be included in the quotation (to the nearest whole $)?

Fabric

$ [   ]

Wood

$ [   ]

27   What cost should be included in the quotation for skilled labour and semi-skilled labour (to the nearest $)?

Skilled

$ [   ]

Semi-skilled

$ [   ]

28   What is the cost which should be included in the quotation for factory overheads (to the nearest $)?

$ [   ]

29   Which statement correctly describes the treatment of the general fixed overheads when preparing the quotation?

○   The overheads should be excluded because they are a sunk cost

○   The overheads should be excluded because they are not incremental costs

○   The overheads should be included because they relate to production costs

○   The overheads should be included because all expenses should be recovered

30   Which **FOUR** of the following statements about relevant costing are true?

☐   An opportunity cost will always be a relevant cost even if it is a past cost

☐   Fixed costs are always general in nature and are therefore never relevant

☐   Committed costs are never considered to be relevant costs

☐   An opportunity cost represents the cost of the best alternative forgone

☐   Notional costs are always relevant as they make the estimate more realistic

☐   Avoidable costs would be saved if an activity did not happen and so are relevant

☐   Common costs are only relevant if the viability of the whole process is being assessed

☐   Differential costs in a make-or-buy decision are not considered to be relevant

(Total = 30 marks)

Section C – Both questions are compulsory and MUST be attempted

31   Carad Co is an electronics company which makes two types of television – plasma screen TVs and LCD TVs. It operates within a highly competitive market and is constantly under pressure to reduce prices. Carad Co operates a standard costing system and performs a detailed variance analysis of both products on a monthly basis. Extracts from the management information for the month of November are shown below:

		Note
Total number of units made and sold	1,400	1
Material price variance	$28,000 A	2
Total labour variance	$6,050 A	3

Notes

(1)   The budgeted total sales volume for TVs was 1,180 units, consisting of an equal mix of plasma screen TVs and LCD screen TVs. Actual sales volume was 750 plasma TVs and 650 LCD TVs. Standard sales prices are $350 per unit for the plasma TVs and $300 per unit for the LCD TVs. The actual sales prices achieved during November were $330 per unit for plasma TVs and $290 per unit for LCD TVs. The standard contributions for plasma TVs and LCD TVs are $190 and $180 per unit respectively.

(2)   The sole reason for this variance was an increase in the purchase price of one of its key components, X. Each plasma TV made and each LCD TV made requires one unit of component X, for which Carad Co's standard cost is $60 per unit. Due to a shortage of components in the market place, the market price for November went up to $85 per unit for X. Carad Co actually paid $80 per unit for it.

(3)   Each plasma TV uses two standard hours of labour and each LCD TV uses 1.5 standard hours of labour. The standard cost for labour is $14 per hour and this also reflects the actual cost per labour hour for the company's permanent staff in November. However, because of the increase in sales and production volumes in November, the company also had to use additional temporary labour at the higher cost of $18 per hour. The total capacity of Carad's permanent workforce is 2,200 hours production per month, assuming full efficiency. In the month of November, the permanent workforce were wholly efficient, taking exactly two hours to complete each plasma TV and exactly 1.5 hours to produce each LCD TV. The total labour variance therefore relates solely to the temporary workers, who took twice as long as the permanent workers to complete their production.

Required

(a)   Calculate the following for the month of November, showing all workings clearly:

(i)   The sales price variance and sales volume contribution variance   **(4 marks)**

(ii)   The material price planning variance and material price operational variance

(2 marks)

(iii)   The labour rate variance and the labour efficiency variance   **(5 marks)**

(b)   Explain the reasons why Carad Co would be interested in the material price planning variance and the material price operational variance.   **(9 marks)**

(Total = 20 marks)

32 Thatcher International Park (TIP) is a theme park and has for many years been a successful business, which has traded profitably. About three years ago the directors decided to capitalise on their success and reduced the expenditure made on new thrill rides, reduced routine maintenance where possible (deciding instead to repair equipment when it broke down) and made a commitment to regularly increase admission prices. Once an admission price is paid customers can use any of the facilities and rides for free.

These steps increased profits considerably, enabling good dividends to be paid to the owners and bonuses to the directors. The last two years of financial results are shown below.

	20X4	20X5
	$	$
Sales	5,250,000	5,320,000
Less expenses:		
Wages	2,500,000	2,200,000
Maintenance – routine	80,000	70,000
Repairs	260,000	320,000
Directors' salaries	150,000	160,000
Directors' bonuses	15,000	18,000
Other costs (including depreciation)	1,200,000	1,180,000
Net profit	1,045,000	1,372,000
Book value of assets at start of year	13,000,000	12,000,000
Dividend paid	500,000	650,000
Number of visitors	150,000	140,000

TIP operates in a country where the average rate of inflation is around 1% per annum.

Required

(a) Assess the financial performance of TIP using the information given above.

(14 marks)

During the early part of 20X4 TIP employed a newly qualified management accountant. They quickly became concerned about the potential performance of TIP; to investigate their concerns, they started to gather data to measure some non-financial measures of success. The data they have gathered is shown below:

Table 1

	20X4	20X5
Hours lost due to breakdown of rides (see note)	9,000 hours	32,000 hours
Average waiting time per ride	20 minutes	30 minutes

Note. TIP has 50 rides of different types. It is open 360 days of the year for ten hours each day.

Required

(b) Assess the **QUALITY** of the service which TIP provides to its customers using Table 1 and any other relevant data and indicate the **RISKS** it is likely to face if it continues with its current policies. **(6 marks)**

(Total = 20 marks)

Formulae sheet

Regression analysis

$y = a + bx$

$$a = \frac{\Sigma y}{n} - \frac{b\Sigma x}{n}$$

$$b = \frac{n\Sigma xy - \Sigma x\Sigma y}{n\Sigma x^2 - (\Sigma x)^2}$$

$$r = \frac{n\Sigma xy - \Sigma x\Sigma y}{\sqrt{\left(n\Sigma x^2 - (\Sigma x)^2\right)\left(n\Sigma y^2 - (\Sigma y)^2\right)}}$$

Learning curve

$Y = ax^b$

Where   Y   = cumulative average time per unit to produce x units
                 a   = the time taken for the first unit of output
                 x   = the cumulative number of units produced
                 b   = the index of learning (log LR/log2)
                 LR = the learning rate as a decimal

Demand curve

P $= a - bQ$

$$b = \frac{\text{change in price}}{\text{change in quantity}}$$

a   = price when Q = 0

MR $= a - 2bQ$

Answers

DO NOT TURN THIS PAGE UNTIL YOU HAVE
COMPLETED THE MOCK EXAM

A PLAN OF ATTACK

Managing your nerves

As you turn the pages to start this mock exam a number of thoughts are likely to cross your mind. At best, examinations cause anxiety so it is important to stay focused on your task for the next three hours! Developing an awareness of what is going on emotionally within you may help you manage your nerves. Remember, you are unlikely to banish the flow of adrenaline, but the key is to harness it to help you work steadily and quickly through your answers.

Working through this mock exam will help you develop the exam stamina you will need to keep going for three hours.

Managing your time

Planning and time management are two of the key skills which complement the technical knowledge you need to succeed. To keep yourself on time, do not be afraid to jot down your target completion times for each question, perhaps next to the title of the question. As all the questions are **compulsory**, you do not have to spend time wondering which question to answer!

Doing the exam

Actually doing the exam is a personal experience. There is not a single **right way**. As long as you submit complete answers to all questions after the three hours are up, then your approach obviously works.

Looking through the exam

Section A has 15 MCQs. This is the section of the exam where ACCA examining team can test knowledge across the breadth of the syllabus. Make sure you read these questions carefully. The distractors are designed to present plausible, but incorrect, answers. Don't let them mislead you. If you really have no idea – guess. You may even be right.

Section B has three questions, each with a scenario and five objective test questions.

Section C has two longer questions:

- Question 31 requires you to calculate sales variances. There are plenty of easy marks in the question. If you get stuck on the details of which numbers to use where, make an attempt at something sensible and move on.

- Question 32 looks at performance measurement. This is a classic performance measurement question with a contrast between the picture painted by financial indicators and that given by non-financial indicators. Start with the ratio calculations and then make sure that you fully analyse what the numbers are telling you.

Allocating your time

BPP's advice is to always allocate your time **according to the marks for the question**. However, **use common sense**. If you're doing a question but haven't a clue how to do part (b), you might be better off re-allocating your time and getting more marks on another question, where you can add something you didn't have time for earlier on. Make sure you leave time to recheck the MCQs and make sure you have answered them all.

Section A

1   The correct answer is: $46.25

Set-up costs per production run = $140,000/28 = $5,000
Cost per inspection = $80,000/8 = $10,000
Other overhead costs per labour hour = $96,000/48,000 = $2

Overhead costs of product D:

	$
Set-up costs (15 × $5,000)	75,000
Inspection costs (3 × $10,000)	30,000
Other overheads (40,000 × $2)	80,000
	185,000

Overhead cost per unit = $185,000/4,000 units = $46.25

2   The correct answer is: $2,346

If the first quarter of 20X5 is quarter 13, the second quarter of 20X7 is quarter 22.
The forecasted sales revenue using the trend line is 2,000 + (25 × 22) = 2,550.
The seasonal variation for quarter 2 is -8%, so the seasonally adjusted sales revenue
forecast is 2,550 × (1 – 8%) = $2,346.

3   The correct answer is: 18,636 units

The number of units required to make a target profit = (fixed costs + target
profit)/contribution per unit of P1.

Fixed costs = ($1.20 × 10,000) + ($1.00 × 12,500) – $2,500 = $22,000

Contribution per unit of P = $3.20 + $1.20 = $4.40

($22,000 + $60,000)/$4.40 = 18,636 units

4   The correct answers are: 'The majority of environmental costs are already captured within
a typical organisation's accounting system. The difficulty lies in identifying them' and
'Environmental life cycle costing enables environmental costs from the design stage of the
product right through to decommissioning at the end of its life to be considered'

Most organisations do collect data about environmental costs but find it difficult to split
them out and categorise them effectively.

Life-cycle costing does allow the organisation to collect information about a product's
environmental costs throughout its life cycle.

The technique which divides material flows into three categories is material flow cost
accounting, not input/output analysis.

ABC does categorise some costs as environment-driven costs, however, these are costs
which are normally hidden within total overheads in a conventional costing system. It is
environment-related costs which can be allocated directly to a cost centre.

5   The correct answer is: The total mix variance was favourable and the total yield variance
was adverse

Mix variance:

Material	AQSM	AQAM	Difference litres	Standard cost $/litre	Variance $
A	800	900	100 A	20	2,000 A
B	1,200	1,100	100 F	25	2,500 F
	2,000	2,000			500 F

Yield variance:

Material	SQSM	AQSM	Difference litres	Standard cost $/litre	Variance $
A	779	800	21 A	20	420 A
B	1,168	1,200	32 A	25	800 A
	(W1) 1,947	2,000			1,220 A

(W1) 1,850 litres of output should use 1,947 litres of input (1,850/0.95)

6   The correct answers are:

Budgeting approach	
Uses adaptive management processes	Beyond budgeting
Builds in previous problems and inefficiencies	Incremental budgeting
Focuses on controlling the causes of costs	Activity-based budgeting
Always extends the one year into the future	Rolling budgeting
Recognises different cost behaviour patterns	Flexible budgeting
Focuses employees on avoiding wasteful expenditure	Zero-based budgeting

Beyond budgeting attempts to move away from conforming to a rigid annual budget and uses adaptive processes to encourage management to be responsive to current situations.

An incremental budget builds from the previous year's figures and so any inefficiencies will be carried forward.

Activity-based budgeting is based on the principles of activity-based costing and will attempt to identify the drivers of costs in order to formulate a budget.

Rolling budgeting are budgets which are continuously updated throughout the year by adding a new budget period once the most recent budget period has ended. This means that the budget is always extended one year into the future and so forces managers to reassess plans more regularly.

Flexible budgets are designed to show the changes in financial figures based on different activity levels and so will recognise different cost behaviour patterns.

Zero-based budgeting starts from scratch with each item justified for its inclusion in the budget and so should encourage the identification of waste and non-value adding activities.

7   The correct answer is: Undertake the minor upgrade

EV for major upgrade = (0.80 × $11m) + (0.2 × $7.5m) = $10.3m

EV for minor upgrade = (0.70 × $9m) + (0.3 × $6m) = $8.1m

Decision

Shutdown and sell $5.75m
Major upgrade (10.3m – 4.5m) $5.8m
Minor upgrade ($8.1m – $2m) $6.1m

As the minor upgrade has the highest expected return that should be the option chosen.

8   The correct answer is:

Ranking	
1st	D
2nd	A
3rd	C
4th	B

In a single limiting factor situation products should be ranked based on their contribution per unit of limiting factor, which in this case is labour hours.

Product	A	B	C	D
Contribution per unit ($)	46	52	21	60
Number of labour hours required per unit	6	8	3	2
Contribution per labour hour ($)	7.67	6.50	7.00	30.00
Ranking	2nd	4th	3rd	1st

9   The correct answer is:

Performance targets	
Efficiency	Increasing number of chargeable hours
Effectiveness	Obtaining a score of 4.7 or above on customer satisfaction
Economy	Cutting departamental expenditure by 5%

Target 1 is measuring the rate of work handled by staff which is an efficiency measure. Target 2 is assessing output, so is a measure of effectiveness. Target 3 is a financial measure and so assesses economy factors.

10   The correct answer is:

Management Information System
Summaries internal data into periodic reports

Transaction Processing System
Facilitates the immediate processing of data

Executive Information System
Utilises dashboard facilities and interactive graphics

Enterprise Resource Planning System
Can be set up with extranet links to customers and suppliers

Transaction processing systems facilitate the immediate processing of data.

Management information systems summarise data from TPS into periodic reports for management to use for decision-making.

Executive information systems draw data from the MIS and support senior managers to make strategic decisions. They usually have dashboard and interactive graphics so that the big picture can be seen.

Enterprise resource planning systems are software packages that integrate all the key processes in an organisation and so this permits data to be shared more easily between departments. It can also have extranet links set up with customers and suppliers.

11   The correct answers are: 'Use of bar coding and scanners' and 'Use of chip readers to read data from chips on customers' bank cards when paying for goods'.

Direct data capture is a type of data input in which there is no data entry but instead uses electronic means. Therefore the use of bar coding and scanners and the use of chip readers are examples of direct data capture costs.

Time spent by the payroll department processing personnel costs is an example of process costs.

The sending of emails to staff regarding matters that are not pertinent to them is classed as an inefficient use of information cost.

12   The correct answers are: 'It can be applied not only to products but also to an organisation's customers' and 'Often between 70% to 90% of costs are determined early in the product life cycle'

Customer life-cycle costing can be used by organisations.

It has been reported that the majority of a product's costs are determined early on, ie at the design phase.

Life-cycle costing does not include any opportunity costs associated with production.

The growth phase is characterised by a rapid increase in demand.

13   The correct answer is: 1.33

Return per factory hour = ($130 – $50)/4 hours = $20
Factory costs per hour = ($20 + $40)/4 = $15
TPAR = $20/$15 = 1.33

14   The correct answer is: Decrease of $78,000

Increase in variable costs per unit from buying in ($140 – $100) =$40
Therefore total increase in variable costs (2,200 units × $40) = $88,000
Less the specific fixed costs saved if A is shut down = ($10,000)
Decrease in profit = $78,000

15   The correct answers are:

The determinants of performance are quality, innovation, resource utilisation and competitiveness		FALSE
Standards are targets for performance and should be fair, achievable and controllable		FALSE
Rewards encourage staff to work towards the standards and should be clear, motivating and controllable	TRUE	
It is a performance measurement framework suitable for service organisations	TRUE	

The determinants of performance are quality, innovation, resource utilisation and flexibility. Competitiveness is a result of the determinants.

Standards should be fair, achievable and staff should have ownership of them. Controllability is a feature of the rewards block.

Rewards should be clear, motivating and controllable, so this is correct.

It is a framework designed to attempt to overcome the problems associated with performance management in service companies.

Section B

16   The correct answer is: 7,200 cuts or 4,800 treatments

Total salon hours = 8 × 6 × 50 = 2,400 each year.

There are three senior stylists, therefore total hours available = 7,200.

Based on the time taken for each activity, they can perform 7,200 cuts (7,200 hours/1 hour per cut) or 4,800 treatments (7,200 hours/1.5 hours per treatment).

17   The correct answers are: Cuts 1.37, Treatments 1.58

Cuts

Return per hour = (Selling price − materials)/time taken on the bottleneck = (60 − 1.50)/1 = 58.50

TPAR = Return per hour/cost per hour = 58.50/42.56 = 1.37 (to two decimal places)

Treatments

Return per hour = (Selling price − materials)/time taken on the bottleneck = (110 − 8.90)/1.5 = 67.40

TPAR = Return per hour/cost per hour = 67.40/42.56 = 1.58 (to two decimal places)

18   The correct answers are:

Identify ways to reduce the material costs for the services

Improve the control of the salon's total operating expenses

Apply an increase to the selling price of the services

The factors which are included in the TPAR are selling price, material costs, operating expenses and bottleneck time. Increasing the selling price and reducing costs will improve the TPAR.

Increasing the time which each service takes on the bottleneck (the senior stylists' time) will only reduce the number of services they can provide, so this will not improve throughput.

Throughput accounting does not advocate the building of inventory as it is often used in a just-in-time environment and there is no point increasing the activity prior to the bottleneck as it will just create a build-up of work-in-progress. Neither of these will improve the rate of throughput through the process.

19   The correct answer is: The senior stylists' time will be a bottleneck for treatments only

The existing capacity for each activity is:

	Cut	Treatment
Assistants	48,000	16,000
Senior stylists	7,200	4,800
Junior stylists	8,000	9,600

If another senior stylist is employed, this will mean that their available hours will be (4 × 2,400) = 9,600.

This will give them capacity to now do 9,600 cuts (9,600 hours/1 hour per cut) and 6,400 treatments (9,600 hours/1.5 hours per treatment).

As a result, the senior stylists will still be the bottleneck activity for treatments but for cuts the bottleneck will now be the junior stylists as they can only do 8,000 cuts compared to the senior stylists of 9,600.

20   The correct answer is: (1) and (2)

The theory of constraints is focused on identifying restrictions in a process and how to manage that restriction (commonly termed a bottleneck).

It is based on the concept of managing throughput, operating expenses and inventory.

It does use a series of focusing steps but it is not complete once the bottleneck has been overcome. In fact it is an ongoing process of improvement, as once the bottleneck has been elevated it is probable that another bottleneck will appear and the process will continue.

It cannot be applied to all limiting factors as some, particularly those external to the organisation, may be out of the organisation's control.

21   The correct answer is: $45.65

Learning curve formula = $y = ax^b$

Cumulative average time per unit for eight units: $Y = 12 \times 8^{-.415} = 5.0628948$ hours.

Therefore cumulative total time for eight units = 40.503158 hours.

Cumulative average time per unit for 7 units: $Y = 12 \times 7^{-.415} = 5.3513771$ hours.

Therefore cumulative total time for 7 units = 37.45964 hours.

Therefore incremental time for 8th unit = 40.503158 hours – 37.45964 hours = 3.043518 hours.

Total labour cost for 8th unit = 3.043518 × $15 = $45.65277

22   The correct answer is: 70.00%

Actual learning rate

Cumulative number of seats produced	Cumulative total hours	Cumulative average hours per unit
1	12.5	12.5
2	?	$12.5 \times r$
4	?	$12.5 \times r^2$
8	34.3	$12.5 \times r^3$

Using algebra: $34.3 = 8 \times (12.5 \times r^3)$

$4.2875 = (12.5 \times r^3)$

$0.343 = r^3$

$r = 0.70$

Therefore the learning rate was 70.00%.

23   The correct answers are:

- Staffing levels were stable during the first manufacturing phase
- Assembly of the chairs was manual and very repetitive
- There were minimal stoppages in the production process
- An 80% learning rate means that the learning was faster than expected.

Factors which are present for a learning curve to take effect are a highly manual and repetitive process (so staff can become quicker the more they perform the same series of tasks), no stoppages to production (so the learning rate will not be lost whilst staff are idle) and a stable workforce (so the learning process does not have to keep restarting).

If there is high staff turnover, stoppages in production and continual design changes, then the learning rate will not be effective and should be slower.

24 The correct answer is: $362,600

As the variable cost per unit is changing depending on the production level, contribution for each level needs to be calculated and then the probabilities applied to the outcomes.

Demand (units)	Contribution (per unit)	Total contribution	Probability	Expected budgeted contribution
10,000	17.00	170,000	0.3	51,000
22,000	17.00	374,000	0.5	187,000
35,000	17.80	623,000	0.2	124,600
				362,600

25 The correct answers are:

Marginal cost-plus pricing is easier where there is a readily identifiable variable cost	**TRUE**	
Full cost-plus pricing requires the budgeted level of output to be determined at the outset	**TRUE**	
Cost-plus pricing is a strategically focused approach as it accounts for external factors		**FALSE**
Cost-plus pricing requires that the profit mark-up applied by an organisation is fixed		**FALSE**

As marginal costing is based on variable costs, it is easier when a readily identifiable variable cost has been established.

The budgeted volume of output does need to be determined for full cost-plus pricing as it would be used to calculate the overhead absorption rate for the calculation of the full cost per unit.

Cost-plus pricing is internally focused and a drawback of the technique is that it fails to consider external influences, like competitor pricing strategies.

The mark-up percentage does not have to be fixed; it can vary and be adjusted to reflect market conditions.

26 The correct answer is: Fabric $3,500 Wood $419

Fabric is in regular use, so the replacement cost is the relevant cost (200 m² × $17.50) = $3,500.

30 m² of wood will have to be ordered in from the alternative supplier but the remaining 20 m² which is in inventory and not needed for other work can be used and then replaced by an order from the usual supplier (30 m² × $8.50) + (20 m² × $8.20) = $419.

27 The correct answer is: Skilled $1,200 Semi-skilled $4,200

Skilled labour:

There is no cost for the first 150 hours as there is spare capacity. The remaining 50 hours required will be paid at time and a half, which is $16 × 1.5 = $24.

50 hours × $24 = $1,200

Semi-skilled labour:

There is no spare capacity, so the company will either need to pay overtime or hire in additional staff. The cost of paying overtime would be $18 per hour, so it would be cheaper to hire in the additional staff for $14 per hour.

300 hours × $14 = $4,200

28   The correct answer is: $1,050

The electricity costs are incremental as the machine will be used more to produce the new order (500 hours × $1.50) = $750.

The supervisor's salary is not relevant as it is paid anyway; however, the overtime is relevant (20 hours × $15) = $300.

29   The correct answer is: The overheads should be excluded because they are not incremental costs

The general fixed overheads should be excluded as they are not incremental, ie they are not arising specifically as a result of this order. They are not sunk as they are not past costs. This is a common misconception.

30   The correct answers are:

Committed costs are never considered to be relevant costs.

An opportunity cost represents the cost of the best alternative forgone.

Avoidable costs would be saved if an activity did not happen and so are relevant.

Common costs are only relevant if the viability of the whole process is being assessed.

An opportunity cost does represent the cost of the best alternative forgone, however, if it is an historic (past) cost, it would not be relevant.

Fixed costs can be incremental to a decision and in those circumstances would be relevant.

Committed costs are costs the organisation has already agreed to and can no longer influence and so are not relevant.

Notional costs are used to make cost estimates more realistic; however, they are not real cash flows and are not considered to be relevant.

Avoidable costs are saved if an activity is not undertaken and if this occurs as a result of the decision, then they are relevant.

Common costs are relevant if the whole process is being evaluated; however, they are not relevant to a further processing decision.

Differential costs are relevant in a make or buy decision as the organisation is trying to choose between two options.

Section C

31

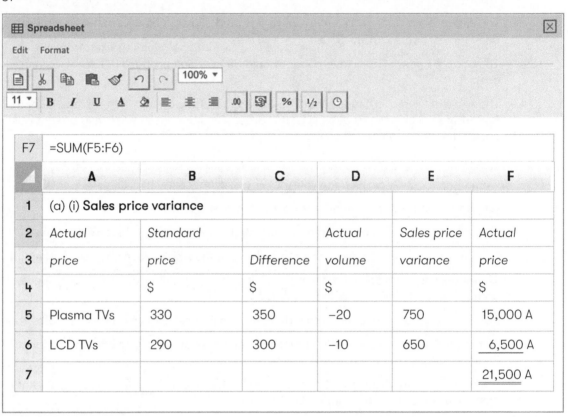

F7	=SUM(F5:F6)					
	A	**B**	**C**	**D**	**E**	**F**
1	(a) (i) **Sales price variance**					
2	*Actual*	*Standard*		*Actual*	*Sales price*	*Actual*
3	*price*	*price*	*Difference*	*volume*	*variance*	*price*
4		$	$	$		$
5	Plasma TVs	330	350	−20	750	15,000 A
6	LCD TVs	290	300	−10	650	6,500 A
7						21,500 A

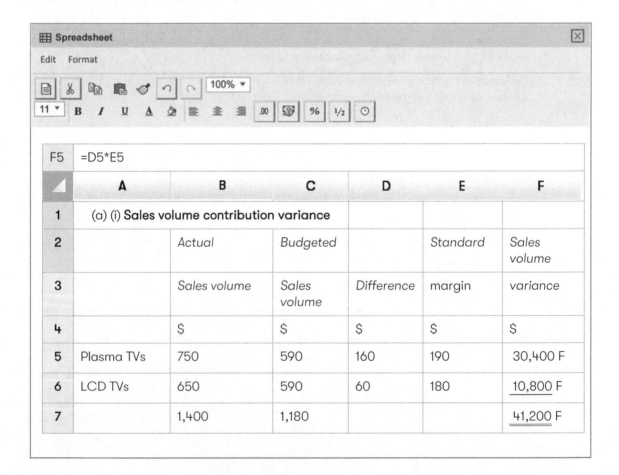

F5	=D5*E5					
	A	**B**	**C**	**D**	**E**	**F**
1	(a) (i) **Sales volume contribution variance**					
2		*Actual*	*Budgeted*		*Standard*	*Sales volume*
3		*Sales volume*	*Sales volume*	*Difference*	*margin*	*variance*
4		$	$	$	$	$
5	Plasma TVs	750	590	160	190	30,400 F
6	LCD TVs	650	590	60	180	10,800 F
7		1,400	1,180			41,200 F

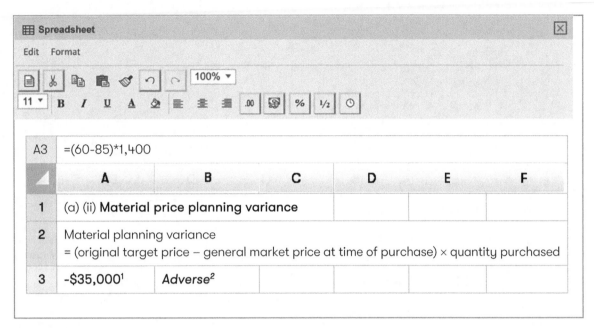

Formulae

1. =(60-85)*1,400

2. =IF(A3>0,"Favourable","Adverse")

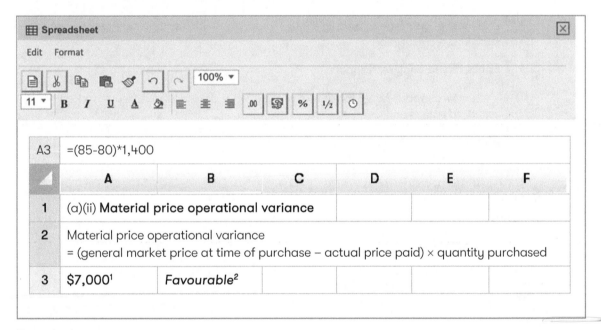

Formulae

1. =(85-80)*1,400

2. =IF(A3>0,"Favourable","Adverse")

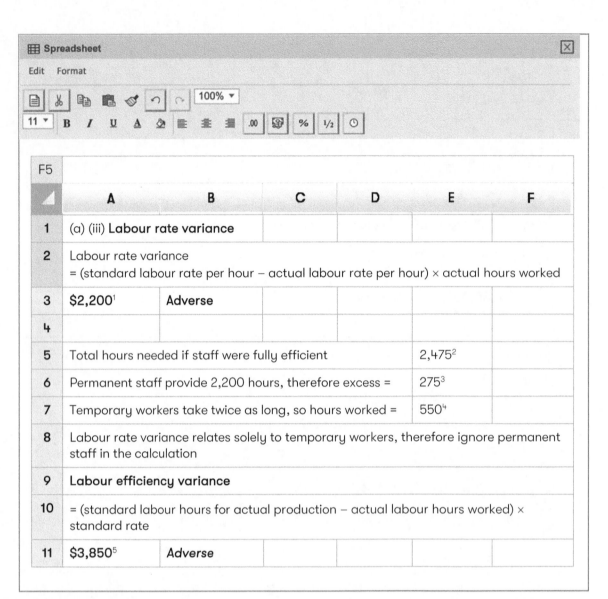

Spreadsheet

Edit Format

100% ▾

11 ▾

F5

	A	B	C	D	E	F
1	(a) (iii) **Labour rate variance**					
2	Labour rate variance = (standard labour rate per hour – actual labour rate per hour) × actual hours worked					
3	$2,200[1]	Adverse				
4						
5	Total hours needed if staff were fully efficient				2,475[2]	
6	Permanent staff provide 2,200 hours, therefore excess =				275[3]	
7	Temporary workers take twice as long, so hours worked =				550[4]	
8	Labour rate variance relates solely to temporary workers, therefore ignore permanent staff in the calculation					
9	**Labour efficiency variance**					
10	= (standard labour hours for actual production – actual labour hours worked) × standard rate					
11	$3,850[5]	Adverse				

Formulae:

1. =(14-18)*E7

2. =(750*2)+(650*1.5)

3. =E5-2,200

4. =E6*2

5. =(E6-E7)*14

(b) **Explanation of planning and operational variances**

Before the material price planning and operational variances were calculated, the only information available as regards material purchasing was that there was an adverse material price variance of $28,000. The purchasing department will be assessed on the basis of this variance, yet, on its own, it is not a reliable indicator of the purchasing department's efficiency. The reason it is not a reliable indicator is because market conditions can change, leading to an increase in price, and this change in market conditions is not within the control of the purchasing department.

By analysing the materials price variance further and breaking it down into its two components – planning and operational – the variance actually becomes a more useful assessment tool. The planning variance represents the uncontrollable element and the operational variance represents the controllable element.

The planning variance is really useful for providing feedback on just how skilled management is in estimating future prices. This can be very easy in some businesses and very difficult in others. Giving this detail could help to improve planning and standard setting in the future, as management will be increasingly aware of factors which could create volatility in their forecasts.

The operational variance is more meaningful in that it measures the purchasing department's efficiency given the market conditions which prevailed at the time. As can be seen in Carad, the material price operational variance is favourable which demonstrates that the purchasing department managed to acquire the component which was in short supply at a better price than expected. Without this breakdown in the variance, the purchasing department could have been held accountable for the overall adverse variance which was not indicative of their actual performance. This is then a fairer method of assessing performance and will, in turn, stop staff from becoming demotivated.

32

(a) TIP's financial performance can be assessed in a number of ways:

Sales growth

Sales are up about 1.3% (W1) which is a little above the rate of inflation and therefore a move in the right direction. However, with average admission prices jumping about 8.6% (W2) and numbers of visitors falling, there are clearly problems. Large increases in admission prices reduce the value proposition for the customer, it is unlikely that the rate of increase is sustainable or even justifiable. Indeed with volumes falling (down by 6.7% (W6)), it appears that some customers are being put off and price could be one of the reasons.

Maintenance and repairs

There appears to be a continuing drift away from routine maintenance with management preferring to repair equipment as required. This does not appear to be saving any money as the combined cost of maintenance and repair is higher in 20X5 than in 20X4 (possible risks are dealt with in part (b)).

BPP
LEARNING
MEDIA

Directors' pay

Absolute salary levels are up 6.7% (W3), well above the modest inflation rate. It appears that the shareholders are happy with the financial performance of the business and are prepared to reward the directors accordingly. Bonus levels are also well up. It may be that the directors have some form of profit related pay scheme and are being rewarded for the improved profit performance. The directors are likely to be very pleased with the increases to pay.

Wages

Wages are down by 12% (W5). This may partly reflect the loss of customers (down by 6.7% (W6)) if it is assumed that at least part of the wages cost is variable. It could also be that the directors are reducing staff levels beyond the fall in the level of customers to enhance short-term profit and personal bonus. Customer service and indeed safety could be compromised here.

Net profit

Net profit is up a huge 31.3% (W7) and most shareholders would be pleased with that. Net profit is a very traditional measure of performance and most would say this was a sign of good performance.

Return on assets

The profitability can be measured relative to the asset base which is being used to generate it. This is sometimes referred to as ROI or return on investment. The return on assets is up considerably to 11.4% from 8% (W8). This is partly due to the significant rise in profit and partly due to the fall in asset value. We are told that TIP has cut back on new development, so the fall in asset value is probably due to depreciation being charged with little being spent during the year on assets. In this regard it is inevitable that return on assets is up but it is more questionable whether this is a good performance. A theme park (and thrill rides in particular) must be updated to keep customers coming back. The directors of TIP are risking the future of the park.

(b)   Quality provision

Reliability of the rides

The hours lost has increased significantly. Equally the percentage of capacity lost due to breakdowns is now approaching 17.8% (W9). This would appear to be a very high number of hours lost. This would surely increase the risk that customers are disappointed being unable to ride. Given the fixed admission price system, this is bound to irritate some customers as they have effectively already paid to ride.

Average queuing time

Queuing will be seen by customers as dead time. They may see some waiting as inevitable and hence acceptable. However, TIP should be careful to maintain waiting times at a minimum. An increase of ten minutes (or 50%) is likely to be noticeable by customers and is unlikely to enhance the quality of the TIP experience for them. The increase in waiting times is probably due to the high number of hours lost due to breakdown with customers being forced to queue for a fewer number of ride options.

Safety

The clear reduction in maintenance could easily damage the safety record of the park and is an obvious quality issue.

Risks

If TIP continues with current policies, then they will expose themselves to the following risks:

- The lack of routine maintenance could easily lead to an accident or injury to a customer. This could lead to compensation being paid or reputational damage.

- Increased competition. The continuous raising of admission prices increases the likelihood of a new competitor entering the market (although there are significant barriers to entry in this market, eg capital cost, land and so on).

- Loss of customers. The value for money which customers see when coming to TIP is clearly reducing (higher prices, less reliability of rides and longer queues). Regardless of the existence of competition, customers could simply choose not to come, substituting another leisure activity instead.

- Profit fall. In the end if customers' numbers fall, then so will profit. The shareholders, although well rewarded at the moment, could suffer a loss of dividend. Directors' job security could then be threatened.

Workings

1   Sales growth is $5,320,000/$5,250,000 = 1.01333 or 1.3%.

2   Average admission prices were:

   20X4: $5,250,000/150,000   = $35 per person
   20X5: $5,320,000/140,000   = $38 per person
   An increase of $38/$35   = 1.0857 or 8.57%.

3   Directors' pay up by $160,000/$150,000 = 1.0667 or 6.7%.

4   Directors' bonuses levels up from $15,000/$150,000 or 10% to $18,000/$160,000 or 12.5% of turnover. This is an increase of 3/15 or 20%.

5   Wages are down by (1 − $2,200,000/$2,500,000) or 12%.

6   Loss of customers is (1 − 140,000/150,000) or 6.7%.

7   Profits up by $1,372,000/$1,045,000 = 1.3129 or 31.3%.

8   Return on assets:

   20X4: $1,045,000/$13,000,000 = 1.0803 or 8.03%
   20X5: $1,372,000/$12,000,000 = 1.114 or 11.4%

9   Capacity of rides in hours is 360 days × 50 rides × 10 hours per day = 180,000.

   20X4 lost capacity is 9,000/180,000 = 0.05 or 5%.
   20X5 lost capacity is 32,000/180,000 = 0.177 or 17.8%.

ACCA

Performance Management

Mock Exam 3

(December 2016 Exam)

Question Paper: 3 hours
This paper is divided into three sections:
Section A – ALL FIFTEEN questions are compulsory and MUST be attempted
Section B – ALL FIFTEEN questions are compulsory and MUST be attempted
Section C – Both questions are compulsory and MUST be attempted

DO NOT OPEN THIS PAPER UNTIL YOU ARE READY TO START
UNDER EXAMINATION CONDITIONS

Section A – ALL FIFTEEN questions are compulsory and MUST be attempted

Each question is worth two marks.

1   A company makes a single product with the following data:

	$	$
Selling price		25
Material	5	
Labour	7	
Variable overhead	3	
Fixed overhead	4	
		(19)
Profit per unit		6

Budgeted output is 30,000 units.

In relation to this data, which of the following statements is correct?

O   The margin of safety is 40%

O   The contribution to sales ratio is 24%

O   The volume of sales needed to make a profit of $270,000 is 45,000 units

O   If budgeted sales increase to 40,000 units, budgeted profit will increase by $100,000

---

2   Which **TWO** of the following statements regarding zero based budgeting are correct?

☐   It is best applied to support expenses rather than to direct costs

☐   It can link strategic goals to specific functional areas

☐   It carries forward inefficiencies from previous budget periods

☐   It is consistent with a top-down budgeting approach

---

3   A manufacturing company decides which of three mutually exclusive products to make in its factory on the basis of maximising the company's throughput accounting ratio.

Current data for the three products is shown in the following table:

	Product X	Product Y	Product Z
Selling price per unit	$60	$40	$20
Direct material cost per unit	$40	$10	$16
Machine hours per unit	10	20	2.5

Total factory costs (excluding direct materials) are $150,000. The company cannot make enough of any of the products to satisfy external demand entirely as machine hours are restricted.

Which of the following actions would improve the company's existing throughput accounting ratio?

O   Increase the selling price of product Z by 10%

O   Increase the selling price of product Y by 10%

O   Reduce the material cost of product Z by 5%

O   Reduce the material cost of product Y by 5%

BPP
LEARNING
MEDIA

4   Which of the following statements about big data is/are correct?

   (1)   Big data is often out of date before it can be used.

   (2)   Big data is only relevant for short term decisions.

   (3)   Big data can be used to predict consumer preferences?

   O   (1), (2) and (3)

   O   (1) and (2) only

   O   (3) only

   O   (2) and (3) only

---

5   Perrin Co has two divisions, A and B.

   Division A has limited skilled labour and is operating at full capacity making product Y. It has been asked to supply a different product, X, to division B. Division B currently sources this product externally for $700 per unit.

   The same grade of materials and labour is used in both products. The cost cards for each product are shown below:

Product	Y	X
	($)/unit	($)/unit
Selling price	600	–
Direct materials ($50 per kg)	200	150
Direct labour ($20 per hour)	80	120
Apportioned fixed overheads ($15 per hour)	60	90

   Using an opportunity cost approach to transfer pricing, what is the minimum transfer price?

   Picklist:

   $270
   $750
   $590
   $840

---

6   Jorioz Co makes joint products X and Y. $120,000 joint processing costs are incurred.

   At the split-off point, 10,000 units of X and 9,000 units of Y are produced, with selling prices of $1.20 for X and $1.50 for Y.

   The units of X could be processed further to make 8,000 units of product Z. The extra costs incurred in this process would be fixed costs of $1,600 and variable costs of $0.50 per unit of input.

   The selling price of Z would be $2.25.

   What would be the outcome if product X is further processed?

   O $600 loss

   O $400 gain

   O $3,900 gain

   O $1,600 loss

---

7   A company has produced the following information for a product it is about to launch:

	20X4	20X5	20X6
Units	2,000	5,000	7,000
Variable production cost per unit	$2.30	$1.80	$1.20
Fixed production costs	$3,000	$3,500	$4,000
Variable selling cost per unit	$0.50	$0.40	$0.40
Fixed selling costs	$1,500	$1,600	$1,600
Administrative costs	$700	$700	$700

What is the life cycle cost per unit (to two decimal places)?

$ [   ]

8   A company manufactures a specific clinical machine used in hospitals. The company holds a 2% share of the market and the total market demand has been constant at 250,000 machines for the last few years. The budgeted selling price for each machine is $10,000 and standard contribution is equivalent to 10% of the budgeted selling price.

An initial performance review of the company's actual results showed a sales volume of 5,600 machines had been achieved. The total market demand for the machines, though, had risen to 300,000 units.

What is the market share variance for the clinical machines?

[▼]

Picklist:

$200,000 favourable
$400,000 adverse
$600,000 favourable
$1,000,000 adverse

9   VC Co is a firm of opticians. It provides a range of services to the public, such as eye tests and contact lens consultations, and has a separate dispensary selling glasses and contact lenses. Patients book appointments with an optician in advance.

A standard appointment is 30 minutes long, during which an optician will assess the patient's specific requirements and provide them with the eye care services they need. After the appointment, patients are offered the chance to buy contact lenses or glasses from the dispensary.

Which of the following describes a characteristic of the services provided by an optician at VC Co during a standard appointment?

O   Tangible

O   Homogeneous

O   Non-perishable

O   Simultaneous

10   Which of the following methods would be **LEAST** effective in ensuring the security of confidential information?

     ◯   Monitoring emails

     ◯   Encryption of files

     ◯   Dial back facility

     ◯   Universal passwords

---

11   A company which makes two products, Alpha and Zeta, uses activity-based costing to absorb its overheads. It has recently identified a new overhead cost pool for inspection costs and has decided that the cost driver is the number of inspections.

The following information has been provided:

Total inspection costs $250,000

	Alpha	Zeta
Production volume (units)	2,500	8,000
Machine hours per unit	1	1.5
Units per batch	500	1,000
Inspections per batch	4	1

What is the inspection cost per unit for product Alpha (to two decimal places)?

$ [＿＿＿＿＿＿＿＿＿＿]

---

12   Indicate, by clicking on the relevant boxes in the table below, whether each of the following statements regarding the existence of multiple objectives in not-for-profit organisations is correct or incorrect.

They ensure goal congruence between stakeholders	**CORRECT**	**INCORRECT**
Compromise between objectives can be problematic	**CORRECT**	**INCORRECT**

---

13   Flow cost accounting is a technique which can be used to account for environmental costs. Inputs and outputs are measured through each individual process of production.

Which of the following is **NOT** a category used within flow cost accounting?

     ◯   Material flows

     ◯   System flows

     ◯   Delivery and disposal flows

     ◯   Waste flows

---

14 A company has used expected values to evaluate a one-off project. The expected value calculation assumed two possible profit outcomes which were assigned probabilities of 0.4 and 0.6.

Which of the following statements about this approach are correct?

(1) The expected value profit is the profit which has the highest probability of being achieved

(2) The expected value gives no indication of the dispersion of the possible outcomes

(3) Expected values are relatively insensitive to assumptions about probability

(4) The expected value may not correspond to any of the actual possible outcomes

- ○ 2 and 4 only
- ○ 2, 3 and 4
- ○ 1, 2 and 3
- ○ 3 and 4 only

---

15 In an investment centre, a divisional manager has autonomy over negotiating all selling prices, has local functions set up for payables, inventory and cash management, and uses a full debt factoring service.

Indicate, by clicking on the relevant boxes in the table below, which of the following the divisional manager should be held accountable for.

The generation of revenues	ACCOUNTABLE	NOT ACCOUNTABLE
Transfer prices	ACCOUNTABLE	NOT ACCOUNTABLE
Management of working capital	ACCOUNTABLE	NOT ACCOUNTABLE
Apportioned head office costs	ACCOUNTABLE	NOT ACCOUNTABLE

(Total = 30 marks)

Section B – ALL FIFTEEN questions are compulsory and MUST be attempted

Each question is worth two marks.

The following scenario relates to questions 16–20.

Hare Events is a company which specialises in organising sporting events in major cities across Teeland. It has approached the local council of Edglas, a large city in the north of Teeland, to request permission to host a running festival which will include both a full marathon and a half marathon race.

Based on the prices it charges for entry to similar events in other locations, Hare Events has decided on an entry fee of $55 for the full marathon and $30 for the half marathon. It expects that the maximum entries will be 20,000 for the full marathon and 14,000 for the half marathon.

Hare Events has done a full assessment of the likely costs involved. Each runner will receive a race pack on completion of the race, which will include a medal, t-shirt, water and chocolate. Water stations will need to be available at every five-kilometre (km) point along the race route, stocked with sufficient supplies of water, sports drinks and gels. These costs are considered to be variable as they depend on the number of race entries.

Hare Events will also incur the following fixed costs. It will need to pay a fixed fee to the Edglas council for permits, road closures and support from the local police and medical services. A full risk assessment needs to be undertaken for insurance purposes. A marketing campaign is planned via advertising on running websites, in fitness magazines and at other events Hare Events is organising in Teeland, and the company which Hare Events usually employs to do the race photography has been approached.

The details of these costs are shown below:

	Full marathon	Half marathon
	$	$
Race packs	15.80	10.80
Water stations	2.40	1.20

	$
Council fees	300,000
Risk assessment and insurance	50,000
Marketing	30,000
Photography	5,000

16 If Hare Events decides to host only the full marathon race, what is the margin of safety?

  ○ 35.0%

  ○ 47.7%

  ○ 52.3%

  ○ 65.0%

17 Assuming that the race entries are sold in a constant sales mix based on the expected race entry numbers, what is the sales revenue Hare Events needs to achieve in order to break even (to the nearest $'000)?

  ○ $385,000

  ○ $575,000

  ○ $592,000

  ○ $597,000

18   Hare Events wishes to achieve a minimum total profit of $500,000 from the running festival.

      What are the number of entries Hare Events will have to sell for each race in order to achieve this level of profit, assuming a constant sales mix based on the expected race entry numbers applies?

      Work to the nearest whole number.

      O   Full marathon: 17,915 entries and half marathon: 12,540 entries

      O   Full marathon: 14,562 entries and half marathon: 18,688 entries

      O   Full marathon: 20,000 entries and half marathon: 8,278 entries

      O   Full marathon: 9,500 entries and half marathon: 6,650 entries

---

19   Hare Events is also considering including a 10 km race during the running festival. It expects the race will have an entry fee of $20 per competitor and variable costs of $8 per competitor. Fixed costs associated with this race will be $48,000.

      If the selling price per competitor, the variable cost per competitor and the total fixed costs for this 10 km race all increase by 10%, which of the following statements will be true?

      O   Break-even volume will increase by 10% and break-even revenue will increase by 10%

      O   Break-even volume will remain unchanged but break-even revenue will increase by 10%

      O   Break-even volume will decrease by 10% but break-even revenue will remain unchanged

      O   Break-even volume and break-even revenue will both remain the same

---

20   Which of the following statements relating to cost volume profit analysis are true?

      (1)   Production levels and sales levels are assumed to be the same so there is no inventory movement

      (2)   The contribution to sales ratio (C/S ratio) can be used to indicate the relative profitability of different products

      (3)   CVP analysis assumes that fixed costs will change if output either falls or increases significantly

      (4)   Sales prices are recognised to vary at different levels of activity especially if higher volume of sales is needed

      O   1, 2 and 3

      O   2, 3 and 4

      O   1 and 2 only

      O   3 and 4 only

The following scenario relates to questions 21–25.

Romeo Co is a business which makes and sells fresh pizza from a number of mobile food vans based at several key locations in the city centre. It offers a variety of toppings and dough bases for the pizzas and has a good reputation for providing a speedy service combined with hot, fresh and tasty food to customers.

Each van employs a chef who is responsible for making the pizzas to Romeo Co's recipes and two sales staff who serve the customers. All purchasing is done centrally to enable Romeo Co to negotiate bulk discounts and build relationships with suppliers.

Romeo Co operates a standard costing and variances system and the standard cost card for Romeo Co's basic tomato pizza is as follows:

Ingredient	Weight kg	Price $ per kg
Dough	0.20	7.60
Tomato sauce	0.08	2.50
Cheese	0.12	20.00
Herbs	0.02	8.40
	0.42	

In Month 3, Romeo Co produced and sold 90 basic tomato pizzas and actual results were as follows:

Ingredient	Kg bought and used	Actual cost per kg
Dough	18.9	6.50
Tomato sauce	6.6	2.45
Cheese	14.5	21.00
Herbs	2.0	8.10
	42	

21   What was the total favourable material price variance for Month 3 (to two decimal places)?

$ [   ]

---

22   What was the total materials mix variance for Month 3?

[▼]

Picklist:

$81.02 adverse
$41.92 adverse
$42.88 adverse
$38.14 adverse

---

23 In Month 4, Romeo Co produced and sold 110 basic tomato pizzas. Actual results were as follows:

Ingredient	Kg bought and used	Actual cost per kg
Dough	21.3	6.60
Tomato sauce	7.5	2.45
Cheese	14.2	20.00
Herbs	2.0	8.50
	45	

What was the total materials yield variance for Month 4?

Note. Calculate all workings to two decimal places.

○ $12.21 favourable

○ $11.63 favourable

○ $21.95 adverse

○ $9.75 adverse

---

24 In Month 5, Romeo Co reported a favourable materials mix variance for the basic tomato pizza.

Which of the following statements would explain why this variance has occurred?

○ The proportion of the relatively expensive ingredients used in production was less than the standard

○ The prices paid for the ingredients used in the mix were lower than the standard prices

○ Each pizza used less of all the ingredients in actual production than expected

○ More pizzas were produced than expected given the level of ingredients input

---

25 In Month 6, 100 basic tomato pizzas were made using a total of 42 kg of ingredients. A new chef at Romeo Co used the expected amount of dough and herbs but used less cheese and more tomato sauce per pizza than the standard. It was noticed that the sales of the basic tomato pizza had declined in the second half of the month.

Based on the above information, which **TWO** of the following statements are correct?

☐ The actual cost per pizza in Month 6 was lower than the standard cost per pizza

☐ The sales staff should lose their Month 6 bonus because of the reduced sales

☐ The value of the ingredients usage variance and the mix variance are the same

☐ The new chef will be responsible for the material price, mix and yield variances

The following scenario relates to questions 26–30.

Sweet Treats Bakery makes three types of cake: brownies, muffins and cupcakes.

The costs, revenues and demand for each of the three cakes are as follows:

	Brownies	Muffins	Cupcakes
Batch size (units)	40	30	20
Selling price ($ per unit)	1.50	1.40	2.00
Material cost ($ per unit)	0.25	0.15	0.25
Labour cost ($ per unit)	0.40	0.45	0.50
Overheads ($ per unit)	0.15	0.20	0.30
Minimum daily demand (units)	30	20	10
Maximum daily demand (units)	140	90	100

The minimum daily demand is required for a long-term contract with a local café and must be met.

The cakes are made in batches using three sequential processes: weighing, mixing and baking. The products must be produced in their batch sizes but are sold as individual units. Each batch of cakes requires the following amount of time for each process:

	Brownies	Muffins	Cupcakes
Weighing (minutes)	15	15	20
Mixing (minutes)	20	16	12
Baking (minutes)	120	110	120

The baking stage of the process is done in three ovens which can each be used for eight hours a day, a total of 1,440 available minutes. Ovens have a capacity of one batch per bake, regardless of product type.

Sweet Treats Bakery uses throughput accounting and considers all costs, other than material, to be 'factory costs' which do not vary with production.

26   On Monday, in addition to the baking ovens, Sweet Treats Bakery has the following process resources available:

Process	Minutes available
Weighing	240
Mixing	180

Which of the three processes, if any, is a bottleneck activity?

Picklist:

Weighing
Mixing
Baking
There is no bottleneck

---

27   On Wednesday, the mixing process is identified as the bottleneck process. On this day, only 120 minutes in the mixing process are available.

Assuming that Sweet Treats Bakery wants to maximise profit, what is the optimal production plan for Wednesday?

O   80 brownies, 30 muffins and 100 cupcakes

O   0 brownies, 90 muffins and 100 cupcakes

O   120 brownies, 0 muffins and 100 cupcakes

O   40 brownies, 60 muffins and 100 cupcakes

---

28   Sweet Treats Bakery has done a detailed review of its products, costs and processes.

Which **TWO** of the following statements will improve the throughput accounting ratio?

☐   The café customer wants to negotiate a loyalty discount

☐   A bulk discount on flour and sugar is available from suppliers

☐   There is additional demand for the cupcakes in the market

☐   The rent of the premises has been reduced for the next year

29   On Friday, due to a local food festival at the weekend, Sweet Treats Bakery is considering increasing its production of cupcakes. These cupcakes can be sold at the festival at the existing selling price.

The company has unlimited capacity for weighing and mixing on Friday but its existing three ovens are already fully utilized, therefore in order to supply cupcakes to the festival, Sweet Treats Bakery will need to hire another identical oven at a cost of $45 for the day.

How much will profit increase by if the company hires the new oven and produces as many cupcakes as possible?

| ▼ |

Picklist:

$55.00
$140.00
$95.00
$31.00

30   In a previous week, the weighing process was the bottleneck and the resulting throughput accounting ratio (TPAR) for the bakery was 1.45.

Indicate, by clicking on the relevant boxes in the table below, whether each of the following statements about the TPAR for the previous week are true or false.

The bakery's operating costs exceeded the total throughput contribution generated from its three products	TRUE	FALSE
Less idle time in the mixing department would have improved the TPAR	TRUE	FALSE
Improved efficiency during the weighing process would have improved the TPAR	TRUE	FALSE

(Total = 30 marks)

Section C – Both questions are compulsory and MUST be attempted

31 Static Co is a multinational consumer goods company. Traditionally, the company has used a fixed annual budgeting process in which it sets quarterly sales revenue targets for each of its product lines. Historically, however, if a product line fails to reach its sales revenue target in any of the first three quarters, the company's sales director (SD) and finance director (FD) simply go back and reduce the sales revenue targets for the quarter just ended, to make it look like the target was reached. They then increase the target for the final quarter to include any shortfall in sales from earlier quarters.

During the last financial year ended 31 August 20X6, this practice meant that managers had to heavily discount many of their product lines in the final quarter in order to boost sales volumes and meet the increased targets. Even with the discounts, however, they still did not quite reach the targets. On the basis of the sales targets set at the beginning of that year, the company had also invested $6m in a new production line in January 20X6. However, to date, this new production line still has not been used. As a result of both these factors, Static Co saw a dramatic fall in return on investment from 16% to 8% in the year.

Consequently, the managing director (MD), the FD and the SD have all been dismissed. Two key members of the accounts department are also on sick leave due to stress and are not expected to return for some weeks. A new MD, who is inexperienced in this industry, has been appointed and is in the process of recruiting a new SD and a new FD.

They have said:

'These mistakes could have been largely avoided if the company had been using rolling budgets, instead of manipulating fixed budgets. From now on, we will be using rolling budgets, updating our budgets on a quarterly basis, with immediate effect.'

The original fixed budget for the year ended 31 August 20X7, for which the first quarter (Q1) has just ended, is shown below:

Budget Y/E 31 August 20X7	Q1 $'000	Q2 $'000	Q3 $'000	Q4 $'000	Total $'000
Revenue	13,425	13,694	13,967	14,247	55,333
Cost of sales	(8,055)	(8,216)	(8,380)	(8,548)	(33,199)
Gross profit	5,370	5,478	5,587	5,699	22,134
Distribution costs	(671)	(685)	(698)	(712)	(2,766)
Administration costs	(2,000)	(2,000)	(2,000)	(2,000)	(8,000)
Operating profit	2,699	2,793	2,889	2,987	11,368

The budget was based on the following assumptions:

(1) Sales volumes would grow by a fixed compound percentage each quarter.
(2) Gross profit margin would remain stable each quarter.
(3) Distribution costs would remain a fixed percentage of revenue each quarter.
(4) Administration costs would be fixed each quarter.

The actual results for the first quarter (Q1) have just been produced and are as follows:

Actual results	Q1 $'000
Revenue	14,096
Cost of sales	(8,740)
Gross profit	5,356
Distribution costs	(705)
Administration costs	(2,020)
Operating profit	2,631

The new MD believes that the difference between the actual and the budgeted sales figures for Q1 is a result of incorrect forecasting of prices; however, they are confident that the four assumptions the fixed budget was based on were correct and that the rolling budget should still be prepared using these assumptions.

Required

(a) Prepare Static Co's rolling budget for the next four quarters. **(8 marks)**

(b) Discuss the problems which have occurred at Static Co due to the previous budgeting process and the improvements which might now be seen through the use of realistic rolling budgets. **(6 marks)**

(c) Discuss the problems which may be encountered when Static Co tries to implement the new budgeting system. **(6 marks)**

(Total = 20 marks)

32 Lens Co manufactures lenses for use by a wide range of commercial customers. The company has two divisions: the Photographic Division (P) and the Optometry Division (O). Each of the divisions is run by a divisional manager who has overall responsibility for all aspects of running their division and the divisions are currently treated as investment centres. Each manager, however, has an authorisation limit of $15,000 per item for capital expenditure and any items costing more than this must first be approved by Head Office.

During the year, Head Office made a decision to sell a large amount of the equipment in Division P and replace it with more technologically advanced equipment. It also decided to close one of Division O's factories in a country deemed to be politically unstable, with the intention of opening a new factory elsewhere in the following year.

Both divisions trade with overseas customers, choosing to provide these customers with 60 days' credit to encourage sales. Due to differences in exchange rates between the time of invoicing the customers and receiving the payment 60 days later, exchange gains and losses often occur.

The cost of capital for Lens Co is 12% per annum.

The following data relates to the year ended 30 November 20X6:

	Division P $'000	Division O $'000
Revenue	14,000	18,800
Gain on sale of equipment	400	–
	14,400	18,800
Direct labour	(2,400)	(3,500)
Direct materials	(4,800)	(6,500)
Divisional overheads*	(3,800)	(5,200)
Trading profit	3,400	3,600
Exchange gain/(loss)	(200)	460
Exceptional costs for factory closure	–	(1,800)
Allocated Head Office costs	(680)	(1,040)
Net divisional profit	2,520	1,220
* Depreciation on uncontrollable assets included in divisional overheads	320	460

	Division P	Division O
	$'000	$'000
Non-current assets controlled by the division	15,400	20,700
Non-current assets controlled by Head Office	3,600	5,200
Inventories	1,800	3,900
Trade receivables	6,200	8,900
Overdraft	500	–
Trade payables	5,100	7,200

To date, managers have always been paid a bonus based on the return on investment (ROI) achieved by their division. However, the company is considering whether residual income would be a better method.

Required

(a) Calculate the return on investment (ROI) for each division for the year ended 30 November 20X6, ensuring that the basis of the calculation makes it a suitable measure for assessing the **DIVISIONAL MANAGERS'** performance.   **(6 marks)**

(b) Explain why you have included or excluded certain items in calculating the ROIs in part (a), stating any assumptions you have made.   **(8 marks)**

(c) Briefly discuss whether it is appropriate to treat each of the divisions of Lens Co as investment centres.   **(2 marks)**

(d) Discuss the problems involved in using ROI to measure the managers' performance.   **(4 marks)**

(Total = 20 marks)

Formulae sheet

Regression analysis

$y = a + bx$

$$a = \frac{\Sigma y}{n} - \frac{b\Sigma x}{n}$$

$$b = \frac{n\Sigma xy - \Sigma x \Sigma y}{n\Sigma x^2 - (\Sigma x)^2}$$

$$r = \frac{n\Sigma xy - \Sigma x \Sigma y}{\sqrt{\left(n\Sigma x^2 - (\Sigma x)^2\right)\left(n\Sigma y^2 - (\Sigma y)^2\right)}}$$

Learning curve

$Y = ax^b$

Where Y = cumulative average time per unit to produce x units

         a = the time taken for the first unit of output

         x = the cumulative number of units produced

         b = the index of learning (log LR/log2)

         LR = the learning rate as a decimal

Demand curve

$P = a - bQ$

$$b = \frac{\text{change in price}}{\text{change in quantity}}$$

a = price when $Q = 0$

$MR = a - 2bQ$

Answers

DO NOT TURN THIS PAGE UNTIL YOU HAVE
COMPLETED THE MOCK EXAM

A PLAN OF ATTACK

Managing your nerves

As you turn the pages to start this mock exam a number of thoughts are likely to cross your mind. At best, examinations cause anxiety so it is important to stay focused on your task for the next three hours! Developing an awareness of what is going on emotionally within you may help you manage your nerves. Remember, you are unlikely to banish the flow of adrenaline, but the key is to harness it to help you work steadily and quickly through your answers.

Working through this mock exam will help you develop the exam stamina you will need to keep going for three hours.

Managing your time

Planning and time management are two of the key skills which complement the technical knowledge you need to succeed. To keep yourself on time, do not be afraid to jot down your target completion times for each question, perhaps next to the title of the question. As all the questions are **compulsory**, you do not have to spend time wondering which question to answer!

Doing the exam

Actually doing the exam is a personal experience. There is not a single **right way**. As long as you submit complete answers to all questions after the three hours are up, then your approach obviously works.

Looking through the exam

Section A has 15 OTQs. This is the section of the exam where the ACCA examining team can test knowledge across the breadth of the syllabus. Make sure you read these questions carefully. The distractors are designed to present plausible, but incorrect, answers. Don't let them mislead you. If you really have no idea – guess. You may even be right.

Section B has three questions, each with a scenario and five objective test questions.

Section C has two longer questions:

- Question 31 requires you to prepare a rolling budget and discuss budgeting systems. There are plenty of easy marks in the question.

- Question 32 looks at performance measurement. This is a classic performance measurement question on return on investment. Start with the ratio calculations and then make sure that you fully explain why you have included or excluded numbers.

Allocating your time

BPP's advice is to always allocate your time **according to the marks for the question**. However, **use common sense**. If you're doing a question but haven't a clue how to do part (b), you might be better off re-allocating your time and getting more marks on another question, where you can add something you didn't have time for earlier on. Make sure you leave time to recheck the MCQs and make sure you have answered them all.

Sections A & B

1   The correct answer is: If budgeted sales increase to 40,000 units, budgeted profit will increase by $100,000

This is because 10,000 more units will be sold at a contribution per unit of $10. The fixed costs would not be expected to change.

2   The correct answers are: It is best applied to support expenses rather than to direct costs and it can link strategic goals to specific functional areas

ZBB is useful for support expenses as they are discretionary and it can be used to link strategic goals to specific functional areas.

3   The correct answer is: Increase the selling price of product Z by 10%

As all three products are mutually exclusive the company would choose to make X as it has the highest throughput return per hour of $2. Of the four possible options only increasing the selling price of product Z by 10% would give a higher throughput return per hour of $2.40.

4   The correct answer is: 3 only

Big Data is relevant to long term as well as short term decision-making and it is updated in real time so is not out of date. It is often used to predict consumer preferences successfully.

5   The correct answer is: $750

The minimum transfer price is $750 and product X should be sourced externally to maximise the profit of the company.

The minimum transfer price is the variable cost of product X ($270) plus the lost contribution from not making product Y ($480).

The lost contribution is from 1.5 units of product Y (as it takes four hours to make product Y and six hours to make product X) which is (($600 – ($200 – $80) × 1.5 = $480.

6   The correct answer is: $600 loss

Before further processing the sales value of X (10,000 units × $1.20) = $12,000.

After further processing:

Sales value of Z (8,000 units × $2.25) = $18,000

Further processing costs ((10,000 units of X × $0.50) + $1,600) = $6,600.

This gives a net return of $11,400 which is $600 less than the sales value of X.

7   The correct answer is: $3.22

Variable production costs ($2.30 × 2,000) + ($1.80 × 5,000) + ($1.20 × 7,000) = $22,000

Variable selling costs ($0.50 × 2,000) + ($0.40 × 5,000) + ($0.40 × 7,000) = $5,800

Fixed production costs = $10,500

Fixed selling costs = $4,700

Administrative costs = $2,100

Total costs = $45,100

Cost per unit = $45,100/14,000 units = $3.22

8   The correct answer is: $400,000 adverse

Market share variance compares revised sales volume to actual sales volume.

Revised sales volume (300,000 units × 2%) = 6,000 units

Actual sales volume = 5,600 units

Difference = 400 units adverse

Valued at standard contribution of $1,000

Variance = $400,000 adverse

9   The correct answer is: Simultaneous

It is simultaneous as there is no delay between the service being provided by the optician and consumed by the patient.

10   The correct answer is: Universal passwords

A universal password would apply to everyone and therefore there would be no way to trace the person responsible for printing/transferring or amending the information. The other three options are common methods for securing the confidentiality of information.

11   The correct answer is: $71.43

Alpha batches (2,500/500) = 5; therefore inspections required for Alpha (5 × 4) = 20

Zeta batches (8,000/1,000) = 8; therefore inspections required for Zeta (8 × 1) = 8

OAR = $250,000/28 = $8,928.57

Alpha cost/unit = (20 × $8,928.57)/2,500 units = $71.43

12   The correct answer is: Compromise between objectives can be problematic

Multiple objectives often conflict and therefore do not ensure goal congruence between stakeholders. Therefore 'They ensure goal congruence between stakeholders' is incorrect. This then can lead to the need for compromise between objectives which can be problematic therefore the second statement is correct.

13   The correct answer is: Waste flows

Waste flows are not a category used within flow cost accounting, however the other three categories are.

14   The correct answers are: 2 and 4 only

- The expected value gives no indication of the dispersion of the possible outcomes
- The expected value may not correspond to any of the actual possible outcomes

The expected value does not give an indication of the dispersion of the possible outcomes; a standard deviation would need to be calculated so Statement 2 is correct.

The expected value is an amalgamation of several possible outcomes and their associated probabilities so it may not correspond to any of the actual possible outcomes so Statement 4 is correct.

15   The correct answer is: The manager will be accountable for the generation of revenues, transfer prices and management of working capital as they have control over these areas.

The manager will not be accountable for the apportioned head office costs as they have no control over those.

16   The correct answer is: 47.7%

Total fixed costs = $385,000

Contribution per marathon entry ($55 − $18.20) = $36.80

BEP = 10,462

Margin of safety (20,000 − 10,462)/20,000 = 47.7%

17   The correct answer is: $592,000

Weighted average C/S ratio (2 × $36.80) + (1.4 × $18.00)/(2 × $55) + (1.4 × $30) = $98.80/$152 = 65%

BER = $385,000/65% = $592,308

18   The correct answer is: Full marathon: 17,915 entries and half marathon: 12,540 entries

Weighted average C/S ratio = 65%

Revenue to achieve target profit = $885,000/65% = $1,361,538

Marathon ($110/$152) × $1,361,538 = $985,324/$55 = 17,915 entries

Half marathon ($42/$152) × $1,361,538 = $376,214/$30 = 12,540 entries

19   The correct answer is: Breakeven volume will remain unchanged but breakeven revenue will increase by 10%

Current contribution = $12
Current BEP = $48,000/$12 = 4,000 units
Current BER = $48,000/($12/$20) = $80,000
Revised contribution = (($20 × 1.1) + ($8 × 1.1)) = $13.20
Revised fixed costs = $48,000 × 1.1 = $52,800
Revised BEP = $52,800/$13.20 = 4,000 units
Revised BER = $52,800/($13.20/$22) = $88,000
The BEP hasn't changed but the BER has increased by 10%

20   The correct answer is: 1 and 2

CVP analysis assumes no movement in inventory and the C/S ratio can be used to indicate the relative profitability of different products so Statements 1 and 2 are correct.

21   The correct answer is: $7.22 favourable

Dough 18.9 kg × ($7.60 − $6.50) = $20.79 favourable
Tomato sauce 6.6 kg × ($2.50 − $2.45) = $0.33 favourable
Cheese 14.5 kg × ($20.00 − $21.00) = $14.50 adverse
Herbs 2 kg × ($8.40 − $8.10) = $0.60 favourable
Total material price variance = $7.22 favourable

22   The correct answer is: $38.14 adverse

	Actual usage/mix kg	Standard mix kg	Mix variance kg	Standard price $ per kg	Mix variance $
Dough	18.9	20.0	1.1 (F)	7.60	8.36 (F)
Sauce	6.6	8.0	1.4 (F)	2.50	3.50 (F)
Cheese	14.5	12.0	2.5 (A)	20.00	50.00 (A)
Herbs	2.0	2.0	−	8.40	−
	42.0	42.0	0		38.14 (A)

23   The correct answer is: $12.21 favourable

	Standard quantity standard mix kg	Actual quantity standard mix kg	Variance kg	Standard cost per kg $	Variance $
Dough	22.00	21.43	0.57 (F)	7.60	4.33 (F)
Sauce	8.80	8.57	0.23 (F)	2.50	0.58 (F)
Cheese	13.20	12.86	0.34 (F)	20.00	6.80 (F)
Herbs	2.20	2.14	0.06 (F)	8.40	0.50 (F)
	46.20	45.00			12.21 (F)

24   The correct answer is: The proportion of the relatively expensive ingredients used in production was less than the standard.

A favourable mix variance indicates that a higher proportion of cheaper ingredients were used in production compared to the standard mix.

25   The correct answers are: The actual cost per pizza in Month 6 was lower than the standard cost per pizza and The value of the ingredients usage variance and the mix variance are the same.

The actual cost per pizza will be lower than the standard cost per pizza because expensive cheese has been replaced with cheaper tomato sauce.

The usage variance equals the mix and yield variance combined. The yield variance is zero as 100 pizzas used 42 kg so the mix and usage variances will be the same.

Sales staff should not automatically lose their bonus as the reduced sales could be a result of the change in mix affecting the quality of the pizza and the new chef will only be responsible for the mix and yield variances as they have no control over the purchase costs of ingredients.

26   The correct answer is: Mixing

Process	Available minutes	Brownies	Muffins	Cupcakes	Total minutes required
Weighing	240	60	45	100	205
Mixing	180	80	48	60	188
Baking	1,440	480	330	600	1,410

The bottleneck is the mixing process as 188 minutes are required to meet maximum demand but there are only 180 minutes available.

Note. Four batched of brownies need to be made in order to have sufficient cakes to meet maximum demand as the cakes must be made in their batch sizes.

27   The correct answer is: 80 brownies, 30 muffins and 100 cupcakes

	Brownies	Muffins	Cupcakes
Throughput contribution ($)	50	37.5	35
Mixing minutes	20	16	12
Throughput per mixing minute ($)	2.50	2.34	2.91
Ranking	2	3	1

Optimal production plan:

Fulfil customer order	Number of cakes	Mixing minutes
1 batch of cupcakes	20	12
1 batch of brownies	40	20
1 batch of muffins	30	16
General production (based on ranking)		
4 batches of cupcakes	80	48
1 batch of brownies	40	20

Therefore the bakery should produce 80 brownies, 30 muffins and 100 cupcakes.

28 The correct answer is: A bulk discount on flour and sugar is available from suppliers and The rent of the premises has been reduced for the next year

Reduction in rent and discounts on materials will reduce costs and will improve the TPAR.

Giving a customer a loyalty discount will reduce sales revenue and as a result the TPAR. Demand for cupcakes can increase but it will not impact the TPAR as demand is not the restriction.

29 The correct answer is: $95.00

Each oven has a capacity of eight hours and each cupcake batch takes two hours so four extra batches can be made.

Extra throughput = four batches × $35 = $140

Less the hire costs will result in an additional profit of $95.

30 The correct answer is: Improved efficiency during the weighing process would have improved the TPAR is TRUE. The other statements are false.

As the TPAR exceeds 1, the throughput contribution exceeds operating costs and so Statement 1 is false.

Less idle time on a non-bottleneck process would not improve the TPAR so Statement 2 is false.

Improving efficiency during the weighing process would improve the TPAR as any actions to improve throughput on a bottleneck will improve the TPAR so Statement 3 is true.

Section C

31 Static Co

Marking scheme

			Marks
(a)	Growth rate		1
	Actual distribution cost %		0.5
	Actual GPM %		0.5
	Use of Q1 actuals		1
	Rolling budget: sales		1
	COS		1
	GPM		0.5
	Distribution costs		1
	Administration costs		1
	Operating profit		0.5
			8
(b)	Problems and improvements		6
(c)	Implementation problems		6
			20

(a)   *Workings*

From budgeted figures: need to work out what the compound growth rate is and the distribution costs as a percentage of revenue.

Compound sales growth: $13,694/13,425 or $13,967/13,694 = 2%

Distribution costs: $671/$13,425 = 5%

From actual figures: GPM = $5,356/14,096 = 38%

Distribution costs: $705/14,096 = still 5%.

Starting point for revenue now $14,096 but compound growth rate still 2%.

Rolling budget for the 12 months ending 30 November 20X7

	Q2 $'000	Q3 $'000	Q4 $'000	Q1 $'000
Revenue	14,378	14,666	14,959	15,258
Cost of sales	(8,914)	(9,093)	(9,275)	(9,460)
Gross profit	5,464	5,573	5,684	5,798
Distribution costs	(719)	(733)	(748)	(763)
Administration costs	(2,020)	(2,020)	(2,020)	(2,020)
Operating profit	2,725	2,820	2,916	3,015

(b)   **Problems and improvements**

Problems

The use of fixed budgeting has caused serious problems at Static Co. The fact it was using inaccurate sales forecast figures led it to invest in a production line which was not actually needed, even though it knew they were inaccurate. This unnecessary investment cost it $6m and caused the return on investment to halve. Had rolling budgets been used at the time, and used properly, the sales forecasts for the remaining quarters would have been adjusted to reflect a fall in demand and the investment would not have been made.

Presumably, inaccurate sales forecasts would have led the business to get its staffing levels and materials purchases wrong as well. This too will have cost the business money. It was forced to heavily discount its goods in order to try to reach its targets at the end of the year, which was simply unrealistic. It can often be difficult to put prices back up again once they have been discounted. However, the actual results from the first quarter suggest that prices have increased again, which is fortunate.

Improvements

The use of rolling budgets should mean that a downturn in demand is adjusted for in future quarters, rather than sales simply being pushed into the last quarter, which is not a realistic adjustment. Management is forced to reassess the budget regularly and produce up-to-date information. This means that accurate management decisions can then be made and mistakes like investing in a new production line which is not needed should not happen again. Planning and control will be more accurate.

(c)   **Problems trying to implement new budgeting system**

The first problem may be trying to obtain the right information needed to update the budget. The FD has been sacked and two other key finance personnel are off work due to stress. This could make it very difficult to obtain information if the department is understaffed and lacking the direction given by the FD. Staff in the finance department may not have the skills to update the budget and roll it forward, having never done it before. Similarly, the sales department is without a SD and they would usually have played a key part in reviewing figures for the sales forecasts. Hence, it may be difficult to obtain reliable sales data.

Even without this staffing issue, obtaining the correct information could be difficult as actually preparing rolling budgets is new for Static Co. Staff will need training. They are only used to preparing fixed budgets, although these have often been revised in the past to move sales into later periods. Staff are not familiar with the process of updating all of their financial information again: reviewing sales demand to realistically reforecast, updating costs, etc. This process takes time and staff may feel resentful about having to do this again, so soon after the annual budgeting process which would recently have been undertaken.

The new MD is new to this industry and therefore lacks experience of how it works. Whilst they are confident that the assumptions of the original fixed budget still stand true, they are not in a good position to know that this is in fact the case. They may be wrong and, if they are, the new rolling budget will be unreliable.

32 Lens Co

Marking scheme

		Marks	
(a)	Calculation of controllable profit	2	
	Calculation of controllable assets	2	
	ROI	2	
			6
(b)	Explanation about controllability	2	
	Inclusion/exclusion explanations	6	
			8
(c)	Description of investment centre	1	
	Application to Lens Co	1	
			2
(d)	Problems with using ROI		4
			20

(a) **Return on investment**

Controllable profit

	Division P	Division O
	$'000	$'000
Revenue	14,000	18,800
Direct labour	(2,400)	(3,500)
Direct materials	(4,800)	(6,500)
Divisional overheads excl. uncontrollable depreciation	(3,480)	(4,740)
Exchange gain/(loss)	(200)	460
Net divisional profit	3,120	4,520

Net assets controlled by the divisions

	Division P $'000	Division O $'000
Non-current assets controlled by division	15,400	20,700
Inventories	1,800	3,900
Trade receivables	6,200	8,900
Overdraft	(500)	–
Trade payables	(5,100)	(7,200)
Net controllable assets	17,800	26,300

ROI for Division P

Controllable profit/controllable assets

= $3,120/$17,800

= 17.53%.

ROI for Division O

$4,520/$26,300 = 17.19%

(b) The ROIs in part (a) have been calculated by applying the principle of 'controllability'. This principle states that managers should only be held accountable for areas which they can control. This means that, when calculating 'profit' for the purposes of calculating ROI, the only revenues and costs included should be controllable by the manager. Similarly, when calculating 'net assets' for the ROI calculation, only assets which the divisional managers can control should be included.

Applying the principles of controllability, treatment of certain costs is explained below:

Gain on sale of equipment

This has been excluded from the profit figure as the decision to dispose of a large amount of equipment in division P was taken by Head Office. The divisional manager had no control over this decision.

Divisional overheads

The depreciation on HO-controlled assets has been excluded when calculating profit for ROI purposes. Again, this is because divisional managers do not control some of the assets.

Exchange gains/losses

These have been left in when arriving at a profit figure for ROI purposes. This is because the scenario states that the divisions choose to give the overseas customers 60 days' credit and it is this delay, between the point of sale and the point of payment, which gives rise to the exchange gain or loss. The managers make the choice to deal with these customers so they have control here.

Exceptional cost of factory closure

The effect of this has been removed from the 'profit' calculation as this decision was made by Head Office, not the manager of division O. It was therefore beyond their control and its effect should be excluded.

Allocated Head Office costs

These have been excluded when calculating profit, as the divisional managers have no control over these and should not be held accountable for them.

Non-current assets controlled by Head Office

These have been excluded from the 'net assets' calculation, as these assets are not under the control of the divisional managers.

(c) **Investment centres**

An investment centre is a type of responsibility centre in which managers have responsibility for not only sales prices, volume and costs, but also for investment in working capital and non-current assets. Both divisions do have responsibility for working capital; that is clear from the scenario. However, they only have responsibility over some of the assets. In the circumstances, it could be argued that it is correct to treat them as investment centres, provided that appropriate adjustments are made when using ROI to assess their performance.

On the other hand, however, managers are only able to sign off $15,000 of capital expenditure, which is a relatively small amount, suggesting that treatment as an investment centre is not appropriate. Bringing the divisions under Head Office control may even be beneficial as exchange rate risk can then be managed more closely.

(d) **Problems of using ROI**

The main disadvantage of using ROI is that the percentage increases as assets get older. This is because the net book value of the assets decreases as a result of higher accumulated depreciation, hence capital employed falls. This, in turn, can lead managers to hold onto ageing assets rather than replace them, especially where their bonuses are linked to ROI. It may be that division P's manager would not have made the same decision which Head Office made to invest in the more advanced technology for this reason.

Another disadvantage is that ROI is based on accounting profits, which are subjective, rather than cash flows. It is therefore open to manipulation.

Additionally, it does not take into account the cost of capital. It merely looks at profits relative to capital employed without taking into account the cost of the capital which has been invested. It is therefore not consistent with maximising returns to investors.

BPP
LEARNING
MEDIA

ACCA

Performance Management

Mock Exam 4

Question Paper: 3 hours
This paper is divided into three sections:
Section A – ALL FIFTEEN questions are compulsory and MUST be attempted
Section B – ALL FIFTEEN questions are compulsory and MUST be attempted
Section C – Both questions are compulsory and MUST be attempted

DO NOT OPEN THIS PAPER UNTIL YOU ARE READY TO START
UNDER EXAMINATION CONDITIONS

Section A – ALL FIFTEEN questions are compulsory and MUST be attempted

Each question is worth two marks.

1   Conference Co has a divisionalised structure. One of its divisions, Division X, sells all its output to other divisions within the company.

Division X's annual budgeted output and costs are as follows:

Units sold	1,050
Direct materials	$22,500
Direct labour	$45,350
Overheads (40% variable)	$37,150

What transfer price per unit will result in a profit margin of 20% for Division X (to the nearest whole $)?

$ _____

2   A company needs 400kg of material Z to fulfil a customer order in one month's time.

It currently has no material Z in inventory. The current purchase price of material Z is $20 per kg and this is expected to rise to $24 per kg in one month's time. Material Z is perishable and normally 20% of stored material is lost per month.

The company expects to have 200kg of material Y in inventory in one month's time with no alternative use other than to sell it for scrap for $18 per kg. The 200kg of material Y could be converted into 200kg of material Z in one month's time at a cost of $4 per kg. Material Y is not perishable.

Which is the total relevant cost of material Z to fulfil the customer order?

$ _____

3   Identify, by clicking on the box below, whether the following statements are true or false.

A transaction processing system collects and records the transactions of an organisation.	TRUE	FALSE
An executive information system is a way of integrating the data from all operations within the organisation into a single system.	TRUE	FALSE

4   X Co uses a throughput accounting system. Details of Product A, per unit, are as follows:

Selling price	$320
Material costs	$80
Conversion costs	$60
Time on bottleneck resource	6 minutes

What is the return per hour for Product A?

[▼]

Picklist:

$30
$40
$1,800
$2,400

---

5   A company grows different types of tea leaves and blends them together. The tea leaves are picked by hand because too many leaves were damaged and wasted when picking machines were used. The tea leaves are then dried and processed and any waste produced is recycled.

The company regularly tests its tea for contaminants, in line with food safety legislation. It recently identified that one tea plantation contained high levels of contaminated soil after the use of a new pesticide.

Identify, by selecting the relevant box in the table below, the environmental cost classification of each of the following costs.

Cost incurred to clean contaminated soil	**PREVENTION**	DETECTION	INTERNAL FAILURE	EXTERNAL FAILURE
Staff cost for picking leaves by hand	**PREVENTION**	DETECTION	INTERNAL FAILURE	EXTERNAL FAILURE
Recycling waste cost	**PREVENTION**	DETECTION	INTERNAL FAILURE	EXTERNAL FAILURE
Cost incurred for testing tea for contaminants	**PREVENTION**	DETECTION	INTERNAL FAILURE	EXTERNAL FAILURE

---

6   A company predicted that the learning rate for production of a new product would be 80%. The actual learning rate was 75%. The following possible reasons were stated for this:

(1)   The number of new employees recruited was lower than expected

(2)   Unexpected problems were encountered with production

(3)   Unexpected changes to Health and Safety laws meant that the company had to increase the number of breaks during production for employees.

Which of the above reasons could have caused the difference between the expected rate of learning and the actual rate of learning?

O   All of the above

O   2 and 3 only

O   1 only

O   None of the above

---

7   Which of the following statements is NOT true about a sales mix variance?

O   If actual sales revenues from two products are in the same ratio as the budgeted sales revenues there is no measurable sales mix variance

O   If all products have the same budgeted margin there is no measurable sales mix variance

O   If actual sales volumes are in the same ratio as the budgeted sales volumes there is no measurable sales mix variance

O   If the actual sales volumes of all products are 10% above the budgeted sales volumes, there is no measurable sales mix variance

8   The following information is available for a manufacturing company which produces multiple products:

(1)   The product mix ratio
(2)   Contribution to sales ratio for each product
(3)   General fixed costs
(4)   Method of reapportioning general fixed costs

Which of the above are required in order to calculate the breakeven sales revenue for the company?

O   All of the above

O   1, 2 and 3 only

O   1, 3 and 4 only

O   2 and 3 only

9   Which of the following statements regarding technologies and systems are correct?

(1)   Networked computers can save costs by sharing hardware, software and data
(2)   An intranet provides quick, effective communication with suppliers
(3)   Wireless networks allow businesses to expand with less disruption than wired networks
(4)   The internet can be used to monitor and measure customer interest

O   2, 3 and 4

O   1 and 2

O   1, 3 and 4

O   1 and 4

10 Maribela Co makes a range of products and sells them online. It uses activity-based costing to allocate costs to its products. Its two most successful products are ABC1 and ABC2 but it makes approximately 20 other products in its factory. The company processes and despatches 12 million orders each year over its entire product range.

Information relating to ABC1 and ABC2 is as follows:

	ABC1	ABC2
Sales volume (units)	10 million	2.4 million
Average order size (units)	8	1.2

The total packing and despatching cost pool for Maribela Co is $18 million each year.

What is the packing and despatching cost per unit of ABC1 (to two decimal places)?

O $5.54

O $0.69

O $1.50

O $0.19

---

11 Which of the following are consequence of using ideal standards?

(1)   Variance analysis is likely to produce adverse results
(2)   Demotivation of staff usually becomes a problem
(3)   Allowances for normal efficiency levels are made
(4)   Standards can become more useful for long-term targets

O   1 and 2 only

O   1, 2 and 4

O   1, 2 and 3

O   3 and 4

---

12 A company wishes to decide on a selling price for a new product. Weekly sales of each product will depend on the price charged and also on customers' response to the new product. The following pay-off table has been prepared.

	Weekly contribution			
Weekly demand	Price P1	Price P2	Price P3	Price P4
Best possible	30,000	31,500	32,000	31,500
Most likely	24,000	26,250	28,000	27,000
Worst possible	18,000	17,500	16,000	13,500

If the choice of selling price is based on a minimax regret decision rule, which price would be selected?

P	

---

13 The following circumstances may arise in relation to the launch of a new product.

Which **TWO** of the circumstances favour a penetration pricing policy?

☐ Demand is relatively inelastic

☐ There are significant economies of scale

☐ The firm wishes to discourage new entrants to the market

☐ The product life cycle is particularly short

---

14 T Co makes and sells two Products X and Y. The two products are sold in a product mix ratio of X:Y = 3:2. T Co's fixed costs per month amount to $30,000 and details of both products are as follows.

	X	Y
Selling price per unit	$58	$28
Marginal costs per unit	$26	$16

T Co wishes to earn a profit of $3,600 next month.

Using the given product mix, what total volume of sales units would be needed to achieve a target profit of $3,600?

| | units

---

15 Log Co has an operating gearing ratio of 33.33%. Its sales are currently $100 million and its operating profit is $20 million. Operating gearing is calculated by dividing fixed costs by variable costs.

What will its operating profit be if its sales increase by 15%?

O $27 million

O $26 million

O $23 million

O $21 million

(Total = 30 marks)

Section B – ALL FIFTEEN questions are compulsory and MUST be attempted

Each question is worth two marks.

The following scenario relates to questions 16–20.

Volt Co generates and sells electricity. It operates two types of power station: nuclear and wind.

The costs and output of the two types of power station are detailed below:

Nuclear station

A nuclear station can generate 9,000 gigawatts of electricity in each of its 40 years of useful life. Operating costs are $486m per year. Operating costs include a provision for depreciation of $175 million per year to recover the $7,000 million cost of building the power station.

Each nuclear station has an estimated decommissioning cost of $12,000 million at the end of its life. The decommissioning cost relates to the cost of safely disposing of spent nuclear fuel.

Wind station

A wind station can generate 1,750 gigawatts of electricity per year. It has a life-cycle cost of $55,000 per gigawatt and an average operating cost of $40,000 per gigawatt over its 20-year life.

16 What is the life-cycle cost per gigawatt of the nuclear station (to the nearest $'000)?

   O $54,000

   O $73,000

   O $87,000

   O $107,000

17 Which of the following will decrease the total life-cycle cost of a nuclear station?

   (1)   Increasing the useful life of the station
   (2)   Reducing the decommissioning cost

   O   1 only

   O   2 only

   O   Both 1 and 2

   O   Neither 1 nor 2

18 How would the disposal cost of spent nuclear fuel be categorised in environmental management accounting (EMA)?

   O   A prevention cost

   O   A detection cost

   O   An internal failure cost

   O   An external failure cost

19   If Volt Co sets a price to earn an operating margin of 40% over the life of a wind station, what will be the total lifetime profit per station (to the nearest $m)?

O $35 million

O $408 million

O $560 million

O $933 million

20   Which of the following are benefits of life-cycle costing for Volt Co?

(1)   It facilitates the designing out of costs at the product development stage

(2)   It can encourage better control of operating costs over the life cycle

(3)   It gives a better understanding of the causes of overhead costs

(4)   It provides useful data for short-term decision-making

O   1, 2 and 3

O   1 and 2 only

O   1 and 4

O   2, 3 and 4

The following scenario relates to questions 21–25.

Cara Co makes two products: the Seebach and the Herdorf.

To make a unit of each product the following resources are required:

	Seebach	Herdorf
Materials ($100 per kg)	5 kg	7 kg
Labour hours ($45 per hour)	2 hours	3 hours
Machine hours ($60 per hour)	3 hours	2 hours

Fixed overheads are $300,000 each month.

The contribution per unit made on each product is as follows:

	Seebach	Herdorf
Contribution ($ per unit)	250	315

The maximum demand each month is 4,000 units of Seebach and 3,000 units of Herdorf. The products and materials are perishable and inventories of raw materials or finished goods cannot be stored.

Cara Co has a legally binding obligation to produce a minimum of 2,000 units of Herdorf in each of Months 1 and 2. There is no minimum production required in Month 3.

The manufacturing manager is planning production volumes and the maximum availability of resources for months 1, 2 and 3 are as follows:

Month	1	2	3
Materials (kg)	34,000	42,000	35,000
Labour (hours)	18,000	12,000	24,000
Machine (hours)	18,000	19,000	12,000

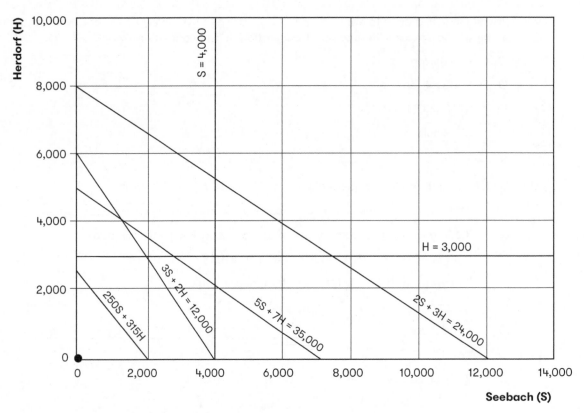

21 What is/are the limiting factor(s) in Month 1?

    ○   Materials, labour hours and machine hours

    ○   Materials and machine hours only

    ○   Materials only

    ○   Labour hours only

22 The production manager has identified that the only limiting factor in Month 2 is labour hours.

What is the production volume for Herdorf for Month 2 (to the nearest whole unit)?

    ○   0

    ○   1,333

    ○   2,000

    ○   3,000

23 If the shadow price for Month 2 is $125 per labour hour, which of the following statements is/are correct?

    (1)   The production manager would be willing to pay existing staff a maximum overtime premium of $125 per hour for the next 2,000 hours

    (2)   The production manager would be willing to pay a maximum of $170 per hour for an additional 2,000 hours of temporary staff time

    O   1 only

    O   2 only

    O   Both 1 and 2

    O   Neither 1 nor 2

24 What is the maximum profit which can be earned in Month 3?

    O $1,080,000

    O $1,380,000

    O $1,445,000

    O $1,145,000

25 Which of the following interpretations of the linear programming graph produced for Month 3 is/are correct?

    (1)   Even if demand for either product increases, labour will be a slack variable if no other resources change

    (2)   If more machine hours were made available in Month 3, they would be used initially to make Herdorfs

    O   1 only

    O   2 only

    O   Both 1 and 2

    O   Neither 1 nor 2

The following scenario relates to questions 26–30.

Marcus manages the production and sales departments for product MN at Grayshott Co. Marcus has been asked to attend a meeting with Grayshott Co's finance director to explain the results for product MN in the last quarter.

Budgeted and actual results for product MN were as follows:

	Budget	Actual
Sales volume (units)	40,000	38,000
	$'000	$'000
Revenue ($65 per unit)	2,600	2,394
Material (5.2 kg at $4 per kg)	(832)	(836)
Labour (2 hours at $8 per hour)	(640)	(798)
Variable overheads (2 hours at $4 per hour)	(320)	(399)
Fixed overheads	(220)	(220)
Profit	588	141

BPP
LEARNING
MEDIA

There was no opening and closing inventory in the last quarter. Grayshott Co operates a marginal costing system.

Marcus is angry about having to attend the meeting as he has no involvement in setting the original budget and he believes that the adverse results are due to the following circumstances which were beyond his control:

(1)   A decision by Grayshott Co's board to increase wages meant that the actual labour rate per hour was 25% higher than budgeted. This decision was made in response to a request by the production department to enable it to meet a large, one-off customer order in the last quarter.

(2)   Due to the closure of a key supplier, Grayshott Co agreed to a contract with an alternative supplier to pay 6% more per kg than the budgeted price for material. The actual cost per kg of material was $4·40.

(3)   Difficult economic conditions meant that market demand for product MN was lower by 10%.

At present Grayshott Co does not operate a system of planning and operational variances and Marcus believes it should do so.

26   What was the market share variance for product MN for the last quarter?

    O $40,400 Favourable

    O $80,800 Adverse

    O $29,400 Favourable

    O $38,000 Adverse

27   What was the adverse materials price planning variance for product MN for the last quarter?

    O $30,400

    O $76,000

    O $45,600

    O $49,920

28   What was the labour rate operational variance for product MN for the last quarter?

    O $159,600 Favourable

    O $159,600 Adverse

    O $160,000 Favourable

    O $160,000 Adverse

29   Which of the following would explain a labour efficiency planning variance?

    (1)   A change in employment legislation requiring staff to take longer rest periods

    (2)   Customers demanding higher quality products leading to a change in product design

    (3)   The learning effect for labour being estimated incorrectly in the production budget

    ○   1 and 2 only

    ○   2 and 3 only

    ○   3 only

    ○   1, 2 and 3

---

30   Which of the following statements regarding the problems of introducing a system of planning and operational variances is/are true?

    (1)   Operational managers may argue that variances are due to the original budget being unrealistic

    (2)   Operational managers may seek to blame uncontrollable external factors for the variances

    ○   1 only

    ○   2 only

    ○   Both 1 and 2

    ○   Neither 1 nor 2

(Total = 30 marks)

Section C – Both questions are compulsory and MUST be attempted

31 Bellahouston Co (Sep/Dec 21)

	Road	Spikes	Trail
	$	$	$
Selling price per pair of shoes	60.00	45.00	52.00
Variable costs per pair of shoes			
Direct material ($5 per metre)	7.50	3.00	6.00
Direct labour ($7 per hour)	7.00	10.50	7.00
Machine hours ($10 per hour)	4.00	2.00	3.00
Fixed overheads absorbed per pair of shoes	4.00	6.00	4.00
Profit per pair of shoes	37.50	23.50	32.00

Bellahouston Co manufactures three types of running shoes which it sells to sports clothing retailers: Road which are for running on roads, Spikes which are used for racing on athletics tracks and Trail which are used for running off-road in rural locations. Each of these products use differing amounts of the same resources. Financial information and the resource requirements related to these products are as follows:

Fixed overheads are absorbed at a rate of $4 per direct labour hour. Bellahouston Co uses a just-in-time production system.

Demand and resource availability for March

Demand for three products for the month of March is expected to be:

Road	2,300 pairs
Spikes	1,400 pairs
Trail	1,650 pairs

Bellahouston Co has received a special order from RunWild, which is not included in the demand estimates above. RunWild are a major sports retailer who have an extensive customer base and are known for stocking the most popular brands of sportwear. The order is to supply a maximum of 200 pairs of each type of shoe at a discount of $8.00 on the standard selling price.

RunWild will charge a financial penalty if the order is not fully complete in March. If this first order is successful, RunWild would be keen to enter into a regular contract.

Usually Bellahouston Co has sufficient resources to meet production, however during March the maximum availability for the following resources has been identified.

Direct material	7,200 metres
Direct labour	6,900 hours
Machine time	1,815 hours

Demand and resource availability for April

Bellahouston Co predicted that the resource availability in March would continue into April, however it has been discovered that the availability of direct material and direct labour will be 15% less than in March. The available machine time and demand estimates are unchanged. RunWild would not be placing an order in April.

Required

(a) (i)   Calculate the optimum production plan and the resulting total contribution earned for March, assuming that the order with RunWild is supplied in full.   **(7 marks)**

(a) (ii) Calculate the maximum financial penalty Bellahouston Co would be prepared to accept from RunWild's order in full.   **(4 marks)**

(b)   Discuss whether Bellahouston Co should fulfil RunWild's order in full in March.   **(4 marks)**

(c)   Define the variables and formulate the constraints and objective function to be used in a linear programming model to determine the optimum usage of resources in April.   **(5 marks)**

(Total = 20 marks)

32 Jayland (Sep/Dec 21)

The country of Jayland has two airlines, Flag Co, its national airline, and Budget Co, a recent entrant into the market.

Flag Co

Flag Co was government owned until ten years ago but is now operated as a private company. Its mission is 'to be the airline of choice for long distance travellers'. It charges premium fares and operates routes from Jayland's capital city to the major airports serving the largest cities around the world. Many of its flights have durations greater than 12 hours. The majority of its passengers are travelling on business and are prepared to pay high prices, however the demand for business travel is very sensitive to economic conditions. Its fleet of aircraft is regarded as 'ageing' by industry analysts.

Budget Co

Budget Co was founded by a wealthy entrepreneur who invested their personal fortune in the company's equity. Its mission is 'to be the lowest fare airline on any route we serve'. It offers flights to destinations up to three hours travel from Jayland. Its fleet of aircraft are generally less than two years old. Most of its passengers are holiday-makers and the demand for its flights appears to be relatively insensitive to economic conditions.

The following information is available for both companies.

Statement of profit or loss extract for year end 31 December 20X6

	Flag Co $m	Budget Co $m
Total revenue	11,333	6,654
Operating profit	1,239	404
Finance costs	250	50
Other non-operating costs	130	76
Profit before tax	859	278

Statement of financial position (summarised) as at 31 December 20X6

	Flag Co $m	Budget Co $m
Non-current assets	11,972	3,177
Current assets (Note 1)	3,404	885
Total assets	15,376	4,062
Total equity	4,598	1,945
Non-current liabilities	5,078	1,001
Current liabilities	5,700	1,116
Total liabilities and shareholders equity	15,376	4,062

Note 1: Current assets include inventory of $2.1m and $1.1m respectively.

Other information for year end 31 December 20X6

	Flag Co $m	Budget Co $m
Aviation fuel litres consumed (millions)	2.434	1.246
Available seat kilometres (millions)	21,423	14,953
Passenger seat kilometres (millions)	14,201	14,206
Operating gearing (contribution/profit before interest and tax)	950%	820%

Required

(a) Analyse the financial performance of the two airlines, including reasons for the differences in the two businesses' performance. **(14 marks)**

   Note: Use the headings profitability, liquidity and risk to structure your answer. There are up to six marks available for calculations.

(b) Briefly explain how Fitzgerald and Moon's building block model could be used to manage the performance of a service business. **(6 marks)**

(Total = 20 marks)

Formulae sheet

Regression analysis

$y = a + bx$

$$a = \frac{\Sigma y}{n} - \frac{b\Sigma x}{n}$$

$$b = \frac{n\Sigma xy - \Sigma x\Sigma y}{n\Sigma x^2 - (\Sigma x)^2}$$

$$r = \frac{n\Sigma xy - \Sigma x\Sigma y}{\sqrt{(n\Sigma x^2 - (\Sigma x)^2)(n\Sigma y^2 - (\Sigma y)^2)}}$$

Learning curve

$Y = ax^b$

Where Y = cumulative average time per unit to produce x units
         a = the time taken for the first unit of output
         x = the cumulative number of units produced
         b = the index of learning (log LR/log2)
         LR = the learning rate as a decimal

Demand curve

$P \quad = a - bQ$

$$b \quad = \frac{\text{change in price}}{\text{change in quantity}}$$

$a \quad$ = price when $Q = 0$

$MR \quad = a - 2bQ$

Answers

DO NOT TURN THIS PAGE UNTIL YOU HAVE
COMPLETED THE MOCK EXAM

A PLAN OF ATTACK

Managing your nerves

As you turn the pages to start this mock exam a number of thoughts are likely to cross your mind. At best, examinations cause anxiety so it is important to stay focused on your task for the next three hours! Developing an awareness of what is going on emotionally within you may help you manage your nerves. Remember, you are unlikely to banish the flow of adrenaline, but the key is to harness it to help you work steadily and quickly through your answers.

Working through this mock exam will help you develop the exam stamina you will need to keep going for three hours.

Managing your time

Planning and time management are two of the key skills which complement the technical knowledge you need to succeed. To keep yourself on time, do not be afraid to jot down your target completion times for each question, perhaps next to the title of the question. As all the questions are **compulsory**, you do not have to spend time wondering which question to answer!

Doing the exam

Actually doing the exam is a personal experience. There is not a single **right way**. As long as you submit complete answers to all questions after the three hours are up, then your approach obviously works.

Looking through the exam

Section A has 15 OTQs. This is the section of the exam where the ACCA examining team can test knowledge across the breadth of the syllabus. Make sure you read these questions carefully. The distractors are designed to present plausible, but incorrect, answers. Don't let them mislead you. If you really have no idea – guess. You may even be right.

Section B has three questions, each with a scenario and five objective test questions.

Section C has two longer questions.

Allocating your time

BPP's advice is to always allocate your time **according to the marks for the question**. However, **use common sense**. If you're doing a question but haven't a clue how to do part (b), you might be better off re-allocating your time and getting more marks on another question, where you can add something you didn't have time for earlier on. Make sure you leave time to recheck the OTQs and make sure you have answered them all.

Sections A & B

1   The correct answer is: $125

The transfer price is calculated by firstly calculating the total cost:

	$
Direct materials	22,500
Direct labour	45,350
Overheads	37,150
Total cost	105,000

The question states that Division A wants to earn a profit margin of 20%, therefore the transfer price per unit is calculated as $105,000 ÷ 0.8 ÷ 1,050 = $125.

This question appeared in the March 2020 exam.

2   The correct answer is: $9,200

The first step is to determine what the company's options are and the cost of those options. They can do the following:

(1)   Buy material Z now and store it for one month but the loss would need accounting for = $20/0.8 = $25 per kg

(2)   Buy material Z in one month's time = $24 per kg

(3)   Convert material Y into material Z in one month's time = $18 + $4 = $22

Based on the cost of the options the company would prefer to convert material Y into 200kg of material Z and then for the remaining 200kg of material Z required for the order, the company would buy it in one month's time.

The total relevant cost is (200kg x $22) + (200kg x $24) = $9,200

This question appeared in the September 2019 exam.

3   The correct answer is:

A transaction processing system collects and records the transactions of an organisation.	**TRUE**	
An executive information system is a way of integrating the data from all operations within the organisation into a single system.		**FALSE**

Statement 2 describes an enterprise resource planning system, not an executive information system.

This question appeared in the June 2015 exam.

4   The correct answer is: $2,400

($320 – $80)/(6/60) = $2,400

This question appeared in the June 2015 exam.

5   The correct answer is:

Cost incurred to clean contaminated soil				EXTERNAL FAILURE
Staff cost for picking leaves by hand	PREVENTION			
Recycling waste cost			INTERNAL FAILURE	
Cost incurred for testing tea for contaminants		DETECTION		

The cost incurred to clean contaminated soil is an external failure cost. This is because this cost has arisen as a result of discharging contaminants into the external environment.

The staff cost for picking leaves by hand is a prevention cost. The picking machines damage too many leaves which causes waste, therefore handpicking leaves prevents this wastage.

The recycling waste cost is an internal failure cost because it is waste which is created by the business but is dealt with by the company so that it is not released into the environment.

The cost incurred for testing tea for contaminants is a detection cost as testing the tea ensures that the company is compliant with legislation.

This question appeared in the September 2019 exam.

6   The correct answer is: 1 only

The learning rate was actually better than expected and only 1 could cause it to improve, because new employees will take time to learn the processes.

This question appeared in the June 2015 exam.

7   The correct answer is: If actual sales revenues from two products are in the same ratio as the budgeted sales revenues there is no measurable sales mix variance.

The first thing to notice about this question is that it asks which of the four options is NOT true. The best way to answer this type of question is to go through all of the options and identify the three statements which are true – the remaining one is false and is the correct answer.

This question relies on knowledge of the sales mix variance. The sales mix variance is calculated as the difference between the actual quantities sold in the actual mix and the actual quantities sold in the standard mix, multiplied by the standard margin.

To have a measurable sales mix variance, the standard margins of the products must be different, and the actual proportions of units sold have to be different from the standard proportions.

If all products have the same budgeted margin there is no measurable sales mix variance, therefore the second option is true.

If actual sales volumes are in the same ratio as the budgeted sales volumes, there is no measurable sales mix variance, therefore the third option is true.

If the actual sales volumes of all products are 10% above the budgeted sales volumes, there is no measurable sales mix variance. Here, there is no change in the proportion of units sold, therefore there is no sales mix variance. The fourth option is true.

The first option is not true as it talks about sales revenues and not sales units. Sales mix variance is based on the difference in sales volume as a result of changes in the proportions of each product sold, not the sales revenue. The proportion of sales revenue can stay the same, but this can hide a change in the volume of units sold. The first option is the correct answer.

This question appeared in the June 2020 exam.

8   The correct answer is: 1, 2 and 3 only

The method of apportioning general overheads is not required to calculate the breakeven sales revenue.

This question appeared in the June 2015 exam.

9   The correct answer is: 1, 3 and 4

Statement (1) is correct. Networked computers can share hardware, such as printers and software, such as accountancy packages. Networks can also share data.

Statement (2) is incorrect. An intranet is an internal network which can be used to share information and communication within the organisation. An extranet would be used to communicate with suppliers.

Statement (3) is correct. Adding additional cabling to a wired network can be disruptive and costly. Wireless networks do not need additional cabling and new users can be added relatively easily.

Statement (4) is correct. Organisations can use the internet to, for example, monitor social media which is a useful way to measure customer interest.

This question appeared in the December 2019 exam.

10   The correct answer is: $0.19

The first step is to calculate the cost per unit of cost driver. In this question, the cost driver for the packing and despatching cost pool is the number of orders. Therefore $18 million/12 million orders = $1.50 per order.

It should then be noted that the question asked for the packing and despatching cost per unit of ABC1. There are eight units of ABC1 in an order therefore the cost per unit is $1.50/8 units = $0.1875, which to two decimal places is $0.19.

This question appeared in the June 2019 exam.

11   The correct answers are: 1, 2 and 4

Ideal standards assume perfect operating conditions exist, with no allowance for wastage or idle time. This is likely to result in adverse variances, therefore statement 1 is correct.

As the standards are set at a higher level than is likely to be achieved, this can cause demotivation amongst staff, therefore statement 2 is correct. Ideal standards can be useful for setting long-term targets as efforts are made to reduce inefficiencies in processes over time therefore statement 4 is correct. Statement 3 is incorrect as it is describing an attainable standard.

This question appeared in the March 2020 exam.

12   The correct answer is: P2

| | *Weekly contribution* | | | |
	Price P1 $	*Price P2* $	*Price P3* $	*Price P4* $
Best possible	30,000	31,500	**32,000**	31,500
Most likely	24,000	26,250	**28,000**	27,000
Worst possible	**18,000**	17,500	16,000	13,500

| | | *Regret* | | |
	Price P1 $	*Price P2* $	*Price P3* $	*Price P4* $
Best possible	32,000 – 30,000 = 2,000	500	0	500
Most likely	28,000 – 24,000 = 4,000	1,750	0	1,000
Worst possible	18,000 – 18,000 = 0	500	2,000	4,500
Maximum regret	4,000	**1,750**	2,000	4,500

The maximum regret is minimised by selecting Price P2

13   The correct answers are:

- There are significant economies of scale
- The firm wishes to discourage new entrants to the market

'Demand is relatively inelastic' is incorrect because a penetration policy is favourable in circumstances where demand is relatively **elastic**. 'The product life cycle is particularly short' favours a market skimming policy, as the firm will want to try and recoup the development costs quickly.

14   The correct answer is: 1,400

Fixed costs + target profit required: $30,000 + $3,600 = $33,600

Weighted average of contributions:

$[(3 \times \$32) + (2 \times \$12)]/5 = \$24$

$33,600/$24 = 1,400 units.

15   The correct answer is: $26m

In order to calculate the operating profit, the total cost must be calculated first. As sales are $100m and profit is $20m, the total cost will be $80m. Given the operational gearing is 33.33%, the fixed cost to variable cost will be in the ratio of 1:3. The fixed cost can be calculated as ¼ × $80m=$20m and the variable cost will be $60m. Contribution will be $40m before the increase in sales. After the 15% increase in sales the new contribution will be 1.15 × $40m= $46m and the new operating profit will be $46m - $20m (FC) = $26m. Selecting $27m calculates the fixed cost as $80m/3=$26.67m which gives the variable cost of $53.33m and a contribution of $46.67m. A 15% increase on this is $7m, hence $27m.

Selecting $23m meant that existing operating profit was increased by 15%

Selecting $21m meant that an increase of 33.33% of 15%= 5% × $20m= $21m

This question appeared in the March 2018 exam.

Questions 16 to 30 appeared in the Mar/Jun 19 exam.

16   The correct answer is: $87,000

Operating cost ($486m × 40 years)	$19,440m
Decommissioning cost	$12,000m
Total life-cycle costs	$31,440m
Total gigawatts (9,000 × 40 years)	360,000
Life-cycle cost per gigawatt ($31,440m/360,000 gigawatts)	$87,333

$87,000 (to the nearest $'000)

17   The correct answer is: 2 only

If the useful life of the nuclear station is increased, the operating cost will be incurred every year thus increasing the total life-cycle costs. Statement (1) is not correct. If the decommissioning cost is reduced, this will reduce the total life-cycle costs. Statement (2) is correct.

18   The correct answer is: An internal failure cost

The disposal cost of the spent nuclear fuel is considered to be an internal failure cost. It is a cost incurred by Volt Co as a result of its activities; however, it is being disposed of in a safe manner to ensure that it does not become a cost borne by society as a whole.

19   The correct answer is: $408m

The selling price is based on the operating margin of 40%.

Selling price per gigawatt ($40,000/0.60)	$66,667
Lifetime profit per gigawatt ($66,667 − $55,000)	$11,667
Total lifetime profit (1,750 gigawatts × $11,667 × 20 years)	$408.345 m

$408m (to the nearest $m)

20   The correct answer is: 1 and 2 only

Statements (1) and (2) are benefits of life-cycle costing for Volt Co. Statement (3) is a benefit of activity-based costing (ABC). Statement (4) is a benefit of relevant costing.

21   The correct answer is: Materials only

	Seebach	Herdorf	Total required	Available
Material (kg)	20,000	21,000	41,000	34,000
Labour (hours)	8,000	9,000	17,000	18,000
Machine hours	12,000	6,000	18,000	18,000

There is sufficient labour hours and machine hours to meet maximum demand but there is a shortage of material, so material is the only limiting factor in Month 1.

22   The correct answer is: 2,000

As labour has been identified as the only limiting factor in Month 2, the two products first have to be ranked on the contribution per labour hour they earn.

	Seebach	Herdorf
Contribution per unit ($)	250	315
Labour hours per unit	2	3
Contribution per labour hour ($)	125	105
Ranking	1st	2nd

On the basis of the ranking, the optimum plan would have been to produce Seebach first up to its maximum demand level. However, Cara Co has a legally binding obligation to produce a minimum of 2,000 units of Herdorf. The remaining hours after the production of the minimum demand of Herdorf has been completed is (12,000 hours – (2,000 units of Herdorf × 3 hours) = 6,000, which will be used to produce 3,000 units of Seebach (6,000 hours/2 hours).

There are no more hours available to make any more products, so the production volume for Herdorf for Month 2 is 2,000 units.

23   The correct answer is: Both 1 and 2

The shadow price is the contribution earned from having one extra unit of limited resource available and is also the extra, on top of the existing cost for that limited resource, which a company would be willing to pay to acquire that extra resource. If the shadow price is $125 per labour hour, it would mean that Cara Co would be willing to pay $125 of overtime premium per hour for the next 2,000 hours. The maximum hourly rate Cara Co would be willing to pay would be ($45 + $125) $170 for an additional 2,000 hours of temporary staff. Therefore both statements are correct.

24   The correct answer is: $1,145,000

To determine the optimum point from the graph, the iso-contribution line (250S + 315H) must be moved at the same gradient through the feasible region until the last point it leaves the feasible region. This is where the machine hours constraint (3S + 2H = 12,000) and demand constraint for Herdorf (H = 3,000) intersect. Reading from that point across to the y axis shows that H = 3,000 and reading from that point down to the x axis shows that S = 2,000

Alternatively, the values for H and S can be determined using simultaneous equations:

H = 3,000

3S + 2H = 12,000

3S + (2 × 3,000) = 12,000

S = (12,000 – 6,000)/3 = 2,000

Maximum contribution ($250 × 2,000 units) + ($315 × 3,000 units) = $1,445,000

Less fixed costs	($300,000)
	$1,145,000

25   The correct answer is: 1 only

A slack variable occurs when there are more resources available than are required.

In the graph, the labour line 2S + 3H = 24,000 is well above the feasible region which means that it is not a binding constraint and there are more labour hours than is required. Even if demand increases for both products, labour would still be a slack variable as machine hours are the binding constraint and that is not expected to change. Statement (1) is correct.

If more machine hours became available in Month 3, they will be used to make Seebach as the maximum demand of Herdorf (3,000 units) has been satisfied already. Statement (2) is not correct.

26   The correct answer is: $40,400 Favourable

The market share variance compares the revised sales volume to the actual sales volume:

Revised sales budget (40,000 units x 90%)	36,000 units
Actual sales	38,000 units
Difference (variance in units)	2,000 favourable
Valued at the standard contribution per unit ($)* 20·20	
Variance ($)	40,400 favourable

*Standard contribution = $65 − (5·2 × $4) − (2 x $8) − (2 × $4) = $20·20

27   The correct answer is: $45,600

The materials price planning variance is calculated by comparing the original standard price to the revised standard price:

Original standard price per kg ($)	4·00
Revised standard price per kg ($)	4.24
Difference ($ per kg)	0.24 adverse
Actual quantity of material used (kg)*	190,000
Variance ($)	45,600 adverse

*Actual quantity of materials used = actual material costs/actual price per kg = $836,000/$4·40 per kg = 190,000 kg

28   The correct answer is: $159,600 Adverse

Labour rate operational variance is calculated by comparing the revised standard rate per labour hour to the actual rate per labour hour:

Revised standard rate per hour ($)	8.00

There is no revision made to the standard rate, as the increase was requested by the production department to meet a large, one-off customer order.

Actual rate per hour (1.25 × $8) ($)	10.00
Difference ($)	2.00 adverse
Number of hours worked*	79,800
Variance ($)	159,600 adverse

*Actual hours worked = actual labour cost/actual rate per hour = $798,000/$10 = 79,800

29   The correct answer is: 1, 2 and 3

Labour efficiency planning variance will occur when the standard hours have to be revised due to factors which are beyond the control of the operational managers.

All the factors would require the original standard hours to be revised and would therefore cause a labour efficiency planning variance.

Therefore statements 1, 2 and 3 are all correct.

30   The correct answer is: Both 1 and 2

Both statements are correct and are known issues with the introduction of a system of planning and operating variances.

Section C

31 Bellahouston Co

> **Workbook reference.** Limiting factors, optimal production plans and linear programming are covered in Chapter 9.
>
> **Top tips.** For part (a)(i) you need to follow the steps to maximise contribution. (1) Determine the limiting factor by producing to maximum demand. (2) Rank products by contribution per unit of limiting factor. (3) Prepare a production plan. For (a)(ii), you need to calculate the contribution amount that would be lost by fulfilling RunWild's order. Part (b) should not cause you any problems. For part (c) you need to define the variables, state the objective function and state the constraints. Don't forget the demand and non-negativity constraints.
>
> **Easy marks.** If you follow a methodical approach for maximising contribution and using a linear programming model, there are lots of easy marks in this question.

Marking scheme

			Marks
(a)	(i)	Production plan	7
	(ii)	Financial penalty	4
(b)		Discussion	4
(c)		Linear programming model	5
			20

(a) **(i)** **Identify the limiting factor:**

	Road	Spikes	Trail	Total required
Direct material/pair (metres)	1.5	0.6	1.2	6,930
Direct labour/pair (hours)	1.0	1.5	1.0	6,750
Machine time/pair (hours)	0.4	0.2	0.3	1,875

Based on the above, machine time is the limiting factor.

Calculate contribution per unit of limiting factor and rank the products:

	Road	Spikes	Trail
Contribution per pair of shoes ($)	41.50	29.50	36.00
Machine hours required	0.40	0.20	0.30
Contribution per machine hour ($)	103.75	147.50	120.00
Ranking	3	1	2

Prepare optimum production plan and calculate resultant total contribution earned:

	Machine hours used (1,815 available)	Contribution per pair of shoes ($)	Total contribution ($)
Fulfil customer order:			
200 Road	80	33.50	6,700
200 Spikes	40	21.50	4,300
200 Trail	60	28.00	5,600
	1,635 remaining		
Apply ranking:			
1,400 Spikes - 1st	280	29.50	41,300
1,650 Trail - 2nd	495	36.00	59,400
2,150 Road - 3rd	860	41.50	89,225
			206,525

(ii) **Calculate the profit maximising mix:**

	Machine hours used (1,815 available)	Contribution per pair of shoes ($)	Total contribution ($)
Apply ranking for the general sales in March:			
1,400 Spikes	280	29.50	41,300
1,650 Trail	495	36.00	59,400
2,300 Road	920	41.50	95,450
	120 hours remaining		
Apply ranking for the special order:			
200 Spikes	40	21.50	4,300
200 Trail	60	28.00	5,600
50 Road	20	33.50	1,675
			207,725

The loss of contribution from fulfilling RunWild's order is $1,200 ($207,725 − $206,525), therefore the maximum financial penalty acceptable would be $1,200.

Alternative approach:

If RunWild's order could only be partially completed, then Bellahouston Co would divert machine hours from making Road shoes for the specific order to making Road shoes for general sale to other retailers. The number of Road shoes for general sale in part (a)(i) fails to meet demand by 150 pairs of shoes and the difference in the contribution earned from making them available for general sale and not to RunWild is $8 per pair. Therefore, the difference in the contribution earned is $1,200 (150 pairs of Road shoes × $8), which would be the maximum financial penalty Bellahouston Co would be willing to accept.

(b) Although the contribution earned is higher if the order is only partially completed, if Bellahouston Co does not fully complete the order, then RunWild may not enter into a regular supply contract and future sales revenue would therefore be lost. In addition, the customer base and reputation of RunWild will help to market Bellahouston Co's products and increase awareness of their products. This benefit will also be lost if RunWild choose not to order from Bellahouston Co again.

It would also not be good for Bellahouston Co's existing reputation if it becomes known for not fulfilling its obligations. This could make other sports retailers reluctant to order from them. It might also impact the end-customer's perception of their product if they cannot buy Bellahouston Co's running shoes due to a lack of availability.

(c)   **Define the variables:**

R = number of pairs of Road shoes
S = number of pairs of Spikes shoes
T = number of pairs of Trail shoes

Constraints:

Direct material	$1·5R + 0·6S + 1·2T \le 6,120$
Direct labour	$1R + 1·5S + 1T \le 5,865$
Machine time	$0·4R + 0·2S + 0·3T \le 1,815$
Demand	$R \le 2,300$
	$S \le 1,400$
	$T \le 1,650$
Non-negativity	$R, S, T \ge 0$

Objective function:
$C = 41·50R + 29·50S + 36·00T$

32 Flag Co and Budget Co

Workbook reference. Performance analysis is covered in Chapter 19.

Top tips. You need to perform some calculations in order to have enough to discuss. Percentage change calculations are key. In your discussion, it is important to suggest why things have changed and how this might affect other parts of the business.

Easy marks. The easy marks are for the percentage change calculations.

		Marks
(a)	Calculations	6
	Discussion	8
(b)	Explanation	6
		20

(a)   **Profitability**

	Flag Co	Budget Co
ROCE	12.8%	13.7%
Operating margin	10.93%	6.07%
Asset turnover	1.17	2.26

Budget Co has a better return on capital employed and is therefore making better returns for its investors. The main cause of this is Budget Co's ability to generate sales. For every $ of capital employed, it generates $2·26 of sales revenue as compared to only $1·17 in the case of Flag Co. Budget Co has much shorter flight times than Flag Co and therefore could be making more journeys and spending less time parked at airports.

Budget Co earns a lower operating margin than Flag Co, as Budget Co's operating costs as a percentage of revenue are 94% compared to Flag Co at 89%. This is probably due to Budget Co's pricing strategy. The lower operating margin is more than offset by Budget Co's higher asset turnover, resulting in a higher capital employed (asset turnover × operating margin = ROCE, therefore 6·07% × 2·26 = 13·7%).

BPP
LEARNING
MEDIA

Analysis of the other information provided shows that Budget Co has a much higher seat occupancy rate.

	Flag Co	Budget Co
Seat occupancy rate	66.29%	95.00%

This is probably a consequence of its low fares policy resulting in higher sales of seats relative to Flag Co and therefore a higher asset turnover.

Budget Co also appears more fuel efficient than Flag Co.

	Flag Co	Budget Co
Available seat kilometre per litre of fuel	8,802	12,001

The better fuel economy is probably related to Budget Co's newer fleet of aircraft. Better fuel economy would tend to improve Budget Co's operating margin, however, it is still lower than Flag Co's.

Liquidity

	Flag Co	Budget Co
Current ratio	0.60	0.79

The current ratios of the two businesses are below the text book norm of 2:1, however, they are both service companies which carry little inventory, so this is not surprising or worrying. There is no apparent reason for the difference between the two companies.

Risk

	Flag Co	Budget Co
Capital gearing (debt:equity)	110.44%	51.47%
Interest cover	4.96 times	8.08 times
Operating gearing	950%	820%

Flag Co has a relatively high level of long-term borrowings. This adds to the risks of the business as interest on these borrowings has to be paid no matter the company's operating profit. At present, its operating profit is nearly five times larger than its interest bill and it appears to be able to comfortably pay its commitments. Its operating gearing is 950%, indicating that if sales volume fell by 10%, then its profit before interest and tax would fall by 95% (that is 950% or 9·5 times more). This would cause Flag Co difficulty in covering its interest payments. As demand for business travel is very sensitive to economic conditions, there is a strong probability that at some point Flag Co will experience a fall in sales volume.

As a result of its owner's equity investment, Budget Co carries less financial gearing than Flag Co and has better interest cover. Its operating gearing is slightly lower and given its relative insensitivity to economic conditions, it can be considered a safer company than Flag Co.

(b) Fitzgerald and Moon's building block model provides a framework for service companies to design performance measurement systems which are linked to management rewards. It provides a system of targets (standards) which will motivate managers to improve business performance.

There are three building blocks in the model. The first block gives six dimensions, meaning the aspects of performance which must be measured in a service business. These are:

- Financial performance, for example, profitability and growth.

- Competitiveness which measures an organisation's standing against its competition.

- Quality of the service offered.

- Flexibility of the organisation in providing the service.

- Innovation which addresses the ability to introduce new processes and services.

- Resource utilisation which measures productivity and efficiency.

These six dimensions should be split into results (financial performance and competitiveness) which are the outcomes of past decisions and determinants (quality, flexibility, innovation and resource utilisation) which drive future performance and results.

The second block relates to setting standards. To motivate managers, it is important that they take ownership of standards (that is accept or internalise them) and the standards appear achievable and equitable (fair).

The third block relates to the rewards managers are offered for achieving the standards. These must have clarity (the performance measurement scheme must be understood by managers), they must be motivating (rewards must be attractive) and controllable (not subject to influences outside the manager's control).

Exam formulae

Set out below are the formulae **which you will be given in the exam** in a formulae sheet. You should learn to use them. If you are not sure what the symbols mean, or how the formulae are used, you should refer to the appropriate chapter in the Workbook.

Exam formulae **Chapter in Workbook**

Regression analysis

14

$y = a + bx$

$$a = \frac{\Sigma y}{n} - \frac{b\Sigma x}{n}$$

$$b = \frac{n\Sigma xy - \Sigma x \Sigma y}{n\Sigma x^2 - (\Sigma x)^2}$$

$$r = \frac{n\Sigma xy - \Sigma x \Sigma y}{\sqrt{\left(n\Sigma x^2 - (\Sigma x)^2\right)\left(n\Sigma y^2 - (\Sigma y)^2\right)}}$$

Learning curve

14

$Y = ax^b$

Where
Y	=	the cumulative average time per unit to produce X units
a	=	the time taken for the first unit of output
x	=	the cumulative number of units
b	=	the index of learning (log LR/log 2)
LR	=	the learning rate as a decimal

Demand curve

10

$P = a - bQ$

$$b = \frac{\text{Change in price}}{\text{Change in quantity}}$$

a = price when Q = 0

$MR = a - 2bQ$

Tell us what you think

Got comments or feedback on this book? Let us know.

Use your QR code reader:

Or, visit:

https://bppgroup.fra1.qualtrics.com/jfe/form/SV_cuphESF344D68Mm